The Fundamentals and Forms of SPEECH

REVISED EDITION

The Fundamentals and Forms of SPEECH

Andrew Thomas Weaver & Ordean Gerhard Ness
THE UNIVERSITY OF WISCONSIN

REVISED EDITION

NEW YORK
THE ODYSSEY PRESS · INC ·

PRINTED IN THE UNITED STATES

Library of Congress Catalog Card Number: 63-12621

A 0 9 8 7 6 5 4 3

Foreword

The first edition of this book has lived through twelve semesters and six summer sessions. During these years, many helpful comments have reached the authors from teachers and students who have used the text. Moreover, the authors have had opportunity to profit from their own classroom experiences with it.

Those who compare the second edition with the first will note many changes, including the following:

A new over-all structure, placing stronger emphasis on those basic informational elements which entitle Speech to its true role as a liberal arts discipline on the college level.

A new chapter on spoken language.

Greater stress on speech forms of greatest practical value to the student and best adapted to classroom teaching.

A reorganized and expanded treatment of public address with more illustrations and examples.

More help to the student in preparing speaking assignments, especially the earlier ones.

A simplified and clarified section on parliamentary procedure, aligned with the best contemporary practice, with a comprehensive chart applying accepted principles to any complex of motions.

Revised and new questions and projects.

Brief bibliographies appended to the chapters, providing additional reading assignments for teachers and students who wish to go more deeply into the various topics.

ANDREW THOMAS WEAVER
ORDEAN GERHARD NESS

Affectionately Dedicated

To My Wife—

A. T. W.

To My Mother—

O. G. N.

Contents

PART ONE

Introductory Considerations

Prologue

I am good speech, the servant of man.

In that dim and misty age, before the dawn of history, I came to man. I was on his tongue and in his ears while he was still an infant on the earth. I was with him when he dwelt in caves and carved crude symbols on the walls, striving to picture me in visible form. By me traditions were preserved and passed along from generation to generation. Through me people learned to live together in families and to cooperate in groups for the welfare of all.

I am good speech. I form that inner stream of awareness that men call mind. I mold human beings in my own image. I teach them to know, and to sympathize with, each other. I enable them to think clearly, feel truly, judge justly, and act wisely.

I am good speech. Were I to fail, man's intelligence would lapse to the level of the beasts', each man would dwell apart from his fellows, the structure of society would crumble, the fabric of life itself would fade, and all the processes of civilization would cease.

I am good speech. I am the history of all that has been and the prophecy of all that is to be. Of me Confucius said, "What man most needs to administer government is that his speech be correct." Of me Dante sang, "It must be done by speech or not at all." And, mindful of me, Mentor Graham, humble teacher of the immortal Lincoln, charged his pupil never to forget that "the right words will rule the world."

I am good speech, the servant of man.

CHAPTER 1

The Role of Speech in Contemporary Society

Speech in the Space Age

It is a trite commonplace that we live in an ever expanding universe. With astronauts and cosmonauts whirling about the earth at five miles a second, with missiles hitting the moon while others float off into light-years of distance, and with yet undreamed of possibilities for pushing human life outward to the nebulae, all of man's communication problems become enormously more difficult and complex. As someone has said: "We have a difficult enough time trying to adapt language to the twilight zones of psychology and metaphysics. When it comes to cosmology we can only throw up our hands in surrender."

But we must not throw up our hands in surrender; speech must be developed along with the other on-going and out-ranging sciences of our age. Scientists are continuing to provide words and transmitting channels for new things and new ideas as they come into our lives. It is the province of speech training to see that our speech is adequate to communicate efficiently under ever changing and expanding conditions.

Speech and Personality

Try to imagine what your life would be like if you were suddenly deprived of the power to speak. Suppose that added to your inability to produce the audible and visible symbols of speech, you should be deprived of the ability to hear and interpret the speech of others. Have you ever known, or heard of, an aphasic patient who has suffered such losses? It is not uncommon for those who have had "strokes," caused by hemorrhages or blood clots in the brain, to lose their power to speak or to understand speech. Such tragic experiences vividly point up the vital role which speech plays in all our lives.

Personality is a social product; it grows out of intercommunication. Speech and personality are always closely associated. The human infant has no real personality as it begins life. The essence of the process by which this relatively simple organism develops into a *person* is socialization, and from this process, which is carried on principally through speech, there eventually emerges the *self*.[1] It is in terms of *self* that personality takes on recognizable form. The vital point is that *self* is a product of contact with others.

At first this contact is mainly physical. The infant has certain constantly recurring needs—hunger, discomfort, etc. These needs are satisfied by the mother or the nurse and, as a result of these ministrations, the infant develops habits. However, these habits, clever and intelligent though they may appear, do not really constitute personality as we think of it. The important element in this situation is the baby's growing realization that he can call out responses in others by his use of gestures and voice. This realization is the beginning of personality.

ROLE-TAKING

Usually, during the second year of life, the child learns to perform imitative acts; he begins to copy the behavior patterns of those about him. He puts himself into the place of these others and tries to behave as they do. Thus he initiates the process which Mead calls "role-taking." At the start, the process is largely unconscious; the imitative behavior is made up of conditioned responses. *Instead of learning by imitation we imitate what we already have learned.*

Later in life this role-taking becomes less automatic, more vol-

[1] George Herbert Mead, *Mind, Self, and Society* (Chicago: University of Chicago Press, 1934), Part III.

untary and conscious, and more meaningful. The child no longer imitates merely to try out the actions of others; he acts *in relation to himself* as he takes the role of others. For example, Johnny, who has learned to toddle about, is constantly busy exploring his environment. He experiments with pushing a dish off the coffee table. His mother catches him doing it and punishes him, verbally or otherwise. The next time Johnny approaches the coffee table, he stops and says aloud to himself, "NO! NO! Johnny!" and retreats from temptation. This simple combination of acts illustrates the *reflexive* stage of role-taking. Johnny begins by acting his own role and then, suddenly, drops that role, assumes the role of his mother, and actually speaks the words his mother probably would speak were she present. He then returns to his own role as an obedient child. This is the stage at which the *self* really begins to take shape. The unique quality of the human personality is this capacity to reflect upon itself; it is both subject and object to itself. Johnny can act; he can react to his own actions as someone else might, and he can adapt his behavior to this other person's imagined reactions. This whole process can be carried out completely within his own thinking and feeling, mainly through talking to himself. This achievement is possible because the child has developed an "image" of the "other" in his own personality.

THE EMERGENCE OF SELF

At first these roles are taken on one at a time. As Johnny approaches the forbidden coffee table he is only Johnny. When he assumes the role of his mother, he is, for the moment, his mother. A further stage in the development of the self occurs when Johnny learns to absorb a number of such roles into his imagination simultaneously and to assimilate them into a "unified self." In order to do this, he learns to internalize these roles so that he can perform them without gesturing or vocalizing aloud. The "unified self," in which several roles are integrated, may result from participating in games. In baseball, for example, the child who is the pitcher must be aware of the batter, the catcher, the infielders, the outfielders, the umpires, and the managers. As Mead says, "The child must have the responses of each position in his own position. He must know what everyone else is going to do, in order to carry out his own play." [2]

SOCIALIZATION

During the period of the child's life which we have been considering, most of the socialization takes place within the family, which is the first and undoubtedly the most important group to which the child belongs. Throughout the remainder of his life, he will become a member of many other groups, some formal and organized and others informal and unorganized. In each group he will take on additional roles. For example, as he grows older, Johnny will join a neighborhood play group and perhaps a Boy Scout troop. He will become a pupil in kindergarten, grade school, and high school. He will be on the football team, in the glee club, and on the school newspaper staff. He will be elected president of the junior class and secretary of the Hi-Y organization. He will be an usher in his church and social chairman of his Sunday School class. He will go to college and join a fraternity. He will become interested in politics and volunteer for service with the Young Republican Club. He will be elected to Phi Beta Kappa and the Order of the Coif. He will become engaged to the girl who sits next to him in his speech class and who will talk him into trying out for a part in a campus Gilbert and Sullivan musical. He will be enrolled in ROTC, and, after graduation, he will enter the Army as a second lieutenant. After three years of service and one promotion, he will be released from service and return to civilian life. He will marry and become the father of a daughter. He will settle in a Midwest community where he will open a law office. He will be an active Army reservist, a member of the Methodist Church, the local chapter of the American Bar Association, the Masons, the Alumni Club, etc. Year after year he will continue to make new associations, join new groups, and take on new roles in old groups.

All groups, especially those which are organized and continuing, develop common attitudes, beliefs, and needs which become parts of the role of each individual who joins them. Communities,

[2] *Ibid.*, pp. 140–41.

cities, states, and nations have certain characteristic attitudes which are reflected in the personalities of their citizens. As these communal attitudes take shape in the organization of the "unified self," a process of *generalization* commences. What to the young child were attitudes of individual "others" now become the attitudes of everybody in a given situation. "Everybody" becomes a sort of "generalized other." Through this "generalized other," society makes sure of its survival by inculcating in the individual its mores and folkways. When a person has taken unto himself this system of organized community attitudes, by assuming his various community roles, he has become a complete "self," a personality, a social product in the fullest sense.

Personality, therefore, is not a single role; it is an integrated system of multiple roles, each colored, to some extent, by all of the others. Thus, a Democrat from a southern community will have characteristics different from those of a Democrat from Chicago, even though many of their political attitudes may be similar. Moreover, the individual's system of roles will show different orders of precedence, or hierarchy, in different circumstances. For example, in church, Johnny's role as a Methodist is in the ascendancy; at home, he is a husband and father; in the office, he is a lawyer; at the university's home-coming, he is an alumnus.

The following dialogue between Ko-Ko and Pooh-Bah in *The Mikado* illustrates, in a facetious and satirical manner, this shift of hierarchy: [3]

Ko-Ko. Pooh-Bah, it seems that the festivities in connection with my approaching marriage must last a week. I should like to do it handsomely, and I want to consult you as to the amount I ought to spend upon them.

Pooh-Bah. Certainly. In which of my capacities? As First Lord of the Treasury, Lord Chamberlain, Attorney-General, Chancellor of the Exchequer, Privy Purse, or Private Secretary?

Ko-Ko. Suppose we say as Private Secretary.

Pooh-Bah. Speaking as your Private Secretary, I should say that, as the city will have to pay for it, don't stint yourself, do it well.

Ko-Ko. Exactly—as the city will have to pay for it. That is your advice.

[3] Gilbert and Sullivan, *The Mikado* (New York: Modern Library, Random House), pp. 12–13.

POOH-BAH. As Private Secretary. Of course you will understand that, as Chancellor of the Exchequer, I am bound to see that due economy is observed.

KO-KO. Oh! But you said just now, "Don't stint yourself, do it well."

POOH-BAH. As Private Secretary.

KO-KO. And now you say that due economy must be observed.

POOH-BAH. As Chancellor of the Exchequer.

KO-KO. I see. Come over here, where the Chancellor can't hear us. (*They cross the stage.*) Now, as my Solicitor, how do you advise me to deal with this difficulty?

POOH-BAH. Oh, as your Solicitor, I should have no hesitation in saying "Chance it—."

KO-KO. Thank you. (*Shaking his hand.*) I will.

POOH-BAH. If it were not that, as Lord Chief Justice, I am bound to see that the law isn't violated.

KO-KO. I see. Come over here where the Chief Justice can't hear us. (*They cross the stage.*) Now, then, as First Lord of the Treasury?

POOH-BAH. Of course, as First Lord of the Treasury, I could propose a special vote that would cover all expenses, if it were not that, as Leader of the Opposition, it would be my duty to resist it, tooth and nail. Or, as Paymaster-General, I could so cook the accounts that, as Lord High Auditor, I should never discover the fraud. But then, as Archbishop of Titipu, it would be my duty to denounce my dishonesty and give myself into my own custody as First Commissioner of Police.

KO-KO. That's extremely awkward.

Pooh-Bah's awkward dilemma points up one of the sources of personal maladjustment frequently encountered in our complex modern society; the roles which people assume often come into conflict with each other. Fortunately, for most of us this conflict is removed before it becomes a serious problem; our primary roles (those stemming from family, church, and school groups) have been so firmly set that later, secondary roles are modified by them so that the conflict disappears or is reduced to a point where it no longer bothers us.

The media of mass communication also deserve mention as sources of roles. Today, both a student and his teacher may play the roles of "Pogo" or "Freddy, the Free Loader." Both the banker and the newsboy may whistle the tunes of the latest musical show. The president of the corporation and the office boy can share the experience of watching and listening to the President of the United States. To a considerable extent, these experiences make possible a core of common roles that millions of personalities can share. Who can say whether this fact is good or bad? To the extent that it causes a deterioration of taste, it probably has detrimental effects. To the extent that it promotes understanding and clearer communication, it is probably good. At any rate, it is important in providing a variety of new roles which people may play.

The process of acquiring a self or a personality is not passive. One of the first lessons the child learns is that, to control what others do to him, he must try to influence them. Personality growth is the result of the speaking which we do and the speaking to which we react. The student should understand this basic function of speaking and listening in the building of personality. As Eisenson says,[4]

> When we use the term *personality* we probably have in mind the effect which an individual's total behavior has on us. A personality may be said to be the totality of the reactive possibilities of the individual. A personality exists only in relation to an organism behaving in an environment. . . . The personal reactions of the individual (his personality) are determined by transactions between himself and his environment. . . .

Every individual has as many personalities as there are people with whom he interacts. Each of us in our time plays many parts and our personalities shift and change with our assumption of different roles in different circumstances. *Each of our roles is a speaking one.* The better we can speak, the better we can play our roles in every situation. Because of the intimate integration of speech and personality, it is only reasonable to conclude that speech training should improve personality. Furthermore, experimental studies have shown that the study and practice of speaking have produced measurable improvements in personality traits. Speech training helps us to perfect ourselves in new roles which increase our social adaptability and usefulness. Nowhere else does the educational process come into such close contact with the factors of personality as it does in the speech classroom.

[4] Jon Eisenson, *The Psychology of Speech* (New York: F. S. Crofts & Co., 1938), p. 145.

Speech and Intellectual Life

It goes without saying that intellectual life and personality overlap; it requires intelligence to assume a variety of roles and play them successfully. All of our higher mental processes are dependent upon our capacity and skill in the use of symbols. For most of us, speech and symbolization are substantially synonymous.

Nearly 200 years ago, the German philosopher, Herder, made the following penetrating observation:

> Nature gives no power in vain. She not only gave man power to invent language but she made that power the dynamic principle of his destiny. Reason was incapable of action without the word symbol, and the first moment of rationality must also have been the first moment of interior language.

This statement focuses attention on the fact that the function of "interior language" (inner or implicit speech—talking silently to oneself) is to create and refine man's intellectual capacities.

IMPORTANCE OF SYMBOLS

Men tend to fall into two classes: (1) those who react mainly to physical objects or situations, and (2) those who react not only to things but also to symbols. The "thinking" of the first type of person is severely limited and earth-bound; with him, out of sight really means out of mind. His powers of memory and imagination are weak; he does little of the constructive and creative thinking of the world. He finds it difficult to react effectively to the symbols of speech when the symbols are detached from an actual physical context. Language is meaningful to such a person only when he can fit it to things he can see, hear, and touch.

To illustrate, an instructor in a "refresher school" for railway personnel read aloud a dispatcher's orders to one of the students and then said, "Now, suppose you were the engineer of train No. 1 and you were pulling out of Station X, eastbound, having just received these orders. At the first block, you find the signals set thus and so. What would you do?" The student seemed puzzled and asked the teacher to restate the problem. After this had been done, he still was confused. "What is your line of work?" asked the instructor. "I'm an engineer," answered the student. "I've been pulling No. 1 for fifteen years and I've never had any trouble. When I'm up in the cab, with my hand on the throttle, I know what those orders and signals mean!"

In sharp contrast to this type of man is one who has learned to be at home in the world of words, to use symbols freely, to breathe the stimulating air of memory and imagination, and to create new patterns of thought and feeling. Speech training can help greatly in developing this capacity to construct a rich and satisfying word world.

Perhaps one caution is needed at this point. It is possible to live so much in the world of words that one loses his anchorage in the world of things. We must maintain the proper correlation between the outer world of time and space and the inner world of symbolic thought and feeling. There is a tyranny of words as well as a tyranny of things! We must always be able to move freely from the world of symbols to the world of objects, and back again, at will. The key to this essential technique is the continual verbalizing of our experiences as they occur. When we meet with anything worth remembering—storing away in our word world—we should talk about it, with others and with ourselves. And we must remember that our words *represent our experiences with situations and things,* not the situations and things themselves.

PHYSICAL BASIS OF INTELLECTUAL LIFE

Strong and startling support for our view of the intimate interrelation of speech and intellectual processes is provided by recent studies of brain structure and function. While we lack space here to examine in detail these findings of neurology, we can sketch in some of the essential outlines.

When we map the human cortex, marking out on it the sensory and motor areas—the former involved in seeing, hearing, touching, smelling, tasting, etc., and the latter enabling us to control muscles and glands—we discover that some parts of the body have only slight representation in the brain, while others have very extensive representation.

The particular sensory areas of the cortex connected with the arms, hands, and fingers are very large. Those related to the legs, feet and toes, while somewhat smaller, are still of considerable size. The part of the cortex associated with the torso is extremely limited. But the sensory areas serving the face, lips, tongue, throat, and jaw are comparatively immense. The motor areas of the cortex which send out nerve impulses to the muscles of the hands, fingers, lips, tongue, throat, and jaw occupy twice as much space as do the areas for all the other muscles of the body put together! The hands alone involve more of the cortex than all the rest of the body exclusive of the face; and the face, more than all else, exclusive of the hands.

Each of the structures of the human body seems to have "voting power" in the cortex proportional to its use. In the long story of evolution, as man's capacity for living in the world of symbols has increased, the neurological organization upon which speech depends has attained increasing dominance in the cortex. The highest possible use-value is placed on the sensory and motor components of gesture and articulate voice. Training in speech exercises man's highest capacities and functions; it cultivates the very core of his neurological being. It seems only reasonable to suppose that practice in speech actually does develop what we loosely call "brain power."

Speech in the Economic Order

Not long ago the Society for the Advancement of Management sent out questionnaires to more than five thousand business executives and five hundred professors and deans of business administration, asking them to list, in the order of relative importance, all the subjects they thought should be included in the curriculum of schools of commerce and business. Eleven hundred and fifty-four replies were received and analyzed. It was found that both business men and educators had rated public speaking at the very top of the list, far above accounting, economics, and all the other technical subjects.

A 1950 survey of one hundred and forty industries, twenty large department stores, and thirty-two agencies of the federal government, employing a total of more than three million persons, showed that 90 per cent of the organizations had active in-service training programs offering courses in conference participation, leadership, and public speaking. A list of these organizations reads like a roster of major American industries and government bureaus. There is a growing conviction that training for business should stress those communication skills which have so much to do with earning a livelihood.

The second survey would seem to indicate clearly that the economic significance of effective oral communication is not confined to individual profit. Communication is the essential means by which all industrial and business groups function. S. M. Vinocour points up industry's growing realization of the importance of speech in its public relations programs: [5]

> The *Wall Street Journal* reported on October 13, 1955, that improved oral communications skills and programs ". . . seem to be paying off for many corporate enterprises, large and small." Some of the corporations cited as utilizing conference-type oral communications programs were Brock-Hall Dairy of Hamden, Connecticut, Johns-Manville, Armco Steel, Pitney-Bowes, Johnson & Johnson, Jersey Standard, Scott Aviation, and R. J. Reynolds Tobacco.
>
> . . . General Electric has organized 11 Speakers' Bureaus in its largest plants, with some 400 speakers on tap. Jones & Laughlin has a special "sales representative" booked for months in advance; he travels about the country talking on all kinds of subjects to all kinds of audiences. Republic Steel, Ford, General Motors, and the American Iron and Steel Institute are also among the industrial leaders promoting speeches as one of their most important public relations media.

B. B. Gardner's study of human relations in industry indicates another value of speech. Gardner says that the "chain of command" or "line of authority" serves as a means of "providing channels of communication extending from top to bottom throughout the structure." If the channels are obstructed in any way, production suffers. Effective communication between workers and foremen and between foremen and executives must be maintained.[6]

To illustrate: after conferring (communicating) with his engineers and technicians, an executive decides that a certain

[5] S. M. Vinocour, "Speech as a PR Tool," *PR,* Vol. 1, No. 4, July, 1956.

[6] B. B. Gardner, *Human Relations in Industry* (Chicago: R. D. Irwin, 1946), p. 46.

line of goods will be produced by his company. Plans are made and explained to (communicated to) the foremen. These men organize the staff and facilities under their supervision (communication) and explain (communicate) the processes to the workers. The workers produce the goods. The foremen note the amount and quality of the product and report (communicate) their findings to the executive. The executive decides, on the basis of the reports, to proceed as scheduled or to make changes in the process. Much of the necessary communication can be carried on through written directives, surveys, reports, etc. But at many points along the line, spoken communication plays a vital role.

An executive's decisions will be effective only when he knows and understands the needs, wants, and attitudes of the men and women who work for him. A foreman's supervision will be effective only when he appreciates the underlying motivations of both his superiors and his subordinates. A worker's performance will be effective only when he is satisfied that his contributions are understood and appreciated and when his physical and emotional needs are being met. How can all these intangibles be dealt with on paper? They simply cannot. It is in recognition of this fact that personnel counselors and labor-management specialists have become so important in our industrial and governmental structure. The full-time job of many of these experts is to facilitate communication among different levels and divisions in business organizations. They function primarily through personal interviews and conferences—speech situations. The most successful business is one in which two-way communication channels are always open between top management and those who form the base of the business pyramid.

Speech and Democratic Citizenship

As Macaulay, Bagehot, and others pointed out long ago, democracy is government by speech; that is why the British call it *parliamentary*. (The term comes from the French verb meaning *to speak.*) Brigance says, "There are only two kinds of nations in the world today, only two: those who in crises want to shoot it out and those who have learned to talk it out."

George Orwell, in his cynical and depressing novel, *1984*, paints a picture of mankind's final ruin under a totalitarian tyranny which destroys the last vestiges of freedom in the world. The central technique by which human beings are reduced to helpless robots is the imposition upon all citizens of a controlled, distorted, and constantly shrinking language, "Newspeak," from which all "dangerous" words have been eliminated by government edict. In this revolutionary "Utopia" it is no longer possible for citizens to commit the crime of thinking; the suppression of speech has deprived them of their power to think.

Free speech is the very lifeblood of democracy, but speech is really free only when it is effective. Of what value is the right to speak, if the would-be speaker is tongue-tied? Freedom of speech is a blessing only to those who have the capacity and skill to use it. In this simple statement is epitomized the whole case for speech training in a democracy.

ACTIVE VERSUS PASSIVE CITIZENSHIP

It is a tragic error for citizens of a democracy to become spectators—passive onlookers and listeners—instead of active participators in civic affairs. But, unfortunately, this seems to be what many of us are doing. We let radio and television commentators do our thinking and exercise our freedom of speech for us. When meetings are held for the discussion of public issues, most of us may be found dozing in easy chairs listening to a broadcast of what others are saying. We are no longer even alert and active listeners and spectators; we have become so accustomed to turning up the volume and watching pictures at close range—to say nothing of being blasted out of our seats at the movies—that we have difficulty in getting meanings from a "live" public speaker or an actor, on a platform or stage.

Profound civic changes are arising from the ever-increasing gadgetry of our technological inventions. Just when we were telling ourselves that democratic processes were breaking down because we had become so numerous that we could no longer talk with each other about our common problems, radio and television came onto the scene with the means of saving the situation. But what happened? How strange it seems that, despite our possession of the means of making ourselves seen and heard around the earth, we now probably have the smallest percentage of our population participating in the discussion of public affairs that we ever have had.

We like to believe that our American government is "by the people." But can we really make this claim? One of the significant trends that we must recognize is the increasing number and importance of professional persuaders, especially in government. Our representatives in our legislatures tell us they vote according to our desires. Many of them try to, but how do they know what we want? How often do we make our opinion known, intelligently and coherently? But, at all times, the professional persuaders, the lobbyists, the special-interest groups conduct systematic, large-scale, effective campaigns both in and out of the hallowed halls of Congress.

Many legislators have noted the decline of old-style floor debate as the decision-making process in our state and national legislatures. Private, informal discussions among legislators and among legislators and lobbyists have become the important decision-making procedures. In part, this trend is understandable. The increasing number of bills and problems confronting lawmakers makes full-fledged debate of each and every issue impossible. But from another point of view, it is regrettable, for it is becoming increasingly difficult for those of us at home to perceive and understand how the decisions are achieved.

Cantril's study of public opinion during World War II showed that Congressional action often lagged far behind the wishes of the public.[7] The lines of communication between constituents and their representatives were not functioning efficiently, while the channels between pressure groups and the Congress were in full operation.

From another point of view, American government has been called "government by information officers." As Wilbur Schramm [8] suggests, the mass media of communication—newspapers, magazines, radio, and television—have taken over the function of interpreting political events for us. To facilitate matters, almost

[7] Hadley Cantril, "Public Opinion in Flux," *The Annals of the American Academy of Political and Social Science*, Vol. 220 (1942), pp. 136–52.

[8] Wilbur Schramm, *The Process and Effects of Mass Communications* (Urbana: University of Illinois Press, 1955), p. 22.

every governmental agency has set up public-information offices to furnish the data to be disseminated and interpreted. The complexity of our federal and state administrations makes direct contact between the average citizen and his government almost too difficult to be feasible. But somehow we must learn about domestic and international problems if we are to exercise our guaranteed right to govern ourselves. As long as the media remain free and competitive in point of view, as long as they inquire diligently and carefully, *and as long as each of us reads and listens critically and talks over what he reads and hears with other informed, discriminating individuals*—our democratic political system can survive. An active, articulate public is requisite to a responsive and responsible democracy.

TOLERANT YET CRITICAL CITIZENSHIP

The open mind is always more important than the open mouth. But the good citizen's mind is not so open that it is drafty. One of the most vital lessons that anyone can learn from participating in discussions is that the world is neither all white nor all black but mostly gray.

We prefer to lend our ears to those who tell us what we already know and believe. Whenever a broadcaster begins to tread on our sensitive mental toes, we flip the dial to another station or snap the turn-off button. There is no better cure for this bad habit than training in the full and free discussion of controversial issues, under competent guidance, in the speech classroom.

But there is a reverse side to this problem: it is possible to be so tolerant as to have no solid opinions at all. While it is important to discover that others may honestly and devoutly hold opinions at variance with our own, we must learn also to be critical of careless, unsupported assertions. One of the most valuable by-products of training in discussion is that it helps to immunize us from the sophistry and hypocrisy in the speaking of demagogues who seek to mislead us.

SPEECH AND OUR LITERARY HERITAGE

The natural world is an ever-vanishing world. Language is man's device for introducing permanence into his ever-dissolving experience. Literature demonstrates to us that the hopes and fears of each generation repeat themselves in succeeding generations. We can meet the issues of our day more constructively if we understand that man's experiences are recurrent phenomena. If we wish to know the truth that shall make us free we must seek it in the heritage of our literature.

The following editorial from one of our leading religious periodicals is a parable of our life today: [9]

> During the recent wildcat strike that tied up the subways just at the rush hour, the hurried, harried millions pushed down the long stairs to the silent underground stations, were turned away at the toll gates, and then pressed back upstairs to seek surface transportation. No one in the ascending stream told anyone in the descending stream on the same staircase that it was pointless to go all the way down. And none of those going down asked anyone going up why they were so suddenly turned around. To have communicated so would have violated New York's unwritten law that no one speaks to anyone. So the morose masses slogged through the same mistake, million by million. Almost you can see the generations of men stumbling down the long staircases of history, coming to impasse, seeking other solutions—and volunteering far too little of their knowledge and wisdom to those who follow, repeating old mistakes. Scholars write books, scientists leave records, the church makes creeds, and all these should be the voice of those who have gone the distance to those who could get farther and go faster if they didn't have to push on into all the same blind alleys. But for the testimony to be telling, those who are on the way back must speak up to those who are on the way in. And those who are going down will do well to ask questions and listen sharply to those who are coming up.

This story illuminates the terrible truth that one is never so alone as he is in a great city where he is surrounded by other human beings who go their separate ways with no concern for him. Quite aside from this literal interpretation is the story's allegorical meaning—that we can, and must, appropriate the experiences of those who have descended the stairway of history before us.

If we are going to make use of our past as we find it in great literature, we must be able to read. The movies, radio, and television have almost robbed us of our ability to read. We are accustomed to being *read to* but not to *reading to ourselves*. All

[9] Reprinted by permission of *The Christian Century* from the issue of July 4, 1956.

reading begins as oral reading, just as all thinking begins as talking to ourselves.

Ormandy and Bernstein can "read" the printed score of a symphony silently and appreciate its meaning. Through years of experience in hearing and conducting symphonies, they have learned to transfer, imaginatively, to their ears what they perceive through their eyes. But those of us who are musical illiterates never can learn to do that by looking at the printed scores of symphonies. If we want to be able to read music silently to ourselves, we must first do a lot of playing and singing.

Until we have learned how literature sounds when read aloud, we cannot make this imaginative transfer from eye to ear. Oratory and poetry, like music, are addressed primarily to the ear, not to the eye. To be understood and appreciated they must be *heard,* either with the ear of the flesh or the ear of the imagination.

SPEECH AND CREATIVE LEADERSHIP

It need hardly be said that creative leadership is indispensable to the safety and progress of society. Kenneth MacGowan quotes Havelock Ellis as saying that there is nothing more fragile than civilization and then asks:

> Have you ever wondered what you would do if you were a cave man? Or what you *could* do?
>
> As you read these words, you may feel secure in your fabulous civilization of machines. But suppose some cosmic calamity destroyed all our cities and factories and railroads and automobiles. In a month most city dwellers would be dead. . . . Farmers would eat their cattle and seed, then start grubbing roots and snaring rabbits.
>
> Out of every thousand men that make, sell and consume, 999 would have no earthly notion of how to get things going again. The few engineers and inventors would starve to death before they could get things up to the level of pre-dynastic Egypt.

Humanity progresses mainly because there are among us those whom Toynbee calls "the creative minority." According to this renowned historian, the paramount problem in every age is to make sure that this constructive minority shall direct the course of the masses of mankind. The point of difference between a *creative* and a *destructive* minority is that the former uses, as its technique of control, *peaceful persuasion,* while the latter employs *force.*

The historian, Ramsey Muir, summarizes the English Civil War by saying:

> The war had taught the English people that even the noblest and the most enlightened aims are vitiated and will eventually be frustrated if those who advocate them try to secure their victory by force, and not by discussion and persuasion. These (discussion and persuasion) were to be henceforth the characteristic notes of the growth of free institutions in the British Commonwealth.

At numerous crises in history, the creative minority has been displaced by destructive leadership. Toynbee says that all progress depends upon the ability of creative leaders to persuade the masses to accept the constructive solutions the leaders have worked out. Failure inevitably precipitates a breakdown in culture, leadership passes from the *minds* of the *creative* to the *hands* of the *destructive,* and, when physical force is substituted for peaceful persuasion, all political and social institutions except those that subsist on violence are swept away.

In a democracy creative leadership alone is not enough. Those who follow must be intelligent, informed, alert, and discriminating. Democracy depends upon a free market place of ideas, where all citizens have the chance to give and take, to persuade and be persuaded. We believe in freedom of speech and of the press with no interference from any authority except the individual's own morality, knowledge, and taste. Without such freedom, a democracy cannot survive, for its very life depends upon what Thomas Jefferson called "the self-righting process." Any such government made up of human beings, as it must be, is apt to err. But in a society where "untrammeled sifting and winnowing of truth" is possible, such errors will not be perpetuated. "The truth will out"; the process will "right itself."

ADDITIONAL READINGS

Baskerville, Barnet, "The Place of Oratory in American History," *Quarterly Journal of Speech,* December, 1953, pp. 459–64.

Nilsen, T. R., "Free Speech, Persuasion, and the Democratic Process," *Quarterly Journal of Speech,* October, 1958, pp. 235–43.

Ewbank, H. L., Baird, A. C., Brigance, W. N., Parrish, W. M., and Weaver, A. T., "What is Speech?—A Symposium," *Quarterly Journal of Speech,* April, 1955, pp. 145–53.

QUESTIONS AND PROJECTS

1. Make a careful, objective analysis of your own personality, listing some of the more important roles which make up your present "self." Check your list against the lists brought in by your classmates. Determine the roles which are most common in the class. Do you think you would find the same common roles in your other classes? Why? Or why not?

2. Prepare and deliver a five-minute speech describing a process or an activity related to your major field of interest. Use visual aids to help you in your description.

3. Is speech a requirement in any of the curricula in your school? If so, interview the deans or other administrative heads of these divisions and get their views concerning the speech requirement. If there is no such requirement in your college, how do you explain the fact? A panel discussion (see Chapter 12) might be arranged on the problem of speech requirements.

4. Plan a symposium of four speeches on the general subject, "Creative Leader-Speakers of History." Each speaker should select one outstanding historical leader who used speech as an essential technique in playing his role. In a speech *to impress* (see Chapter 11), make the point that there is a close relationship between speech ability and leadership.

5. Using a diagram of the human brain—or a model, make a 3- to 5-minute speech on the subject of "Speech Ability and Brain Power."

6. Interview an outstandingly successful businessman in your community and report what he thinks about the role of speech in his occupation and success.

7. Find out what you can about the speech-training program being carried on in an industry and make an expository speech to the class on what you learn.

8. Select passages from Orwell's *1984* which illustrate the importance of speech to citizenship. Read them to the class and comment on them.

9. Who are some of the "creative leaders" in the United States at the present time? Select one and tell the class about him in a 5-minute speech, stressing his uses of communication as a means of leadership.

10. Study the origin and development of democracy in ancient Greece. What role did speech and speech training play in this development? Or, obversely, what relationships can you find between the democracy of ancient Greece and the development of oratory?

CHAPTER 2

The Nature of Communication and Speech

Measured in terms of its effects upon the individual and upon society, speech is incomparably man's greatest invention. All down through the ages, speech has been the instrument by which human beings have influenced and manipulated their world and reached new dimensions of life and thought.

Learning to substitute pictographs, hieroglyphics, and finally, written and printed symbols for spoken language marked another tremendous advance in intellectual powers and culture. It remained for the second half of the nineteenth century to produce the telephone, and for the first half of the twentieth to bring in the miracles of radio and television which have made possible instantaneous intercommunication among men anywhere on earth and even far into outer space. Everywhere speech is at the center of these extended relationships between man and his universe and between man and his fellow men.

There are many differences between human beings and the other animals but none so vital as in their capacity for intercommunication. Of course the lower animals do communicate with others of their own species in limited ways but man so far surpasses them in this type of activity that the difference in degree becomes a difference in kind.

Since speech is the principal form of communication and is most often thought of as practically equivalent to communication, it may be advantageous for us to begin our study by considering the question, What is communication? Then we shall raise the

further question, Just how does speech fit into the more general concept of communication?

Communication Defined

We should begin by noting that we are here dealing with an enormously complex process which sometimes seems deceptively simple until we try to analyze, explain, and define it. Communication is the most intricate and elaborate type of behavior in which human beings engage. If we could understand it in all of its branches and phases, we should be able to explain practically all of the mysteries of life and thought and feeling.

THE FACTORS OF COMMUNICATION

There are always six factors in every act of communication: (1) the *communicator* or encoder, (2) the *code*, (3) the *channel*, (4) the *communiqué* or message, (5) the *communicatee* or decoder, and (6) the *result* or meaning.

The *communicator* is the initiator of the whole process; something within his nervous system causes him to feel that, in order to adjust himself to the situation, he needs to communicate with some other person or persons. He needs to share an experience, to solicit assistance, to secure approval, or merely to feel that he is in contact with someone. In other terms, we may say that he wants to send a communiqué or message to someone.

Now there is no way in which a communiqué or message can be transmitted by thought waves. Few scientists accept the alleged phenomena of telepathy; the message has to be encoded and sent over a physical channel which can carry it across the gap between two minds.

The *codes* most commonly used are: spoken language, written language, visible speech (gesture, facial expressions, etc.), painting, sculpture, music, and mathematics.

The usual *channels* of communication are air vibrations, light vibrations, and electronic impulses.

When the signals which constitute the code reach the *communicatee* or decoder, they have to be interpreted or decoded into a message.

The communicatee then reacts to the message, *as he under-*

stands it. These reactions constitute the result of the communication. The result is in the form of another message, usually encoded in the visible and audible behavior of the communicatee and "sent" back to the communicator. Thus communication normally is reciprocal; the encoding and decoding shift back and forth as the communication proceeds.

We may diagram the communicative process in the following schema:

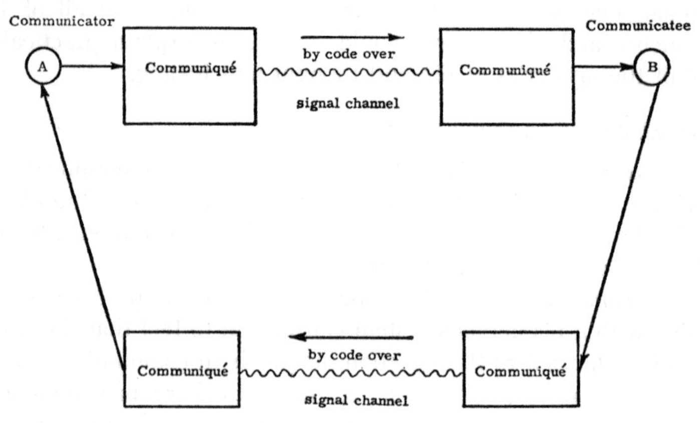

Of course, there are situations in the field of mass communication where immediate and direct reciprocal interaction between the sender and the receiver is impossible. In conversing over the telephone, the roles of sender and receiver alternate but neither speaker can react to the visible behavior of the other except, of course, as he *imagines* it or detects it in the vocal code. In radio and television, the communicator receives neither visible nor audible responses from the communicatee; it is a one-way type of communication. Yet, even in such situations, there may be some delayed responses from the audience which make the communication in a sense reciprocal. Through fan mail, public opinion polls, etc., real, though delayed, reactions may affect the behavior of the communicator.

FEEDBACK

Webster's Third New International Dictionary defines *feedback* as "the return to the input of a part of the output of a machine, system, or process." For example, a person changes the position of his arm; the muscle movements involved in the change of position send return reports in to his central nervous system and these movements, in turn, tell him that his arm has changed its position. The sensations which arise as the result of the movement are feedback. This type of feedback is called *self-regulatory;* it may be illustrated by self-regulating machines such as thermostatically controlled heating systems, automatic lighting plants, etc. All of our learned behavior patterns—standing, walking, vocalizing, etc.—are operated through feedback. As Brown explains the mechanism: [1]

> Feedback is the scanning of behavior for success or failure in order to determine how to modify future behavior. It tells the heating plant when to shut off. It keeps the automatic pilot on course. It makes you adjust your walk when you step on a pebble. It tells you when you have mispronounced a word, spoken too loudly, or insulted your listener. . . . The point is that a self-adjusting mechanism, whether man or radar, works toward its purpose by a flow of messages which inform it of its progress. . . . Upset it (feedback) and behavior goes berserk; destroy it, and the machine or organism is helpless.

This type of feedback depends upon what psychologists call movement-produced stimulation. As we have said, whenever we move, our movements stimulate us. Whenever we speak a word, we hear our own voice, we feel the movements of our tongue, our jaws, and our other articulators and these sensations (feedback) trip off the ensuing movements.

Our speech patterns are held together by movement-produced stimulation or feedback. Each movement brings stimulation which touches off the following movement. It would be quite impossible for anyone to learn elaborate serial responses without the help of feedback. Indeed, the deaf child, because he gets no auditory feedback from the movements of his voice muscles cannot learn to speak unless, through special training, he substitutes some other form of feedback (visual, tactile, etc.) for the auditory. When we start to speak a sentence, we normally keep going until we have finished it—just as when we start to yawn we do not stop until we have completed the series of movements involved in yawning.

In a number of ways, the self stimulation involved in speaking

[1] Charles T. Brown, *Introduction to Speech* (New York: Houghton Mifflin Co., 1955), p. 22.

is of immense significance in our lives. No matter whom else we may speak to, we always speak to ourselves, and the stimulations which we receive from our own speech make up a large share of the world in which we live. Dr. Wendell Johnson has dealt brilliantly with this point. The student will profit much from a careful reading of what he has to say.[2]

But there is also a second type of feedback—the social. This type we already have discussed in terms of the reciprocity of stimulation and the alternation of the roles of speaker and listener. The speaker not only stimulates himself directly but, through the responses which he stirs up on the part of the listener and to which, in turn, he reacts, he stimulates himself indirectly.

A good deal of the social feedback in a speech situation is imaginary; that is, the responses which the speaker *thinks* he is producing in his listener stimulate him. When Mr. A and Mr. B are conversing, six persons are present in the situation: Mr. A, Mr. A's idea or image of himself, Mr. A's idea or image of Mr. B, Mr. B himself, Mr. B's idea or image of himself, and Mr. B's image of Mr. A. The fact that each of the two persons, A and B, may be quite different from his own idea of himself or from his idea of the other often results in confusion and disappointment with the effects of attempts at communication. As we have noted in Chapter 1, every human personality is made up of a large number of "roles," which are reflections of other personalities. In communication it is of the greatest importance to get an accurate and adequate image of the roles of others, and of one's own "self."

Speech Defined

It often is difficult to define terms which are used glibly in daily conversation. So it is with the word *speech.* As we think together about speech, we may have an experience something like that which Wendell Johnson describes when he says that, if one looks at one's own father long enough, one may begin to see him as a perfect stranger. Gilbert Chesterton once said: "You can look at a thing 999 times and be perfectly safe. But if you look at it the thousandth time you are in danger of *seeing* it." These sen-

[2] Wendell Johnson, *Your Most Enchanted Listener* (New York: Harper and Brothers, 1956).

tences epitomize the history of science and invention. We may learn a great deal about any familiar object or idea if we can manage to see it *as if for the first time.*

People are always more interested in *ends* than in *means,* in *products* than in *processes.* For example, although we all cherish memories of pleasant experiences, we usually are very little concerned as to *how* these memories are stored within us and kept available for recall and review. Or, we like or dislike people without bothering to ask ourselves *why.* When we come up against problems we cannot solve or obstacles we cannot surmount, we often escape through sublimation or rationalization, usually without suspecting what we are doing. Just so, we all use speech with our attention focused on what it secures for us but with little awareness of just how it works. Usually, in all of our experiences we are more concerned with the *what* than with the *why* and the *how.* In some measure, education should serve to reverse this tendency. Therefore, we shall begin by concentrating on speech as an *agency* or a *means* through which we seek to secure success in the intricate enterprise of living satisfactorily with other people.

At this point we offer a carefully considered definition of speech: *it is the psycho-physical process by which one person attempts to influence another person (or other persons) through light waves and/or sound waves produced solely and directly by the action of his own muscles.* (We might add, as a corollary: *and is usually stimulated and influenced by the light waves and/ or sound waves fed back to him by the one or ones whom he is trying to influence.*) Note that under this definition, a smile, a shrug, a lifted eyebrow, a growl, or a spoken word, phrase or sentence—any one of these alone or any combination of these may be speech.

To illustrate the speech process, let us look at a comparatively simple situation in which speech is being used for informational purposes only; the communicator desires to tell the communicatee about some physical object or occurrence. Schematically, this speech process can be represented as follows: [3]

[3] This diagram is adapted from one used by Wendell Johnson, "Speech and Personality," in L. Bryson (ed.), *The Communication of Ideas* (New York: Harper and Brothers, 1948), p. 56.

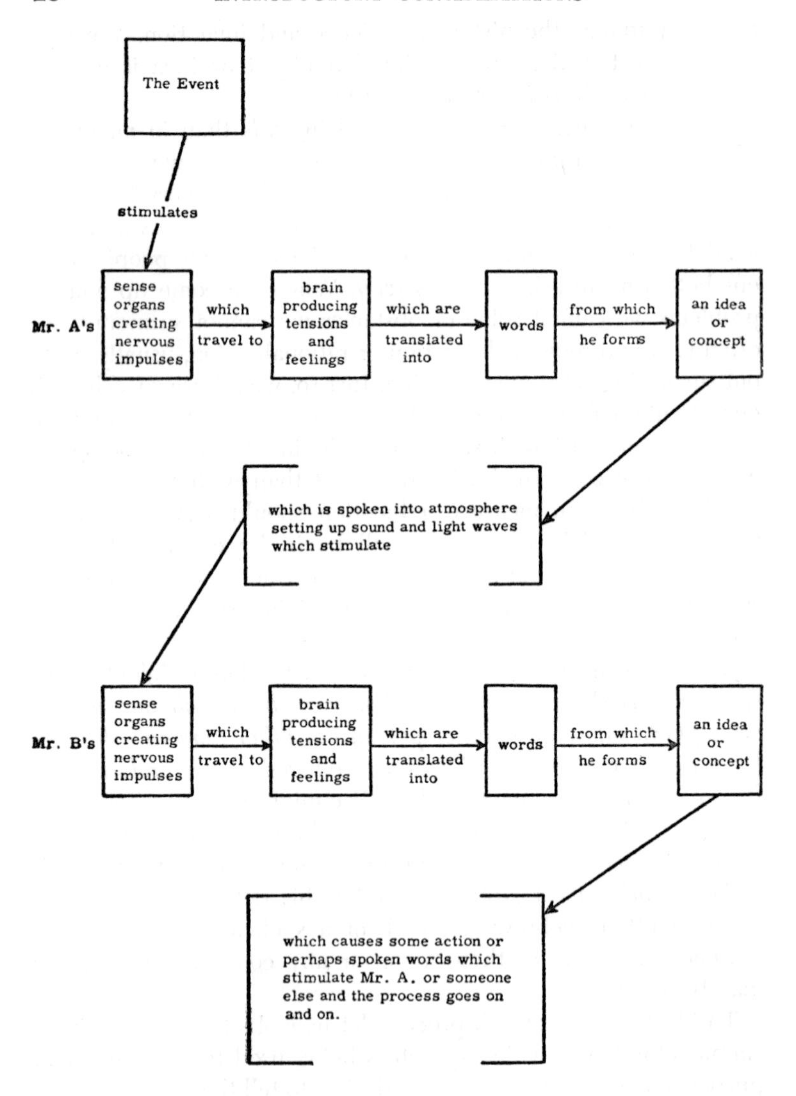

Diagram of Speech Process

It will be observed that the foregoing actually is an elaboration of the diagram of the communication process on page 24. The four blocks in line 2 and in line 4 represent the steps in the creation of the message which we showed by single blocks in the earlier diagram.

One basic fact about the speech process is that absolutely nothing, actually or literally, is *transferred* from the speaker to the listener through speech. Speech is not a process of wrapping up thoughts and feelings in a package and depositing it in a communicatee's mind. Nothing passes between the speaker and the listener but light waves and sound waves. Speech is always a pattern of these waves by which the communicator stirs up meanings in the communicatee by getting him to recall his own experiences. No one can ever tell another man a story; all he can do is try to stimulate him to tell himself a story. The best we can do is to use light waves and sound waves which may awaken those particular elements of the listener's past experience needed to reproduce within him the patterns of thinking and feeling we want him to have.

The Physical Aspects of Speech

From the physical point of view, speech consists of light waves and/or sound waves. The human eye is sensitive to light waves from infra-red to ultra-violet, i.e., from 300,000,000,000,000 to 800,000,000,000,000 vibrations per second. Above and below these limits we can see nothing and, therefore, vibrations of the ether outside this relatively narrow band of frequencies can stir up no responses in us through our sense of sight. The range of our hearing is also limited; our ears are sensitive to vibrations—rhythmic pressure changes—from about 16 to 20,000 per second. Above and below these frequencies we hear nothing. As Wendell Johnson explains: [4]

> Our sensory receptors are capable of responding only to relatively small segments of the total ranges of energy radiations. That is, the wave lengths to which the eye responds are but a small part of the total spectrum of wave lengths. We register as sound only a narrow

[4] Wendell Johnson, "The Spoken Word and the Great Unsaid," *Quarterly Journal of Speech,* Vol. 37, December, 1951, p. 420.

band of the full range of air vibrations. Noiseless dog whistles, "electronic eyes," and radar mechanisms—to say nothing of homing pigeons—underscore the primitive nature of our sensory equipment.

Of course air and ether vibration rates extend from zero to infinity, but human sensory capacity does not. Therefore, the physics of speech is centered on the light and sound within the rather narrow range to which eyes and ears make us sensitive. The implications of this fact are significant for the student of speech.

Obviously, light waves are of no use as a communication channel in the dark or when the communicatee is blind. Likewise, sound waves are ineffectual when they are drowned out in noise or when the communicatee is deaf. Movements which do not generate visible light waves or vocal sounds too faint to be audible are of no use in speech. If a communicatee is so near-sighted that he cannot see the movements of a speaker's facial muscles or of his hands, the channel of light waves is blocked. Similarly, it is of no use to bombard deaf ears with vocal vibrations.

The Physiological Aspects of Speech

The physics of speech seems simple when compared with the physiology of speech. Practically everything about the human body is germane to the scientific study of speech—the breathing mechanism, nerve impulses, action of muscles, blood pressure changes, glandular secretions, etc., etc.

From the physiological point of view, speech should be considered an overlaid or superimposed function—i.e., a process making use of structures and mechanisms which serve more basic biological needs, such as, chewing, swallowing, breathing, protecting the air passages from the entrance of foreign substances, etc. Thus an overlaid function is a secondary function. The point here is that speech is produced, not by muscle systems with which human beings are provided primarily that they may speak, but rather by the specialized use of muscle systems which perform more vital biological services.

Sapir points out the inaccuracy of referring to "organs of speech." He says: [5]

[5] Edward Sapir, *Language* (New York: Harcourt, Brace and Co., 1921), p. 7.

> . . . There are only organs that are incidentally useful in the production of speech sounds. The lungs, the larynx, the palate, the nose, the teeth, and the lips are all so utilized but they are no more to be thought of as primary organs of speech than are the fingers to be considered as essentially organs of piano-playing or the knees as organs of prayer. . . . Physiologically, speech is an overlaid function, or, to be more precise, a group of overlaid functions. It gets what service it can out of organs and functions, nervous and muscular, that have come into being and are maintained for very different ends. . . .

Even the vocal folds themselves are essentially concerned with valvular functions of the glottis, e.g., keeping food and drink out of the respiratory passages. When the folds are brought tightly together they impound the air in the lungs and thus provide firm leverages on the chest walls for the arm muscles. The primary physiological function of the breathing apparatus is to get oxygen into the blood and carry off carbon dioxide. The primary function of the teeth is to masticate food. The primary functions of the tongue are to taste food, to push it between the teeth in chewing, and to facilitate swallowing. Calling attention to these primary physiological functions does not imply that vocal speech is not an important function. Nevertheless, it is well to understand that speech is not as vital to life processes as are these other fundamental functions.

The Psychological Aspects of Speech

The psychology of speech centers around the basic concept of stimulus and response. From one point of view, speech consists of stimuli and responses.

The relatively new science of semantics helps us to understand the psychological nature of speech. Semantics seeks to explain the processes by which meanings become attached to symbols and the difficulties in using symbols accurately and effectively. Semantics stresses the vital distinction between the symbol and the experience for which it is a substitute. It emphasizes the point that we talk and think, not about the objective world of things around us, but only about our experiences with this world.

Paralleling the development of semantics has been the growth of "Information Theory" or "Cybernetics." Investigators in this field are attempting to work out the laws which govern the transmission of messages through symbols and to formulate mathematical statements governing the selection of the symbols to be used by the sender. An important contribution of information theorists is their definition of "noise" as any factor impeding the transmission of a message or distorting its meaning.

NOISE IN SPEECH SITUATIONS

There are many types of "noise" in our everyday speech communication and the effectiveness of our speaking depends upon our being able to reduce or eliminate them. There are physical "noises" and there are psychological "noises." A course in speech should alert us to perceive and deal with "noise." Unfortunate visible and audible mannerisms, colorless and monotonous language, mispronunciations, harsh and unpleasant voice quality, discourtesy, and like faults may constitute "noise." We draw our communication diagram once more, this time adding a representation of "noise" and self-regulatory feedback:

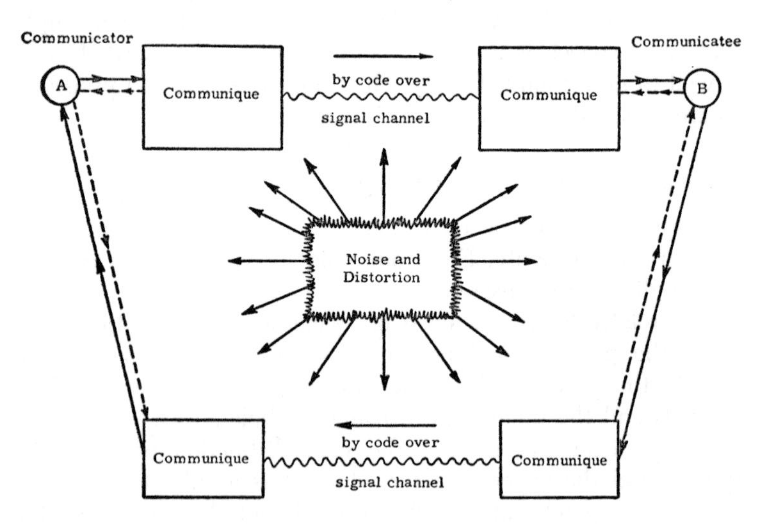

The communication may break down anywhere along the line because of the presence of noise. For example:

1. The communicator's sense organs may not be acting normally or at full efficiency. Thus the originating stimuli which

trip off the whole communication cycle may suffer from built-in noise.

2. The communicator's past experience may not have prepared him to react normally and, therefore, he may not interpret his present experiences normally. His imperfect interpretation will produce noise.
3. Limitations in the communicator's vocabulary may constitute noise.
4. The communicator's lack of ability to organize ideas and think clearly and logically may introduce elements of noise.
5. The communicator's inaccurate image of himself and/or the communicatee may be noise.
6. The communicator may have a speech defect which is noise in the encoding process.
7. Outside interference with the channel—noise in the sound and/or light waves—may obliterate or dim the audible or visible signs being transmitted.
8. The communicatee's sensory preoccupation with irrelevant stimuli is noise when it closes the avenues to stimuli furnished by the speaker.
9. Deficiencies in the experience of the communicatee may be noise.
10. Vocabulary deficiencies on the part of the communicatee produce noise.
11. Etc., etc., etc.!

The list might be continued almost indefinitely. The essential point is that the chances for noise in communication are legion and the possibility for completely "noiseless" communication are very slight indeed. In speech there is many a slip between the lip and the mind.

Nevertheless, despite all these difficulties communication satisfactory for all practical purposes can be achieved. We are all moderately successful in our efforts to communicate. Our purpose in elaborating the various forms of noise is to emphasize the complexities and pitfalls in communication. Speaking effectively requires the learning of principles and techniques, a task which demands the best that we have to give in careful study and constant practice.

The Social Aspect of Speech

Finally, we come to the obvious, but frequently ignored, social nature of speech. It is the need for cooperative action in the social situation which gives rise to speech. The prime motivation is the individual's need to reach some satisfying cooperation with other people. A person reared in complete isolation from other human beings would have no need for speech and would not develop it. It is notable that among the lower animals the purposive use of behavior to secure the cooperation of other members of the species is directly proportional to the importance of group activity in the animal's life economy. Most birds have well developed social lives and, consequently, they are voluble vocalizers. Animals which live isolated, relatively independent lives vocalize comparatively little.

We cannot understand speech unless we view it in its social matrix. The dominant drive back of speech is to bring about cooperative living. It is scarcely an overstatement to say that speech and society, if not practically identical, at least are indissolubly bound together.

The Four Elements of the Speech Process

There are four basic elements or ingredients in the speech process: *mental activity, language, voice,* and *visible action.*

Often a speaker seems to succeed in spite of obvious weaknesses in some of the basic elements. When this happens, he undoubtedly has compensating strength in some of the other elements. The only safe advice to the student speaker is: Cultivate your capacities in all of the elements, bringing your use of each of them up to the highest possible level of efficiency. It is foolish to jerk along on one or two cylinders when all four should be furnishing smooth power and speed. You should: (1) think clearly and feel deeply, (2) use words precisely and colorfully, (3) employ voice expressively and communicatively, and (4) act as if you mean what you are saying.

MENTAL ACTIVITY

As we have seen, speech originates in the nervous system of a speaker. Prior to and back of the visible and audible behavior of the speaker, lie the mental processes which prompt the speaking. This mental activity includes such factors as the speaker's purposes, his attitudes and feelings toward himself and his listener(s), his characteristic reactions to the world about him, his experiences, and even his dreams. No speaking can ever rise higher than its source; confused mental processes always show through the other elements and limit or destroy their effectiveness.

LANGUAGE

In one sense, it is probably correct to say that spoken language is the most artificial and conventional element in speech. Man speaks in many languages which depend upon the place in which he learns his language, his parentage, and many other accidental and fortuitous circumstances.

Spoken language, like written language, is made up of syllables, words, phrases, and sentences. But careful studies have revealed some important differences between the language of conversation and public address on the one hand, and the language of the pen and the printing press on the other. Professor Winans once said that a speech is not just an essay "standing on its hind legs." We shall have a good deal more to say about this element in Chapter 8.

VOICE

Everything that one hears in listening to speech, above and in addition to the spoken language, is included in the *vocal* element. In includes the loudness, quality, pitch, and duration of the vocal sounds and all the infinite permutations and combinations of these factors. When the language elements are voiced, tone, inflection, timing, diminuendo and crescendo effects—all these *say* something that the words alone do not and cannot say. Our words usually have many possible meanings and shades of meaning. Variations in voice indicate which meanings we intend. Voice is the matrix of sound waves in which oral language is set. Voice may make "No" mean "Yes" or "Maybe" or "NO!"

VISIBLE ACTION

This is the element of the speech code which uses the light waves channel in communication. It includes posture, movement, gesture, facial expression, etc.—in short, its comprises *all* of the visible behavior of the speaker which stirs up meaning in the communicatee. This visible code will be discussed in detail in Chapter 6.

We have presented the four elements of speech in the order which they normally seem to originate, from the point of view of the speaker; he thinks of speech, first, as thoughts and feelings (the message); second, as language forms into which his thoughts and feelings are cast; and finally, as the vocal and visible behavior which he can use to produce and modify the language forms. However, as we look at and listen to one who is speaking, these four elements affect us in exactly the reverse order; this is also the sequence in which they develop in the life of the child.

Characteristics of the Good Speaker

Before proceeding to a fuller consideration of the total activity which constitutes speech, we will take up rather briefly some of the principal characteristics of the good speaker which you should seek to acquire or develop through your classroom training.

1. *The good speaker is a keen and careful observer.* He sharpens his senses and learns to use them accurately and fully. He is sensitive to the world about him, especially to people. He sees, hears, touches, tastes, smells, and handles interesting objects. Because he has his senses working and is in vital contact with the external world, he is in a position to *talk sense.* The insensitive, non-observant person spins his messages out of his own inner consciousness and is never able to develop a working relationship with external things. Other factors being equal, the more completely a communicator senses what is outside his own central nervous system, the better speaker he is.
2. *The good speaker builds up a broad background of knowledge.* It is not enough to *sense* the world; he must, in some

measure, come to organize and *understand* it—or at least those aspects of it about which he wants to talk. He must learn to abstract and generalize from the information that comes to him through his senses. Unless he can interpret sense experience and build concepts from it, he cannot establish frames of reference which will give meanings to sensory data. An idiot may have keen senses but he lacks the power to abstract, generalize, and build concepts.

3. *The good speaker develops the capacity to think purposefully and logically.* It is quite possible to reach the mental level covered by the preceding characteristics without being able to sustain a line of connected, logical thinking. The problem here is to relate a series of ideas to each other according to some predetermined pattern. It is essential that a speaker possess the capacity for building meaningful patterns out of the smaller units of discourse so that the whole structure may effectively influence the thinking of others.
4. *The good speaker knows his own abilities and his own limitations.* The good speaker realizes how his peculiar and personal experiences, prejudices, feelings, fantasies, etc. affect his message and meanings. He knows that his own reactions are bound to be different from those of his communicatees; he will be careful not to be too positive and dogmatic. He will use such qualifying phrases as, "It seems to me," "In my judgment," "As I see the matter," etc. Such expressions assure the communicatee that the communicator properly evaluates his own points of view and is tolerant of differences of opinion.
5. *The good speaker has an accurate "image" of the communicatee.* The good speaker seeks to know the communicatee as completely as he can. He fashions his message and encodes it to fit the communicatee. He realizes that the meanings which arise from the communication will be joint products of the encoder and the decoder and, therefore, recognizes the need for the fullest possible cooperation between them. The more accurate the speaker's "image" of the listener, the more wisely he can select from all the things that he *might* say the specific things that he *should* say.

6. *The good speaker appreciates the personal equation in communication.* The personal relationship of the communicator to the communicatee is of very great importance in determining what the effects of communication will be. There is power in a strong personality. As the speaker learns to adjust himself to different "others," he grows in what we loosely call personality, and, as he grows in personality, he increases his capacity for social adaptation—it is a circular process. The more attractive the personality of the speaker, the better are his chances of stirring up in the listeners the meanings he wants them to have.
7. *The good speaker uses every opportunity for practice.* It has been suggested that the old adage, practice makes perfect, should be revised to read, practice makes permanent. Nevertheless, it still is true that *intelligent* practice does tend to improve skills. Despite all that may be done in the speech classroom to shorten the process of learning to speak well, a good deal of error always remains. No substitute for practice has been found in learning to do anything well. Nobody becomes a champion golfer by reading about golf or by following tournament players in the "gallery" at an exhibition or TV match; he has to *play* golf often and intelligently. The good speaker knows it is so with speech.
8. *The good speaker knows that voice and action are vital in speech.* There is much more to speech than the message and the language code; there are also the vocal and visible codes which must be mastered and used skillfully. The good speaker knows that when there are conflicts and inconsistencies between voice and visible action, or between visible action and language, the communicatee has to make choices between meanings and may choose incorrectly. The good speaker does not make the mistake of downgrading any part of the code to which he has to entrust his message; he does not depreciate the technical skills of vocal and visible action.
9. *The good speaker is an intelligent self-critic.* If the speaker is to engage in the intelligent practice which makes perfect, he has to be his own teacher; he must study his own speaking, estimate his own success or failure, and prescribe for

himself what he must do to improve. He studies the results of his efforts to communicate, the responses he gets and fails to get; he figures out reasons, explanations, and causes; and he constantly gives himself advice on remedial and corrective procedures. Only as a speaker becomes an intelligent self-critic of his own speaking can he hope to reach high-level accomplishment in the art of communication. The best that the instructor can do is to furnish the student with the criteria of excellence and the tools for self-improvement.

10. *The good speaker realizes his ethical responsibilities.* Society thrives on interaction but only on interaction based on high moral values. Over nineteen hundred years ago, the great Roman teacher, Quintilian, defined the orator as a good man skilled in speaking. No one has yet improved that statement. Communication divorced from *ethos* (character, integrity) is bound to fall short of the best. Demagoguery, no matter how immediately effective it may be, is not the proper goal of speech training. The good speaker is keenly and continually aware of his obligation to do and say only that which will promote the welfare of others. All of the commonly accepted standards of honesty, fairness, decency, and concern for others apply to speech, as much as to any other human activity.

How the Child Learns Speech

We are all born speechless. No one starts to speak naturally and instinctively; speech has to be learned. In understanding how speech originates and develops in the child, we must begin with a consideration of the factors or forces which operate in all human learning.

FACTORS IN THE LEARNING PROCESS

Biological Drives. The behavior of a living creature is always driven by forces within itself. To have these inborn, inner drives is to be alive, and vice versa. Without these urges, there would be no reaction or response to the stimulations from the outer world; to put the matter another way, the world around us would not really stimulate us at all, for to be stimulated is to react. Interaction between the forces within and those without is the very essence of being alive. Such imperative inner motives as hunger, pain, sex, etc. constitute the source of all human adjustment activity, including speech.

Stimulation. As we have just suggested, the essential difference between a living organism and an inanimate object lies in the capacity of the former to react to stimulation. This ability to react depends upon the possession of certain specialized neurological and physiological structures: (1) *sense organs* (*receptors*), (2) *nervous system,* and (3) *muscles and glands* (*effectors*). The forms of energy which call the various sense organs into action are called stimuli. The different sense organs make the organism sensitive to different kinds of energy; the eye makes it sensitive to light waves; the ear makes it sensitive to sound waves; the sense endings in the skin make it sensitive to contact, pressure, heat, cold, and pain. All of our contact with the world both outside and inside our bodies begins with the action of sense organs.

What happens when a sense organ is aroused? A nerve impulse begins in the sense organ, travels to a sensory center in the spinal cord or some part of the brain, is switched over to a motor center, and sent out over another nerve pathway to a muscle and/or a gland. The muscle then contracts or the gland secretes. Every human activity, simple or complex, involves this threefold process—stimulation, nerve conduction, and muscular and/or glandular response. This principle holds true all the way from the simplest reflex to the most complicated intellectual behavior. Here are to be found all the elements that later constitute the elaborate response patterns we call "speech."

Fixation of Responses. Once having responded to stimulation, we tend to react to the same or similar stimulation by repeating our responses. Thus our behavior becomes set or fixated. Our responses become set in two ways: (1) No matter how many false or erroneous responses we may make in trying to adjust ourselves to situations, we persist until we have found the correct one. Thus, the nerve pathways involved in the correct response are left open and ready to respond again. (2) A successful response is accompanied by a pleasant feeling which tends to reenforce it and keep it ready to act again. These two factors form the basis for the formation of useful habits at all levels of behavior. Of course, they apply to speech habits as they do to other useful habits. We strive to satisfy our inner needs, we respond to stimulation, and we are so constructed that responses which serve our needs will be retained, repeated, and built into habits.

Conditioning. Two types of stimuli call out our responses: (1) original, unlearned stimuli and (2) substitute or conditioned stimuli. The first type of stimulus calls a sense organ into action without the intervention of learning; the pathways from the sense organ to the nerve center and from the nerve center to the muscle or gland have been established by nature prior to any learning. We all come into the world with certain inborn connections between our sense organs and our muscles and glands, for example, in such reflex actions as blinking, swallowing, etc. These relatively simple reflexes form the basis for all our complex future behavior which is constructed from them by conditioning.

Although conditioning had long been discussed by psychologists, it was the great Russian physiologist, Pavlov, who gave new dimensions to the concept by his experiments on the salivary reflex of dogs. The original stimulus for the action of the saliva glands is the presence of food in the mouth. Pavlov found that if a metronome were started ticking every time the dog was eating, soon the sound of the metronome alone would make the dog's "mouth water." This substitution of the auditory stimulus for the original stimulus, he called conditioning. It is to be observed that the ticking of the metronome originally had no power to make the saliva flow; it acquired power by being applied with a stimulus which, by nature, already had power.

Later investigators demonstrated that the same reflex in human beings can be similarly conditioned. All of us know that the sound of the refrigerator door closing, the smell of food cooking, the verbal description of an appetizing meal, or even the thought of food, may make our mouths water. More than half a century ago Twitmyer experimentally conditioned the knee-jerk reflex to the ringing of a bell; every time he tapped the patellar tendon, he rang a bell or sounded a buzzer. Eventually the auditory stimulus from the bell or buzzer caused the knee jerk. The pupillary reflex (changes in the size of the pupil of the eye), originally caused by changes in illumination, also has been conditioned by the sound of a bell.

Human emotional behavior is especially susceptible to conditioning. There are probably only three unlearned emotions—fear, anger, and love—and these are called out by a limited number of stimuli. But when we are behaving emotionally, any chance stimulus in the total stimulating situation may "get into the act" and become a substitute for (may condition) the original stimulus. Thus we may develop all sorts of strange and inappropriate emotional behavior—phobias, manias, etc.

Conditioning accounts for most of human learning. If it is once clearly understood in the foregoing rather elementary examples, it may be extended to explain such intricate learned habits as those which make up human speech, and thought, which, for the most part, is talking to one's self.

Adaptation. By this factor in the learning process, we mean changes in the efficiency of learned responses, both simple and complex. Gains in efficiency are called *positive adaptation;* losses in efficiency are called *negative adaptation.*

Increased efficiency of behavior may be indicated in two ways: (1) lowering the threshold of stimulation and (2) speeding up the responses. Both of these changes are the normal results of the repetition of responses.

As we perform any act again and again, we become more and more sensitive to the stimuli which cause us to respond; the threshold of stimulation is lowered. Furthermore, we speed up our actions. If we get up every time the alarm goes off, we become so positively adapted that eventually the slightest tinkle will awaken us. On the other hand, if we are slow to respond or fail to respond at all when the alarm sounds, we become *negatively* adapted, and the threshold of stimulation rises until, eventually, we do not hear the alarm even though it may continue to ring for a long time. Positive adaptation produces skill in any activity, be it piano playing, golf, typing, or speaking. First, conditioning, and then positive adaptation—these are the two major ingredients of artistry in any activity.

Telescoping. Very closely allied to positive adaptation is *telescoping*, the shortening of a series of acts through the dovetailing of successive elements. As we go through a serial act such as walking, we do not complete each movement before starting the next; we start each movement while the preceding movement is still doing on. The skilled typist or pianist could never attain the necessary speed if each movement were made separately; the movements must overlap and blend together into larger units. In speaking, as we utter a syllable, we simultaneously make advance adjustments for vocalizing the syllable that is to follow. The sentences are compressed in a way analogous to the way in which a telescope is when its overlapping parts are slipped over each other and the instrument is shortened. So, at last, we speak not in separate isolated sounds, but in smooth-flowing larger patterns of integrated language.

STAGES IN THE SPEECH-LEARNING PROCESS

For purposes of convenience we may designate four stages through which the child passes in learning to speak. These stages are not discrete, or clearly separate steps; they are not sharply delineated; there is a great deal of overlapping among them.

The Stage of Unsatisfaction. William James described the world into which the infant is born as "a blooming, buzzing confusion." It is a world of unorganized stimulation and of random responses. Sense organs are being bombarded by a multitude of stimuli. The responses of the infant, aside from a few simple reflexes, are general and random—kicking, twisting, turning, arm waving, gurgling, cooing, crying, etc. Doubtless the value of all this rather accidental behavior is the discovery of responses which may contribute to the satisfaction of the needs of the child who is struggling to bring itself into such relationships with its environment as will promote its well-being. There is a sense in which this stage is not true speech at all. It is set forth here as a stage because the element of social control is foreshadowed in these early, unorganized efforts to modify the environment in ways which will satisfy the child's needs.

The Stage of Gesture. When the baby "discovers" that the movements of its hands, arms, and facial muscles influence the activities of nurses and parents in ways beneficial to it, speech definitely begins. The infant soon learns to use its visible behavior to control the behavior of other persons and then all the essentials of speech are present.

Students who are trying to improve their speech should note the fact that in the development of speech, the visible symbols come first. Judd says: [6]

> Gesture, or gesture language as it is called, is thus seen to be not merely a complex form of behavior but one which expresses a new type of relationship between the reactor and his environment. Gesture is a social form of behavior involving attention to persons as well as to objects. Indeed, gesture supersedes the more direct forms of attack on objects.

Allport sums up this gesture stage by saying: [7]

> The language of gesture develops from natural and serviceable movements originally of purely individualistic significance. The head-shaking gesture illustrates the genetic process. At the beginning, the baby turns his head away so as to prevent undesired substances which touch his lips from entering his mouth. This is the stage of simple *avoidance* or *withdrawing*. By conditioned response the sight of the undesirable object later calls forth the same reaction, and the effect is now avoidance, or *refusal*. The movement serves as a sign which is readily understood and reacted to by the person offering the rejected substance. Since the action serves thus to control the behavior of others in a manner useful to the individual, it is fixated according to the principles of arc fixation in learning it. It is now *used as a sign;* in other words, it has become a gesture. The movement therefore has passed from a simple avoiding response of no social significance to a truly expressive one valuable in the control of the social environment for the prepotent interests of the individual who uses it. [*Prepotent interests* is a term synonymous with *biological needs*.]

Another explanation of what is taking place at this stage is suggested by Sullivan who says that speech arises from simple empathic responses and that long before the infant actually *understands* either his own behavior or that of others, he will react with responses which result from emotional contagion or "communion." The mechanism of empathy will be discussed at greater length in Chapters 6 and 9, but here it is sufficient to explain that

[6] C. H. Judd, *Psychology* (Boston: Ginn & Co., 1917), p. 217.

[7] F. H. Allport, *Social Psychology* (Boston: Houghton Mifflin Co., 1924), p. 54.

empathy is a projection of one's own feelings into what one sees and hears. According to this view: [8]

> It is biological for the infant when nursing to show certain expressive movements which are called the satisfaction response, and it is probably biological for the parent concerned to see these things. Due to the empathic linkage, this, the reaction of the parent to the satisfaction-response of the infant, communicates good feeling to the infant and thus he learns that this response has power.

This empathic communion seems to consist of a combination of facial expressions, postures, and gestures which constitute for the child a system of non-linguistic symbols which have meaning.

At first the baby's gestures are full, graphic, and pantomimic; they have a rather obvious meaning. But, as time goes on, the gestures are reduced to remnants or clues, only a small part of the former gestures being needed to give the observer the intended meaning. There is a deep-seated drive on the part of the organism to conserve energy. This tendency toward minimum effort is a powerful incentive to substitute activity of the vocal folds for gestures, voice production being relatively effortless.

The Stage of Pre-language Voice. Of course, there is a considerable overlapping of this stage and the preceding one; while the child is learning to use gestures for purposes of social control, he is also learning to use the vowel and consonant sounds which will later be combined into syllables and words. He is building up a vocabulary of vocal tones which will finally make it possible to use the conventional symbols of language.

Both gesture and voice begin in the random activity of muscles. When the infant is hungry or uncomfortable, it moves and utters vocal sounds. In this period all the sounds out of which spoken language can be made are produced and practiced. Next to gesture, this tone code is the most primitive and fundamental element in speech.

The tone "language" of the child lasts throughout all the later adult forms of speech. Under emotional stress, grownups may revert to this infantile type of speech; profanity often is merely a meaningless combination of words the uttering of which permits

[8] Harry Stack Sullivan, *Conceptions of Modern Psychiatry* (New York: W. W. Norton and Company, 1947), p. 17.

the speaker to employ this infantile tone code. The meaning of many of our interjections lies in the tones rather than in the words. Sometimes, people under violent provocation, slip back even beyond pre-language vocalization into pantomime. Consider the tantrums of adults and the other types of spoiled-child behavior which adults use to influence the behavior of others.

The Stage of Articulate Language. The pre-language vocalization of the child begins with the open tones which we call vowels. Then these tones are interrupted by random movements of the tongue, lips, soft palate, and jaw which produce the consonants. This period of babbling and cooing is a form of play.

> The chief significance of the vocal play of babies seems to be in establishing circular reflexes between the sound of the syllable and the response of speaking it. Let us suppose, for example, that the baby utters the symbol *da*. By so doing he stimulates himself through two channels. He receives certain kinaesthetic sensations from the movement of the vocal organs and certain auditory sensations from the sound which he produced.[9]

As the child makes the sound "da," he stimulates his own ear. This auditory feedback, through circular conditioning, is substituted for the stimulus which originally caused him to utter the sound. The infant does not speak the sound "da" just once at a time; he repeats it over and over again, thus circularly conditioning his own activity.

It is easy to understand why the child born deaf fails to develop the sound system upon which language is based. He starts the spontaneous babbling and cooing of the hearing child but, since he cannot hear the sounds he produces, he never arrives at the stage where the feedback becomes a stimulus for sound production. Congenitally deaf children may be taught to articulate words through the substitution of visual or tactile stimuli for auditory stimuli, but their spoken language can never have the delicate and accurate sounds of normal speech.

When the child has "learned" to produce vocal sounds in response to the hearing of sounds he himself utters, his ear-voice reflexes have been so conditioned that he can speak sounds which he hears others speak. When he hears others utter sounds, he automatically responds by producing the sounds in his "vocabulary"

[9] Allport, *op. cit.*, p. 182.

that come closest to them. He does not learn new sounds; he produces, through conditioning, the sounds he already has mastered. This reproducing process we loosely call "imitation."

Children can learn the sound systems of several languages rather easily, whereas older people find it hard to learn to speak foreign languages. The child has a large vocabulary of circularly-conditioned vocal sounds, many of which later will prove useless for mastering his own language and, therefore, will be dropped. The adult, having stereotyped the sound system of one language, will speak another language with an accent, that is, with the use of the sounds of his own language which are the closest approximations to those of the second language.

When the essential ear-voice reflexes have been established in the child, the parent begins to teach the child the names of things. For example, the parent shows the object and says "doll." The child responds with the sounds that represent his closest approach to "doll," perhaps only "da." When this has been repeated a few times, the sight of the object is substituted for the sound of the word and the child responds to seeing the doll by calling out his closest approximation of the name. In this way the child learns to react to objects with the specific vocalization conditioned by them.

ADDITIONAL READINGS

Brown, Charles T., *Introduction to Speech* (Boston: Houghton Mifflin Co., 1955).

Cicero, *Orator*, translated by H. M. Hubbell (Cambridge, Mass.: Harvard University Press, 1942).

Schramm, Wilbur, "How Communication Works," in *Process and Effects of Mass Communications* (Urbana: University of Illinois Press, 1955).

Thonssen, Lester, *Selected Readings in Rhetoric and Public Speaking* (New York: H. W. Wilson Co., 1942).

Thonssen, Lester, and Baird, A. Craig, *Speech Criticism* (New York: The Ronald Press, 1948).

QUESTIONS AND PROJECTS

1. Think back over your speaking experiences on important occasions, both formal and informal. Pick out one speech situation which you feel you handled with success, and one in which you feel that

you failed. Analyze these two contrasting experiences in terms of what you have read in the foregoing chapter, trying to explain your success and your failure. Tell the class about the experiences.

2. Analyze the next speech you hear either over radio or television or on the platform. How much "noise" was there in the communication process? What was the nature of the "noise" and how did it affect the message for you? How well did the speaker deal with the "noise" in the situation? Did you contribute some of the "noise"?

3. Prepare a short (3-minute) speech about yourself, concentrating not on "vital statistics," but on your attitudes, feelings, beliefs, likes, and dislikes, or on interesting personal experiences. The aim of the speech should be to enable other members of the class to feel that they know you better.

4. In lieu of Project 3, you might introduce another member of the speech class to the group. Spend some time with this person. Try to find out as many interesting things about him as you can, and then present this information accurately and in a stimulating way. (While the class are engaged in either Project 3 or this one, a member can keep a tabulation of the various group memberships that are represented. This summary can then be read to the class as a helpful beginning step in audience analysis.)

5. Make an analysis of the speaking requirements of the profession or career you expect to enter. It may be helpful to interview successful individuals in this field regarding their speech experiences. Report your findings and conclusions to the class in a 3- to 5-minute speech.

6. Discuss Lytton Strachey's statement: "Perhaps of all the creations of man, language is the most astounding." Criticize and evaluate.

7. Consider George DuMaurier's unusual description of speech: "Language is a poor thing. You fill your lungs with wind and shake a little slit in your throat, make mouths, and that shakes the air, and the air makes a pair of little drums in my head—a very complicated arrangement—and my brain seizes your meaning in the rough." Analyze and evaluate this statement.

8. Make a careful inventory of yourself as a speaker. Try to pick out your assets and liabilities and jot down your reasons for thinking of them as such. You might also support these reasons by specific examples from your experience. Furnish a copy of this inventory to your instructor and keep one for yourself. This sort of inventory can be very helpful to you, but only if you really take the time to do a thoughtful job on it; otherwise you are wasting your time and your teacher's.

CHAPTER 3

The Function of Stage Fright

Stage Fright Defined

One of the clearest and most satisfactory definitions of stage fright is that of Floyd I. Greenleaf,[1] who says that stage fright

> . . . is an evaluative disability, occurring in social speech situations, and characterized by anticipatory negative reactions of fear, avoidance, and various internal and overt manifestations of tensions and behavioral maladjustment.

Eisenson in his treatment of stage fright stresses the view that it originates in a Freudian conflict between avoidance and approach responses which are touched off by the audience situation. The speaker desires an audience and at the same time fears it; he is, therefore, at once attracted to and repelled by the audience. The attraction stimulates approach responses while the repulsion stimulates withdrawal or avoidance responses. The result is conflict and confusion of attitude and feeling.[2]

Emotional Nature of Stage Fright

Clearly then, stage fright is an emotional response, not an intellectual one; it arises from automatic, reflex reactions rather than from conscious, reasoned reactions. If we want to understand it, we should begin by considering the nature of emotional behavior and its place and function in our lives.

[1] Quoted in Theodore Clevenger, "A Synthesis of Experimental Research on Stage Fright," *Quarterly Journal of Speech*, Vol. 45 (1959), p. 134.
[2] Jon Eisenson, J. J. Auer, and John V. Irwin, *The Psychology of Communication* (New York: Appleton-Century-Crofts, 1963).

EMOTION DEFINED

An emotion is a general stirred up physical and mental state; it is a condition of excitement characterized by tension in muscles and activity in internal organs, particularly the endocrine glands, such as the thyroid, the adrenals, and the pituitary, which pour powerful energizing substances called hormones directly into the blood. The person who is experiencing emotion is affected by increased blood pressure, quickened pulse, rapid breathing, and tensed muscles. His mouth may feel dry, he may perspire, his knees may shake, and his hands may feel cold and clammy. If his emotion is violent, he may have difficulty in articulating his words clearly, he may stutter and stammer. In short, all his finer muscular controls and coordinations are impaired. Some of the common phrases we use to describe emotional behavior shed light on its essential nature: "He lost his head," "He blew up," "He flew all to pieces," "He was blind with rage," "He flew off the handle," etc., etc. All such expressions suggest that in an extreme emotional state discrimination and control are absent. One cannot be highly emotional and dominantly intellectual at the same time.

ELEMENTS OF EMOTION

Two elements are present in every emotion: (1) feedback into consciousness from disturbed internal conditions and (2) an awareness of a causative factor which has produced the widespread reverberations. The first of these taken by itself is not really an emotion; it is simply a jittery, upset bodily state. By itself, the second is a purely intellectual condition. But when the two are combined, we have an emotion. Since all emotions are alike in their physiological components, it is the second factor—the intellectual—that furnishes the basis for differentiating one emotion from another. The muscular, respiratory, circulatory, visceral, and glandular elements in fear are the same as those in anger, love, or any other equally violent emotional state. The fact that we call the emotion "fear" in one instance and "anger" or "love" in another does not mean that there is any essential difference in their physiological nature.

Now we ask: What are emotions for? What role do they play

in human life? Why should we experience emotion at all? Wouldn't we be better off if we were coldly logical, intellectual machines? To answer this question, we turn to William James' explanation of the function of emotion in our lives.

THE DYNAMOGENIC NATURE OF EMOTION

James stressed what he called the dynamogenic nature of emotion. The word *dynamogenic* comes from two Greek roots meaning *power* and *birth* or *beginning*. Emotion then is an energy-generating process; emotional states make available powers not ordinarily at our disposal. When we experience fear, we may be able to run faster than we otherwise could; when we are angry, we may strike a harder blow than we could in an unemotional state. Thus, we see that emotions are emergency mechanisms which make it possible for us to exert powers which we do not ordinarily seem to possess.

An English novelist, I. A. R. Wylie, writing under the interesting title, "I Enjoy Myself Most When I'm scared," says: [3]

> When was I the happiest? When did I enjoy myself most? And I came on an unexpected answer: I had enjoyed myself most when I had been at my best, and I had been most often at my best when I'd been badly scared. By 'enjoying myself' I mean feeling that I have done a good job or reacted to some challenge in a way that makes it possible for me, in the face of difficulty and danger, to trust myself.

The writer goes on to tell about her first experiences of utter panic when she was called upon to make speeches and the sense of triumph and satisfaction which came from meeting the challenge and acquitting herself creditably. She testifies that stage fright arouses within her "unsuspected powers" and that fear is a stimulant which enables her to surpass her normal self. She says further that when she begins a speech feeling perfectly comfortable, she is usually a flat failure; she needs the spur of emotional excitement in order to do her best.

NEUROLOGICAL ASPECTS OF EMOTION

From the viewpoint of the nerve centers involved, the thalamus, one of the lower parts of the brain, plays the leading role in

[3] I. A. R. Wylie, "I Enjoy Myself Most When I'm Scared," *Reader's Digest,* Vol. 62, March, 1953, p. 17.

emotional excitement. However, as we have seen, the higher centers in the cortex are also involved; it is through their action that we become aware of the exciting cause of our emotion. These cortical centers have sufficient influence over the lower ones so that we can continue some measure of control and discrimination even in face of the tendencies toward disorganization touched off by the action of the thalamus. Thus, the cortex and the thalamus contend for domination of behavior. No one is ever either one hundred per cent emotional or one hundred per cent intellectual.

In a speaker, too much cortical dominance means coldness and uninterestingness; too much thalamic dominance means instability and confusion. The personality best adapted to civilized society is one in which there is a nice balance between the emotional and the intellectual, the former providing the driving energy and the latter, the guidance.

One psychologist says: [4]

> Emotion is aroused whenever the higher centers of the brain fail to find a fitting response to the perceived situation or when a doubt is aroused as to our ability successfully to respond to it. . . . Emotional reactions are inversely proportional to the ability of the higher centers of the brain to meet a given situation.

Most of us, in emotion-arousing situations, are faced with the problem of strengthening the action of the cortex rather than allowing the thalamus to dictate our behavior. Here we have the gist of the matter; if, through cortical processes, we can work out ways of meeting adequately the speech situations we face, we will reduce the excessive and disabling emotion.

Causes of Stage Fright

We already have indicated that emotions are tripped off by any situation which seems to present an emergency. While stage fright is so named because it so frequently affects public performers on some sort of stage, in reality we all experience similar feelings in a great variety of social situations. When an employee is suddenly summoned to the foreman's office, he is quite likely

[4] Frederick A. Hodge, "The Emotions in a New Role," *Psychological Review,* 42:555.

to experience apprehension or alarm. He may have feelings of inferiority, inadequacy, and self-distrust. When a salesman approaches a prospect, he may feel his courage oozing away; he may be afraid that he will not be able to present his product persuasively enough to get the potential buyer to sign on the dotted line. As he waits in the reception room, he may find his muscles tense, his heart pounding, his breathing irregular and shallow, and an "all-gone" feeling in the pit of his stomach. When a student is called to the dean's office at the end of a term, he may be very frightened. Ordinarily we do not say that these people are suffering from stage fright, but they feel exactly the way the insecure person feels in a threatening speech situation.

One of the strange paradoxes of human nature is that we want an audience and yet fear one. We all like to be in touch with others; there is no experience more painful for the normal person than to be isolated from his fellow men. We all enjoy attention. Many a problem child or maladjusted adult is simply a person who has failed to find acceptable ways of getting attention. Driven to desperation, he employs objectionable devices for attracting attention and becomes a nuisance to other people. It is out of this almost universal desire for attention that the craving for an audience arises. The trouble is that, as we have seen, often when we have secured an audience, we are afraid of it; our approach and avoidance tendencies pull us in two directions at once.

Naturally and instinctively we seem to feel that when we enter into communication with even one person, we face the question, Which of us is going to control the other? When we stand before a number of people, we feel an inner realization that we are up against a difficult problem. Almost every successful speaker testifies to the exhilaration which comes from a successful speech; this sense of triumph derives from the feeling that he has met and surmounted a challenge.

UNIVERSALITY OF STAGE FRIGHT

There is nothing strange or abnormal about stage fright; the experience is practically universal. A speaker who does not feel any stage fright is more peculiar than one who feels it strongly.

There is nothing unnatural about feeling that a speech is important and fraught with difficulty.

Stage fright usually does not appear in children until about the age of puberty. Why should this be so? It seems that, as the child matures, he becomes concerned about his place in the social order and anxious to win the approval of others. Yet, it is difficult to understand why he should suddenly become the victim of stage fright. It would seem that some way might be found to bridge the gap between the easy comfort of the earlier years and the unhappy tensions of the later.

One investigator[5] found that he could classify high school speakers into three groups: (1) those who do not experience any stage fright, (2) those who do experience stage fright in beginning to speak but whose fears diminish as they proceed, and (3) those who are afraid as they begin and grow increasingly afraid as they continue. It was found that those in the second group were the best speakers.

ABSENCE OF STAGE FRIGHT A LIABILITY

Perhaps you know someone who is so completely lacking in sensitiveness that he is completely at ease in any and all social situations. His attitude is one of continuous self-satisfaction. He is not the least afraid of people, individually or collectively; he feels superior and secure. Such a person is seriously maladjusted socially; he is bound to be a failure in speech, public or private.

Controlled sensitiveness is a tremendous asset to a speaker. The sensitive person is not likely to offend others; he notices and interprets the outward signs of their inner feelings and adjusts what he is saying accordingly. He knows, almost instinctively, when others are bored, puzzled, or irritated. Many great public speakers and distinguished actors never face an audience without twinges of stage fright. William Jennings Bryan, one of the greatest American orators, often said that if the time ever came when he could face an audience without feeling any trace of stage fright he would know that he had lost an essential part of his equipment for public speaking.

[5] Charles W. Lomas, "The Psychology of Stage Fright," *Quarterly Journal of Speech*, February, 1937, Vol. XXIII, No. 1, p. 41.

The great ancient teacher of speech, Quintilian, wrote in his textbook more than nineteen hundred years ago: [6]

> . . . I am not unwilling that the man who has got to make a speech should show signs of nervousness when he rises to his feet, should change colour and make it clear that he feels the risks of his position: indeed, if these symptoms do not occur naturally, it will be necessary to stimulate them.

And Cicero, the foremost orator of Rome, said: [7]

> . . . the better qualified a man is to speak, the more he fears the difficulty of speaking, and the expectation of the audience.

Two points in these quotations deserve special notice: (a) Quintilian's view regarding the necessity for an emotional approach to an audience and (b) Cicero's phrase implying the need for meeting *"the expectation of the audience."*

Making Stage Fright Work for You

We have now seen that a normal amount of stage fright is potentially good and can become a real asset to a speaker if properly handled. In a sense it does not need to be *converted* into an asset; it already *is* one. What then can you do to make sure you are letting this asset work for you?

First, cultivate a positive mental attitude. Dismiss from your mind the unjustified notion that those with whom you speak would enjoy seeing you embarrassed and ill-at-ease. Be smart enough to realize that others in whose presence you act frightened and upset will feel your distress *empathically.* Other people want you to succeed; they would do almost anything to help you. Strive to develop and hold an adequate and fair image of your listeners, who usually are kindly and friendly folks; don't treat them as if they were enemies. Try to see them as actual individuals rather than a vague "sea of faces."

As William James long ago pointed out, we can do a great deal to substitute confidence for fear by acting as we do when we feel confident. We can change depression into exhilaration by throw-

[6] Quintilian, *Institutio Oratoria,* translated by H. S. Butler (Harvard University Press, 1921), Vol. 4, p. 411.

[7] Lester Thonssen, *Selected Readings in Rhetoric and Public Speaking* (New York: The H. W. Wilson Co., 1942), p. 86.

ing our shoulders back, standing straight and erect and speaking in strong, positive tones. The governess in *The King and I* uttered a profound truth when she said that she always whistled when she was afraid and that, by doing so, she fooled not only others into believing that she *was* brave, but more important still, she fooled herself as well!

Second, make thorough preparation. Prepare so fully that you can stand some shrinkage of your intellectual powers during the actual speaking. It is not enough that you know *beforehand* what you want to say and how you expect to say it. You must be so thoroughly prepared that when you come to the act of communication you can lose some of your muscular skill and even some of your ideas and still retain enough to do the job. The next chapter tells in detail what preparing to speak involves.

Often the novice speaker says, "I went over my material three or four times before I came here and I thought I had it well in mind. Now I forget what I had planned to say!" The speaker should overlearn his speech to a point from which he can forget some of it and still carry on adequately. He should resolve not to be like Mark Twain's steamboat, the engine of which was so small that every time its whistle blew, it stopped!

Third, persevere until you succeed. When an aviator has survived an accident, he loses no time in getting back into the air. If he were to sit around the hangar talking about his narrow escape and reliving his panic, he might develop such a state of nerves that he would never be able to climb into the cockpit again. When the speaker has the painful experience of "goofing," he should not dodge future speech situations; he should seek them out and keep plugging away. Here is where the principle of negative adaptation comes in.

NEGATIVE ADAPTATION

By *negative adaptation* we mean raising of the threshold of stimulation and the weakening of responses. When we refuse to respond to a stimulus, we set up a condition in which it will take a stronger stimulus to trip off the response. When a child does not come at his mother's call, and is allowed to ignore the summons, it will take a louder call the next time to make him come.

By refusing to let the fear of an audience prevent us from speaking, we eventually wear out the fear stimulus and become more comfortable.

We have explained that emotions are emergency mechanisms which make available to us reserve energies. But why should they overshoot the mark as they frequently do? Why, in a sudden crisis, do we find ourselves paralyzed with fear and unable to meet the situation? Why should we be frozen to the spot and unable to move? Why should we become so angry that we lose our heads and act foolishly? Why should a simple speech situation throw us into such an emotional turmoil that we cannot speak effectively? The answer to such puzzling questions is that we begin life with an oversupply of emotional behavior because it inevitably will be reduced by negative adaptation. If we did not have too much emotion at the start, we should have too little later.

Perhaps the clearest illustration of negative adaptation is the development of "tolerance" for medicines or drugs. For example, the doctor is hesitant to prescribe antibiotics for minor illnesses lest the patient become immune to their effects through negative adaptation. The ancient tyrants who lived in constant dread of assassination by poisoning negatively adapted themselves to various poisons by taking small doses of them at first and gradually increasing the quantity until they had built up their resistance to them. The structural steel worker becomes negatively adapted to walking an I-beam forty stories above the street. Often, negative adaptation goes too far and skilled workers in dangerous occupations become foolhardy.

Negative adaptation is the friend of the sufferer from stage fright; by speaking whenever good opportunities present themselves, he can become negatively adapted and eventually will be able to meet speaking situations with just enough stage fright to release the appropriate amount of energy for the work at hand. Most students are in no danger of getting too well adapted and losing the values of a reasonable amount of emotionality in their speech. However, even the beginner should know that it is possible to become so dead and colorless emotionally that he will cease to be alert and effective.

In this speech course, you have the opportunity to decide whether the emotional excitement within your own bodies during speech situations is going to be a handicap or a help to you; whether the extraordinary energies it makes available will generate effective visible action, voice, language, and mental processes or be drained off into random, aimless, hampering behavior; whether you will permit emotion to use you or resolve to use it; in short, whether stage fright is to be your master or your servant. Faced with these alternatives, an intelligent person, ambitious to make the most of himself, should be able to make the right choices.

EXPERIMENTAL EVIDENCE

After studying the published results of many investigators, Clevenger[8] concludes that as stage fright is reduced from its more extreme forms to a reasonable amount, speaking ability rises proportionately. He also observes the very interesting fact that women suffer more from excessive stage fright than men do but that they *seem* to those who judge their effectiveness less subject to it. Or conversely, men testify that they are less handicapped by stage fright but *seem* to observers more handicapped. In this rather paradoxical set of circumstances there is one rather clear lesson for the beginning speaker, namely, that what matters most is not how much stage fright one experiences; what matters is how much evidence one gives of the stage fright he feels.

Robinson[9] urges the speaker to avoid the mistake of assuming that the audience is evaluating him instead of his message; by reminding himself of the fact that what he is saying is more important than anything else in the situation, he can do much to lessen his fears. The four big words in Robinson's advice to novice speakers who are bothered by excessive stage fright are: *Practice, Preparation, Attitude,* and *Rehearsal.*

[8] *Op. cit.,* p. 140.
[9] Edward R. Robinson, "What Can the Speech Teacher Do About Students' Stage Fright?" *Speech Teacher,* Vol. 8 (1959), pp. 8–14.

ADDITIONAL READINGS

Brigance, William Norwood, *Speech, Its Techniques and Disciplines in a Free Society*, 2nd edition (New York: Appleton-Century-Crofts, 1961), pp. 68–74.

Clevenger, Theodore, Jr., "A Synthesis of Experimental Research in Stage Fright," *Quarterly Journal of Speech*, April, 1959, pp. 134–45.

QUESTIONS AND PROJECTS

1. An English poet, John Saxe, gave us the following:

> A centipede was happy quite
> Until a frog in fun
> Said: "Pray which leg comes after which?"
> This raised her mind to such a pitch,
> She lay distracted in the ditch,
> Considering how to run.

What relation do you perceive between the predicament of the centipede and that of a speaker suffering from stage fright?

2. In a 3- to 5-minute speech, tell the class simply and directly about your own experiences, if any, with stage fright.

3. Your class will be your audience throughout this course. What is your "image" of the various people in the class? Describe three of your classmates *as you see them and think of them* at this point in the course. Write out your descriptions and read them to the class.

4. What is your "image" of yourself as a member of the class? If anyone else has described his "image" of you, what corrections or changes do you think should be made?

5. Exactly what procedures are you following in attempting to make the best possible use of whatever stage fright you experience? Be as specific as you can.

CHAPTER 4

Preparing Speaking Assignments

What can I speak about? Where do I get material for my speech? How shall I plan it? Shall I write it out? Understandably, these are questions often asked by beginning speech students. In this chapter we shall suggest some answers. We are going to concentrate on preparing public-speaking class assignments; recommendations for preparing discussion and oral interpretation assignments will be found in the chapters devoted to these other speech forms. Also, we urge you to study carefully other portions of this book (especially the chapter on public speaking) along with this chapter.

Choosing a Subject

To be satisfactory, the subject of a speech should *fit the speaker, the audience, the occasion, the time limits, and the purpose.*

1. *The subject should fit the speaker.* If any of the requirements in the choice of a subject is the most important, it is this one. Unless you have more than a passing interest in, and a superficial understanding of, the ideas you communicate, you will be less than completely successful. But if you can personally identify yourself with your subject, if you know whereof you speak, you have taken an important step toward effectiveness. "Do I have the right to speak on this topic?" should be the basic question you ask yourself in choosing a subject. This "right to speak" is

a relative qualification only; it does not imply absolute authority, for no human being is capable of speaking with absolute authority on any topic.

Ask yourself these questions when you have tentatively chosen a subject: Have I ever been personally involved in any situation related to this subject? Do I have available resources for gathering information about it? Are any of these sources open to me, but not to the majority of my audience? Do I know something first-hand about this subject before starting my research on it? If you can answer "yes" to any or all of these, you probably have found a topic on which you have the right to speak.

The world in which you live, have lived, and will live is filled with subjects on which you can speak with personal authority. No other person ever has had, or ever will have, the same experiences as you have had. By reflecting on what has happened *to you* and what *you* hope will happen *to you* in the future, you will find many available speech ideas. For example, suppose that last summer you worked as a counselor at a camp for underprivileged children. From this experience you probably developed some attitudes and knowledge about such subjects as, "What it means to be underprivileged," "The mind of a child," "How to stem the tide of juvenile delinquency," "Training a child," etc. Whatever specific area you worked in at the camp (sports, dramatics, etc.) may furnish another list of possible subjects for a serious discussion. An entertaining speech based on camp experiences may be a further possibility. Obviously, your summer's experience alone will not be an adequate source of material. You will want to do more research. But such experience is an example of the personal involvement we have been talking about, and will make the speech more meaningful to you and to your audience.

Here is a list of areas you might think about as sources for speech material:

Your religious beliefs
Your home town
People who have influenced you
Your hobbies

Your career plans
Courses you have taken or are taking
Your political beliefs
Your favorite poem, novel, play, movie, TV program, etc.
Your favorite author, actor, playwright, artist, etc.
Your favorite sports and performers
Jobs you have held
Vacations you have enjoyed
Organizations to which you belong
Your educational experiences

2. *The subject should fit the audience.* In the speech class you have an advantage that you will not frequently find in other public-speaking situations. You already have learned much about your audience, and as the term progresses, you will learn more. And you yourself are a member of that audience most of the time. When you are choosing a subject, you must keep in mind what you know about your classmates' interests, information, and attitudes. These, however, are not factors that need to limit your choice to any great extent. You have before you an audience who are inquisitive and tolerant. Their interests are broad and varied. Your task is not so much to choose a subject of interest to the class as to make the subject interesting to the class. It is probably true that almost any subject can be adapted to any audience. One of the most important questions to ask yourself is, "Will my audience find any value in what I have to say about this subject?"

3. *The subject should fit the occasion.* Here again the class situation presents few problems. This test of a topic will be much more important in situations outside the classroom. But you certainly can be aware of occasion here, too. A speech about football probably would be appropriate during the football season. A "get-out-and-vote" appeal would fit particularly well when a campus election is in the offing. "Archibald MacLeish: An Appraisal" would be especially good before or after a public lecture by the poet on your campus. Here again it is a matter more of adapting your topic to an occasion or an event than of letting the occasion restrict your choice of subject.

4. *The subject should fit the time limit.* This is a real problem

in any speaking situation. In the speech class the time given you must be brief, and the limits will be enforced by your instructor.

Most of the time you will find yourself choosing a general subject area, and then by the process of limitation, selecting the specific topic that will fit the time restrictions. For example, it is fall; football is in season. This is your favorite sport; you also know that most of your audience are interested in it. Your assignment is a seven-minute speech to inform. Obviously, you can't explain the game in seven minutes. You cannot detail in full the history of the game. But there are specific aspects of the game that you understand and can adequately discuss within the time limit. Some rule changes have been adopted since last season and these may provide a topic. Or, you play an end position on the team and you may describe in some detail the job of an end. Or, realizing that most of the class have not seen football gear except from the stands, you may give a demonstration speech showing and describing the equipment.

On some other occasions, you may want to speak about some specific event that you have witnessed, but you doubt that it will fill the five or ten minutes you have been allotted. In such a case, look about you for other similar events or situations; perhaps through generalization you can hit upon a subject worthy of your audience's time. For example, you attended last week's football game. You noticed a lack of enthusiasm around you. But this single observation doesn't seem sufficiently provocative for a speech. You do some further observing. You read in your school paper that the recent election brought out only fifteen per cent of the student body. On a walk around the campus one day you find the sidewalks littered with scrap paper. Out of these and similar specific experiences you decide to prepare a speech on "school spirit."

5. *The subject should fit your general purpose.* In your speech class, the purpose will usually be assigned to you. In other situations you may be allowed to determine your own purpose. Occasion, audience, and purpose often are closely related. Most subjects can be made to fit any of the general ends of speech. Perhaps television interests you as a possible topic. You might inform your audience about some phase of the industry;

or you might want to persuade them to become more critical viewers; or you might entertain them with the story of your first appearance before the camera.

Developing Your Specific Purpose

Your specific purpose states concisely your central idea and what you propose to accomplish with it. You must work out the precise goal before you can begin to plan what you are going to say. Here are some samples of specific purposes: in a speech to inform, "My object is to explain to the class the new football rules"; in a speech to impress, "I want the class to appreciate the values of school spirit"; in a speech to convince, "My object is to get the class to believe that final examinations should be abolished"; in a speech to actuate, "My purpose is to get the class to contribute to the Campus Chest."

Gathering Material for Your Speeches

The five best ways of securing material for a speech are observing, thinking, reading, interviewing, and corresponding.

Observing. The very best way to learn the facts on most subjects is through using your own powers of direct observation. If you can make a personal investigation of the subject you are going to discuss, you should do so. If you can learn about your topic first hand, that is the best way to learn about it. If you can watch the process you are going to explain, you should watch it. You should know from personal observation all that you possibly can about every subject upon which you are going to speak. You will think more clearly and feel more deeply about material thus gathered than you can about material gained from talking to other people about their experiences or from reading of their experiences. But, do not trust your unaided powers of recall; make notes on your experiences as soon as possible after they occur.

Thinking. One of the first things to do about any subject upon which you have to make a speech is to think it through for yourself and to organize your own thoughts about it. What does it mean *to you?* What type of problem does it present—ethical, economic, political, aesthetic? Answer such questions and jot the answers down before turning to one of the other types of investigation. Above all, do not slight this method while following any of the others. Do not stop thinking actively about the subject until you leave the platform after your speech is over.

Reading. There usually is a large amount of material available in the library on any subject. It is impossible to read everything. What you do read should be determined by the precise nature of your subject and the quality of the available material. If there is time to read three books on a subject, do not read the first three you come upon; spend some time in selecting the three that will be most helpful. When investigating a new subject, it is well to begin with general information and move later to the specific. If you have not already learned how to use your campus library, do so immediately. Most libraries have well-stocked reference rooms—and reference librarians who are eager to help you find what you need. Make use of these facilities.

Interviewing. Talking to people from whom you wish to get information on the subject of a speech has one very distinct advantage over reading books—you can ask questions. This is not to suggest that in your interviews you should indulge in cross-examination, but simply that you should be sure you have found out what you wanted to know and have an accurate record of the material.

Corresponding. Corresponding with those who know, and who are willing to answer questions, is a common and often effective method of investigation. This method is to be used when the material can be covered in a reasonably short questionnaire. If you have to ask a few simple questions, a letter is probably better than an interview. Do not write to authors asking their opinions when you can glean these from their published works.

It is important not only to be able to find the right kind of material, but also to have it in convenient form, so that you can refer to it again and again without wearing it out, rubbing it out, or losing it.

Every note you take should carry an accurate reference to its source—the writer or speaker, and the book, article, letter, conversation, or speech from which the material was secured. An accurate reference is one so clear and detailed that from it another person could locate the material without difficulty. We suggest that you use note cards, placing all references at the top of the card for easy filing, as in the following sample:

Subject	Writer	Where Found
"Ghostwriting"	E. G. Bormann	"Ghostwriting and the Rhetorical Critic," *Quarterly Journal of Speech,* October, 1960, p. 284.
"In contemporary history only a few statesmen such as Churchill, Wilson, and Theodore Roosevelt have had enough faith in their rhetorical skill to withstand, for the most part, the pressure of using ghostwriters."		

Building Your Speech

We now shall consider the processes by which the raw materials you have gathered can be molded into your finished speech. We begin by examining the general features of rhetorical structure.

Three main divisions of a speech are commonly recognized: (1) the *introduction,* (2) the *discussion,* and (3) the *conclusion.*

THE INTRODUCTION

We first will consider the introduction and proceed chronologically, through the discussion, to the conclusion. We are not suggesting, however, that this should be the time arrangement of your preparation. Your first obligation is to study the collected materials and ideas in support of your principal thesis, then to arrange and re-arrange these until you have found the most satisfactory organization. When all this has been accomplished, you are ready to consider your introduction and conclusion.

Perhaps the best-known statement concerning the purpose of the introduction is Cicero's: "To render hearers well disposed toward the speaker, attentive to his speech, and open to conviction." The introduction should also furnish the audience whatever *information* may be necessary to understand the discussion.

And, usually, it should give the audience a first look at the speaker's theme and purpose.

The chances are that your audience are attending to you as you get up to speak because you are a moving object, something new to look at. You want them to continue to attend to you, voluntarily, because they have become "well-disposed" toward you. But more important, you want them to attend to your ideas and develop an interest in them. When you have the attention and interest of your audience, you can lead them to your main proposition.

An introduction should make an audience feel that they have reasons for listening to the speech and to the speaker. It should be of sufficient length to accomplish this purpose, and no longer. Some speech authorities insist, with considerable reason, that *every* speech should contain a "need-to-know" step. The introduction seems to be the place for such motivational matter—unless the need is complex and not readily discernible, in which case perhaps it deserves attention as the first major issue of the discussion.

Some subjects and situations require only brief introductions. If you know that your audience is vitally concerned with your subject, you can state your specific purpose without lengthy preliminaries. In other instances you may be facing a hostile audience—or one that is tired, bored, or preoccupied. Here you have a challenge. You must make the audience like *you;* you must make them realize that you have something to say to *them* specifically; you must show them that what you have to say will be of value to them. In still other instances, you may find it necessary to use much of your introduction in giving information which the audience will need to understand the discussion to follow, e.g., explanations of important terms, historical background, indications of material to be excluded because it is irrelevant, etc.

Do not make excuses in the introduction to a speech. It is well to understand the difference between excuses and legitimate explanations. A speaker who has known that he is to discuss his subject before a certain audience on a certain occasion should not open his remarks by stating that he does not understand why he should be called upon to speak, or that he is quite uninformed and unprepared, or that someone else could speak very much better! If you feel this way about a speaking engagement, decline it. If you do not feel this way, you should have enough honesty and self-respect to refrain from making such insincere statements.

There is a widespread and wholly mistaken notion that the only proper way to start a speech is with a funny story. Sometimes the purpose of the introduction can be served by a humorous story, well-told. If there is actually something in the subject, the speaker, the occasion, the environment, or the audience that can be turned to advantage by a humorous story in the introduction, then telling the story is justified.

Using false leads in the introduction is a common error; the speaker, instead of going directly into the proper work of the occasion, wanders around, refers to all sorts of irrelevant matters and arouses the interest of the audience in a number of subjects that have nothing to do with his purpose. This procedure simply throws up barriers that he later has to break down.

A complete classification of all the techniques you can use in an introduction is not practical, but we shall mention a few common ones.

The *headline* technique serves the same purpose in a speech as large print does in a newspaper. In his introduction the speaker presents certain bold statements, startling statistics, or a striking question, designed to arouse the interest of the audience. He dips into the material of his discussion, selects a few headline items and presents them vividly to the audience at the beginning, with the promise of developing them later.

Comparison is another common technique of introduction. The speaker draws an interesting comparison between one of the elements of the particular speech situation and an element in some other situation with which the audience is familiar. Using the *familiar* is effective. The speaker mentions some person or event known to the audience. Or he refers to what the master of ceremonies or the previous speakers have said, if there have been such.

A *text,* or *quotation,* furnishes another way to begin a speech.

When the text or quotation is familiar to the audience and well liked by them, it serves as an excellent point of departure.

The *common bond* technique of introduction, which seeks to establish a basis of agreement between the speaker and his audience, is very effective. The speaker tries to make the audience feel that he and they are alike in some important respect; he dwells upon common beliefs or attitudes. If he is going to talk to a group of citizens of the United States on a political issue, he may begin by referring to the fact that the people on both sides of this issue are Americans, that they are all interested in the welfare of their country, etc. If a speaker from England is addressing an audience in the United States on a topic upon which Englishmen and Americans differ, he may well begin by referring to the common traditions of English-speaking peoples. A speaker representing one Christian denomination, talking to an audience of another denomination, may try to get together with them on a common platform of Christianity before he goes on to discuss issues upon which they are divided. It is always possible to find some common bond.

To prepare an adequate introduction, then, you must consider your subject matter and purpose, your audience, the situation, and your relation to each of these. In later chapters we discuss the forms of support, the kinds of materials, used to develop ideas. Obviously, almost any of these can be used to form the detailed content of your introduction—example, analogy, testimony, visual aids, statistics, etc.

The following are the opening paragraphs of student speeches.[1] After reading these introductions carefully, preferably aloud, see if you can answer the following questions:

1. What type of introduction is each? What kinds of material are used?
2. Can you tell from the introductions what the speeches are about? What are the speakers' themes or central ideas?

[1] Excerpts from the following speeches made by winners of the Northern Oratorical League contests: (I) Albert Adelman, "Merely Players" (1937); (II) Eleonor Luse, "Driftwood" (1928); (III) R. C. Grignon, "Tarpaper Tepees" (1952). Reprinted by permission of the Executive Committee of the Northern Oratorical League.

3. Do the introductions awaken your interest in the speakers' topics? Do they make you want to hear more?
4. Do the introductions give you any impressions of the speakers' personalities? Do you think that you would like the speakers personally?
5. Rate the introductions as excellent, good, fair, or poor. What standards or tests do you apply in evaluating the introductions?

I

Take yourself back with me to a dank autumn day two years ago in the Northwestern football stadium. The scoreboard tells a catastrophe, not altogether unprecedented: the University of Wisconsin has been defeated. During the excitement of the contest Don Heap was knocked out, and with no one else to put into the game, the coach, in desperation, called upon me. Quaking in my shoes, I stumbled out on the field, and while Jankowski was looking at an airplane I managed to wriggle and crawl to a touchdown. While carrying the ball through a hole about as big as the dancing space at the Junior Prom, I had but one idea: get across that goal line—nothing more! Truly, my perspective of football as a mere player was just about as narrow as the hole I was knifing through.

Not so today! The curtain is now drawn on that act. I take a seat, figuratively, on the goal post. From this position I can see the game as it really is. I see it now as an appealing dramatic spectacle: the frenzied fans, the anxious coaches, the high-strung players. The whole scene rolls before me in a colorful panorama. The band blares out a marching-song as eleven bright-suited warriors take the field. The gold-tinted helmets, the crunching bodies, the clashing of cleats, all give it a fascinating glamour. Something primitive crops out when 60,000 people roar for a touchdown, and as the game tightens there is fear . . . anger . . . fear again . . . amazement . . . credulity . . . exultation. Every elemental emotion sweeps through their hearts in this Roman holiday.

These gladiatorial combats have spread throughout our modern empire. Think of the "big" games played every year, each a spectacle drawing from fifty to one hundred thousand people: Southern California versus Notre Dame, Army against the Navy, Harvard's classic with Yale, Minnesota and Michigan. Football—a mere harmless sport? It may have started so, but it has become one of our great educational problems. Its influence, magnified by our universities, touches every playground, every home, every office. It is written about in every newspaper from the tabloid to the *Christian Science Monitor*.

After three years of competition, I'd like to scrutinize the effects of this game.

II

One exhilarating spring day I dodged the fear of overcutting and escaped for a short time the throes of classes and assignments to wander through the woods. I reveled in the freedom of choosing my own direction: of following my own inclination. Suddenly I stopped before an onrushing stream. It was racing away from all the peace and quiet which I enjoyed. Lost in its current were twigs and logs and grasses. They rushed past me as the current carried them on, where no one knew. A peculiar sensation came over me, a feeling I had often experienced. The sensation became more intense as I thought of the logs and twigs never to be released from that current; for no matter how narrow the confines of the bank might be, the stream would drag everything with it relentlessly.

As I stood there I realized that college life is like a rushing stream and we are lost in its current—intellectually, socially, politically, religiously lost. For four years we are borne relentlessly through narrow confines of critical situations without thought or aim. A typical and probably the most realistic example of students moving in this college current is the football rush to the stadium. Lost in that stream of people we don't think whether or not we might save time by turning down a side street. Laughing and talking, we needlessly follow the mob. The closer we come to the stadium, the greater the crowd becomes, and more intense the onrush. This human stream pours through the gates and on to the bleachers. We are lost in the enthusiastic cheering crowd.

III

One summer night when I was sixteen, I was left alone at our cottage on Round Lake, Minnesota. Ours was the only house on the bay and except for the frogs and the crickets, the evening was still. Around bedtime there was a knock on the door and before I could answer, an Indian boy stepped into the room and ordered me to put out the lights. His voice and manner were so commanding that I did what he said, and seconds later I heard the cries of men coming down the road. I ran to the window and stared out. There were ten Indians—all of them wearing ceremonial costumes and all of them very drunk. They danced past the window and, single file, climbed up on our long flat roof where they continued their antics in the moonlight.

As I started for the door, I noticed car lights flashing through the trees. People from the resort across the lake had heard the yells and had come to watch. After a long half hour, the Indians became tired or thirsty and the tourists left. The big Pow-Wow was over.

The Indian boy, sitting by the fireplace, stood up and introduced himself. He was John Blue Pony from the Chippewa reservation a mile away. The roof dancers were his relatives and friends. They had sent him to forewarn me so that I wouldn't get worried. It seems the local resort trade had been quiet all summer, and the ingenious barkeep had made a deal with the Indians—free beer for a good show.

To those Americans who live near reservations there's nothing unusual about this story.

IV [2]

I'm no authority; I'm not an expert or a big wheel. I don't know anything that any boy from Nebraska couldn't tell you. But I know this: I fought with a lot of men in this war, all kinds—a Polish gunner, a Jewish engineer, a German bombardier, and even a full-blooded Dakota Indian. I saw men wounded, and whatever land their grandfathers came from, their blood was always the same color. And whatever church they went to, their screams of pain sounded just about the same.

I had fifty-eight bombing missions, and I'm still tired enough so my hands shake, and plenty of nights I don't sleep so well. I'd like to go home to Nebraska and forget the war, and just lie under a tree somewhere and just take it easy. It's hard for me to realize that the war is not over for me. Not for a lot of us, Jewish-Americans, Italian-Americans, Negro-Americans, Japanese-Americans. While there is still hatred and prejudice, our fight goes on. Back in Nebraska on our farm, when I planted seed I knew that after a while I'd get a crop. That's the way it was with a lot of us in this war; we went to plant the seeds to bring in a crop of decency and peace for our families and our children.

Back in high school in Nebraska, one of the things that they taught us was that America is a land where it isn't race or religion that makes free men. That's why I went to Tokyo. I went to fight for my country where freedom isn't color but a way of life, and all men are created equal until they prove it otherwise. That's an old idea we have in Hershey, Nebraska, just down the highway from Cozad, which is near North Platte.

THE DISCUSSION

The principal work of the speech is done in the discussion; it contains the basic substance upon which the speaker relies for accomplishing his purpose.

[2] Ben Kuroki, title and date unknown.

How you organize your discussion is going to depend primarily on your subject and your purpose. There are many possible methods. You first will study your central idea to determine how it can be broken down into major sub-ideas. Any central theme can be divided into several different sets of sub-ideas, depending on the way in which you analyze it. We will consider briefly the most common methods of analyzing and organizing the discussion of a speech.

Chronological ("Time-Order") Arrangement. If you are narrating an incident, lecturing on a period of history, or explaining a process, this is an advantageous method of organization. You start at the beginning and follow through in time order to the end. In this method you analyze your central idea to find events in the incident or major steps in the process. These will become your main sub-points. However, do not simply string together a series of events or steps just because they occur chronologically. Here, as in any other method of organization, it is wise to present only a few major ideas, which your audience can recognize as major. Perhaps what you will do is to group together several events or steps. For example, you are going to explain the problems involved in raising potatoes. You decide to do so by tracing the process from beginning to end; these are the steps you wish to include:

1. Kind of soil and climate
2. Preparation of soil
3. Preparation of seed potatoes
4. Planting
5. Cultivation and care
6. Harvesting
7. Storing
8. Marketing

Although treating eight main points is not impossible, your audience may understand and recall better if you group these into three broader steps:

I. Preliminary Preparations
   A. Selecting proper soil and climate
   B. Preparing the soil

C. Preparing the seed potatoes
II. The Field Work
A. Planting
B. Cultivation and care
C. Harvesting
III. The Final Steps
A. Storing
B. Marketing

There are several methods of organization which are similar to the chronological. One frequently used is the "*space-order,*" which is particularly successful if you are explaining a subject which has spatial or geographical characteristics. In describing your college, for example, you might take your listeners on a tour of the campus, discussing points of interest as you come to them "in space." Other similar methods include:

1. From the known to unknown;
2. From the simple to the complex (or vice versa);
3. From large divisions to small divisions (or vice versa);
4. From exterior to interior; from near to far (or vice versa). (This is very much like the "space-order" method.)

Logical ("Reason-Order") Arrangement. In many persuasive speeches you may find it best to seek acceptance of your proposal by detailing a series of main and subordinate reasons for accepting it. First, you determine the two, three, or four principal reasons that seem adequate to prove the proposition. Then, under each of these, you arrange the two or three reasons that support it.

The following discussion illustrates how a speech might be planned using logical organization as the basic pattern:

For his principal thesis, the speaker proposes:

The Federal Communications Commission should have *no* direct control over television programming.

He determines three major arguments in support of this proposition:

I. Control over ideas—censorship—is alien to American political and social ideals.

II. Federal censorship of programming would at best be arbitrary—at worst, it would be dangerous.
III. The "natural" and rightful controls of public taste and morality are adequately being exercised.

Then he supports each of these with sub-arguments:

I. Control over ideas—censorship—is alien to American political and social ideals.
  A. A democracy depends on the free market place of ideas.
  B. The United States Constitution guarantees freedom of expression.
  C. Except for times of national emergency, the federal government has never exercised such control over the other media of communication or entertainment.
II. Federal censorship of programming would at best be arbitrary—at worst, it would be dangerous.
  A. The FCC already is overburdened with the responsibilities given them by federal law.
  B. No group of seven—or even eleven—men can be expected to serve as arbiters of the taste and needs of 185,000,000 people.
  C. Imposition of "standards" would stultify creativity, rather than promote excellence.
  D. Control by any human being is subject to misuse.
III. The "natural" and rightful controls of public taste and morality are adequately being exercised.
  A. The TV industry listens to expressions of public interest and needs.
  B. Citizen organizations interested in better broadcasting are increasing both in number and in influence.
  C. Never in the history of American television has programming shown the diversification and quality it does today.

The speaker now has the argumentative framework for a persuasive speech. Notice that, if you read the proposition and add the word "because" after it, the three main points follow as "logical" reasons for accepting the proposition. The same is true in each of the three main points. Obversely, if you read the main points first, then interpolate the word "therefore," the proposition will follow "logically." This is a good test of the logical plan of organization.

Now, each of the speaker's sub-arguments will require support. He will support these by citing evidence (statistics, examples, testimony, etc.), by further reasoning, or by arousing the emotional needs and desires of his audience. His organization of these supporting materials may vary from point to point; at this time, he chooses for each of the sub-arguments the pattern that can best present his point of view.

For example, let us take the first major argument—that government control is alien to American political and social ideals. The first sub-argument could be developed chronologically by citing the important philosophies stressing the freedom of the individual and his rights of free speech, free worship, and political freedom. He might start with John Milton or John Locke, progress through John Stuart Mill and Thomas Jefferson to Justices Oliver Wendell Holmes and Felix Frankfurter. In addition (or instead), he might briefly review significant federal and state court cases which have set the precedents functioning in our society, perhaps ending with the famous *Lady Chatterley's Lover* case.

This review of court opinions might serve as major support for the second sub-argument, if not used for the first. Or, the speaker might proceed by first citing the appropriate sections of the Bill of Rights, following this with an analysis of how the American courts have clearly applied this freedom to broadcasting. To do this, he might again use examples of court cases involving the FCC and use, as testimony, significant declarations by the judges involved in these cases.

The third sub-argument (that no other medium is so controlled) might best be handled "topically," with a brief consideration of the other principal media—the press, the movies, and the theater—showing the "hands-off" policy followed by the government in each. This argument would probably include a sub-point in which the speaker recognizes the differences between broadcasting and the other media—its pervasiveness, its presence in the home, its easy availability to greater numbers of people, regardless of age and literacy. Then, he might counter this by (1) pointing to the industry's recognition of the pervasive power of television and the self-regulation established to control it; (2) citing the opinions of sociologists and psychologists who generally minimize the impact of the mass media on overt behavior; (3) suggesting the responsibility of parents to guide and control the viewing habits of their children, in the same way they probably have controlled reading materials and movie attendance. In debate, such recognition and disposition of counter-argument is called "anticipatory rebuttal." It has the effect of deflating the impact of the counter-argument before it is even presented. It also impresses on the audience the speaker's awareness of the whole problem and his willingness to consider the viewpoints of others.

Similarly, he would prepare the other two main arguments, with appropriate support and varying plans of presentation.

In setting up a logical plan, you have to answer the question, In what order shall I arrange the main reasons? It has long been taught that, in presenting a series of points or arguments, we should follow the principle of climax, moving from the least important to the most important. Recent experimentation brings this order into question. The importance of an idea does not always reflect its interestingness. The fatigue of an audience increases as the speech goes along, and, therefore, arguments presented early in the speech may have a greater effect than they would were they presented later. Probably a bit of advice, which goes back to Cicero, is still worth taking—place one of the strongest reasons first, another strong one last, and the weaker ones in the middle.

Problem-Solution Arrangement. Another successful plan of organization, frequently used in persuasive speeches, is based on John Dewey's five-step method of problem solving, which we can paraphrase as follows:

1. Defining and outlining the problem;
2. Analyzing it to determine causes, extent, etc.;
3. Suggesting all possible solutions;
4. Examining each of the suggested solutions to determine the "best";
5. Testing the "best" solution.

This method is followed generally in our suggestions for organizing group discussion in Chapter 12. It can also be adapted easily to the public speech. For example, in the introduction, you describe the problem vividly, pointing out its importance. If the causes are self-evident or easy to explain, you can include the second step in the introduction also; or if this step needs greater development, it might be used as the first main point in the discussion. Steps 3 and 4 become part of the discussion. You wish to make a strong plea for the acceptance of your "best" solution as your conclusion. Here is an outline of a speech using "problem-solution" organization:

Central Idea: What can be done to improve TV programming?

Introduction

I. American TV programming is in a sorry state today.
   (In sub-points, describe the situation.)
II. Three factors are principally responsible for the mess.
   (In sub-points, discuss such reasons as financial competition, apathy, the reluctance of the Federal Communications Commission to act.)

Transition: What can be done?

Discussion

I. Three suggestions for improving TV programming have received special attention in recent months:
   A. Government ownership of the media. (Explain briefly.)
   B. Some system of "pay-TV." (Explain briefly.)
   C. Congressional action to strengthen the powers of the FCC. (Explain briefly.)
II. Let us examine each of these proposals.
   A. Arguments pro and con "government ownership."
   B. Arguments pro and con "pay-TV."
   C. Arguments pro and con "strengthening the FCC."

Transition: Which of these seems the most practical and effective?

Conclusion

I. The most feasible proposal seems to be more effective guidance and control by the FCC.
   A. There are dangers in adopting this proposal; however,
   B. These dangers can be minimized or eliminated; and
   C. The advantages outweigh the disadvantages.

II. I urge your acceptance of this point of view.
(Here, if desirable, call for specific action by the audience, e.g., writing to the FCC, to their Congressmen, etc.)

This method of organization has some psychological advantages, particularly in situations where you are advocating a new or unpopular proposal. You are trying to "motivate" your audience to accept your solution by leading them through the same series of steps that you used in arriving at your conclusion. You are showing them that you have carefully considered a number of alternatives. You are comparing these for them, and in so doing, may be answering some of the objections they might raise were you presenting only one solution. This plan is useful in all three types of persuasive speeches, and in some speeches to inform.

Variations of this method also should be noted. The first represents a cut-down version of the original by grouping some of the five steps and by eliminating the consideration of alternative proposals:

I. Problem or need (Why something must be done).
II. Solution (What should be done).
III. Effect or satisfaction (What benefits will accrue if the solution is adopted).

Another variation reverses the order of the steps and includes a "plan of action," specific suggestions as to how the solution can be effected. This method, of course, would work best where the audience's acceptance of the solution can be gained easily.

I. Proposal (What should be done).
II. Reasons for adopting proposal (Why it should be done—need and satisfaction).
III. Implementing the proposal (How it can be done).

Topical Arrangement. The most common form of organization is the *topical,* one made up of a list of main points and subdivisions that may be put together on any principle that seems best suited to the occasion. If you were to make a speech telling the story of Franklin Roosevelt's life, you probably would follow a chronological outline. If you were to give a speech to prove that Franklin Roosevelt was justified in his attack on the United States Supreme Court, you probably would follow a logical plan. If you were to give a speech entitled, "The Essential Greatness of Franklin Roosevelt," aimed at impressiveness as a general end, you might follow a topical outline. Here you would choose a list of qualities you wish to discuss and arrange them in the order that seems best for the audience and the occasion. The order that is best for one audience may not be best for another. It is quite possible that the same list of qualities might be arranged in one order for a meeting at Harvard University, in a different order for a meeting of the Congress, and in still another for a convention of the American Historical Association. You might also select different qualities as topics for the three situations.

The topical method is most useful for speeches to inform or to impress. Classroom lectures are often organized in this manner, as are many speeches of eulogy, dedication, commemoration, and the like. Most of the chapters of this text are so arranged. The following shows topical arrangement:

Specific Purpose: To explain how the content of American TV programs is controlled.

Introduction

I. More than ever before, the public's attention is focusing on TV programming.
   A. The quiz and "payola" scandals.
   B. Increased activity by listeners' groups and civic organizations.
II. The basic question is the matter of control.
   A. Who should exercise it?
   B. How much should be exercised?
III. To help you better to understand the problem, I will describe the most significant sources of control now operating in the American TV scene.
   A. Government agencies.
   B. The broadcasting industry.
   C. The sponsor.
   D. Pressure groups.
   E. The public.

Discussion

I. Control by government agencies.
  A. The Federal Communications Commission.
  B. The Federal Trade Commission.
  C. State and local governments.
II. Control by the industry.
  A. The National Association of Broadcasters Radio and TV "Codes."
  B. Network codes.
  C. Station policies.
III. Control by sponsors.
  A. Economic factors.
  B. Role of the advertising agency.
IV. Control by pressure groups.
  A. The American Bar Association.
  B. The American Medical Association.
  C. The National Association for the Advancement of Colored People.
  D. Others.
V. Control by the public.
  A. Through ratings.
  B. Through fan mail.
  C. Through listeners' organizations.

Conclusion

I. How effective is this control?
  A. Answer depends on how one looks at it.
    1. Those who favor the present system.
    2. Those who would change the system.
  B. It is obvious that the controlling agents are often at cross purposes with each other.
II. We must be aware of the situation as it now exists.

After you have selected and arranged the main headings of your discussion, you should turn your attention toward coordinating and integrating them so that the entire speech will seem *whole*, or *unified*, and not a mass of unrelated ideas. Three devices are especially valuable in achieving this integration. They are *transitions, summaries*, and *partitions*.

A *transition* is a word, a phrase, or a sentence by which attention is shifted from one idea to another. Few experiences in listening to a speech are more disconcerting than to find that, without proper notice from the speaker, it has been assumed that we would cease focusing our attention on one thought and move on to another. Such expressions as "sometimes," "on the other hand," "moreover," "however," "on the contrary," "and yet," and "next" are transitional words and phrases.

In the "problem-solution" outline on pages 78 and 79, we have put into the outline two questions which serve as major transitions. If we had developed the outline in greater detail, including all the necessary sub-points, we would have set down many more transitions. In fact, we urge you to note precisely on your outlines every transition that you use—at least at the beginning of your speech work.

A *partition* is a list of steps yet to be taken, or of points the speaker hopes to develop during the remainder of his speech. A *summary* is a statement of steps he already has taken, or of what he already has accomplished. The partition looks forward, and the summary, backward. Point III of the Introduction on page 80 is a *partition.* In that same outline, we might well have used a *summary* at the end of the discussion, restating (in slightly different language, perhaps) the five forms of control. Note that such a summary followed by the question asked in Point I of the Conclusion would serve quite satisfactorily as a *transition.*

We may use *summary* and *partition* in combination, for example, "Up to this point I have attempted to do three things, namely, one, ——; two, ——; and three, ——. I shall now attempt to present two more considerations before closing, namely, one, ——; and two, ——."

Summaries and partitions make it easier for the audience to pay attention. An audience does not enjoy being jolted roughly from one point to another. If you help your audiences to follow your discourse carefully step by step, allowing them at times to glance back over the way along which you have come, and forward down the line over which you are about to lead them, you will find them more ready to accept your guidance. A partition can frequently be used as a means of leading from the introduction to the discussion; summaries are sometimes effective as the first part of a conclusion. Such usage is like that suggested by the legendary Negro minister whose formula for a sermon was as follows: "Fust, Ah tells 'em what Ah's gwine tell 'em; then Ah tells 'em; then Ah tells 'em what Ah tol' 'em." He began with a partition and closed with a summary.

Of course, the discussion of a speech consists of more than main points and sub-points. Each of these must be supported, proved, explained, illustrated, or amplified. To do this a speaker uses what we call the *forms of support*. These we will discuss in Chapter 10 and in the chapter describing the general and special purposes of public speaking (Chapter 11).

THE CONCLUSION

The form and content of the conclusion must fit the audience, the subject, and the occasion. In the history of rhetoric there have been many statements of what the conclusion of a speech should contain or attempt to accomplish. As in most other rhetorical matters, it is worth while to turn back to Aristotle, who wrote that the purposes of "the epilogue" are:

1. To make the audience well disposed toward the speaker and ill disposed toward his adversary.
2. To amplify and diminish—that is, to amplify the merits of the speaker's case and to diminish the effect of what opponents may have said or may say.
3. To arouse the required state of emotion in the hearers.
4. To recapitulate or to summarize.

The conclusion should connect the most important elements in the speech as effectively as possible with the interests and desires of the audience. A variety of forms of conclusions may be used. Some of these are:

1. A summary, or recapitulation, of the main points, giving the audience a condensed, bird's-eye view backward over the speech.
2. An emotional appeal in which the speaker tries to attach the fundamental attitudes of the audience to his cause.

3. A plea for specific action in line with the argument that has been presented in the discussion.

4. An anecdote that vividly epitomizes the whole speech.

5. A literary quotation that performs the same function as the anecdote in No. 4.

The conclusion, like the introduction, should be as brief as possible, consistent with its function. Too often the speaker is reluctant to stop; he goes over and over again what he already has said, with the result that his long, rambling conclusion damages rather than helps the speech. An overly repetitious conclusion irritates and alienates an audience; to say, "Now in conclusion—" and then fail to conclude is a crime that an audience does not readily forgive.

Here are three conclusions which belong with the first three of the introductions on pages 70–72.[3] Read them aloud, study them for both structure and content, and then try to answer the following questions about them:

1. How do you estimate the effectiveness of the various conclusions?
2. Do the conclusions make you feel that the body of the speeches would have been worth hearing? How do you judge?
3. What motives or appeals, expressed or implied, can you identify in the several conclusions?

I

You must change your attitude toward the athletes themselves. Encourage them to be students preparing for life; keep them off the pedestals. Keep them "merely players." Tell them frankly that as players they have not yet done one single thing of permanent value to the world. Newspapers do not play them up because they have achieved something for society; they are used merely as commercial commodities to run the presses and the schools. No business will pay a man because he once kicked an inflated object sixty yards. The professionals might buy his skill, but how many Wildcats, Badgers, and Gophers want to become Bears, Packers, and Giants for life?

Help make these men human beings, working, living as you live—asking no quarter, giving no quarter—on an intellectual par with

[3] See reference, page 69.

every student in the university. In the splendor of it all make these words ring in their ears: Keep it a game, keep it fun. Life does not end with the captaincy of the football team nor with a place on the All-American. You go on from there stripped of your glory to compete in a tougher world of men in the battle of life. Play the game, don't live it.

II

My plea is for the thousands of college students who are lost in the onrushing current of our college life. This current must be abated. College students must dip below the surface intellectually and socially and throw off this superficiality if they are to leave their impress on society. Is college a preparation for the future when it gives us false standards for judging individuals? How can we solve the race problem if within our own college group there exist snobbery and prejudice? Is college a preparation for the future when it sets up for us false standards of success? Is striving for mere prominence in college a preparation for constructive citizenship? The college woman who strives for prominence will be the social climber in society—a liability to the human race. Is college training statesmen when we are blindly following the crowd, never thinking for ourselves? When university elections reveal "ballot-stuffing," there is little hope that we, the future politicians of America, will clean up the political world.

The significance of this situation is apparent. As college students we realize that something must be done to the present situation; but this realization is not enough. In cooperation with the faculties, we, the college students, must organize an educational system which forces us to develop our individualities and to be independent in our thinking; which creates within us a deep and vital concern with true culture; a system which will retain in us our intellectual and spiritual ideals and which will send out its graduates to be tolerant, broad-minded, able citizens.

III

Obviously there is no single solution to these problems. For nearly one hundred years the United States has tried to free itself from its responsibilities to the red man. Treaties have been signed and broken. Promises have been made and forgotten. Time and again the government has blundered in its search for a plan of universal salvation. Every year appropriations to the Bureau of Indian Affairs have risen until we are now paying $40,000,000 per annum. And still poverty, ignorance, and carelessness infest the reservations.

Today there are several programs before Congress which attempt to meet the three major problems I have just discussed. Proposals have been made for better housing, public schools, land management, and state jurisdiction. But the cornerstone of all these programs is the ultimate integration of the Indian with the rest of the population. Each year small groups free themselves and leave their antiquated customs behind them in the tarpaper tepees. Only when this is done can we be sure that the Indians will be independent and will have a chance for adequate education, for an improved standard of living, and for participation in the political life of America. With proper guidance and understanding, we can open the Indian's eyes. Then once again Blue Pony, Running Elk, Charlie Big Bear, and Silver Smoke will move on to a new land. This time we must see to it that they do not move away from us, but rather that they move toward us and civilization.

Outlining Your Speech

An outline is a blueprint for a speech. It is the written outcome of your method of organization. An outline can guide you in the work of preparation, and it also may be the basis for the presentation of your speech to an audience. However, you may find it desirable to make two separate outlines for these two purposes; the one used in preparing the speech may be detailed and complete while the one for delivery is a simplified version.

In our discussion of organization we really have considered indirectly the process of outlining. We have used various forms of outlines to illustrate the different methods of organization. A few additional general suggestions may be appropriate here.

When you construct your outline, always follow a careful and consistent use of symbols. The following system is recommended for elaborate and detailed outlines:

I. Use Roman numerals for the most important divisions below the centered headings: Introduction, Discussion, and Conclusion.
    A. Use capital letters next.
    B. . . . .
    C. . . . .
        1. Then Arabic numerals.
        2. . . . .
        3. . . . .

a. Then small letters.
b. . . . .
c. . . . .
(1) If another set is needed, use Arabic numerals in parentheses.
(2) . . . .
(3) . . . .
(a) Then small letters in parentheses.
(b) . . . .
(c) . . . .

Outlines for simple informative speeches and speeches to entertain may be built satisfactorily out of single words or short phrases, especially if the arrangement is topical or chronological. When you are attempting to motivate belief or action, you probably will want to put most of your main and sub-points in complete sentences. Indeed, this may be desirable in all your outlining at first because it will help you clarify your thinking and assist you in testing the efficiency of your organization. Such a procedure also insures that you will word your main ideas effectively, a result which your audience will appreciate.

ADDITIONAL READINGS

Arnold, Carroll C., Ehninger, Douglass, and Gerber, John C., *The Speaker's Resource Book* (Chicago: Scott, Foresman and Co., 1961).
Black, Edwin and Kerr, Harry P., *American Issues, A Sourcebook for Speech Topics* (New York: Harcourt, Brace and World, 1961).
Braden, Waldo W. and Gehring, Mary Louise, *Speech Practices* (New York: Harper and Brothers, 1958), Chapters 3 and 5.
Parrish, Wayland Maxfield and Hochmuth, Marie, *American Speeches* (New York: Longmans, Green and Co., 1954).
Wrage, Ernest J. and Baskerville, Barnet, *American Forum: Speeches on Historic Issues* (New York: Harper and Brothers, 1960).
Wrage, Ernest J. and Baskerville, Barnet, *Contemporary Forum: American Speeches on Twentieth-Century Issues* (New York: Harper and Brothers, 1962).

QUESTIONS AND PROJECTS

1. Write out in full and hand in a 1000-word speech. When you turn in this manuscript to your instructor, attach a statement of the

procedures and methods you employed in securing your materials. The three best manuscripts can be selected for presentation to the class.

2. Secure the approval of the instructor on the choice of a subject that you will then proceed to look up in the library. Hand in the cards on which you take your notes.

3. With some other person in your group, work up and present an interview, illustrating the proper techniques for securing the opinions of an authority on some controversial issue.

4. Find what seems to you an excellent introduction to a speech. Learn all you can about the situation in which it was delivered, and present it to the class with a brief statement supporting your choice of it and your opinion that it was effective.

5. Do the same for a conclusion to a speech.

6. Select a subject of interest to you. Then pick out three different situations in which you might speak about this subject. (A) Write out your specific purpose for each of these three speeches. (B) Prepare an introduction to fit each of the three speeches. (C) Outline the main points and major sub-points to show the method of organization you would use for each speech. (D) Be ready to defend your work in each of the preceding steps.

7. Choose a speech reprinted in a newspaper or periodical (e.g., the *New York Times, Vital Speeches,* etc.). Attempt to determine the method of organization used by the speaker. Outline his main points and major sub-points to illustrate the organization. Evaluate the speaker's method of organization.

8. Prepare an outline for each of your classroom speaking assignments during the remainder of the term. (Your instructor may ask that each be handed in several class periods before you are scheduled to speak.) Keep a copy of each of these outlines. At the end of the term, analyze them to note your progress in organization skill: (A) Do you find that you constantly used the same method of organization? (B) What changes in organization would you now make in any of these speeches? (C) Which outline and organization method served you best in the final presentation of your speech? Why was this so?

PART TWO

The Fundamentals of Speech

CHAPTER 5

Listening Effectively

The Importance of Effective Listening

Marcus Aurelius, the wise Roman emperor of the second century, in Book VI of his *Meditations*, wrote, "Accustom thyself to attend eagerly to what is said by another; be in the speaker's mind." There could scarcely be a better suggestion as to how to listen effectively. Somewhere in his essays, Thoreau said, "It takes two to speak truth—one to speak and another to hear." And Emerson once remarked that in order to have great speakers, we must have great audiences, too. In fact, speaking and listening are as closely related as the outside and inside of a cup.

We have emphasized the view that speech is a circular or reciprocal process, which is to say that, in the normal speech situation, there must be at least two participants, a *sender* and a *receiver*, who alternate in their roles as the speaking proceeds. The fact that the *sender* (speaker) usually is more active than the *receiver* (listener) should not deceive us into concluding that the *receiver* plays a passive role; the effective listener is always creatively active.

Listening is more than *hearing;* we hear with our ears but we listen with our minds. We listen by combining what comes in through our ears with relevant past experiences. Listening is the dynamic, active process of *interpreting* the sound waves that strike our eardrums. Sound waves of and by themselves have no meaning; meaning is something we *do* when our auditory nerves are stimulated by vibrations in the air about us.

Dr. Ralph Nichols of the University of Minnesota, the foremost authority on listening, tells us that effective listening is closely correlated with effective speaking; good speakers are almost always good listeners. He says, "When we have spotted the best speakers in a class, we have, at the same time, spotted those who are most successfully improving their speech by listening attentively to their classmates."

The following brief passage from a rather humorous essay on listening carries a message we all should ponder thoughtfully:

> To many people listening is a tepid affair compared to the high joy of keeping the larynx in motion. Such people like to talk as though they were taking part in a filibuster. . . . The occupational hazard of a professional talker is that he shirks his obligation to listen and consequently learns little. Not long ago a preacher's wife asked her husband to go with her to a concert. He begged off by saying that he had just finished a speaking engagement and was too tired. Whereupon she warned him solemnly: "You had better watch out or your tongue will wear out before your ears do." And that would be a terrible calamity. Save your tongue and give your ears some exercise.[1]

An ancient Greek proverb tells us that man was created with one tongue and two ears so that he might listen twice as much as he talks.

In a speech course, we need to emphasize the role of the listener. Speaker and listener are mutually dependent upon each other for the results of every attempted act of communication. Only when genuine cooperation is attained does the speaking become really effective.

To achieve this vital cooperation, the speaker must get to know his listeners; he must build up in his mind a satisfactory "image" of them. No such image can be perfect; we cannot know everything about other persons. We cannot predict accurately all of their reactions. Therefore, even when the speaker is fully aware of his responsibility and does his best to meet it, communication will not be 100 per cent effective.

Moreover, the listener must accept his share of the joint responsibility for the success of the communicative enterprise. He must build up an accurate image of the speaker. Irving Lorge

[1] "Listening," by Simeon Stylites, Copyright 1960, Christian Century Foundation. Reprinted by permission from *The Christian Century*, June 15, 1960.

says that communication always involves interaction between the knowledge, attitudes, and skills of the speaker and those of the listener.[2] If there is serious distortion on the part of either, the resultant "noise" causes the communication to break down. In other words, essentially the same problem faces the speaker and the listener; both have to get away from conscious or unconscious egocentrism. So far as is humanly possible, each must understand the person or persons at the other end of the communication process.

Most people spend far more time listening than speaking. The difference in favor of listening is especially great during the years spent in gaining an education. College students rely upon listening for a large part of their learning. The two principal means of education are reading and listening and, sad to say, many students have never learned either to read or to listen. Weaknesses in reading and listening bear melancholy fruit at examination times. The task of developing silent-reading skills may be left to specialists in remedial reading, but the building of listening techniques must be undertaken in speech courses, if it is to be attended to anywhere in the curriculum.

The Techniques of Effective Listening [3]

BE INTERESTED

As listeners we all have been spoiled by radio, television, public address systems, and the movies, which make listening as effortless as possible. When the speaker's object is to give us information, we expect that he will water down his data, simplify them, and dress them up in a format designed to catch and hold our involuntary attention. Our easy-hearing experiences predispose us to feel that, as listeners, we bear little or no responsibility for the success of the communication process. When the speaker's subject-matter is at all difficult to understand, we dismiss it and excuse ourselves by saying, "We could not listen because it wasn't interesting." If we want to be good listeners

[2] Irving Lorge, "The Psychologists' Contribution to the Communication of Ideas," in Lyman Bryson (ed.), *The Communication of Ideas* (New York: Harper and Brothers, 1948).

[3] Thomas R. Lewis and Ralph G. Nichols, *Listening and Speaking* (Dubuque, Iowa: William C. Brown Company, 1954), pp. 11–26.

we must resolve to pay attention even when listening is not easy. We must exert our will-power and determine to be interested. After all, there really are no completely uninteresting speeches or subjects, though, all too often, there are uninterested listeners. Perhaps a special warning is needed here concerning our natural reluctance to listen when difficult expository material is being presented. Unless facts are closely related to our basic interests, we are likely to shrug them off by calling them "dry as dust," or by asking, "Why should I care about that?" or "What good will it ever do me to know that?"

When you find it difficult to listen to informational speaking, which makes up a very large share of what you hear in classroom lectures, remind yourselves that information is the stuff out of which knowledge is made and that anyone who cannot listen well to expository speaking can scarcely expect to succeed as a college student.

FOCUS ATTENTION ON THE *WHAT*, RATHER THAN ON THE *HOW*

Make a conscious effort not to be distracted by any of the shortcomings or faults in the speaker's delivery. Focus your attention on what the speaker is trying to tell you. Try constantly to look *through* whatever peculiarities or mannerisms the speaker may have to his meanings. Picking out flaws in the speaking may be desirable in the speech classroom where you are trying to help one another to become better speakers, but you should realize that, when you are doing this, you are not in the best frame of mind to listen effectively to subject matter. Paying attention to the *how* may cause you to miss the *what*.

MAINTAIN EMOTIONAL BALANCE

While it is true that we should listen with our emotions as well as with our intellects, we must remain calm if we are to be discriminating and clear-headed listeners. It is easy to become over-stimulated by some relatively unimportant detail in the material and, in our excitement, lose the main thread of the message. Sometimes the speaker says something which seems so important that we are lured into stopping to consider it and explore its implications. While we are doing this, the speaker continues and, when we try to get back to his main line of thought, we find it impossible to do so. The more excited a listener becomes, the less discriminating he is and the less capable of appreciating the total pattern of the meaning; inevitably, he will over-value some elements and depreciate others. Therefore, strive to keep calm and let your intellectual processes control your feelings. If, eventually, you are carried away by enthusiasm for the speaker's message, you will at least have made a reasonably deliberate choice as to the direction in which you are headed.

Strong, and even violent, patterns of emotional behavior become attached to particular words and phrases called *stereotypes* which are said to be "loaded" or "charged." The world seems to be full of speakers who are unaware of the emotional explosions they cause by their unwitting use of such words and phrases. When the speaker is careless in this respect, the listener must become doubly careful. This is especially true of expressions which arouse hositility to the speaker personally. The listener should resolve not to give way to negative attitudes precipitated within him by unintentionally loaded words. He should say to himself: "I will not allow my feelings of antagonism toward the speaker to throw me off the track of his meanings. I shall postpone my personal quarrel with the speaker at least until I am sure that I have his message."

IDENTIFY MEANINGS

In listening, it is of great importance to know what sort of meaning you are trying to get. Seldom, if ever, is a speaker's message made up entirely of factual meanings; there are almost always feelings and emotions connected with the facts and ideas. However, if the speaker is dealing mainly with ideas—denotative meanings—the listener should concentrate on the factual elements in what is being presented. On the other hand, if the speaker's meanings are primarily emotional—connotative—then the listener wastes time and effort in trying to grasp and arrange facts. If the speaker's message consists of opinions, one should listen for and evaluate the opinions. If the message is a composite of images, one should alert one's powers of imagination.

If the speaker is asking for the recall of a mood or an emotion, the listener should cooperate by re-living the sort of experiences for which the speaker is asking.

Many speeches are not well organized. For example, it is practically impossible to outline Ralph Waldo Emerson's most brilliant lectures. A desperate attempt to find structure and pattern where they do not exist may cost the listener his opportunity to get the speaker's real message. Even when you are taking notes in a classroom lecture, it may be unwise to try to figure out an over-all outline as you go along. The lecturer may, or may not, be working from a logical outline. You may find it well to wait until after you have heard the entire lecture before you try to determine how it was organized.

RESIST DISTRACTIONS

There are many potential distractions in every speech situation. The poor listener allows himself to be diverted by incidental happenings around him. Instead of keeping his eyes on the speaker, he shifts his gaze to the window and observes the passing clouds or the fluttering leaves of the trees. Or he focuses his attention on his neighbors, he watches their hands as they take notes. He hears the sounds of traffic on the street, the wail of a distant ambulance siren, or the squeal of automobile brakes at the street intersection. The least that may be expected of a listener is that he should maintain an attitude of attention and really try to listen. Assuming the right posture will help a listener to maintain the effective internal patterns of listening. Slouching down in the seat, relaxing muscles, and closing the eyes may lead to sleepy indifference and destroy all chance of real listening.

TAKE ADVANTAGE OF THOUGHT SPEED

Experimental studies have shown that we can talk to ourselves four or five times as fast as we can talk to others. This means that as we are listening to a speaker we can do a lot of talking to ourselves. In the pauses between the speaker's phrases and sentences we can say to ourselves four or five times as much as the speaker can say to us.

Now this is all very fine, *providing we talk to ourselves about what the speaker is saying.* The trouble is that there is always a temptation to talk to ourselves about something else, and when we do this, we create a gulf between ourselves and what we are supposed to be listening to. Suddenly, we are brought up short by a rhetorical question or some other attention-getting device, and find that we no longer know what the speaker is talking about or what he already has said. It is of utmost importance, therefore, to utilize thought speed constructively in the listening process. The following are some questions which you may ask yourself as you think actively while you wait for the speaker to proceed:

1. What have been the speaker's main points thus far?
2. How does the idea he is now presenting fit in with what he already has said?
3. What will he say next?
4. Is he presenting facts or opinions, or both?
5. Are his personal prejudices creeping into his statements?
6. How is this specific statement related to the speaker's theme or main purpose?
7. How does what I am now hearing fit into what I have previously heard on this subject?

A Method for Improving Your Listening

At one university, students taking a course in listening improved their scores by an average of 16 per cent after only three brief periods of training. At another university, the lowest 10 per cent of the freshmen who took an entrance test in listening made scores equal to the average of all freshmen after a short training period. These gains in listening efficiency seem to indicate clearly that bad habits in listening can be eliminated and better ones established rather quickly under proper instruction.

College is the best possible environment for establishing good listening habits. You are listening to lectures every day and every lecture provides a training period in listening. Moreover, your motivation is strong, for your grades depend, in large measure, on how well you listen. What you should do is to develop listening techniques which will work for you and then use them until they become habitual.

The following suggests one method which seems effective for application to classroom lectures.

Before the Lecture

1. Motivate yourself to listen. Tell yourself what the lecture may mean to you in terms of your grade in the course, if you must, but better, in terms of the long-range use of the subject matter which will be presented.
2. Be sure that you have an accurate "image" of the lecturer. Learn all you can about him, his point of view toward his subject, etc.
3. Review your notes on previous lectures in the course and the assigned sections in your textbook.
4. Try to anticipate what will be covered in the lecture.

During the Lecture

1. Pay close attention, no matter what the internal or external distractions may be.
2. Keep your wits alert and don't allow yourself to become excited or emotional.
3. If the lecture seems to have been clearly outlined, follow its development, point by point.
4. Note the ways in which the lecturer proves his points or supports his views.

After the Lecture

1. If you have the opportunity, ask questions about any matters that are not clear to you. (Your notes should make such questions stand out clearly and you should not be satisfied until, by asking the lecturer or someone else, you have the answers.)
2. Talk over what you have just heard with other members of the class.
3. Try to fit the lecture into your over-all picture of the course.

4. At your first opportunity, organize and re-work your notes, adding details which you remember but have not recorded.

Listening to Persuasion

In answer to the question: "Do you know how to listen?" Wendell Johnson says,[4]

> Sound is so much with us that we perform the wonders of listening almost as unconsciously as the beasties afield. We listen for the most part as artlessly as we breathe. But, while under practically all circumstances Nature and the *medulla oblongata* will attend to our breathing for us, we can entrust our listening to our reflexes only at the risk of losing our birthrights.
>
> As speakers, men have been schooled in the arts of persuasion, and without the counter-art of listening a man can be persuaded . . . to eat foods that ruin his liver, to abstain from killing flies, to vote away his right to vote, and to murder his fellows in the name of righteousness. The art of listening holds for us the desperate hope of withstanding the spreading ravages of commercial, nationalistic and ideological persuasion. Unless the gentle watchword, "Listen," becomes an arresting command, we may not halt in time the stampede of humanity in pursuit of the enchanting tootling of the Pied Piper of Doom.

It is well to pause and think just how critical listening may be the antidote for false and harmful persuasion and propaganda. More than ever before in history we are being bombarded by persuasive speaking. Radio, television, and the movies have immeasurably increased our opportunities to absorb worth-while ideas. But, unfortunately, these mass media also subject us to the wiles of false and self-seeking persuaders. Careful, discriminating listening is the best defense against the siren songs of persuaders who, by slick phrases and beguiling rhythms, try to lure us into thinking, believing, and doing what alert and critical listening might warn us against as false and harmful. It is quite possible to lend our ears to a speaker, with no intention of committing ourselves to his cause, only to awaken later to the sad realization that we have been led in directions of which our better judgment cannot approve.

Professor Johnson stresses the three following questions for the

[4] Wendell Johnson, "Two Views on Listening, I. Do You Know How to Listen?" *ETC.*, Vol. VII, No. 1, Autumn, 1949, p. 3.

listener to keep in mind as he listens to speakers who are trying to persuade him:

What does the speaker really mean? Discounting his language, his vocal patterns, his facial expressions, his postures, and his gestures, what is his real, stripped-down meaning? What are his fundamental purposes? What is he driving at? What does he want me to believe? What action does he want me to take?

How does the speaker know? What are his credentials? What opportunities has he had to find out, first-hand, the "facts" he is using? What experiences has he had which give him the right to tell me what I ought to think and believe and do? What are the sources of his authority?

What is the speaker omitting? The good listener learns to hear more than the speaker says; he hears what the speaker *might* have said also. And it often happens that what the speaker is carefully refraining from saying renders what he is saying inadequate, irrelevant, or even misleading.[5]

An intelligent, experienced listener who follows a speaker carefully should be able to fill in the gaps in the speaker's presentation. Such a listener will be keenly aware of the incompleteness of what the speaker actually says, the many reservations and modifications which he neglects, and the bald assertions for which he gives little or no proof. So, while it is, of course, unreasonable to expect any speaker to say everything that might be said on any subject or occasion, it still is proper and necessary to scrutinize what he *does say* from the point of view of what he *does not say.*

The concept of propaganda is a concern of many teachers, sociologists, psychologists, and men in public office—and rightly so. Doob defines propaganda as "the attempt to affect the personalities and to control the behavior of individuals toward ends considered unscientific, or of doubtful value, in a society at a particular time." [6] It is evident to students of propaganda that the only effective way of combating it is to educate the people at whom it is directed. The primary purpose of such education

[5] *Ibid.*, p. 8.

[6] Leonard W. Doob, *Public Opinion and Propaganda* (New York: Henry Holt and Co., 1948), p. 240.

should be to inform the listener of the techniques the propagandist is likely to use so that the listener—or the reader—can recognize them and defend himself against them.

Propaganda analysts have described a number of the devices used by the "mass persuader." The following are some of these which we may expect when we are exposed to this potentially dangerous type of persuasion: [7]

1. Giving a person, idea, or cause a bad label without any support for so doing, e.g., "Joe Smith is a Red," "This is a left-wing, un-American proposal," etc. If the listener is careful to see such statements as merely unsupported assertions for which no evidence is offered, he will not be easily misled. When you hear such statements, you should ask yourselves, "Who says so?" or "Why should I credit a rumor like that?"

2. Associating the person, idea, or cause with some emotional symbol that has a positive value for most people. In a sense, this is the reverse of No. 1, e.g., "The Mothers of America want John Jones in Congress!" or "A vote for this proposal is a vote for the sanctity of the home!" The propagandist may say that his cause has been endorsed by a group of Christian ministers or by a professor from the State University. We may not know anything about the group of ministers. The professor's name may mean nothing to us; perhaps he no longer teaches at the University, if he ever did! But the prestige of the Christian ministry or of the University faculty may cause the unwary listener to accept the speaker's idea unquestioningly. Again, the listener should protect himself from going off the deep end by asking himself, "What *evidence* has the speaker given us?" "Does this general statement really *prove* the point he is trying to make?"

3. Giving the impression that the cause or the idea is "for the people," "the plain folks," "the common man," and has their support. This is a distortion of the honorable concept of "the common good" or "the general welfare." When a speaker uses this false appeal, we are in danger of accepting a doubtful cause for what sounds like a worthy reason but which, in reality, is only

[7] See Alfred McClung Lee and Elizabeth Briant Lee, *The Fine Art of Propaganda* (New York: Harcourt, Brace & Co., 1939).

empty talk. We should remind ourselves that the speaker has not proved anything and that the probability is that he would not resort to such false appeals if he could prove what he claims.

5. The "band-wagon" device. The propagandist tries to get the listener to forego any careful examination of the proposition on the ground that "everybody" already has accepted it. We are told that a public opinion poll has shown "overwhelming support" for a plan but, often, concrete figures are omitted. The speaker relies upon the normal, natural desire of all of us to be on the winning side. Often the results of public opinion polls are manipulated to mean what a fuller examination would reveal that they do not mean at all. Before a listener follows the crowd, he should find out just where the crowd is going!

6. Selecting only those facts which support a given point of view and omitting those on the other side. The speaker says that he has asked ten people what they think of his proposal and that they are all for it. He may also have asked ten other people what they thought and found that none of them agreed with him, but he doesn't mention them! Or, he has been careful to poll only those who he knows in advance are in favor of his plan. Facts are often taken out of context and misinterpreted. The listener to such persuasion may well remind himself that it is possible to assemble an imposing array of facts by simply throwing out the contrary facts.

All of the foregoing devices are designed to gain uncritical acceptance from a listener.

Chart for Analysis of Listening Habits

How often do you indulge in the following bad listening habits? Check yourself carefully on each one as follows:

For every "almost always" checked, score	2
For every "usually" score	4
For every "sometimes" score	6
For every "seldom" score	8
For every "almost never" score	10

(*Chart for Analysis of Listening Habits,* continued)

HABIT	FREQUENCY					SCORE
	Almost always	Usually	Some-times	Seldom	Almost never	
1. Dismissing the subject as uninteresting	______	______	______	______	______	______
2. Finding fault with the speaker's delivery	______	______	______	______	______	______
3. Getting excited by material in the speech	______	______	______	______	______	______
4. Listening for facts only	______	______	______	______	______	______
5. Trying to outline everything	______	______	______	______	______	______
6. Becoming distracted	______	______	______	______	______	______
7. Avoiding difficult expository material	______	______	______	______	______	______
8. Giving way to feelings of personal antagonism	______	______	______	______	______	______
9. Wasting the advantage of thought speed	______	______	______	______	______	______
					Total	______

Interpret your score as follows:

Below 60: definitely need training in listening
60–80: satisfactory listening
80–90: excellent listening

Criticism and Evaluation of Speaking

One of the basic functions of listening is to form judgments as to the quality of the speaking we hear. Only a good listener can be a good judge. A poor listener is not only a handicap to the speaker but he really has little or no right to criticize the speech or the speaker.

As we already have said, in your speech courses you will be listening to other student speakers more often than you yourselves will be speaking. Listening forms the basis of criticism and evaluation and will be a worth-while learning experience for you if you will do it carefully and thoughtfully. It will teach you how to distinguish poor speech from good speech. One caution may be needed at this point—listening in order to form judgments of the quality and effectiveness of speaking is quite different in many ways from listening to understand subject matter. In the former type of listening, we pay conscious attention to the voice, action, language, and mental processes of the speaker; whereas, in the latter, we try to concentrate on the meanings which the speaker is seeking to communicate.

THE TESTS OF GOOD SPEECH

To listen critically is to apply some sort of predetermined measures or tests of skill and effectiveness. Therefore, at this point, we must try to answer the question, What are the fundamental characteristics of good speech?

First, good speech is purposive. It is not intended primarily to relieve the speaker's feelings or clarify his thinking; it is designed to influence the listener in specific ways.

Second, good speech is seen and heard easily. Unless the visible and audible symbols used by the speaker are clear enough and strong enough to reach the listener's mind through his eyes and ears, the speech is ineffective—if indeed any real speech occurs at all!

Third, good speech gains and holds attention. When the listener ceases to pay attention, the speech stops.

Fourth, good speaking seems confident and poised. Unless the listener gets the impression that the speaker is competent to lead and direct his thinking and feeling, he will not follow the speaker.

EVERY SPEECH IS UNIQUE

When we attempt to go beyond these rather general tests and to set up more detailed or specific standards, we face many puzzling problems. "Circumstances alter cases"; every speech differs from every other speech in speaker, setting, audience, and occasion. It is easy to formulate general laws and principles but these are likely to break down when we begin to apply them to specific speech situations. As critics of speaking, we are likely to say "always," when we should say "usually," and "never," when we should say "seldom." Therefore, we should be cautious about proclaiming absolute criteria of right and wrong. The better informed one is about speech, the more wary one is of insisting upon just one "right" way. It is safer to start with the assumption that there is no single recipe for good speech. About all we can say is that the speaking must be appropriate to the speaker, the listener, the subject, and the occasion.

TESTS OF SPEECH

In the final analysis, speech cannot be weighed or measured objectively. This is not to say that there are no standards; it is only to insist that standards are subjective. Standards are derived from the reactions and evaluations of trained listeners. Moreover, standards change with time and place.

Notwithstanding the difficulties in establishing bases for evaluation, there seem to be two common and useful criteria, the *pragmatic* and the *artistic.*

The Pragmatic Test. Two opposing candidates run for a political office. Both do a lot of talking and speech-making. It is a temptation to think that the one who is elected is the better speaker. Two lawyers face each other in court. The plaintiff's attorney wins the case. It is easy to assume that he must have been a better speaker than the defendant's attorney. Two salesmen call on the same prospect. One comes out of the office with a signed order while the other emerges empty-handed. We instinctively conclude that the fellow who got the order must have made the more effective presentation.

But there are obvious flaws in this pragmatic test. The trouble may lie in one or both of two errors: (1) our failure to prove a causal connection between the speaking and the outcome, and (2) the unwarranted assumption that success was equally possible for the two speakers. Perhaps the campaign speaking had little or no effect on the voting. Suppose that Mr. B was a Republican running in a Democratic district and that Mr. A was a Democrat, already in office and running for re-election. Suppose that in the lawsuit, the facts and the law were all on the plaintiff's side. Or, suppose that Salesman X was selling a product that the prospective customer wanted, while Salesman Y was trying to sell something that the customer neither wanted nor needed. Before we can compare the effectiveness of two speakers, we have to have an accurate knowledge of many factors in the situation not easily accessible to an outside observer. To say that, other factors being equal, the better speaker is the one who can get his audience to react as he wants them to in the shortest time and with the least effort for all concerned is justifiable only if and when other factors actually are equal.

Therefore, almost inevitably, we conclude that the pragmatic test alone is not very satisfactory; we feel the need of getting onto firmer and higher ground and we proceed to a consideration of a second type of test, the artistic.

The Artistic Test. We postulate the existence of some stable and approved values in our society and believe we may base our value judgments on them. Some of these factors are accuracy of statement, validity of evidence, soundness of logic, good taste, fairness, honesty, etc. In terms of ethics and morals, we do not hesitate to place a good many qualities of speaking above effectiveness in terms of end results. We dare not omit such values from our tests of speech. Then, too, we must take into account such formal elements of speech as pronunciation, syntax, and style.

Yet, when all is said, we must recognize some limitations in the artistic test. Those who think most highly of this approach frequently seem to overlook the pragmatic aspects of speech. It appears that if speech is to maintain its touch with reality, a sensible combination of the pragmatic and the artistic standards is necessary.

ELEMENTS AND TOTAL IMPRESSION

What shall we say about speech which has many specific weaknesses and yet makes a strong total impression? Or, what shall we say about speech which seems flawless in technique but which makes a weak total impression? It seems wise to keep in mind the idea that the total impression is always more important than part impressions. Flaws in the elements of speech must be viewed in the light of the speaker's total effectiveness. When a speaker violates the "standards" we have set up and still has marked success, we should begin to suspect that our "standards" may need some revision. Even so, genuinely basic principles cannot be transgressed without serious damage to the total effect of the speech.

ADDITIONAL READINGS

Barbara, Dominick A., *The Art of Listening* (Springfield, Ill.: Charles C. Thomas, 1958).

Chase, Stuart, *Guide to Straight Thinking* (New York: Harper and Brothers, 1956).

Flesch, Rudolf, *The Art of Clear Thinking* (New York: Harper and Brothers, 1951).

Nichols, R. G. and Lewis, T. R., *Listening and Speaking—A Guide to Effective Oral Communication* (Dubuque, Iowa: William C. Brown Co., 1954).

Thonssen, Lester and Baird, A. Craig, *Speech Criticism* (New York: The Ronald Press, 1948).

QUESTIONS AND PROJECTS

1. Listen to radio or television discussions on public issues at least five times during the semester. When each discussion is completed, outline the major ideas presented by the participants, including as much of the pertinent evidence as you can recall. Hand these reports to your instructor or to a classmate to see if they can understand the material.
2. Attend a public speech and apply the techniques of good listen-

ing before, during, and after the talk. When you return home, write a condensed version of the speaker's ideas and an evaluation of his techniques.

3. While attending a public speech, notice the reactions of the rest of the audience. How would you classify the listening that you observe? When you note any sort of overt reaction, observe also what the speaker is doing and saying at these moments. Does there seem to be a cause-effect relationship between these reactions and the speaker's performance?

4. Criticize Lord Chesterfield's advice to his son: "If people don't want to listen to you, it is better to hold your tongue than to hold them."

5. In Shakespeare's *King Henry IV*, Part II, Act 1, Scene 2, the buffoon, Falstaff, accounting for his failure to appear before the Chief Justice when summoned, explains that he suffers from a peculiar sort of deafness which he aptly describes as "the disease of not listening, the malady of not marking." What do you make of his excuse?

6. Read the text of a recent public speech (either in a newspaper or in a periodical such as *Vital Speeches*). Write a criticism of this speech.

7. Listen to or read a political campaign speech. Analyze it for any of the propaganda techniques discussed in this chapter. On the basis of your findings, how would you evaluate the speech?

8. Perform the same sort of analysis as you did in Project 7, using radio or television commercials as subject matter.

CHAPTER 6

The Visible Code

In oral communication, a speaker uses both verbal and non-verbal symbols to express his ideas and feelings; he sets up both sound waves and light waves as he speaks; usually he stimulates both the ear and the eye of the listener or observer. In this chapter and the next we are going to look at the physical nature of speech—to see how the speaker's body sets up the sound waves and light waves which stimulate his listener's ears and eyes, and how these actions can be improved to make communication between speaker and listener more meaningful and effective.

Right from the start, it must be understood that a firm differentiation between "body" and "voice" in speech is simply impossible. First, in face-to-face speech, the two codes operate together, in integrated fashion, to communicate meaning. The ideal public speaker was described by someone who said of Barton Booth, the famous English actor (1681–1733), "The blind might have seen him in his voice and the deaf have heard him in his visage." Also, voice is just as physical as are other bodily actions. Satisfactory voice control, involving as it does the coordinated operation of a large number of relatively small muscles, can be acquired only after general muscular control has been established. The separation of the visible code from the audible in these two chapters is an arbitrary one, to permit us to point up the principles of effectiveness in each.

Visible speech and thinking are closely related. We actually think with our muscles; our skill in thinking depends upon the degree of control we have over them. True intellectual processes require a very high degree of selective physical action. Thinking depends largely on the action of the same muscles used in speaking. Our thinking proceeds in terms of abbreviated, fragmentary, and partial movements of these muscles. In developing efficient thinking we carry this reduction of speech movements to such an extreme that it is very difficult to keep the two processes, thinking and speaking, running along together simultaneously. Thinking is speech shorthand, and therefore, when we think and speak at the same time we are attempting the difficult task of combining the complete overt muscular behavior of the speaking process with the simplified inner behavior of thinking. Yet we must learn to do just this if we are to succeed in meaningful oral communication with our fellow men. This suggests that we need to develop delicate control over our muscles.

Principles of Effectiveness

There are four general principles of effectiveness in the use of visible speech: (1) *animation,* (2) *strength,* (3) *coordination,* and (4) *variety.* These are but variant aspects of the one inviolable law of visible action—*everything the speaker does should help him stir up those meanings and only those meanings that will help him accomplish his purpose.*

A speaker's visible action is seldom neutral; every posture he assumes and every motion he makes are almost certain either to increase or to decrease his effectiveness. He cannot dodge the issue of visible action; if he tries to get along without visible action, the most obvious and significant aspect of his behavior will be his deficiency in this fundamental part of the speech code.

One factor which makes the visible code so important is *empathy.* As we have seen, when we watch a speaker, we enter into certain physical activities which that speaker's behavior stimulates us to copy. For the most part, our imitative actions are slight and more or less unconscious. We may frown, smile, sit up in our chair, slump down, and thus follow every movement of the speaker. If what we do as we observe him is a part of the reaction he wants to elicit from us, his visible code is operating successfully in helping to stir up meanings within our minds. If not, he is failing.

ANIMATION

No healthy, living muscle is ever completely relaxed; some degree of contraction is always present. This slight contraction is called *muscular tone.* Differences in the degree of tone are made possible by varying the number of muscle fibers which are contracted. Each so-called "muscle" actually consists of a large number of individual fibers. Any single fiber can be only either fully contracted or completely relaxed—a principle known in physiology as the "all-or-none" law. Some fibers of every muscle are always contracted; the number contracted determines the muscle's tone at any particular moment.

One of the most significant differences among people is in muscular tone. The high-strung, nervous, excitable person presents a picture of high muscle tone. The lethargic, easy-going, slow-moving person shows low tone. One of the characteristics of emotional behavior is a general heightening of tonicity all over the body, to facilitate quick and vigorous action when required by the situation.

The speaker should manifest sufficient general muscular tone to appear alert and ready for action. Listeners unconsciously interpret liveliness as meaning that the speaker is free from hampering inhibitions, in good health, and interested in communicating with them. In speech, the active individual has a great advantage over the inert individual. We find it difficult enough to stir up meanings in the minds of others when we are using all our speech resources. It is impossible for us to do our best when we are immobile. Many speakers seem to use their bodies merely as mechanisms for uttering language; those who observe them *see* little that helps in understanding what is being said. Partly, this is a matter of empathy. Low tone in the performer empathically begets low tone in the observer.

The opposite also is true. A nervous, high-strung speaker who is in a perpetual whirl of motion cannot help but cause considerable restlessness in his audience. The result may be either distraction or embarrassment, or even amusement.

STRENGTH

Sufficient muscle tone and animation will help to give a speaker the dynamic quality necessary for effective communication. Alertness and animation, however, may be superficial. Strength, on the other hand, is present only when the speaker vigorously wants to communicate. Obviously the degree of strength which he may use in his physical actions should vary from situation to situation, from purpose to purpose, and from audience to audience. When a person speaks to a large group, his visible symbols will have to be enlarged and produced more slowly than when he is talking in conversation. As listeners, children usually like greater vigor in gesture and movement on the part of a speaker than adults do. A speaker trying to arouse action on the part of his listeners probably will exhibit greater strength than he would if his purpose were strictly informative.

COORDINATION

Before we can effectively use the basic patterns of visible speech, we must establish proper coordination among our various muscle systems. If a speaker's action is to be pleasant to contemplate, it must be graceful, smooth, and economical, rather than awkward, jerky, and wasteful. That is to say, the speaker's intellect must control his emotions in the use of the visible code. However, coldly intellectual speaking is no more effective than overly emotional speaking. We should seek a nice balance between the two.

Not only must each physical action appear to be coordinated and smooth within itself, it must also be synchronized with the other elements of speech. The visible code must be closely integrated with the audible. Movement of any sort does not exist for the sake of the movement itself, but for the contribution it will make to the speaker's total communicative effort.

VARIETY

Speaking is, in a very real sense, living. So variety, "the spice of life," is a very important ingredient of speech. A "point of diminishing returns" in the use of visible action is very definitely a physiological and psychological reality; constant repetition of any stimulus, no matter how effective it may have been at first, will eventually wear out or fatigue the reacting organism which becomes negatively adapted. We have seen the importance of variety in maintaining attention; we have stressed it as an essential characteristic of subject matter and language style; later its function in effective voice will be noted. Here we suggest that it must be used in the visible code. A speaker who does not vary his posture, who repeats the same movements intermittently throughout his speaking, who "saws the air" with the identical gesture again and again, or whose face is in a perpetual frown (or smile), eventually will "wear out" his audience physically, and the effectiveness of his visible code will diminish.

The Elements of the Visible Code

A speaker's visible code consists of *posture, bodily movement,* and *gesture.* We shall consider these, pointing out common errors and faults in the use of each, and suggesting techniques for their effective utilization in the communication process.

POSTURE

Many of the most fundamental impacts of a speaker upon the mental processes of those to whom he speaks come from his posture. Some speakers, by the unfortunate physical attitude they assume, negate everything else they put into the visible and vocal codes. Not only does bad posture have unhappy consequences in the reactions of others, but it may make it difficult if not impossible for the speaker himself to maintain a clear and vigorous line of thought and to use all his physical resources. For example, if a speaker drapes himself over a desk in such a way as to tie up his hands and arms, he may find that he cannot use them effectively when he needs them and he may also find that he is not sufficiently alert to follow his own line of reasoning clearly and forcefully.

Common Errors in Posture. One of the typical mistakes in posture is too much relaxation of the muscles that hold the body erect; the bearing of the speaker suggests an indifferent attitude toward himself, his subject, and most important of all, his audience. The other extreme is equally to be avoided; the speaker who maintains a rigid, immobile physical attitude is likely to suggest inflexible mental attitudes. Too much tension in the speaker's muscles makes the audience uncomfortable. Furthermore, such tensions reduce his capacity for easy and forceful movements and contribute to his own feeling of awkwardness.

Characteristics of Effective Posture. Keep in mind that your listeners will take note of your posture, not only when you are standing in front of them, but also when you rise to speak, when you walk toward the platform, and when you leave it. A satisfactory posture is one which permits you to control all your muscles with a minimum of effort. Posture should suggest self-respect, confidence, and a proper attitude toward the audience. To stand with feet wide apart suggests mental instability. To keep the feet too close together may make the audience feel that they, too, are likely to lose their balance. To stand with one foot behind the other and with the major share of the weight settled back away from the audience is also likely to stir up meanings that will not help you.

Inexperienced speakers are often concerned about what to do with their hands. For some reason or other, we are never so conscious of these appendages as when we stand in front of an audience. *Do not worry about them.* They don't look like hams to your listener; they only feel that way to you. Let your arms hang relaxed at your sides. In this position, they are easily available for any gesturing you may need. But placing a hand occasionally in the pocket, or resting it on the podium, or behind the back is by no means wrong or bad. It may be just the right touch, in certain circumstances. An effective speaker finds many good uses for his hands; the general position of your hands should be such that it will promote these uses. You should realize, however, that when you place your hands behind you or in your pockets, your audience may find it impossible to do likewise, and, consequently, the empathic effect can be unfortunate.

In many public speaking situations you will use a lectern or stand. It is a convenience to you, a place where you can unobtrusively place your outline or notes. It is not, as so many speakers seem to feel, a physical support for the body. No doubt an inexperienced speaker may find some comfort in standing near or behind a lectern, especially during the first moments of his speech. But the lectern must not be a barrier between you and your audience. If the stand is too high or too low for you, don't use it. If possible, find out about the physical arrangements in advance, and adapt your style of delivery and use of notes to the situation.

There are, therefore, no strict rules for effective posture. Just remember that your speaking posture should indicate (1) a desire to communicate directly with your audience, (2) a reasonable degree of confidence in yourself, and (3) mental and physical stability.

MOVEMENT

By movement we mean shifts in the speaker's position or location. A moving object is likely to catch our eye, especially if it moves in a field of relatively motionless objects. So, one of the principal functions of physical movement in speaking is to get and hold attention.

When we read printed material, we are aided in understanding how the author develops his ideas and how he progresses from one idea to another by certain devices of punctuation, particularly the indentation scheme in paragraphing. A speaker can use movement similarly to mark his transitions from one point to the next so that the audience may follow the development of his thought patterns. Printed punctuation also indicates shifts in emotional attitudes. An exclamation point has a significance different from that of a period; italics are often used to emphasize words or concepts that have special importance; and quotation marks often denote unusual meanings. Skillful use of movement can add similar significance to the spoken word.

Common Faults in Movement. Perhaps the most common fault observed among speakers is irrelevant movement. Because of nervousness, the speaker may be unable to control his muscles and use them purposefully. He wanders about the platform, giving the impression of taking time out as he does so. Such movement suggests lack of poise and balance; the speaker is saying, "I am ill at ease." The other extreme, unnatural immobility, is just as bad; the speaker freezes to the spot and seems unable to move away from it. In a quite different way, he says to the audience a good deal of what the over-active speaker says by too much movement.

Principles of Effective Movement. The paramount principle here is that all movement must be motivated, i.e., *it must spring from a specific intent to communicate meaning.* Movement isn't something added onto speaking; it is a vital and integral part of it. When you have finished your first major idea and you take a step to one side before starting your next point, you should not be saying to yourself, "I will move here because I need to introduce some movement into my delivery." Rather you move because you want to point up the fact that you have completed one phase of your thinking and are about to start on another. Unmotivated movement seldom is neutral in its effect; it is usually distracting—*meaningful in the wrong way.*

How much movement is needed depends on various factors in the speech situation. A sleepy or uncomfortable audience may react favorably to more movement than will a refreshed audience who are sensitive to more delicate types of stimulation. A large audience usually wants more movement than does a small one, perhaps because they may find more distractions around them. Audiences made up of people who live active lives and who work with their hands usually enjoy more movement on a speaker's part than do other kinds of workers. Young children require more physical activity with which they can empathize than do more mature audiences.

Study the situation, learn about the habits and tastes of your audience and adapt your action to the requirements of the particular situation. Of course, the principles of control and variety also apply. When you wish to emphasize a shift in the over-all organization of your ideas by a movement to the side, you may not get your point across if you have been moving constantly from one side of the platform to the other.

GESTURE

Gesture consists of visible signs made with the hands, arms, head, face, and eyes. Since gesture is more definitely conventionalized than are posture and movement, there are some special principles to guide the speaker in its use.

The visible speech of gesture renders more specific the meaning of the general postural symbols. Total bodily action involving posture, movement, *and* gesture is more meaningful than the action of any single part of the body. Other factors being equal, the ease with which we interpret visible speech is directly proportional to the number of physical agents employed in producing it.

Common Faults in Gesture. Awkward gestures call attention to themselves. They lose their symbolic character in the general feeling of strain and even shock that they produce empathically. Gestures should be graceful, not to evoke the comment that they *are* graceful, but because when they are not so, they draw attention to themselves and away from the ideas and feelings they should symbolize. Gestures must seem a part of total bodily action. The hand must not be used as an isolated agent; it is a part of the arm and the arm is a part of the whole body.

Gestures of the hand and arm usually should begin near the midline of the body and move away from it, rather than vice versa. Usually, the hand should not cross the vertical center line of the body or in front of the face. The eyes of the audience tend to focus on the speaker's face and on the vertical midline of his figure and any hand action that interferes with a full and continuous view of the face or cuts this line is likely to call attention to itself and thus be distracting.

The speaker's eyes are probably his most effective agents of gesture. It is a mistake not to *make and maintain eye contact* with the audience. When a speaker looks out of the window or just over the heads of his audience, he is misusing one of the best means at his disposal for controlling their behavior. Some speakers resort to all sorts of unfortunate expedients for avoiding the eyes of their audience. It really is not difficult to look people squarely in the eyes as you talk to them. But it is difficult to convince an audience that you are deeply concerned about their reactions if you don't give them the feeling of person-to-person relationship which comes from a meeting of eyes.

Successful communication is a reciprocal process. A speaker

will succeed more easily if he can establish a circular response between himself and his listener. The feedback he receives from the listener serves as his best index of how well he is communicating. The area around the eyes reveals most clearly how a listener is reacting. If the speaker is not "contacting" the eyes of his listeners, he is depriving himself of one of the most important methods of controlling his own communicative behavior.

Principles of Effectiveness. We have already suggested some of the principles of effectiveness in gesture. There are three additional fundamentals that need to be considered: (1) *timing,* (2) *reserve,* and (3) *habitualization.*

(*1*) *Timing.* Just as gesture develops before language in the child's speech, so gesture should precede the utterance of words in adult speech. A reversal of this normal order produces a comic effect. Suppose when someone asks you, "Where is the house?" you look straight at your questioner and answer, "Right over there." Then, after you have finished speaking the words, you turn and point to the house. You will find that the effect is ludicrous. The proper sequence of events is (1) turn the body, (2) point to the house, and (3) then utter the words. Gesture and vocalization normally overlap, of course, but the gesture starts first.

(2) *Reserve.* In speaking to the players, Hamlet put the principle of reserve about as well as it can be stated: ". . . for in the very torrent, tempest, and, as I may say, whirlwind of your passion, you must acquire and beget a temperance that may give it smoothness." *Temperance* is a synonym for what we call *reserve.* We never like to watch a speaker who seems to be exerting himself to the uttermost; we want to feel that, if he had something still more important to say, he would have adequate available resources. Therefore, avoid all-out types of action, in favor of moderation.

Reserve, however, does not imply weakness. Strong, well-defined action, which stems from genuine motivation, should characterize every element of the visible code. What we have said about reserve is also related to variety. Just as any single gesture must be kept under control, so you must avoid the over-use of any one gesture or movement.

(3) *Habitualization.* No part of the speech code ever can

function at its best so long as it is produced consciously and voluntarily. So it is with gesture. When you have to stop what you are saying to think up and execute a gesture, that gesture cannot serve effectively as a symbol. You must acquire a set of unconscious habits that will take care of gesture during speaking. The objective is to train your muscles to the point where you safely can trust them to their own inner feedback controls while you concentrate on what you are saying, the reactions you are getting, and the purposes you are trying to accomplish.

Kinds of Gestures. There are probably as many kinds of gesture as there are speakers, subjects, and situations. However, it may be helpful to make a rather general classification of three principal types: (1) *descriptive gestures,* (2) *suggestive gestures,* and (3) *emphatic gestures.*

(*1*) *Descriptive Gestures.* Descriptive gestures are literal, denotative, and objective. They are used to produce clear mental pictures of size, shape, position, and physical relationships. When we say, "The pitcher stands there, the first baseman there, and the catcher here," we probably use descriptive gestures. When we say, "The tube was about *so* long and *so* big around," we use descriptive gestures.

(2) *Suggestive Gestures.* Suggestive gestures are figurative, connotative, and subjective. Such gestures stir up mental concepts of entities that cannot be seen by the physical eye; they are symbols of feelings and attitudes. A shrug of the shoulder indicating indifference, a shake of the head that says "No," a wave of the hand that stands for "Good-bye"—these are suggestive gestures.

(3) *Emphatic Gestures.* The emphatic gesture ordinarily is not substituted for words as is the suggestive gesture; it is used to reinforce words. When we say, "It's no use for you to tell *me* that. I will *not* believe it!" or, "Never! *Never! NEVER!*" we may shake our head, stamp our foot, slap our hands together, or pound the desk to emphasize what we are saying; these actions are emphatic gestures.

Directness

Good speaking, regardless of the form, is as much like good conversation as circumstances permit. Of course, the circumstances in which one is speaking in public often make it desirable that the variation from ordinary conversation be considerable. It is impossible to speak properly to twelve thousand people using the same vocalization, the same visible action, or the same language as would be adequate in presenting similar meanings to one or two people in conversation. Or, a public reading of a lyric or a Shakespearean soliloquy will require a delivery more emotionally stimulating than that which should be used in an informative speech. But, as a general principle, we suggest that you will find the conversational manner of delivery effective for most speaking situations. It certainly is the most communicative—and adaptable.

There are amazing differences between the speaking techniques of the mediocre and the skilled conversationalist. The positive quality of dynamic conversation results to a considerable extent from the speaker's lively, intelligent use of the visible code. He is physically alert and active, he reinforces his ideas with movement and facial expression, he describes with gesture, and—perhaps most important—he makes direct eye contact with his listeners.

Directness is the essential quality of effective speaking. In Professor Winans' phrase, directness means speaking with a "lively sense of communication." It means really *saying something to somebody,* and not simply *delivering a speech in the presence of somebody.* A very amusing little cartoon which appeared in a daily newspaper recently showed a pompous looking speaker, standing before an audience saying, "Ladies and gentlemen, before I begin my speech, I want to say something." It is not difficult to imagine what his speech was going to be like!

From the physical point of view, the one best way of achieving directness is to establish *eye contact* with individuals in your audience. Looking in the direction of the audience will not do it; you actually must *see* them. Think of good conversationalists you have met; when they are talking to you, they look you in the eye. The eye, more than any other member of the body, can reveal what you are thinking. When you make contact with your listeners' eyes, you show them that you mean what you say, that you want them to grasp what you say, and that you want to see their reaction to what you say. Let your eye contact be made with individuals in all sections of the audience. *But* let your eyes rest for a moment on each person you select so that you make real contact with him. The speaker whose eyes flit rapidly here and there creates a feeling of restiveness just as surely as does the speaker who gazes out the window or over the heads of his audience.

Intelligent Self-Criticism

The ultimate goal of training in the use of visible speech can be reached only if you become an intelligent self-critic of your own posture, movement, and gesture. We do not mean that you necessarily should seek to perfect yourself by studying your own speaking behavior in a mirror, but we do mean that you should diligently analyze your own successes and failures. Furthermore, watch other speakers as occasions permit (here is one point at which the classroom situation functions very effectively) and seek to understand the factors that make their efforts meaningful or meaningless. You must become a candid and competent critic of the mechanics of your own speech and of the speech of others.

ADDITIONAL READINGS

McBurney, James H. and Wrage, Ernest J., *Guide to Good Speech* (New York: Prentice-Hall, 1955), Chapter 10.

Brigance, William Norwood, *Speech, Its Techniques and Disciplines in a Free Society* (New York: Appleton-Century-Crofts, 1961), Chapter 16.

Parrish, Wayland Maxfield, "The Concept of Naturalness," *Quarterly Journal of Speech*, December, 1951, pp. 448–54.

Winans, James, *Speech Making* (New York: Appleton-Century, 1938), Chapters 20 and 21.

QUESTIONS AND PROJECTS

1. Demonstrate three ineffective public speaking postures and explain to the class why they are likely to interfere with the work of the speaker.
2. Demonstrate a negative type of adjustment on the part of a speaker toward an audience.
3. Illustrate right and wrong ways of making the three different kinds of gestures.

4. Speak the following with appropriate vocalization and gesture:
   a. I ask you to consider this proposition fairly.
   b. There are just two questions to be answered: First, do we need a change? and, second, is this change the right one?
   c. Behold! Hundreds of square miles of territory lie waste and desolate.
   d. A week, a month, a year, and then a decade passed—but nothing more was heard of him.
   e. Specterlike, a figure glided out of the shadows, across the moonlit clearing, and disappeared again into the shadows on the other side.
   f. On the one hand is peace, and on the other, war. You must choose this day.
   g. "What is it that the gentlemen wish? What would they have?"
   h. "The war is inevitable—and let it come! I repeat it, sir, let it come!"
   i. "If I were an American as I am an Englishman, I would never lay down my arms! Never! Never! Never!"
   j. "The past rises before me like a dream."
   k. No, that is not the man. He is over there.
   l. On this very spot, history was made.
   m. The car dashed up the hill, over the bridge, and passed from view.
   n. He stood rooted to the spot.
   o. Before him was the vast Pacific, and behind him the snow-capped peaks.
   p. "Oh guns! fall silent till the dead men hear
Over their heads, our legions pressing on."
   q. Come one step nearer at your own risk. My blood is up and I am not afraid of you!

r. HAMLET'S ADVICE TO PLAYERS

Speak the speech, I pray you, as I pronounced it to you, trippingly on the tongue; but if you mouth it, as many of your players do, I had as lief the town-crier spoke my lines. Nor do not saw the air too much with your hand, thus; but use all gently: for in the very torrent, tempest, and—as I may say—whirlwind of your passion, you must acquire and beget a temperance, that may give it smoothness. O! it offends me to the soul to hear a robustious periwig-pated fellow tear a passion to tatters, to very rags, to split the ears of the groundlings, who for the most part are capable of nothing but inexplicable dumb shows and noise: I would have such a fellow whipped for o'erdoing Termagant; it out-herods Herod: pray you, avoid it.

Be not too tame neither, but let your own discretion be your tutor: suit the action to the word, the word to the action; with this special observance, that you o'erstep not the modesty of nature; for anything so overdone is from the purpose of playing, whose end both at the first, and now, was and is, to hold, as 'twere, the mirror up to nature; to show virtue her own feature, scorn her own image, and the very age and body of the time his form and pressure. Now, this overdone, or come tardy off, though it make the unskillful laugh, cannot but make the judicious grieve; the censure of which one must in your allowance o'erweigh a whole theatre of others. O! there be players that I have seen play, and heard others praise, and that highly, not to speak it profanely, that, neither having the accent of Christians nor the gait of Christian, pagan, nor man, have so strutted and bellowed that I have thought some of nature's journeymen had made men and not made them well, they imitated humanity so abominably.

—Shakespeare

s. SAIL ON, O SHIP OF STATE

Thou, too, sail on, O Ship of State!
Sail on O UNION, strong and great!
Humanity with all its fears,
With all the hopes of future years,
Is hanging breathless on thy fate!
We know what Master laid thy keel,
What Workman wrought thy ribs of steel,
Who made each mast, and sail, and rope,
What anvils rang, what hammers beat,
In what a forge and what a heat
Were shaped the anchors of thy hope!
Fear not each sudden sound and shock,
'Tis of the wave and not the rock;
'Tis but the flapping of the sail,
And not a rent made by the gale!
In spite of rock and tempest's roar,
In spite of false lights on the shore,
Sail on, nor fear to breast the sea!
Our hearts, our hopes, are all with thee,
Our hearts, our hopes, our prayers, our tears,
Our faith triumphant o'er our fears,
Are all with thee,—are all with thee!

—Longfellow

CHAPTER 7

The Audible Code

Section One—Voice Production

Possible relationships between voice and personality have long fascinated psychologists and speech scientists. Their experiments and empirical observations reveal that, although voice is not a wholly accurate index of personality, it most certainly does influence the responses of the listener, particularly because it affects the image of the speaker in the listener's mind. Some of the experimental findings are worth noting here.

As might be expected, a judgment as to a speaker's sex can quite accurately be made from listening to the voice, except in the case of a child or of a man whose pitch never has changed. By listening to a voice, one usually can make a fairly accurate determination of the speaker's age also. One study revealed a moderate tendency for people low on the social-adjustment scale to have unpleasing voices.[1] The speaking voice seems to reveal whether an individual is essentially dominant or submissive; aggressiveness and a strong vibrant voice quality are positively correlated, while nervousness and such a quality are negatively correlated.[2]

One of the most interesting and significant conclusions drawn from these experiments is that listeners tend to "stereotype" rela-

[1] M. F. Hurd, *A Study of the Relationships between Voice and Personality among Students of Speech*, Ph.D. dissertation, University of Minnesota, 1942.

[2] W. E. Moore, "Personality Traits and Voice Quality Deficiencies," *Journal of Speech Disorders*, No. 4, 1939, pp. 33–36.

tionships between voice and personality.[3] This seems to be the case especially in judging the occupation or the dominant "life pattern" of the speaker. Listeners tend to ascribe a particular type of voice to the teacher, another to the clergyman, still others to the policeman, the politician, the person with aesthetic interests, the socially-minded individual, etc. It has also been found that radio listeners create mental full-length portraits of speakers, based only on how the voices sound; and there is an amazing uniformity in certain aspects of the portraits of the same speaker as seen in the minds of a number of listeners—especially the aspects of height, build, and weight.[4] Though listeners tend to agree on these judgments, their composite judgments appear to be generally incorrect so far as the actual speakers are concerned.[5] However, the fact that people do base judgments on voice, that emotional characteristics can be discerned from the voice, is sufficient reason for scrutinizing this element of speech in some detail.

It is small wonder that voice is related to personality and that voice reveals the speaker; the so-called vocal organs are integral parts of the vegetative, life-giving, and life-maintaining mechanisms of the human body. As has been observed earlier, man has no voice organs as such; the voice is produced by structures the primary functions of which are to keep the body alive and working. Voice production is an "overlaid" process—certain vegetative organs have assumed the additional duty of creating the sounds we call voice. Anything that affects these vital organs in the performance of their more basic functions will also affect their performance in the production of voice.

The Voice Mechanism

Voice is the purposive production of sound by means of the breathing and laryngeal mechanisms. Voice is the raw material

[3] G. W. Allport and H. Cantril, "Judging Personality from the Voice," *Journal of Social Psychology,* No. 5, 1934, pp. 37–55.

[4] In T. H. Pear, *Voice and Personality* (New York: John Wiley & Sons, 1931).

[5] Many radio "stars" who attempted to switch to television in the early 1950's found that they were not accepted by their former radio audiences—because they didn't look like the images the audience had created from voice alone.

out of which speech sounds are made, but this raw material may be used for purposes of social control without converting it into articulate speech.

There are four main parts of the voice mechanism: *the motor, the vibrator, the resonators,* and *the articulators.*

THE MOTOR

The motor of the voice is composed of the muscles used in breathing. Although we often talk about "lung-power" when we speak of a baby's crying, or an opera singer's vocal strength and control, we are speaking metaphorically. The lungs are wholly passive in the breathing process. They are spongy sacks into which, in inspiration, the air is drawn. They are suspended in the chest cavity and open to the outer air only through the bronchial tubes, bronchi, trachea, larynx, pharynx, and mouth and nose. When certain muscles contract, the chest cavity is enlarged, creating a potential vacuum around the lungs. Air rushes into the lungs to produce an equilibrium of pressure outside and inside. In expiration, these muscles relax, the chest cavity shrinks, and air (breath) is squeezed out of the lungs. Inspiration is active; normal, *quiet* expiration is passive. Expiration *during vocalization* becomes more forceful and active.

The principal muscle used in breathing is the *diaphragm,* which is an arched, tendinous-muscular sheet, forming the floor of the chest and the roof of the abdomen. It is attached to the breast bone and the ribs in front, to the ribs at the sides, and to the spinal column in the rear. In its relaxed position, it is somewhat domelike. When it contracts, its central portion moves downward with a piston action and it becomes slightly flattened. This action increases the vertical diameter of the chest cavity, presses the diaphragm down upon the stomach and the liver, and thus causes the walls of the abdomen to bulge outward.

Three sets of muscles control the action of the ribs in breathing —*the scaleni, the intercostals,* and *the elevators.* The scaleni raise the first two ribs. The intercostals and the elevators expand the rest of the rib-cage, causing the chest to enlarge from front to back and from side to side.

When the diaphragm, the intercostals, and the elevators relax, the ribs fall back into place and the diaphragm recoils upward, thus diminishing the size of the chest cavity and forcing the air out.

In breathing for speech more muscular action is necessary than in quiet breathing, particularly during expiration. At the same time that the diaphragm and the chest muscles are relaxing to permit the rib-cage to return to its normal "rest" position, the abdominal muscles contract and push the viscera up against the diaphragm, thus aiding considerably in the forced expiration necessary in forceful speech.

The rate of respiration usually is speeded up during vocalization, and, usually, a somewhat greater amount of air is moved into and out of the lungs. In normal breathing, expiration takes about the same length of time as inspiration; during speech, the inspiratory phase is shortened and the expiratory prolonged.

Adequate breathing for speech purposes shows these characteristics:

(1) Both inspiration and expiration are kept under a certain degree of cortical control to insure a steady flow of air during expiration and to set up a rhythm and rate which correspond with the thought units or phrasing of the speaker.

(2) The speaker is able to vary the rate and vigor of breathing to effect the changes of force necessary for varying situations, moods, and meanings.

(3) The inhalation process is as silent as possible; this is especially necessary when the speaker is in front of a highly sensitive microphrone which greatly magnifies the noise of a raspy breath intake. During speaking, the breath is usually drawn in through the mouth rather than through the nose since this process permits greater speed of inhalation and lessens the chance for noise effects.

(4) While there is little scientific proof that any one method of respiration is best, "diaphragmatic," "lower chest," or "abdominal" breathing is most generally used by experienced speakers. The chest is larger at its base than at its apex and can be expanded to a larger capacity in its lower area. It is most efficient, therefore, to utilize this larger space and greater expansion in the function of speech which requires considerable volume of

breath. There is also evidence to indicate that the muscles of the lower chest and the diaphragm can be most easily controlled in their operation. Then, too, overuse of the upper chest muscles is likely to create a "carry-over" tenseness in the region of the larynx, and thus distort the tones produced.

THE VIBRATOR

In the larynx, voice box, or "Adam's apple" the vocal vibrations are started. Although the larynx developed biologically as a protective valve to prevent the entrance of food or water into the air passages during swallowing, it has come to play the primary role in producing voiced sounds. The essential vibrator is composed of the vocal cords—or, more accurately, the vocal *folds.* The front ends of these folds are inserted into the thyroid cartilage just below the notch in the Adam's apple and extend back to the two small arytenoid cartilages. The average length of the vocal bands or folds in the adult male is about nine-tenths of an inch; in the adult female, about seven-tenths of an inch.

In vocalizing, we draw these folds together in such a way as to block the breath channel and then force the breath up against them through the windpipe. When the pressure builds up sufficiently, the folds are blown apart. Thus a series of puffs of breath (vibrations) is released into the upper portion of the larynx, from where the vibrations travel out through the pharynx, the mouth, and/or the nasal passages.

The muscular structure of the larynx provides a mechanism capable of a practically infinite number of adjustments. The most important voice function of these muscles is to vary the tension of the vocal folds. When the tension is high, the vibrations are rapid; when the tension is lower, the vibrations are slower. These changes in tension change the pitch of the voice. When the folds are tense, there usually is greater energy in the puffs of air emitted under pressure and vocalization is louder; when they are less tense, the voice usually is weaker.

Paradoxically, voice is made up of "voiceless" as well as "voiced" sounds. When the vocal folds are not drawn together, we can still produce whispered, or voiceless, sounds merely by actively moving the breath column through the airway and acting upon it with the articulators. In ordinary voiced speech (with the folds in operation) many of the components of the total product actually are voiceless. In speaking the word *feet,* for example, the *f* sound is voiceless, as is the *t*. The vocal folds are used only in producing the long *e* vowel.

THE RESONATORS

If there were no more to the mechanism than the motor and the vibrator, we should be at a loss to account for the strength of the human voice. But in the voice, as in all other musical instruments, the tones initiated by the vibrators are reinforced by resonators. If a violin string is stretched between two posts and then bowed, it will give forth a weak and colorless tone. However, when the same string is stretched over the bridge of a violin and set into vibration, the body of the instrument (the resonator) adds power to the tone and gives it the characteristic violin quality. The piano has a sounding board. The brass wind instruments, such as the cornet and the French horn, are really little more than complicated resonators; the human lips themselves start the vibrations that are resonated by the metal tubes. The principal voice resonators are the *pharynx,* the *mouth,* and the *nasal cavities.*

The Pharynx. The pharynx, commonly called the throat, is a relatively large, baglike structure, the walls of which are muscles covered with mucous membrane. These muscles operate in such a way as to produce almost all conceivable modifications in the size and shape of the pharynx; it can be left wide open at the top and pursed at the bottom, or it can be left relaxed at the bottom and constricted at the top. The modifiability in the shape and size of the pharynx gives it great potentialities as a resonator.

The most important modifications of the pharynx for purposes of resonance are doubtless those in length. In order to understand the effect of varying the length of the pharyngeal resonator, place a glass tube in a jar of water and hold a tuning fork over the open end of the tube. By moving the tube up and down, you can locate a point at which the length of the portion of the tube above the water is just right to resonate the vibrations of the particular tuning fork. When you reach this point, there is a surprising increase in the strength of the fork's tone. Just so can the pharynx be fitted with great precision to the different pitches initiated by the larynx.

The Mouth. In the mouth also, we find many of the features of an effective resonator. It has at least one point of superiority over the pharynx; several of its surfaces—the teeth and the hard palate—cause the vibrations that strike them to reverberate. By the movements of the jaw and the tongue the mouth can be tuned to various pitches in the voice. Skill in making these adjustments is of prime importance in producing pleasant and effective voice.

The Nasal Cavities. The nose is a complex set of small bony caverns lined with mucous membrane. The shape, size, and openings of these chambers are relatively fixed, but they have extremely important resonance functions.

THE ARTICULATORS

The articulators transform the raw materials of voice into the specific patterns of spoken language. There are four principal articulators that must operate effectively if we are to produce satisfactory speech: the *tongue,* the *teeth,* the *lips,* and the *soft palate.*

The Tongue. The importance of the tongue as an articulator can scarcely be overstated; its name is often used as a synonym for oral language in such expressions as "the mother *tongue*" and "they spoke different *tongues.*" The tongue is a complex bundle of muscles capable of elaborate movements. Much slovenly and careless voicing of consonant sounds is caused by an uncontrolled or awkward tongue. When a student finds his speech deficient in articulation, he will do well first of all to consider his control of his tongue.

The Teeth. The role of the teeth in articulation may readily be noted in the peculiarities of speech produced in the absence of some or all of them. Without the teeth, it is practically impossible to produce properly certain high-frequency consonants such as *f, s,* and *th.*

The Lips. There are two principal ways in which the lips work in articulation. First, they are brought together to produce the pressure that is released in such sounds as *p* and *b*. Second, in producing sounds such as *f* and *v*, the lower lip must be brought against the tips of the upper front teeth.

The Soft Palate. The soft palate controls the passageway between the mouth and the nose. When it is tight against the back wall of the throat, the voice comes out through the mouth. When it hangs relaxed, the sound issues through the nose and the mouth. During the production of all speech sounds, except *m*, *n*, and *ng*, the soft palate should be drawn backward and upward. A lazy soft palate, like a lazy tongue and lazy lips, is responsible for much poor speech.

The Tone Code

The product of the combined activities of all of these organs is voice. Like all sound, voice can be examined from two points of view, the physical and the psychological.

From the viewpoint of the physicist, sound consists of pressure changes. A vibrating body crowds the molecules of air together in one phase of its movement and then allows them to spring apart in the other phase. If a strip of spring steel is clamped into a vise and its free end is pulled to one side and then released suddenly, its oscillations will cause alternate condensations and rarefactions in the surrounding air. These changes in air pressure are propagated by the impact of the particles adjacent to the vibrator upon those about them in all directions. The same thing happens when a violin string is bowed, when a drumhead is struck, or when the vocal folds are vibrated.

For the psychologist, sound is a living being's awareness of and reaction to air vibrations which impinge upon the tympanic membrane. The ear is an organ with special sensitivity to pressure changes occurring at certain rates. As the air particles set into motion by the vibrating body strike the eardrum, the delicate diaphragm moves in and out at the rate with which the pressure changes reach it. This process starts nerve impulses in the inner ear, which are transmitted to the hearing center in the temporal lobe of the brain. Vibrations with a frequency of 20 or less are not heard as continuous tones; they are felt merely as rhythmic pulsations in the air. At the upper extreme, our capacity for hearing stops somewhere between 20,000 and 30,000 vibrations per second.

The psychological properties of sound most concern the speech student. The same characteristics that differentiate all tones are operative in vocal tones as well—*quality* (timbre), *force* (intensity and volume), *time* (duration and rate), and *pitch* (frequency).

QUALITY

The first and basic element of the vocal tone code is *quality.* Quality is determined by the particular combination of vibrations which compose it. Most vibrators move in complex ways; they oscillate as units and as parts at the same time. A violin string vibrates over its entire length, and, simultaneously, in segments that are fixed fractions of the whole—halves, thirds, fourths, fifths, etc. The whole string moves more slowly than do its parts; this slower total movement produces what is called the *fundamental.* The segments give off more rapid vibrations, which are called *overtones,* or *upper partials.* The overtones fuse with the fundamental. Other things being equal, the greater the number of overtones, the more pleasing the quality will be. It is also important that the overtones be exact multiples (harmonics) of the fundamental and that their relative strengths be in proper proportion to each other and the fundamental. When a sound is made up of a number of irregular pressure patterns, it is a noise rather than a tone. When the pressure patterns occur regularly and the ear can integrate them nicely with each other, the tone seems of good quality.

The human voice mechanism, like all other musical instruments, produces both fundamentals and overtones. The function of the resonators—pharynx, mouth, and nasal passages—is to reinforce the various partials in the composite tone. Any individual's characteristic voice quality depends upon how his resonators work, which partials they reinforce and which they tend to damp out. Large resonators strengthen the lower tones; small ones, the higher. The muscle tonus of the walls of the respiratory passages undoubtedly affects their efficiency as resonators. If the muscles are flabby, the resonance is weak and the quality poor. If the muscles are firm, the resonance is strong and the quality brilliant. Unless the soft palate works properly, the nasal chambers cannot be used effectively as resonators; they will be used when they should not be, and vice versa.

Quality is perhaps the first aspect of an individual's voice that is noted and evaluated by a listener. If it is pleasant, if it seems to suit the speaker's feelings, ideas, and mood, the quality will be accepted as adequate and appropriate. But if it is not pleasing—if it is nasal, harsh, guttural—and the meaning context does not suggest such unpleasantness, the quality will call attention to itself and interfere with communication. It will produce "noise." Quality changes can convey fine shadings of meaning. An actor can show fear by increasing nasality, strong hatred by using harsh, guttural sounds, wistfulness by adopting an aspirate quality, and so on. In any speech situation, quality will affect connotation—meaningfully, if it seems appropriate to idea and mood.

FORCE

The second element of the tone code, *force*, is sometimes called *volume* and sometimes *intensity*. We control the intensity of a vocal tone principally by regulating the impact of the breath stream against the vocal folds. The stronger this impact, the greater the distance through which the folds will vibrate, if their tension is not altered. This distance variable, *amplitude*, is the factor which—pitch remaining constant—produces degrees of "loudness." However, an increase in air pressure against the folds usually makes them more tense and this increase in tension causes them to vibrate more rapidly. An increase in loudness often also contributes to a rise in pitch. To maintain a relatively constant pitch level during changes in intensity, we must learn to control the tension of the vocal folds.

The whole problem of vocal force is related more closely to breathing than to any other factor. Most speakers have sufficient breath capacity for the production of any useful degree of vocal force; the question is how to control and use a moderate amount of breath *economically*. The most important muscles for the production and control of vocal force are the muscles of the abdominal walls.

Vocal force requires breath support. However, greater vocal force can be achieved without expending a greater volume of breathed air. A recent study shows that, among the 140 subjects examined, about a third actually used less breath in speaking loudly than in speaking normally.[6] In these cases intensity change seems to have resulted from more efficient use of the resonators.

In addition to its importance in creating a "signal" strong enough to be received without strain, force functions in meaning, especially as it helps to suggest the emotional character of the message. Three types of force can be distinguished—*effusive, expulsive,* and *explosive*. These are not sharply defined categories but represent a continuum, with the *effusive* and the *explosive* as the extremes.

Effusive Force. In the effusive form, the tone begins gently, gradually rises to a level that is not especially strong, and continues so to the end. This sustained, "drawn out" force is associated with strong yet quiet emotions, and is especially suited to material characterized by one dominant tone throughout—for example, Hamlet's soliloquy which begins, "To be or not to be . . . ," or T. S. Eliot's "The Hollow Men," or The Twenty-Third Psalm.

Expulsive Force. The expulsive form demands more energy, more abruptness of initiation, than does the effusive. This form is characterized by variety—in attack, in the levels of intensity reached in single phrases, and in the *stress* given individual words. (Although stress also may involve pitch and rate change, it often is partly a function of force change.) Lively, interesting conversation exhibits expulsive force; because it is suited to expressing a variety of intellectual and emotional meanings, it serves a speaker well in most public speaking situations.

Explosive Force. The explosive form of force is notable for its extreme and sometimes violent fluctuations. It requires a maximum of power and efficiency in the abdominal muscles. It

[6] Cited in Giles W. Gray and C. M. Wise, *The Bases of Speech*, Third Edition (New York: Harper & Brothers, 1959).

is used to express intense emotions; it gives the hearer a definite sense of shock. The breathing action required for the explosive form of force is not unlike that which takes place in a sudden cough or a quick burst of laughter. The action often is sharp and vigorous. Although explosiveness is not characteristic of conversation or most public speaking, it has uses for the actor or the oral interpreter. The opening lines of Carl Sandburg's well-known "Chicago," passages of Vachel Lindsay's emotional tone-poems ("The Congo," for instance), Stanley Kowalski's violent scenes in Tennessee Williams' *A Streetcar Named Desire*, or the comic rantings of Volpone seem to call for the kind of intensity provided by the explosive.

TIME

The third element in the tone code is *time*. Every tone possesses *duration;* it may be designated as short, long, or intermediate. Moreover, tones succeed each other at varying intervals. The speed at which this shift occurs is called *rate*. *Duration* and *rate*, taken together, constitute *movement*. Movement is a large part of *rhythm*. A term closely associated with rate, suggesting the dynamic values of time changes, is *tempo*.

In voice, we think of rate as the speed at which an individual speaks. Normal rate varies from 125 to 185 words per minute. Actually, rate, or speed of speech flow, is a combination of two more-or-less separate elements—*quantity* and *pause*.

Quantity. The vowel sounds are the tones in speech, and many of these can be prolonged easily. The amount of time consumed in uttering vowel sounds is what we mean by *quantity*. Other things being equal, sounds which occupy more time in utterance are considered more important than those which take less time. Within reasonable limits, when a speaker is deliberate, he creates the impression of saying something important and seems to be giving his hearers a chance to develop more meaning. When the speaker's use of quantity is discriminating and purposeful, he is employing one of the most effective types of vocal variety.

Pause. Pause, rightly handled—*and by pause we mean the significant and purposeful cessation of utterance*—may be eloquent and expressive. *Pauses are not hesitations.* Hesitations may stir up meanings, but usually meanings not helpful to the speaker. We pause, not because we cannot think of anything to say, but because we want to give the hearer time to respond to what we already have said or to prepare for what we are about to say. Experimental results indicate that speakers spend about one-half as much time pausing as they do in uttering language.

A grammatical pause indicates the essential relationships between parts of sentences and between major and minor ideas as expressed in sentences and paragraphs. It has been estimated that over three-fourths of the use of the pause is to show these relationships. Pauses also can be used for emphasis and for awakening emotional responses in the listener. A pause will frequently show the speaker's attitude. It will indicate his desire for a full and complete reaction from the hearer either to what has preceded or to what is about to follow. A pause is often designed to concentrate the hearer's attention on the meanings.

Rhythm. In quantity and pause, we have considered two elements of rhythm. One other element is *stress.* Just as soon as we give up vocal *monotony,* we are committing ourselves to either *chaos* or *rhythm,* and, of course, in these circumstances the only choice is rhythm.

Rhythm is the pattern of strong and weak beats, of utterance and pause, of slow and fast movement set up by combining quantity, pause, and stress. Every person has his own characteristic speech rhythms, which are normally subject to many adjustments in meeting the needs of varying situations.

PITCH

The fourth, the final, element of the tone code is *pitch.* Pitch depends upon frequency of vibration. It is the most useful of the four elements for indicating those fine distinctions that are the very essence of intellectual processes.

The most striking difference between the voice of a woman and the voice of a man is in pitch. Within the same sex, of course, some people have deep, low-pitched voices, while others have high, shrill voices. The primary factors determining an individual's vocal pitch are the size and length of his vocal folds, the size and shape of his resonators, and the level of tension in his folds.

Every speaker tends to vary his pitch above and below what might be called his "normal" or "habitual" pitch. A number of speech authorities recommend that each person should develop a "normal" pitch that is best for him, i.e., one which permits maximum reinforcement from the resonators. You can approximate this optimum pitch by singing up and down the musical scale, going as low as you can each time and fixing on the lowest tone which you can produce with full resonation. Your optimum pitch usually will be found about four or five full tones above this lowest level.

Section Two—Improving Vocal Skills

Now that you have learned how the human voice is produced and what its basic elements are, you are ready to take an inventory of your own vocal habits and begin a plan of study and drill to improve them. The suggestions we shall make presuppose "normal" physical and emotional adjustment; we shall be dealing only with minor faults or weaknesses which result from poor voice habits or wrong mental attitudes. If you have any reason to suspect that your voice problems are the result of anatomical malformations or serious emotional disturbances, you should seek the services of a trained speech clinician or a physician before undertaking any program of drills and exercises.

Since voice training is usually a matter of unlearning old habits and learning new ones to replace them, it is a long-range task which requires perseverance, day-to-day attention, and, most of all, a sincere desire to achieve vocal improvement.

Characteristics of A Good Speaking Voice

The following are the characteristics of a good speaking voice:

1. It is *pleasant.* It has a quality of warmth, which makes the listener like and respect the speaker. It also reveals the speaker's respect for the listener. The emotional attitude of the speaker is a determining factor in producing this characteristic of voice. If

you have a deep-seated desire to speak and derive personal satisfaction from communicating with others, your voice will tend to reflect that attitude and feeling.

2. It is *unobtrusive.* The sound of the voice doesn't stand out apart from the total complex of meanings being communicated. It shows a proper balance among the various elements—rate, force, pitch, and quality; no single element is noticeable. The voice is free of obvious faults or weaknesses. The pitch fits the sex and age of the speaker. The articulation is clear enough to be understood with ease. The pronunciation reflects the best standards of the speaker's community.

3. It is *adaptable.* It can be adjusted to each of a large number of variables—occasion, audience, mood and purpose of the speaker, subject matter, strength of external distractions, etc.

A Plan of Drill and Exercise

Before making specific suggestions for overcoming common faults of vocalization, we shall recommend one method of planning your exercise periods. Because of the nature of your special voice problems, your instructor may recommend a different approach, or you yourself may find one that is more suitable. However, any long-term attempt to improve voice should incorporate the following suggestions:

1. Plan and maintain a *daily* exercise period, Saturdays, Sundays, and holidays included.

2. Begin each exercise period with about five minutes of practice in relaxation. Here are some recommended relaxation exercises:

a. Seat yourself comfortably in a chair with your feet flat on the floor. Let your arms lie loosely in your lap. Close your eyes. Drop your head so that it lies easily on your upper chest. Maintain this relaxed position for a few moments, keeping your mind from any organized purposive thoughts.

b. Assume the same position as in *a,* except place your arms loosely on a table in front of you. Close your eyes. Drop your head so that it lies easily on your arms. Maintain this position for a few moments.

c. From the same position as in *a* above, drop your head so that it rests on your chest; then slowly lift your head and let it drop backward as far as you can easily. While you are doing this, relax your jaw and facial muscles. A variation of this exercise is to rotate your head slowly, letting it fall as far to the side, front, and back as possible, always keeping face and jaw muscles relaxed.

d. Repeat the movement of *c* while in a standing position with the arms hanging loosely at your sides.

e. While in a comfortable seated position, tense all of the muscles that you can. Keep the tension for a moment or two and then relax as many of these muscles as possible. Note the differences, in your kinesthetic sensations, between the relaxed and tensed situations.

f. Yawn for approximately one minute. Laugh heartily for another minute.

3. During your early drill periods include a number of voice-recording sessions, followed by analytical listening sessions, preferably in the presence of your speech teacher. Voice recordings should be made periodically throughout your entire training program so that you yourself can assess the extent of your improvement.

4. Spend part of each drill period with another speech student, listening to and criticizing each other's performance of the exercises.

Problems in Breathing

Exercises in breathing should accomplish two major objectives: (1) to assure a sufficient supply of breath, and (2) to develop such control of the breathing process that both life and speech requirements can be met simultaneously.

SUFFICIENT BREATH

This first set of exercises is designed to make sure that your breathing is taking place mostly in the lower chest:

a. Sit comfortably, but erect, in a chair. Place your hands so that your thumbs touch the lower ribs at your sides and your fingers are placed over the abdomen. Exhale as much as you can; push in your lower ribs and abdomen with your hands. Next, inhale as much air as you can, keeping your hands in constant pressure against the ribs and abdomen. Next, exhale with a slow steady inward and upward movement of the ribs and abdomen. Repeat this cycle 20 to 25 times. (During some of your drill periods this exercise should be varied to include a constant speeding up of inspiration and slowing down of expiration as you perform the 20 to 25 cycles of breathing.)

b. Keep your right hand in the same position as in *a* above, but place your left hand on your upper chest. Repeat the exercise making sure that there is little movement of the upper chest, but full movement of the lower chest and abdominal regions. As you are performing this exercise and that in *a* above, try to become aware of the sensations which you feel in the lower and upper chest regions.

c. Now repeat this exercise without using your hands as a guide or control.

CONTROL OF BREATH

The next set of exercises is intended to improve your control over the expiration phase:

a. Take a deep breath, using the lower chest regions predominantly. Whisper "ah" as long as you can, keeping it steady and constant in force.

b. Now do the same thing with a phonated or voiced "ah."

c. Next, whisper "ah" in staccato notes as many times as you can in one breath.

d. Repeat this with a voiced "ah."

e. Count as far as you can easily on a single expiration, using whispered speech.

f. Do the same, using voiced sounds.

g. Prepare a group of sentences of approximately 10–20 words each. Read each of these on a single expiration. While you are reading them, check your expiration with your hands to make sure that you are not wasting breath either at the beginning of your expiration or at the end.

h. Prepare a group of paragraphs that include sentences which are not too long or complex for easy oral reading. Practice reading these paragraphs until you are certain that you have mastered the technique of breathing during "natural" pauses in the meaning of the written material.

Problems in Pitch Level

The two most common faults in the use of vocal pitch are (1) monopitch and (2) an average pitch level either too high or too low.

MONOPITCH

Speaking within a very limited pitch range is one of the most noticeable vocal weaknesses. This fault may result from lack of emotion or from a failure to see and appreciate fine distinctions in meanings. Furthermore, some people are practically pitch-deaf, and this deficiency incapacitates them for any satisfactory use of vocal pitch. There is another and larger group of people who, while not pitch-deaf, simply pay little or no attention to pitch. Apparently, they never are conscious of pitch changes and therefore do not appreciate their usefulness.

There are two ways in which vocal pitch changes occur—the *step* and the *slide*. In the *step* there is a distinct change in pitch from one syllable or word to the next. The *slide* (or inflection) is a smooth shift in pitch during the uttering of a syllable or word. Here are a few exercises suggesting the type of drill which will enhance pitch variety in your speaking:

Exercises in the Use of Steps:

a. Read the following sentences. Pause slightly between the two words in each sentence and on the second word raise your pitch definitely enough so that the change can be heard.

Get up.	Speak up.
Jim swam.	Let's go.
Come home.	Who won?
It's here.	He does.
Now what?	He goofed!

b. Now read the sentences above with a lower pitch on the second word.

c. Make up sets of two-clause sentences similar to the following:

If it rains today, the game will not be played.
Since it rained today, the game wasn't played.
It's raining today and the game has been called.

In the first of these sentences, you will note that normal reading calls for a shift or step downward in the second clause; in the second sentence, the latter clause is normally raised in pitch over that used for the introductory one; in the last sentence there is little or no shift between the two clauses. Practice this set of sentences and others which you work out for yourself, making the shifts as strong and definite as you can.

d. Often a whole phrase will be spoken in a general pitch level different from that used in the remainder of the sentence. Usually this occurs when we insert a parenthetical phrase between parts of the main idea of a sentence. Note in the following that, in order to maintain the meaning of the main part of the sentence, you probably will shift the whole underlined parenthetical expression into a lower pitch level:

A stitch in time, *my mother told me,* will save time.
It would be desirable, *to our way of thinking,* that speech courses be required for all professional men and women.

Exercises in the Use of Slides:

a. Analyze the following words in relation to the parenthetical sentence after each. Then read the words in such a way that they will suggest the meaning of the corresponding sentence. Exaggerate the slide you are using.

Yes.	(That's what I mean.)
Now.	(I mean immediately.)
What?	(What did you say?)
Where?	(I don't see it.)
Joan?	(Was she present?)
Good!	(That's fine!)
Oh.	(It makes no difference.)
Well?	(What are you doing here?)
Hush!	(Don't speak.)
Green?	(She wore a green dress?)

b. Slides are used to give meaning, not only to individual words, but also to whole phrases and sentences. Statements of fact (declarative phrases and sentences) usually require a downward inflection at the end, as in the following:

This is where I live.
I am an American.
That's what I mean.

Imperative sentences or commands likewise take this downward slide:

Don't move.
Bring me a drink.
Take care of yourself.

Questions which call for a "yes" or "no" answer usually require an upward inflection, especially in American usage:

Is this the place?
Ready, Jean?
Wasn't it worthwhile?

However, when a question calls for more than a simple affirmation or negation, when you are asking for information that requires a statement, the inflection at the end of a question is likely to be downward:

When did this happen?
Where did you go yesterday?
How do you know all this?

When we attach a question to the end of a declarative sentence, we may use either a downward or upward inflection depending on the meaning we are trying to suggest or the answer we are looking for. Take the declarative statement, "John was with you." Now add, "wasn't he?" It reads:

John was with you, wasn't he?

Read this question with an upward slide. You will note that you are asking for a "yes" or "no" answer. In effect, you are asking, "Was John with you?" Read the question with a downward slide. Now you seem to be demanding a confirmation. You are suggesting, "I am sure John was with you—deny it if you can." Work out a set of sentences of this type. Read them with both upward and downward inflections and note the change in meaning which results.

c. There are many other important relationships which are shown by steps and slides in the pitch pattern. Good speech drillbooks and manuals contain many more exercises than we are able to list here. Your instructor also can recommend specific drills to assist you in planning a training program.

AVERAGE PITCH LEVEL

Excitable, nervous people are likely to have high-pitched voices; phlegmatic, easy-going people, low-pitched voices. *Practically the only way of securing any permanent readjustment of general vocal pitch level is through modifying bodily tensions generally.*

Every normal voice has a very considerable range in pitch. Each of us should find his normal key, or so-called "optimum pitch," and use it as a starting point in practicing pitch changes, employing just as much variety as possible, consistent with our meanings, of course.

The following exercises should be helpful in assisting a speaker to develop a register or key suitable to his personality and speech needs:

a. With the aid of a musical instrument find your best pitch level. The method for determining this is described on page 137.

b. With the aid of your instructor and a recording device, determine whether or not you are using your best level.

c. If you find that your general level is too low, the best exercise will probably be the reading and speaking of materials which are difficult to put across, and which demand a great deal of concentration.

d. If your pitch level is too high, select a conversational bit of prose that has no strong emotional meaning. At first, read the passage at a general pitch level above that which you normally use. Then drop the whole pitch level one full octave and read the passage again. Repeat this exercise a number of times. This lower level will be below your optimum pitch. After you find that you can easily read a passage at the lower level, begin gradually to raise the pitch level until you arrive at the one which you have decided is best suited to your voice. This exercise needs to be repeated again and again over a period of many weeks, until eventually you will be able to hit your optimum pitch at the first reading. Record your voice as often as possible during the training.

Problems in Time

The most common faults in the use of the time element of voice are:

1. A rate too rapid or too slow;
2. Phonation either too prolonged or too staccato;
3. Monotony of rate;
4. Faulty phrasing;
5. Rhythmic patterns too regular and recurrent.

Exercises in Timing:

a. With the assistance of your speech instructor, determine whether your basic tempo is too rapid or too slow. This can be done by recording your speech and then comparing it with a recording of another student who is adjudged to have an effective rate. Or this can be done by reading a passage and then determining the number of words per minute that you speak. If the rate exceeds 185 words per minute, it is probably too rapid; or if it is less than 140 words per minute, it is too slow.

b. If your rate is too rapid:

(1) Consciously use a slow rate in reading a prose passage, at first slowing it down to the point where it is almost meaningless and gradually increasing the rate until you reach one which seems to communicate its meaning.

(2) Choose subject matter which reflects emotions or feelings that call for a slow rate—sadness, grief, awe, homesickness, etc.

(3) Practice reading or speaking in a large room. Try to make yourself easily heard at the back of the room.

(4) Practice relaxation exercises, since too much tension is a common cause of an excessively rapid rate.

c. If your rate is too slow, the chances are that you are too phlegmatic. Find materials either in poetry or prose that interest you very much and that are full of action. Practice reading these, with as much enthusiasm as possible. When you practice your speeches or your readings, use a large number of gestures, walk about the room, get as much bodily activity into your practice speaking as possible.

d. Read the following selections with especial attention to the use of the time element to help you get the mood and meaning across. If the selection seems to demand a rapid rate, note also that it will probably benefit from greater use of staccato tones, that is, a shortening of the time you take to vocalize the vowel elements of the words. If it calls for a slower, more measured rate, the vowel sounds probably will be prolonged.

TO SLEEP

A flock of sheep that leisurely pass by,
One after one; the sound of rain, and bees
Murmuring; the fall of rivers, winds, and seas,
Smooth fields, white sheets of water, and pure sky;
I have thought of all by turns, and yet do lie
Sleepless! and soon the small birds' melodies
Must hear, first uttered from my orchard trees;
And the first cuckoo's melancholy cry.
Even thus last night, and two nights more, I lay,
And could not win thee, Sleep! by any stealth:
So do not let me wear tonight away:
Without Thee what is all the morning's wealth?
Come, blessed barrier between day and day,
Dear mother of fresh thoughts and joyous health!

—Wordsworth

From "SONG OF THE BROOK"

I come from haunts of coot and hern,
  I make a sudden sally,
And sparkle out among the fern,
  To bicker down the valley.

By thirty hills I hurry down,
  Or slip between the ridges,
By twenty thorps, a little town,
  And half a hundred bridges.

I chatter over stony ways,
In little sharps and trebles,
I bubble into eddying bays,
I babble on the pebbles.

With many a curve my banks I fret,
By many a field and fallow,
And many a fairy foreland set,
With willow-weed and mallow.

I chatter, chatter, as I flow
To join the brimming river,
For men may come and men may go,
But I go on forever.

—Tennyson

A hurry of hoofs in a village street,
A shape in the moonlight, a bulk in the dark
And beneath, from the pebbles, in passing, a spark
Struck out by a steed flying fearless and fleet:
That was all. And yet, through the gloom and the light,
The fate of a nation was riding that night;
And the spark struck out by that steed, in his flight,
Kindled the land into flame with its heat.

—Longfellow

e. Note especially the differences in rhythms among the three selections in *d* above. The first and third, though in poetic form, have a less definite pattern of stressed and unstressed beats than does the second. With the guidance of your instructor, practice developing a rhythm appropriate to each of the three selections.

f. Few selections from good literature rely entirely on one rhythm or rate to achieve their effectiveness. Therefore, variety in reading is essential. Practice the following with this in mind, using appropriate quantity, pauses, movement, stress, and rhythm as the meaning and the mood demand.

From "PIPPA PASSES"

The year's at the spring
And day's at the morn;
Morning's at seven;
The hill-side's dew-pearled;
The lark's on the wing;
The snail's on the thorn:

God's in his heaven—
All's right with the world!

—Browning

PROSPICE

Fear death?—to feel the fog in my throat,
The mist in my face,
When the snows begin, and the blasts denote
I am nearing the place,
The power of the night, the press of the storm,
The post of the foe:
Where he stands, the Arch Fear in a visible form,
Yet the strong man must go:
For the journey is done and the summit attained,
And the barriers fall,
Though a battle 's to fight ere the guerdon be gained,
The reward of it all.
I was ever a fighter, so—one fight more,
The best and the last!
I would hate that death bandaged my eyes, and forebore,
And bade me creep past.
No! let me taste the whole of it, fare like my peers
The heroes of old,
Bear the brunt, in a minute pay glad life's arrears
Of pain, darkness and cold.
For sudden the worst turns the best to the brave,
The black minute 's at end,
And the elements' rage, the fiend-voices that rave,
Shall dwindle, shall blend,
Shall change, shall become first a peace out of pain,
Then a light, then thy breast,
O thou soul of my soul! I shall clasp thee again,
And with God be the rest!

—Browning

Problems in Force

The speaker should strive to develop the ability to use all degrees of vocal force from *pianissimo* to *fortissimo*.

Many cases of faulty use of force may be the result of poor judgment on the part of the speaker; he is not adequately aware of the requirements of the situation in which he is speaking. However, other causes also may be operative: (1) Weak voices may be caused by using pitch levels that are too low; therefore, drill in raising pitch levels may be the best remedy for force problems as well. (2) Vowels have the greatest carrying power of all speech sounds. A person whose speech is characterized by too short vowel sounds (i.e., overuse of the staccato) will probably have less success in employing strong vocal force and so should benefit from exercises in timing. (3) An individual whose breathing is faulty may have difficulty in using the element of force; especially is this true of the person who expels much of his breath before he starts vocalizing a phrase or sentence. Breathing habits should be checked when starting to work on vocal force.

a. At your optimum pitch, sing a loud "ah." The loudness should be at a level of force which requires some effort. Sustain this tone at the same intensity as long as possible. An intensity meter will measure the amount of force you are using and will assist you in keeping the amount steady. (Certain types of tape recorders have such meters.) Make a written record of the length of time you can hold the tone at the same force level. Practice this exercise several times a day, always striving for the same intensity level. Record the number of seconds you hold the tone each time. Note the progress you make in duration. The average individual can sustain a loud tone for 20 to 25 seconds. (Obviously, if you are using an intensity meter to check your force level, you must keep the same distance from the microphone each time you try the exercise.)

b. Sing the vowel "ah" at your natural pitch level. Starting at that level, sing up the scale one octave; sustain the tone as loudly and as long as you can on each note of the scale. You will note that as you go up the scale you will be producing louder tones. When you get to the top note of the scale, sing back down it, still prolonging each note and making each one as loud as possible. When you come back to your natural pitch, you should be getting a louder tone on that pitch than when you started the exercise. Repeat this drill from time to time during all your practice periods.

c. Sing "ah" at your natural pitch. Keeping pitch constant, start with a loud degree of force and gradually decrease the loudness to the point where it is barely audible. Use a meter to show you what you are doing and to help you keep the decrescendo even and smooth. Reverse this procedure, starting with a soft tone and gradually increasing it to a loud one.

d. Select a paragraph of prose. Read it first at a very soft level, but making certain that you are using vocalized tones at all times (i.e., avoid the whispered quality as a means of securing softness). Next, read the same paragraph as loudly as you can. Then read it at a medium level of force.

e. If possible, find a large room in which you can practice reading aloud. Take a friend along with you. Have him sit at the front of the room first; read to him at that position. Then have him move half-way toward the back of the room and repeat your reading. Finally, have him sit at the extreme rear of the room, and again read to him. Notice the differences in your loudness and intensity as you try to make your reading intelligible.

Problems of Quality

One of the most common faults in vocal quality is monotony. You should strive to build as large a *vocabulary of tones* as possible; the first consideration is to gain flexibility and versatility. Monotony of quality may be caused by too low a tension of the bodily muscles generally. Another prime cause of vocal monotony is embarrassment, or stage fright. Such an emotional state tends to produce a quality characteristic of fear; fear-induced laryngeal tensions, harmful to the voice, are present. Training in vocal quality means developing a large number of normal emotional responses; it involves also the full and versatile use of the resonators.

It is obvious that, although variety of quality is desirable, there will be one basic quality which distinguishes the voice of the individual and which he will use most. The best habitual quality, which each of us should strive to achieve, is one we call *normal.* The term "normal" here means the right tone for ordinary, informal situations. This quality is clear and agreeable. It employs all of the resonators; it is free from improper nasality and from guttural growl, hollow pectoral (chest) murmur, and oral and falsetto thinness and squeakiness. All of the breath is vibrated; none of it is allowed to escape unvocalized as it does in the whispered quality.

Under certain circumstances, an individual's normal quality may be enlarged and expanded into what we call the *orotund.* By derivation, orotund means "with a round mouth." This quality is produced very much as is the normal except that it involves greater force and more attention to those resonance characteristics which make for audibility at a distance. Both the normal and the orotund at their best probably have an admixture of the nasal quality to give them sharpness; this element is added by allowing the soft palate to relax slightly from its contact with the pharyngeal wall. A person can learn to *feel* the position of the soft palate by producing nasal and non-nasal tones in quick succession.

The most common faulty deviations from normal and orotund quality are *excessive nasality, breathiness, harshness,* and *hoarseness.*

EXCESSIVE NASALITY

This quality is primarily the result of improper functioning of the resonators; it results from keeping the nasal cavities open at the back, when they should be closed off. A person whose voice is unpleasantly nasal should first of all determine if it is so as the result of such a pathological disorder as a cleft palate or paralysis of the velar (palatal) muscles. If it is not, the nasality probably stems from a lazy soft palate, ineffective operation of the jaw muscles, or improper elevation of the tongue in the rear of the mouth. Frequently people are lazy with their soft palates, lips, and tongues. The result is that vibrating breath passes out through the nose during the vocalization of sounds that should not be nasalized.

Another objectionable quality, which frequently is miscalled "nasal," is that produced when there are obstructions in the nasal passages. This condition interferes with proper nasal resonance and is more properly termed "denasality" or "negative nasality."

Exercises to eliminate excessive nasality can and should take many forms. We can present only one here.

While observing your mouth in a mirror, yawn as vigorously as you can. You will note that the velum comes into contact with the back wall of the throat at the opening into the nasal cavities. Now sustain the sound "ah" while watching your velum in the mirror. Make sure that the velum remains in contact with the pharyngeal wall during the entire time you are making the vowel sound. While you are producing this sound, alternately hold your nose and release it. If the velum is functioning properly, there should be no noticeable difference in the quality of the sound you are making. Next, prolong the same sound and alternately lower and lift the velum. Notice the change in quality. Come back to these exercises frequently during your voice training until you have achieved considerable voluntary control over the velum.

BREATHINESS

Breathy quality arises from a failure to bring the vocal folds together completely. There may be a pathological defect which prevents this closure (for example, singer's nodes—small growths on the folds themselves). If there is no such condition, the poor quality may be caused by other improper speech habits. Upper-chest breathing, a pitch level that is lower than it should be, insufficient muscular tone throughout the entire body, all may produce the quality. Therefore, exercises to remove such faults should be utilized in trying to overcome breathy quality. Other exercises that should be useful include the following:

a. Practice some of the breathing exercises already recommended. After you have checked up on your breathing habits for the moment, sustain the vowel "ah" as long as possible, avoiding all signs of breathiness.

b. Prepare and read several sentences which include a number of words beginning with the "h" sound and with plosives ("p," "b," "t," "d") and fricative sounds ("f," "v," "s," "z," "th"). While breathing out gradually and steadily, read these sentences, checking yourself to make sure that you are not permitting a large fraction of your breath to escape before you begin the first word. Try to equalize the amount of breath that you use for all parts of the sentence.

c. While performing the exercises and practicing your readings, sit or stand erect, though not stiff. Assume a mental attitude of animation and enthusiasm. This will increase the general tonus of your body, including your throat muscles.

d. Read the following word pairs. The first word requires an aspirate attack which should be stopped as soon as you get into the vowel sound.

hid	id	ham	am
heal	eel	has	as
hold	old	hair	air
had	add	hail	ail
high	eye	hand	and

Read these word pairs until you can make the second word of each pair completely free of breathiness.

HARSHNESS

This quality is noisy, rasping, and unmusical. It is frequently described as a growl, especially when it is characterized by a low pitch. Teachers of vocal music try to rid their pupils of the harsh quality by advising them to "place the voice forward in the mouth." Those who habitually use a growl should try to shift their attention in voice production from the laryngeal muscles to the breathing muscles, particularly the abdominal muscles. Many speakers, in situations that demand more than ordinary vocal force, fall into the habit of constricting their throat muscles, instead of pumping more vigorously with their abdominal muscles, and thus lapse into this unpleasant harsh quality. *But the best way to get rid of a chronic harshness is to break up the bad emotional habits which cause it.*

a. Use relaxation exercises frequently. Immediately following a period of relaxation, inhale easily, letting your jaw drop relaxed. Start a yawn. As you start the exhalation for the yawn, easily and smoothly say "hah." Keep your throat as open as possible. Follow this exercise with one that includes all the vowel sounds, prefacing each with the aspirate "h"—"hah," "hay," "he," "hi," "ho," and "hoo."

b. Use the word pairs in exercise *d* of the breathiness section. Read the pairs, keeping in mind that a word beginning with "h" is favorable for a gradual initiation of the vowel sound that follows. Try to carry over the gradual vowel initiation in the first word to the vowel of the second word. Avoid any abrupt glottal "attacks," that is, clicks or coughlike explosions, before any of the vowels.

HOARSENESS

This quality, a combination of harshness and breathiness, frequently is associated with laryngeal infection. Chronic hoarseness should be diagnosed by a physician whose advice should be followed before beginning any exercises. If there is no physical cause for the condition, the exercises designed to correct harshness and breathiness should prove most beneficial.

Section Three—Pronunciation and Enunciation

The problem involved in pronunciation can perhaps best be realized by noting the observations of several authoritative lexicographers and linguists:

The term *correct pronunciation* is often used. Yet it is probable that many who use the term would find it difficult to give a precise and clear definition of the sense in which they use it.[7]

I have no intention of becoming either a reformer of pronunciation or a judge who decides what pronunciations are "good" and what are "bad."[8]

I do not consider it possible at the present time to regard any special type as "Standard" or as intrinsically "better" than other types.[9] . . . Pronunciation varies from district to district, from class to class, from character to character, in proportion to the local, social, or moral difference that separates them.[10]

The English language is spoken all around the world and many varieties of pronunciation have grown up. Some of the forces that cause these differences are climate, contact with native languages, commercial dealings with people of other nationalities, etc. Despite its vast area, the United States has relatively few major dialects, only three as a matter of fact, and all of these are intelligible to nearly every English-speaking person in the entire country. There is no serious problem of pronunciation among those who speak the three dialects of American English no matter where they may go in the United States.

The dialects spoken in this country are the Eastern, the Southern, and the Midwestern (General American). The Eastern dialect is limited principally to New England and to the most highly literate people of New York City; the Southern is found mainly in the states that composed the Confederacy; and the General American is spoken throughout the rest of the United States. These areas are not sharply separated from each other geographically, and, along the borders between them, dialects are considerably mixed. Furthermore, in each region, there is a generous admixture of the speech of both of the others, because of the presence of natives from the other sections. And each of the major dialects reveals many variations within its primary characteristics; often these variations, some of which can be called

[7] "Guide to Pronunciation," *Webster's Third New International Dictionary*, G. & C. Merriam Company, 1961, p. 40a.

[8] Daniel Jones, *English Pronouncing Dictionary*, New York, 1956, p. xvi. (Cited in Reference No. 7 above.)

[9] Daniel Jones, *An Outline of English Phonetics*, 8th ed., New York, 1956, p. 12. (Cited in Reference No. 7 above.)

[10] A. Lloyd James, *Broadcast English*, I., 2d ed., London, 1931, p. 11. (Cited in Reference No. 7 above.)

nothing but sub-standard, result from geographical isolation or social provincialism. Radio and television seem to be having some influence in modifying the variant pronunciations of the different dialect regions.

Each of the major dialects has its characteristic pronunciations, but the differences among them are relatively minor. Nevertheless, there are differences. A distinguished lexicographer remarked recently that it would be difficult to find two cultivated speakers who would pronounce the words in the following sentence exactly alike: "*When Mary Harris was married in Marion, various hilarious associates made merry a hundred ways and shared the hospitable home of her parents.*"

In addition to variations existing among geographical areas, and among social and cultural communities within these areas, pronunciation changes in the course of time. Every time a new edition of a dictionary appears, it records many pronunciations that have come into vogue since the preceding edition was published.

The problem is further compounded by the many discrepancies between letters and sounds in the English language. The person who looks at a printed "word" and pronounces it is translating a visual stimulus into an auditory one. We need to begin by realizing what a gulf there is between living and audible human speech and the cold, inert written or printed shadows of it. Basically, language should always be thought of as produced by the vocal mechanism and acting upon the ear and not as something made with a printing press or a pen, affecting us merely through the sense of sight. We should realize that, at best, the printed signs through which language is recorded and preserved are only crude representations of oral language. From these facts arises a fundamental difficulty. How shall we translate written language back into living (spoken) language with any assurance that we are using the sounds the writer thought he was indicating?

In English, the same combinations of letters have many different sound values, while different combinations have the same sound values. For an example of the first, take *ough* in the following—*ought, bough, dough, through,* and *enough.* Or *oes* in *shoes, floes,* and *does.* Different combinations that have the same sound value are *ff*, *gh*, and *ph*, as in *off*, *laugh*, and *philosophy*. The reason for these and for many other similar inconsistencies is that the spellings of words have continued unchanged over long periods of time while the sounds for which they originally stood have shifted radically. The sound of *e* is represented by *ee* in *see*, by *ea* in *each*, by *ie* in *believe*, by *ei* in *seize*, by *i* in *machine*, by *eo* in *people*, by *ay* in *quay*, by *oe* in *Phoebe*, and by *ae* in *Caesar*. The letter *a* has a great variety of sound values, as in *name, any, bear, man, father, watch, village, all, sofa,* and *beat.*

George Bernard Shaw's classic satire on this confusion is worth noting. He suggested "*ghoti*" as a perfectly "logical" spelling for the more recognizable word *fish*, by combining the *gh* sound in *cough*, the *o* sound in *women*, and the *ti* phoneme in *notion*.

In order to have a spelling system that would correspond exactly to speech sounds, it would be necessary to have one invariable letter symbol for each separate speech sound, as is true in the International Phonetic Alphabet. Our English spelling has lost touch with our pronunciation; these two have drifted so far apart in many instances that only a radical spelling reform will bring them together again. Someone has said that there probably isn't a single word in the English language the spelling of which would be a sure guide to its pronunciation. Those who try to pronounce according to spelling find themselves in a morass of inconsistencies.

From all this, it would seem that the problem is so great that nothing can be done about it. If there is no such thing as "correct" pronunciation, what difference does it make? But just stop a moment to recall an instance when you heard a word "mispronounced," according to your idea of usage. You did notice it and, for a moment, communication was interrupted. You perhaps formed an impression of the speaker, an impression based at least in part on that "mispronunciation." Many of the most vital impressions others make upon us and we, in turn, make upon them spring from pronunciation, or mispronunciation.

In speaking, *the word as pronounced* IS THE ONLY WORD the hearer gets. How can he tell whether you mean *fallow, fellow,* or *follow; sailor* or *seller; tail, tell,* or *tall* or *toil* or *toll; merry* or *marry;*

vary or *very;* except by the slight difference you make in the leading vowel in each case? Hence, every word should be rightly pronounced. It is true we do guess out much of very imperfect speech by context; but a person of any education should be ashamed to have others guessing out his utterances. . . . Moreover, mispronounced words may be misunderstood or absolutely lost; if you say *hor'i · zn,* your hearer may not know that you mean *ho · ri'zn.*[11]

THE SOLUTION

Although there is no "correct" pronunciation of a particular word, there certainly is a "satisfactory" or "appropriate" one. The pronunciation of a word is satisfactory if (a) it makes the word instantly recognizable; (b) it does not call undue attention to itself; (c) it follows the usage of the leaders of the social and cultural community; and (d) it fits the context (for, as we shall note later, words in isolation may be pronounced differently from words in phrases or sentences).

You *know* satisfactory pronunciations of most words you use. If you do not *know,* you owe it to yourself to investigate them. You can follow the social and cultural leaders of your community. When there is a difference of practice among leaders, adopt the form that seems to be preferred by the majority of leaders. If, on the basis of your own personal observation you cannot be sure which is the preferred form, consult a good dictionary.

Using a Dictionary. There is a good deal of misunderstanding about what a dictionary actually is. Many people regard it as an arbitrary authority that sets up standards out of thin air or the imagination of the editors. The dictionary-maker tries his level best, by all the means at his disposal, to ascertain the pronunciations preferred by the people who are most worthy of imitation. He sets down the pronunciations of such persons for the information of those who want to know what they are.

Pronunciation is a matter of syllabication, accentuation, and articulation of individual sounds. A good dictionary assists its user in each of these.

Syllabication. A syllable is defined as "one or more speech

[11] "How to Use *The New Standard Dictionary,*" leaflet in *The New Standard Dictionary* (New York: Funk & Wagnalls Co., 1956).

MERRIAM-WEBSTER PRONUNCIATION SYMBOLS

ə .....**banana, collect**

ˈə, ˌə **humdrum**

ə̄ .....as in one pronunciation used by *r*-droppers for **bird** (alternative \əi\)

ə̇ .....two-value symbol equivalent to the unstressed variants \ə\, \i\, as in **habit, duchess** (\ˈhabət\ = \ˈhabət, -bit\)

ᵊ .....immediately preceding \l\, \n\, \m\, \ŋ\, as in **battle, mitten**, and in one pronunciation of **cap and bells** \-ᵊm-\, **lock and key** \-ᵊŋ-\; immediately following \l\, \m\, \r\, as in one pronunciation of French **table, prisme, titre**

əi ....as in one pronunciation used by *r*-droppers for **bird** (alternative \ə̄\)

ər ...**operation**; stressed, as in **bird** as pronounced by speakers who do not drop *r*; stressed and with centered period after the \r\, as in one pronunciation of **burry** (alternative \ə̄r\) and in one pronunciation of **hurry** (alternative \ə·r\); stressed and with centered period between \ə\ and \r\, as in one pronunciation of **hurry** (alternative \ər·\)

a .....**mat, map**

ā .....**day, fade, date, aorta**

ä .....**bother, cot**; most American speakers have the same vowel in **father, cart**

ȧ .....**father** as pronounced by speakers who do not rhyme it with **bother; farther** and **cart** as pronounced by *r*-droppers

aa ...**bad, bag, fan** as often pronounced in an area having New York City and Washington, D. C., on its perimeter; in an emphatic syllable, as before a pause, often \aaə\

ȧi ....as in some pronunciations of **bag, bang, pass**

aů ...**now, loud**, some pronunciations of **talcum**

b .....**baby, rib**

ch ....**chin, nature** \ˈnāchə(r)\ (actually, this sound is \t\ + \sh\)

d .....**elder, undone**

d· .....as in the usual American pronunciation of **latter, ladder**

e .....**bet, bed**

ˈē, ˌē **beat, nosebleed, evenly, sleepy**

ē .....as in one pronunciation of **evenly, sleepy, envious, igneous** (alternative \i\)

ee ....(in transcriptions of foreign words only) indicates a vowel with the quality of *e* in *bet* but long, not the sound of *ee* in *sleep: en arrière* \äⁿnáryeer\

eů ...as in one pronunciation of **elk, helm**

f .....**fifty, cuff**

g .....**go, big**

h .....**hat, ahead**

hw ...**whale** as pronounced by those who do not have the same pronunciation for both *whale* and *wall*

i ......**tip**, one pronunciation of **banish** (alternative unstressed (\ē\), one pronunciation of **habit** (alternative \ə\; see ə̇)

ī .....**site, side, buy** (actually, this sound is \ä\ + \i\, or \ȧ\ + \i\)

iů ....as in one pronunciation of **milk, film**

j ......**job, gem, edge, procedure** \prəˈsējə(r)\ (actually, this sound is \d\ + \zh\)

k .....**kin, cook, ache**

k̲ .....as in one pronunciation of **loch** (alternative \k\), as in German **ich-laut**

l ......**lily, pool**

m ....**murmur, dim, nymph**

n .....**no, own**

ⁿ .....indicates that a preceding vowel is pronounced with the nasal passages open, as in French *un bon vin blanc* \œⁿbōⁿvaⁿbläⁿ\

ŋ .....**sing** \ˈsiŋ\, **singer** \ˈsiŋə(r)\, **finger** \ˈfiŋgə(r)\, **ink** \ˈiŋk\

ō .....**bone, snow, beau**; one pronunciation of **glory** (alternative \ȯ\)

ȯ .....**saw, all, saurian**; one pronunciation of **horrid** (alternative \ä\)

œ ....French **bœuf**, German **Hölle**

œ̄ ....French **feu**, German **Höhle**

ȯi ....**coin, destroy, strawy, sawing**

ōō ...(in transcriptions of foreign words only) indicates a vowel with the quality of *o* in *bone* but longer, not the sound of *oo* in *food: comte* \kōōⁿt\

p .....**pepper, lip**

r .....**rarity**, one pronunciation of **tar**

s .....**source, less**

sh ....with nothing between, as in **shy, mission, machine, special** (actually, this is a single sound, not two); with a stress mark between, two sounds as in **death's-head** \ˈdeths,hed\

t .....**tie, attack**; one pronunciation of **latter** (alternative \d·\)

th ....with nothing between, as in **thin, ether** (actually, this is a single sound, not two); with a stress mark between, two sounds as in **knighthood** \ˈnīt,hůd\

t̲h̲ ....**then, either** (actually, this is a single sound, not two)

ü .....**rule, fool, youth, union** \ˈyünyən\, **few** \ˈfyü\

ů .....**pull, wood, curable** \ˈkyůrəbəl\

ue ....German **füllen, hübsch**

ue̅ ....French **rue**, German **fühlen**

v .....**vivid, give**

w ....**we, away**

y .....**yard, cue** \ˈkyü\, **union** \ˈyünyən\

ʸ .....(in transcriptions of foreign words only) indicates that during the articulation of the sound represented by the preceding character the tip of the tongue has substantially the position it has for the articulation of the first sound of *yard*, as in French *digne* \dēnʸ\

yü....**youth, union, cue, few**

yů....**curable**

z.....**zone, raise**

zh....**vision, azure** \ˈazhə(r)\ (actually, this is a single sound, not two) sounds constituting an uninterrupted unit of utterance and forming either a whole word (man) or a division of a word (A-mer-i-ca)." There are certain rules of syllabication—the breaking up of words into syllables. However, there are so many inconsistencies of practice in this matter and so much difference of opinion that, again, the only way to be sure is to consult a good dictionary. Until we have done so, we are in danger of making a mistake as to just what the separate elements in a polysyllabic combination are. The following are characteristic examples of English syllabication: *mill·stone, or·tho·dox·y, prec·i·pice, ac·knowl·edge, con·science, con·grat·u·late, anx·ious, re·bel·lion, cau·sal·i·ty, log·i·cal, beau·ti·ful, hab·it, val·iant, ter·ri·ble, de·scrip·tion, aus·pi·cious, hast·i·ly, in·ci·den·tal, chasm.*

Accentuation. By accent is meant the prominence of a syllable, that which makes it stand out above surrounding syllables. The principal element in accent is stress; that is, the degree of vocal force applied to it. Frequently, in a polysyllabic word, there are two or more stressed syllables, although almost always there is one syllable that gets more stress than any other. This fact gives rise to what are called primary and secondary accents. We use a [ˈ] above the line preceding the syllable which gets the primary accent, and a [ˌ] below the line preceding the syllable getting a secondary stress. Examples of words in which there is just one syllable accented are *ˈaccent* (n), *acˈcent,* (v); *adˈdress* (n), *adˈdress* or *ˈaddress* (v), *hexˈameter, inˈquiry.* Examples of primary and secondary accent are the following: *inˌquisiˈtorial, ˌdisoˈbedience, ˌgalvanoˈmetric, ˌhelioˈcentric.* Occasionally we have a word with two syllables accented equally, e.g., *ˈred-ˈhot, ˈthirˈteen, ˈwell-ˈknown, ˈlong-ˈlived, ˈNew ˈYork.*

Diacritical Markings. There are something like sixty-five recognizably different sounds in spoken English, but only twenty-six letters with which to represent them. Obviously, then, if we are going to write down anything like exact representations of the sounds of spoken English, we must devise a set of symbols more elaborate than our alphabet. One way of doing this is to attach to the letters signs which enable us to differentiate the various sounds for which a particular letter may stand. Such signs are called diacritical marks. These are found in the dictionary key to pronunciation included on page 157.[12] The dictionary indicates the pronunciation of a word by respelling it in letters to which diacritical marks have been attached.

Words in Connected Speech. Thus far, we have been dealing with the pronunciation of isolated words. However, we do not usually speak words singly; we speak them in sentences. The way in which we commence the pronunciation of a word depends in some measure upon the final sounds of the preceding word. Likewise, the way in which we produce the final sound of a word depends upon the initial sound of the following word. Through long usage, the syllables within separate words already have been subjected to these influences which account for some of the inconsistencies of English pronunciation. With sixty-five different sounds in the language, the number of combinations in which they may appear is practically infinite. Therefore, the possibilities of modifications of the separate sounds are also infinite. Moreover, the length of each of the several sounds is dependent upon the entire pattern. This principle holds true especially for the vowel sounds since these are more easily varied in duration than are most consonants.

COMMON ERRORS IN PRONUNCIATION AND ENUNCIATION

Many of the following "errors" involve, not pronunciation defects as such, but enunciation or articulation faults. The majority of pronunciation variations in American English result from variance in the habitual or *customary articulation of vowel sounds.*[13]

"Mispronunciation" also may stem from faulty articulation. Both vowels and consonants must be acceptably articulated to insure clear, understandable pronunciation. Vowels furnish the basic tone and quality of speech; consonants, the distinctness and precision necessary for most meanings.

[12] The system of markings in the *Third New International Dictionary* shows a number of changes from earlier editions. It makes use of a few International Phonetic Alphabet symbols and markings. The system seems to us to make possible considerable precision in pronunciation, and with a little preliminary study we believe you will find it helpful.

[13] Phonetically, the word park, for example, usually is [pak] to the Bostonian, [pɑ:k] to a Southerner, and [pɑrk] to the Midwesterner.

Faulty articulation of vowels is often a problem in resonance. Improper nasalizing of vowels results from improper control of the soft palate—for instance, allowing nasal resonance to intrude on the quality of a vowel that should be non-nasal. The unpleasant "flat" Midwestern *a*, (phonetically [æ]), is caused by excessively stretching the corners of the lips sideways, thus altering the shape of the resonant chamber, the mouth, and elongating and narrowing the space between the lips.

Resonance defects may also make difficult the proper articulation of consonants, especially [p], [b], [t], [d], [f], [v], [ʃ] and [ʒ]. The medial [d] in *madam* or *medium* is almost obliterated in the speech of a person with too much nasality. A much more common cause of consonant misarticulation is laziness of the lips and tongue. Occasionally problems stem from setting one or more of the articulatory organs in improper placement in relation to other organs. For example, the [l] sound should be made with the tip of the tongue touching the front part of the hard palate, just back of—or even touching—the upper teeth; when the tongue tip curls back, touching the roof of the mouth, a defective, unpleasant, sometimes completely indistinguishable sound is heard.

Of course, physical defects or malformation of the articulators may be the problem—too much "overbite," lack of "overbite," malformed or missing teeth, cleft palate, etc. Speech correction specialists can be very helpful in re-training these organs and should be consulted in such cases. However, we repeat, most articulation problems are the result of laziness and misuse, and can be alleviated by understanding, drill, and diligence.

Test yourself on the following list of common errors in articulation and pronunciation: [14]

1. Mistakes in the *ŋ* and *g* sounds.
   a. Final *ŋ* changed to *n*. (bringing, singing, coming)
   b. Final *ŋ* changed to *ŋ-g*. (sing, bring)
   c. Medial *ŋ* changed to *ŋ-g*, and vice versa. (hanger, singer, anger, finger, single)
   d. Omission of *g*. (recognize)
2. *w* substituted for *hw*. (what, white, while, whisper)

[14] Pronunciation symbols used are those of *Webster's Third New International Dictionary*.

3. *s* confused with *z*, and *sh* with *zh*. (increase, absurd, confuse, design, assure, leisure, measure, usual)
4. Voiced <u>th</u> and voiceless <u>th</u> interchanged. (with, pith, moth, thither)
5. *t* substituted for voiceless th. (thick, think, thought)
6. *j* and *ch* confused. (edge, judge, besiege)
7. *r* mispronounced.
   a. *w* is substituted for *r*, as in baby talk. (red, run)
   b. the so-called linking *r* is inserted between words ending with a vowel and beginning with a vowel, respectively. (the ide*a* of, the la*w* of)
8. *ü* substituted for *yü*. (opportunity, student, duty)
9. Difficult consonant combinations slighted. (te*sts*, clo*thes*, ho*lds*, ke*pt*, ta*sks*, fa*cts*)
10. Vocal fadeout on final consonants. (ma*de*, mean*t*, migh*t*)
11. *d* substituted for *t*. (little, metal)
12. *i* substituted for *e*, and vice versa. (men, many, strengthen, since)
13. *j* substituted for *zh*. (garage, rouge)
14. *o* substituted for *a*. (park, remark)
15. *tü* or *chü* substituted for *tù*. (literature)
16. *ȯ* substituted for *ȧ*. (dog, cough)
17. Suppression of syllables and sounds. (re*a*lly, gener*al*ly, gover*n*ment, fun*d*amental, pro*b*ably, Pres*id*ent of the Un*it*ed States)
18. Insertion of extra syllables and sounds. (mayoralty, municipal, athletic, column, mischievous)
19. Incorrect accentuation. (incomparable, mischievous, hospitable)
20. Failure to shorten vowels before consonants. (*e*ffect, *o*pponent, d*i*ssect, p*o*ssess)
21. Pronouncing silent, or mute, consonants. (a*l*mond, com*b*ing, ve*h*ement, fore*h*ead, of*t*en, wais*t*coat, ve*h*icle, victuals, *h*erbage, blac*k*guard)
22. Mistakes from false analogy in spelling. (sacrilegious, hiccough, breeches)
23. *j* inserted into words where it does not belong. (duty, literature)
24. *l* slighted or omitted; sometimes a dark *l* made with the back of the tongue is substituted for a clear *l* made with the tip of the tongue. (twelve, self)
25. Broad *ä* is used where it does not belong, in place of the correct short *a* or *ȧ*. (and, hand, grand)
26. Overstressing the words *a* and *the* in unstressed positions. (I saw a man, the dog runs)
27. Eliding the weak form of <u>*thē*</u> with vowel sounds beginning the next word. (the ocean, the operation)
28. Transposition of sounds. (hun*dr*ed, child*re*n, mod*er*n)

29. Hard *ch* substituted for soft *ch* or mute *ch*. (chaise, schism)
30. *i* or *ė* substituted for 'ə. (just, study)
31. *ä* substituted for ə. (unless, until)
32. ə substituted for *ō*. (fellow, potato, widow)

Section Four—Phonetics

As we have seen, the sounds of spoken language are constantly changing while the written representations of them remain pretty much the same. Thus it comes about that the relatively static written forms are less and less accurate indicators of the sounds of oral language. The need for unambiguous spellings which would represent pronunciations accurately led a group of language scholars from a number of nations to devise an International Phonetic Alphabet (IPA) in 1887. In this alphabet each symbol stands for one distinctive sound (*phoneme*), no matter what conventional letters may be used in spelling it. A *phoneme* may be defined as a group of sounds so closely interrelated that they are merely minor variants of one basic sound which is significantly different from all other language sounds.

Phonetics is not a language; it is simply a set of symbols by which pronunciations may be accurately indicated and recorded. The IPA includes the phonemes of many languages; a person familiar with it can pronounce correctly the transcriptions of any of these languages. The respelling of words in phonetic characters is a much more satisfactory guide to their pronunciation than is respelling in the regular English letters with supplementary diacritical markings as shown in the conventional dictionary.

We present here a glossary of the standard *phonemes* of American English with the IPA symbols which represent them. If your speech instructor plans to use phonetics in teaching pronunciation, you will need to memorize this code.

Consonants

The IPA uses conventional English symbols for most of the consonants:

[b]	*b*it	[n]	go*n*e
[d]	*d*eem	[p]	*p*in
[f]	*f*all	[r]	*r*ing
[g]	*g*one	[s]	*s*ing
[h]	*h*is	[t]	bi*t*
[k]	*k*ing	[v]	*v*ine
[l]	fa*ll*	[w]	*w*alk
[m]	dee*m*	[z]	*z*ebra

Some consonant sounds have been given special symbols:

[j]	*y*es	[ʃ]	*sh*ow
[ʍ] or [hw]	*wh*en	[ʒ]	vi*s*ion
[θ]	*th*ing (voiceless)	[tʃ]	*ch*alk
[ð]	*th*is (voiced)	[dʒ]	*j*ump
[ŋ]	si*ng*		

The word *consonant* originally implied a sound capable of being pronounced only with another sound, i.e., with a vowel. This early conception does not hold, for some consonants can be sounded alone; some—as [m], [s], [z], [ʃ], etc.—are as easily sounded alone as vowels. Most consonants except the voiceless ones—[p, t, k, θ, f, s, ʃ, h, hw]—have some sonority or musical quality.

Vowels

The most sonorous phonemes are the vowels. These are made with free vibration of the vocal folds and are therefore fully voiced in normal speech.

English spelling is especially inadequate in presenting vowel sounds. The IPA uses the following symbols for simple vowels—as heard in General American speech:

[i]	d*ee*m	[o]	*o*bey (lightly stressed)
[ɪ]	b*i*t	[ʊ]	f*oo*t
[ɛ]	y*e*s	[u]	p*oo*l
[e]	ch*a*otic (lightly stressed)	[ɝ, ɜr]	b*ir*d (stressed)
[æ]	h*a*t	[ɚ]	weath*er* (unstressed)
[ɑ]	b*al*m	[ə]	*a*bout (always unstressed)
[ɔ]	h*aw*k	[ʌ]	*u*p (always stressed)

Certain additional symbols should be added to the above:

[a], a vowel half-way between [ɑ] and [æ], most frequently heard in New England in *half, park, dance.* Frequently heard elsewhere in the United States in a*sk*, and as the first element of the diphthong [ɑɪ] in *fine.*

[ɒ], a vowel half-way between [ɑ] and [ɔ], heard sometimes in *hot, God, dog, office, song.* Most Americans use [ɑ] or [ɔ] in these words.

[ɜ], a vowel without *r*-quality heard in England and eastern New England in *bird.*

DIPHTHONGS

Two vowel sounds spoken consecutively and thought of as a single sound are called *diphthongs.*[15] The most common in General American speech are:

[aɪ, ɑɪ]	f*i*ne
[aʊ, ɑʊ]	c*ow*
[eɪ]	d*a*te (strongly stressed)
[oʊ]	t*o*e (strongly stressed)
[ɔɪ]	b*oy*
[ju]	imb*ue*

THE VOWEL CHART

The most satisfactory scheme of classifying vowels for speech training purposes is that of relative tongue position as the sound is produced. The high point of the tongue in the mouth is used to place the vowel in relation to other vowels. When [i] is pronounced, the high point of the tongue comes much closer to the hard palate than it does for [ɑ]; therefore [i] is a higher vowel than [ɑ]. In pronouncing [u], notice that the high point of the tongue is the back portion of the tongue; in [i], it is the front portion that is the high point. Hence [u] is called a "back" vowel and [i] a "front" vowel. There are so many variations possible in the production of vowel sounds that any system of classification can at best be a relative one.

[15] [ə] appears as the second element of the diphthongs [ʊə], [ɔə], [ɪə] and [ɛə], where the letter *r* appears after the vowel and the person normally "drops the *r* sound. E.g., *fare* is heard as [fɛə] instead of [fɛɚ] or [fɛər] or [fɛr], depending on which phonetician is doing the transcribing.

The following figure shows the American vowels arranged roughly according to the position of the high point of the tongue. The left hand side represents the front of the tongue; the right, the back.

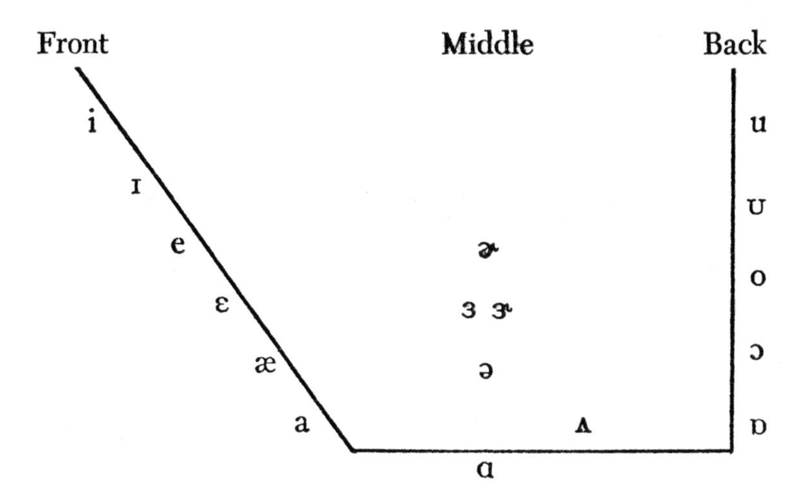

Special Symbols

The following symbols are used to show accents, length of utterance, nasalization, and other sound characteristics:

[ː]. This time length mark placed after a sound shows that the sound was held longer than usual. For example, a Southerner might pronounce *park*, [pɑːk]; this indicates that, in addition to dropping the *r* sound, he has lengthened the utterance time of the vowel.

[ˈ]. This mark is placed before a syllable to show that it has primary accent, as in *began*, [bɪˈgæn].

[ˌ]. This mark is placed before the syllable having secondary accent, as in *conversation*, [ˌkɑnvɚˈseɪʃən].

[ˌ]. If placed below [l] or [n], this mark indicates that the consonant is syllabic in nature; e.g., *hidden*, [hɪdn̩], or *mantle*, [mæntl̩].

[ʔ]. This mark stands for the glottal stop, a staccato click, or cough-like explosion of the vocal folds. Sometimes this sound is heard at the initiation of vowel sounds. Sometimes it is medial, as in *bottle*, [bɑʔl], where it takes the place of the properly produced [t]. (The glottal stop is not an acceptable language phoneme from the point of view of pronunciation, although it often is heard.)

[˜]. This circumflex accent placed over a vowel indicates that the vowel has been nasalized in pronunciation, as in the French word *champs*, [ʃɑ̃].

IPA Symbol	Key Word	Webster's Third New International Dictionary	Webster's New Collegiate Dictionary
[i]	eat [it]	ˈē, ˌē	ē
[ɪ]	it [ɪt]	i	ĭ
[e]	chaotic [keɑtɪk]	ā	ȧ́
[ɛ]	end [ɛnd]	e	ĕ
[æ]	at [æt]	a	ă
[a]	ask [ask]	ȧ	ȧ
[u]	pool [pul]	ü	o͞o
[ʊ]	pull [pʊl]	u̇	o͝o
[o]	obey [obeɪ]	ō	ṓ
[ɔ]	all [ɔl]	ȯ	ô
[ɑ]	dog [dɒg]	—	ŏ, ô
[ɒ]	father [fɑðɚ]	ä	ä
[ʌ]	up [ʌp]	ˈə, ˌə	ŭ
[ə]	above [əbʌv]	ə	*ă, ȧ, ŏ, ĭ*
[ɝ]	bird [bɝd]	ər	ûr
[ɜ]	bird [bɜd]	ə̄	û
[ɚ]	weather [wɛðɚ]	ə(r)	ẽr
[ɑɪ, aɪ]	time [tɑɪm] [taɪm]	ī	ī
[ɔɪ]	boy [bɔɪ]	ȯi	oi
[ɑʊ, aʊ]	sound [sɑʊnd] [saʊnd]	au̇	ou
[eɪ]	day [deɪ]	ā	ā
[oʊ]	go [goʊ]	ō	ō
[m]	may [meɪ]	m	m

IPA Symbol	Key Word	Webster's Third New International Dictionary	Webster's New Collegiate Dictionary
[n]	not [nɑt]	n	n
[ŋ]	sing [sɪŋ]	ŋ	ng
[p]	pay [peɪ]	p	p
[b]	bed [bɛd]	b	b
[t]	test [tɛst]	t	t
[d]	dime [daɪm]	d	d
[k]	come [kʌm]	k	k
[g]	gone [gɔn]	g	g
[f]	feel [fil]	f	f
[v]	verse [vɝs]	v	v
[θ]	thin [θɪn]	th	th
[ð]	then [ðɛn]	t̲h̲	t̶h̶
[s]	sank [sæŋk]	s	s
[z]	zebra [zibrə]	z	z
[ʃ]	ship [ʃɪp]	sh	sh
[ʒ]	garage [gərɑʒ]	zh	zh
[h]	how [haʊ]	h	h
[w]	well [wɛl]	w	w
[hw]	when [hwɛn]	hw	hw
[j]	yes [jɛs]	y	y
[r]	ring [rɪŋ]	r	r
[l]	length [lɛŋθ]	l	l
[tʃ]	church [tʃɝtʃ]	ch	ch
[dʒ]	judge [dʒʌdʒ]	j	j

ADDITIONAL READINGS

Anderson, Virgil, *Training the Speaking Voice,* 2nd edition (New York: Oxford University Press, 1961).

Fairbanks, Grant, *Voice and Articulation Drillbook,* 2nd edition (New York: Harper & Brothers, 1960).

Kenyon, John S. and Knott, Thomas A., *A Pronouncing Dictionary of American English* (Springfield, Mass.: G. & C. Merriam Co., 1953), pp. xv–xxvii.

Thomas, C. K., *An Introduction to the Phonetics of American English,* 2nd edition (New York: The Ronald Press, 1958).

CHAPTER 8

The Language Code

As we have explained in the first chapter, there are four elements of speech: *visible action, voice, language,* and *mental processes.* In speech classes and in speech textbooks, the most frequently neglected of these elements is *language.* We can prescribe definite rules for organizing materials, reasoning, and testing evidence; we can make students conscious of their deficiencies in visible action and voice; but the improvement of language presents very complex problems to both students and teachers.

Consider the following penetrating comments by Jenkins: [1]

> Verbal style impresses all observers as a most complex multidimensional entity (if indeed it can be conceived of as an entity at all). The variety of expressive features that may be incorporated in language . . . is manifestly enormous, and the number of combinations of features or patterns is staggering to contemplate. An individual uttering a single sentence makes a surprising number of "choices" in the "simple" act . . . the problem of accounting for them is far beyond the scope of any current theory.

Vocabulary

While there are more than 450,000 words in *Webster's Third New International Dictionary,* and thousands of technical and

[1] James J. Jenkins, "Commonality of Associations as an Indicator of More General Patterns of Verbal Behavior," reprinted from *Style in Language,* edited by Thomas A. Sebeok, by permission of The M.I.T. Press (published jointly by The Technology Press of Massachusetts Institute of Technology and John Wiley and Sons, Inc., New York). Copyright 1960 by The Massachusetts Institute of Technology.

scientific terms not listed there, the average American has a working vocabulary of only 3000 words. Even professional men seldom use more than 20,000 words. Notwithstanding the fact that we all understand many more words than we use in our own speech, most of us are severely handicapped in our communication by limitations in our listening vocabularies as well as in our speaking vocabularies.

How pitifully inadequate are our vocabularies when we try to talk about the space age into which we now are well launched. How sadly restricted is our understanding of the terms used by our men of science who are trying to tell us about the universe in which we live. How many people really understand what is meant by such terms as *nuclear fission, fallout, plutonium, transistor, isotope, cyclotron, jet propulsion, vitamin*? Most people *use* and react to these words (*after a fashion*) but only with vagueness and considerable confusion of mind. And think of the exactness, the nuances and depths of meaning we cannot stir up in others because we lack the "right" words. If we would unlock the minds of others, we must be able to find and use the appropriate key words.

The problem most of us face is not how to expand our vocabularies by adding long and unusual words but rather to learn to use simple variants of language which will accurately express our specific meanings.

Grammar

As speakers we must be aware of the fact that every time we use an ungrammatical expression we run the risk of interrupting our communication—of introducing "noise" into the process. When the listener notices a mistake in grammar, he is more than likely to lose the meaning. This result is closely analogous to what happens when the speaker mispronounces a word. Broadcasters testify that a slip in pronunciation or grammar brings more "fan mail" than the ideas which the speaker was presenting when he committed the error!

Here are some of the common rules and principles of grammar which seem to be violated most often:

RULES INVOLVING PRONOUNS

1. After forms of the verb *to be,* used the nominative case, e.g., "It is *she,*" not "It is *her,*"; "It is *we* who must act," not "It is *us* who must act."

2. After transitive verbs and prepositions, use the objective case, e.g., "This is between you and *me,*" not "This is between you and *I,*" "He told my brother and *me,*" not "He told my brother and *I*"; "A group of *us* students did it," not "A group of *we* students did it."

3. Pronouns must agree with their antecedents in person, number, and gender, e.g., "Each one must do *his* best," not "Each one must do *their* best"; "Neither of them realized *his* responsibility," not "Neither of them realized *their* responsibility."

4. Use *who* as subject and *whom* as object of verbs and prepositions, e.g., "He is the man *who,* we knew, was right," not "He is the man *whom,* we knew, was right"; "He is the man *whom,* I think, we should follow," not "He is the man *who,* I think, we should follow."

RULES INVOLVING PREPOSITIONS

1. Do not use propositions where they are not needed, e.g.: "Where are you going?" not "Where are you going *to*?"; "Where are you?" not "Where are you *at*?"

2. Do not put unnecessary words between a preposition or verb and its object, e.g.: "What kind of man is he?" not "What kind of *a* man is he?" "Close the house," not "Close *up* the house."

3. Learn the distinctions between:

between and *among*
angry with and *angry at*
like and *as*

MISCELLANEOUS DISTINCTIONS

1. "Different *from,*" not "different *than.*"

2. When "kind" and "sort" are singular be sure that demonstrative words modifying them are also singular, e.g.: "*that* kind of men," not "*these* kind of men"; "*this* sort of book," not "*those* sort of books."

3. Avoid double negatives.

4. Differentiate: *good* and *well, less* and *fewer, if* and *whether, most* and *almost.*

5. Do not confuse the intransitive verb, *lie,* and the transitive verb, *lay*. Say "I am *lying* on the ground," not "I am *laying* on the ground"; "I *lay* on the ground yesterday," not "I *laid* on the ground yesterday"; "I now *lay* the book on the table"; "Yesterday I *laid* it there." The principal parts of the intransitive verb are: *lie, lay, have lain;* the principal parts of the transitive verb are: *lay, laid, have laid.*

An English grammar should be a vital part of your working library and you should refer to it when you are in doubt as to any phrasing. While the authors of this textbook are well aware that many of the traditional rules of grammar have been relaxed in recent years and that speakers now are freer than they once were to make up their own rules, nevertheless it usually pays a speaker to be on his best behavior; he can better afford to err on the side of accuracy and conventionality than to commit what others may regard as serious errors in language forms.

Jargon

Almost every occupation or profession creates a vocabulary of its own. Such specialized language forms are useful for communication among members of these groups. However, the danger is that those who use these highly specialized vocabularies may fail to communicate with those outside their groups. In a democratic society, it is of tremendous importance that specialists should be able to talk about their specialties with non-specialists. Professors of theology and homiletics are becoming concerned with the prevalence of "Gospel gobbledygook" in the sermons of many clergymen. These ministers fill their pulpit discourses with phrases which have little or no meaning in terms of the world in which their congregations live. The politician perhaps offends more often than any other speaker. He intones, "To meet the challenge of our times, when the world is at the crossroads, America cries out for that Great American, that man of proven courage and ability," and so on and on for thirty minutes. Admen, lawyers, doctors—and teachers—often sin in this manner.

"Logolalia"

Many speakers suffer from this verbal disease. Their speech is interspersed with meaningless phrases or words, continuously repeated. We know of one intelligent young lady who cannot speak a sentence without introducing, at least once, the phrase, "You know." She is never aware of the phrase; she has no reason for using it; often she splits a prepositional phrase with the two words. "You see," "you know what I mean," "in any way, shape, or form," "if you please," "well," "and then," and "now" are some of the repeated expressions that we all have heard. "Logolalia" is a habit similar to the constant use of verbal pauses—"er's" and "uh's." Capable and intelligent individuals unknowingly suffer from such meaningless verbalization.

Redundancy and Flowery Language

A similar fault is using needlessly long phrases when a single word would do. "The fact that" is such a phrase which many of us use without reason. The following examples are typical:

"because of the fact that" instead of "since" or "because"
"in spite of the fact that" instead of "though" or "although"
"remind you of the fact that" instead of "remind you"
"unaware of the fact that" instead of "did not know"
"the fact that he was not present" instead of "his absence"
"the fact that I was there" instead of "my presence"

Sometimes style suffers from a desire to be impressive. We have said that public speaking should emulate conversation at its best. Conversation depends on verbs, nouns, and adverbs for its impact. We seldom decorate it with empty frills. Political speaking frequently abounds in overblown ornamentation. Commenting on this fault, Benjamin Franklin once remarked: "Here comes the orator with his flood of words and his drop of reason." Finley Peter Dunne's famous "Mr. Dooley," in explaining to his friend Hennessey what oratory is tells him that when an orator means "No," he says, "The answer is in the negative," and when he refers to the sky, he calls it "the jeweled canopy of the heavens."

Consider the following example of high-flown language in

which the meaning is obscured by the elaborate and insincere wording:

> Regardless of their pigmentation or coloration under normal illumination, felines of all species, it has been learned authoritatively, have been found to be cinerous when the earth becomes enveloped in tenebrosity.

The simple straightforward meaning of all this verbiage is: "All cats are gray in the dark."

People who work for government agencies may talk in terms which seem designed to give the impression of profundity and importance to ideas of small intrinsic consequence. Consider the following notice posted on the bulletin board of a federal bureau in Washington:

> Employees should not hold counterproductive bi-lateral counterpart meetings.

A simple English translation of this warning is: "Employees should not waste time talking to others."

The title of a graduate thesis was "Emotional Coefficient Correlative in Interpersonal Relationships between Management and Supervisory Echelons." When the author was asked what the title meant, he said simply, "Why the foreman hates the boss."

Someone has said that people sometimes cultivate obscurity in order to sound learned. They think that their ordinary ideas may seem more impressive in a dimmer light. There is a Chinese proverb which says that when a piece of paper blows into a courtroom, it will take a team of oxen to pull it out again. Clarity and simplicity of language most often reflect a well-ordered, intelligent mind.

It is calculated that the average American speaks something like 16,000 words a day. If we figure on the basis of 175,000,000 people of speaking age, we come up with the astronomical total of 2,800,000,000,000 words spoken every twenty-four hours in the United States. Remember that the average vocabulary consists of only 3000 words and you get some idea of the amount of repetition. To much of what is said, of course, nobody listens. Bishop Shipman used to tell about a man who circulated among a crowd at a cocktail party saying to everybody, "My mother committed suicide this morning." A good many people replied, "Really? How charming!"

Slang and Colloquial Speech

Recently one of our popular weekly magazines carried an article on the language forms in use among our more sophisticated contemporary teen-agers. Some of the popular terms they are using are:

big daddy—any older man	pad—home
cube or square—a normal person	beatsneaks—tennis shoes
ankle-biter—a child	the tube—television
bread—money	flip flop—convertible

Some of the current expressions seem too vague even to translate—e.g., "Kinda like never," "Kill it, Dad, before it spreads," and "Who stole the astronaut's crayons?" However, such expressions as the following seem to have fairly stable and explainable significance: "cool" (excellent or wonderful); "swinging" (pleasant); "What's your mob adjustment?" (How are you feeling?); "You bug me" (I can't stand you); "I dig you the most" (I like you very much); "Who rattled your cage?" (Who asked for your opinion?); "I was shot down" (I failed the examination); "Let's put it in orbit" (Let's go); "You've got a real cool set of threads" (Your sport coat is very attractive); "Shoot low, they're riding Shetlands" (Be careful).

Such expressions may seem more than a trifle silly, but several of them are both ingenious and amusing. Moreover, they do demonstrate considerable originality and creativeness. The problem for the older people in the community is to understand and react appropriately to the language they hear. At times, one half suspects that the motivation back of this "Youthese" is the desire to talk without being understood by parents and other older people.

Colloquial speech may be usable in some speaking situations. Such idioms, mutually understood by speaker and listener, actually can be more precise and more effective than "correct" dictionary wording. Will Rogers' style was clearly colloquial; it fit the speaker, the audience, and the occasion. Harry S. Truman sprinkled his extempore campaign speaking with slang, apparently with real effectiveness.

A speaker's style must properly reflect his "image"; it must reveal his recognition of his audience's "images"; it must fit the "image" of the situation. If these requisites are not violated in its usage, colloquial, idiomatic speech can be a successful communication tool.

Style

Most writers on language improvement stress the need for developing "style." This emphasis frequently is misunderstood to mean the cultivation of mannerisms and peculiarities—even eccentricities—in language. Style is, however, something quite different from such superficial types of wording. Originally the word *style* was derived from the Latin "stilus," meaning a writing instrument. In classical Latin, *style* came to signify a manner of writing, and later, a manner of expressing ideas. Finally, it came to mean good technique in expressing thoughts and feelings in words—its present denotation.

In a very real sense it is true that style is character revealed in language. The ancient rhetorician, Longinus (213–273 A.D.), told his students that great style is the echo of a great personality. Edward Gibbon said almost the same thing, "Style is the image of character." Buffon, the French scientist and philosopher, epitomized this point of view in his memorable and oft-quoted statement, "Le style est l'homme même" (Style is the man himself). Roger Brown observes that language style is as individual as a fingerprint.

Novices in the use of language tend to think of style as a way of speaking and/or writing which is used by literary artists, orators, and statesmen. A student is likely to say, "Why do you tell me about style? I am not going to be an essayist, a novelist, or a platform speaker." The answer is that every one of us is going to talk and write and therefore all of us face the problem of expressing ourselves either effectively or ineffectively, i.e., either with or without style. With equal justification, a person might say that he is indifferent to style in clothes because he is not aiming to be one of the ten best-dressed men in the country. Who would deliberately choose to dress so that it would be said of him that he lacks style? (Only a beatnik!) The basic assumption which lies back of this book and back of all courses in speech is that it is worth while learning to say what we have to say in the best style of which we are capable.

FUNDAMENTALS OF STYLE

1. *Simplicity* is one of the basic elements in language style. It has been said that schooling sometimes seems to result in a decrease in the ability to use language effectively. Frequently the child has style in his use of language but, as he grows older and more "learned," he covers up this early style with complexities and obscurities. The expressions of the poor and the illiterate often possess style superior to the pompous and overblown language of the sophisticated, whose language forms seem to muddy the waters of their thought and feeling. We all have met plain folks who speak with great precision and with flashes of true style; theirs is the living language born of actual experience as contrasted with the ponderous phraseology of artifice and contrivance. As Lucas says, "Primitive language seems often a kind of magic, intellectual language, a kind of algebra."[2] In this connection one remembers Gilbert Murray's remark to the effect that it would be better if more people in colleges spoke with the simplicity of Polynesians!

Quintilian urged the speaker to aim at not being misunderstood rather than at simply being understood. He said, "We think ourselves geniuses simply because it takes geniuses to understand us." In our misguided attempts to be impressive, we succeed merely in being pretentious and obscure. A great deal of the charm of great speeches is that they are so simple in their language. No one in the audience at Gettysburg would have needed a pocket dictionary to understand and appreciate what Abraham Lincoln was saying. All of us should beware of the temptation to show off our vocabulary by using big words when shorter, simpler ones will stir up the meanings just as well, or better. It is a crime to use speech for the purpose of demonstrating how intellectual and how brilliant we are when we should

[2] F. L. Lucas, "Style," in *Cambridge Reader in English* (London: Cassell & Co., Ltd., 1955), p. 31.

be trying to communicate meanings worthy of the attention and consideration of our listeners.

Ralph Waldo Emerson tells of lending a copy of Plato's *Republic* to an old farmer who said when he returned the book, "That fellow, Plato, has a lot of my ideas!"

2. *Brevity*, the next fundamental of style, is closely related to *simplicity*. One who aspires to good style should never use more words than are necessary to accomplish his purpose. Brevity shows consideration for others; to use ten words when one would do as well, or better, is discourteous. Excess verbiage wastes time, and life is made of time. When a speaker talks ten minutes to 100 people, he uses up a thousand minutes of other people's time—sixteen and two thirds hours!

Sparta (Laconia) left the legacy of a precious word to the world—*laconic*. The Spartans were notable for the terseness of their speech. They have been called "a land of iron courage and iron speech." Once Philip of Macedon sent them a threat that he was about to destroy them. He wrote, "If I come to your land, I shall exterminate you." The reply of the Spartans was one word—"If"! One of the perfect speeches of our history was uttered by Ulysses S. Grant at Appomattox—"Let us have peace."

3. *Variety* lends charm to language. There are many types of variety available to the speaker. He can vary the length of his sentences; he can vary the structure of his phrasing, using interrogative, declarative, and imperative forms; he can use words derived from Latin and words that come from Anglo-Saxon. The speaker should beware of unbroken uniformity in language; the French philosopher La Motte once said, "Ennui is born of uniformity."

4. *Courtesy* in speech frequently brings unexpectedly rich rewards. Courtesy implies understanding, sympathy, and consideration, and it arouses similar attitudes and sentiments in those on whom it is brought to bear. In the choice of language, there is no substitute for the Golden Rule.

The philosopher Whitehead, said, "Style is the ultimate morality of the mind." Confucious once said, "The gentleman is courteous but not pliable; the common man pliable, but not courteous."

5. *Restraint* is a too often neglected characteristic of good

style. The effective speaker's language is free of exaggeration, it undershoots rather than overshoots the mark. Restraint and conservatism in phrasing leave the listener with the feeling that the speaker is careful, reasonable, and concerned not to overstep the limits of accuracy. It is much better to have the listener say, "Yes, that is well within the truth," than, "Well, now, I wonder if that really is true."

Consider Wendell Phillips' use of restraint in his great lecture on the Negro leader, Toussaint L'Ouverture. After describing Toussaint's military exploits and comparing them with those of Cromwell, he concluded by saying, "Now, if Cromwell was a general, at least this man was—a soldier." As his audiences listened, they must have expected that he was going to make the extravagant claim that Toussaint was a Field Marshal. But when he made the lesser assertion, the effect was to secure agreement in the minds of the audience. Speakers tempted to exaggerate in order to be impressive often defeat themselves.

6. *Sincerity* breeds good style in language. Sincerity suggests honesty, integrity, and frankness. As Lucas says, "Many writers, especially of an academic or aesthetic kind, seem to me to stultify themselves because they are neither clever enough to be brilliant, nor honest enough to be simple." [3] Homer wrote:

> I hold that man hateful as the
> gates of Hell
> Who says one thing, while another
> in his heart lies hidden well.

It often is quite difficult to tell whether or not a speaker *is* truly sincere but we can tell whether or not he *seems* sincere. The best way to make sure of *seeming* sincere is to *be* sincere. You can never be sure that you are not going to *seem* insincere but you can at least resolve that you will not *be* insincere. The one question that you should ask yourself as you speak each sentence is: Am I absolutely sure that I really *mean* that?

Sometimes we are betrayed into thinking that, because a statement sounds good, it must be true. Francis Bacon warned that speaking in perpetual hyperbole is justifiable only in love! Of course, this warning is not intended to endorse emotionless and

[3] *Ibid.*, p. 125.

unenthusiastic language where feeling and enthusiasm are spontaneous and genuine. A biographer of Rupert Brooke wrote, "Rupert left Rugby in a blaze of glory." The poet's mother, in reading the manuscript, crossed out "a blaze of glory" and substituted "July."

7. *Specificity* is a most desirable quality in oral style. We cannot get along wholly without abstract and general terms but we should not use them to excess and we should employ concrete and specific terms to supplement them wherever possible. References to actual objects which can be seen and touched bring an impression of reality into the use of language. Pictures are only one step removed from objects, and word pictures are only one step further removed. When we are using language about concrete and specific things which we can contact through our sense organs, we are "talking sense." When we are using abstract language which has little or no connection with our senses, we are in danger of talking nonsense!

Good style is replete with illustrations and specific examples which give a touch of reality to language. It is much easier to demonstrate the meaning of patriotism by citing examples from history than it is to define it in abstract words.

Metaphors and similes are useful in giving specificity to language. Vividness is a characteristic of the specific and the concrete and can be promoted through appropriate metaphors and similes. Aristotle emphasized the value of metaphor in rhetoric.

Metaphor comes naturally in simple language because of the desire to make the new and unfamiliar vivid and comprehensible by stressing its likenesses to the old and familiar. One wonders who it was who first saw and called attention to the "eye of the needle" and to the "teeth of the saw." Of course some of these metaphors have grown stale with long usage but the speaker who has the ingenuity to see subtle similarities and mold them into metaphors has learned to employ one of the basic devices of style.

But we must beware the mixed metaphor which produces only ludicrous effects. The speaker who announced with great unction that he smelled a rat and proposed to nip it in the bud undoubtedly made an impression, but certainly he was not demonstrating effective style. Neither were the speakers who were guilty of the following:

We will burn our ships and steer boldly out into the open sea of freedom.

We must resolve to iron out the vicious circles in all these bottlenecks.

This proposal would be a mortal wound to the very keystone of good government.

Note Jonathan Swift's skillful use of metaphor when he says, "The reason why so few marriages are happy is because young ladies spend their time in making nets, not in making cages." Or consider the figure of speech in Ingersoll's tribute to the heroic dead: "Their victories made us free and rendered tyrannies in other lands as insecure as snow upon the volcano's lip." Winston Churchill once remarked, "Trying to maintain good relations with a Communist is like wooing a crocodile. You do not know whether to tickle it under the chin or beat it over the head. When it opens its mouth, you cannot tell whether it is trying to smile or preparing to eat you up."

8. *Euphony* is the final element in good language style; it means pleasing or agreeable language sounds. It is very important that the speaker's language should sound good. Harsh and jarring combinations of sounds should be avoided; they are almost certain to call attention to themselves and away from their meaning. Phrasings that sound awkward should be modified until they can be spoken easily. Empathy is involved in listening to a speaker as well as in looking at him. Listeners tend to imitate the sounds they hear and if, in so doing, they develop a feeling of muscle strain, the sounds will seem awkward and unpleasant to them. A tongue-twister becomes painful to the listener's ear. The speaker should beware of words and phrases which are difficult to articulate. Remember that what is hard to say is also hard to hear; and what slips easily off the tongue of the speaker insinuates itself smoothly into the ear and mind of the listener.

Alliteration, skillfully used and not over-used, may make a marked contribution to euphony. Consider the following passage from Lord Macaulay:

Meanwhile the disorders of Cannon's camp went on increasing. He called a council of war to consider what course to take. But so soon as the council had met, a preliminary question was raised. The army was almost exclusively a Highland army. The recent victory had been won exclusively by Highland warriors. Great chiefs who had brought six or seven hundred fighting men into the field did not think it fair that they should be outvoted by gentlemen from Ireland, and from the Low Countries, who bore indeed King James's commission, and were called colonels and captains, but colonels without regiments and captains without companies.

Like many other good things, alliteration can be carried to a fault. The rule that should guide the speaker is—never let devices sink to the level of mere tricks; use them with discrimination and economy always.

One of the best ways to develop a good oral style is to read aloud good style as exemplified in really fine speeches as they appear in print. No one can study music without ever hearing music.

ADDITIONAL READINGS

Brigance, William Norwood, *Speech Composition*, 2nd edition (New York: Appleton-Century-Crofts, 1953), Chapter 6.

Bryant, Donald C. and Wallace, Karl R., *The Fundamentals of Public Speaking* (New York: Appleton-Century-Crofts, 1960), pp. 251–83.

Parrish, Wayland Maxfield and Hochmuth, Marie, *American Speeches* (New York: Longmans, Green and Co., 1954), pp. 1–20.

Potter, Simeon, *Our Language* (Baltimore: Pelican Books, 1950), Chapter 11.

QUESTIONS AND PROJECTS

1. Bring to class two or three paragraphs which you think exemplify good oral style. Read them aloud and comment on their distinctive characteristics.

2. Select two or three paragraphs from a magazine or newspaper which, you think, are in acceptable written style but lack some of the essentials of good oral style. Re-write the paragraphs in better style for your speaking. Read aloud the originals and your revisions, pointing out the special features of each.

3. Compare and contrast a passage from some English essay which is considered excellent style with a passage of equal length from some

great public address. The two examples which follow may point the way:

a. If it be affirmed that rhyme and metrical arrangement of themselves constitute a distinction which overturns what has just been said on the strict affinity of metrical language with that of prose, and paves the way for other artificial distinctions which the mind voluntarily admits, I answer that the language of such poetry as is here recommended is, as far as possible, a selection of the language really spoken by men; that this selection, wherever it is made with true taste and feeling, will of itself form a distinction far greater than would at first be imagined, and will entirely separate the composition from the vulgarity and meanness of ordinary life; and, if meter be super-added thereto, I believe that a dissimilitude will be produced altogether sufficient for the gratification of a rational mind.

—William Wordsworth

b. Shakespeare was an intellectual ocean whose waves touched all the shores of thought; within which were all the tides of destiny and will; over which swept all the storms of fate, ambition and revenge; upon which fell the gloom and darkness of despair and death, and all the sunlight of content and love; and within which was the inverted sky, lit with the eternal stars—an intellectual ocean toward which all rivers ran, and from which now the isles and continents of thought receive their dew and rain.

—Robert Green Ingersoll

4. The following paragraphs represent the introduction and the conclusion of an address by General of the Army Douglas MacArthur to the graduating class of the United States Military Academy at West Point on May 12, 1962, when he was given the Sylvanus Thayer Award for service to his nation. ("The general spoke without a prepared text and without notes"—*U.S. News and World Report,* June 4, 1962.) Read the excerpts aloud several times and form your own opinion as to their quality. Then read them to the class, telling the class how you like the excerpts and why.

No human being could fail to be deeply moved by such a tribute as this, coming from a profession I have served so long and a people I have loved so well. It fills me with an emotion I cannot express. But this award is not intended primarily for a personality, but to symbolize a great moral code—the code of conduct and chivalry of those who guard this beloved land of culture and descent.

Duty, Honor, Country: Those three hallowed words reverently dictate what you want to be, what you can be, what you will be. They are your rallying point to build courage when courage seems to fail, to regain faith when there seems to be little cause for faith, to create hope when hope becomes forlorn.

. . . .

The shadows are lengthening for me. The twilight is here. My days of old have vanished—tone and tints. They have gone glimmering through the dreams of things that were. Their memory is one of wondrous beauty, watered by tears and coaxed and caressed by the smiles of yesterday. I listen then, but with thirsty ear, for the witching melody of faint bugles blowing reveille, of far drums beating the long roll.

In my dreams I hear again the crash of guns, the rattle of musketry, the strange mournful mutter of the battlefield. But in the evening of my memory I come back to West Point. Always there echoes and re-echoes: Duty, Honor, Country.

Today marks my final roll call with you. But I want you to know that when I cross the river, my last conscious thoughts will be of the Corps, and the Corps, and the Corps.

I bid you farewell.

CHAPTER 9

Meaning

Definition of Meaning

No term that we use in discussing speech is less precise and more elusive than the word *meaning*. What do we *mean* by *meaning?*

First of all, what we call meaning in speech originates within the nervous system of the speaker who seeks to awaken a counterpart in the nervous system of the listener. We should always think of speech as a *stirring-up* process rather than as a *transmitting* process. All that any speaker can do is to issue "sight and sound drafts" on his listener's bank account of experience. Too often we use such phrases as "getting meaning" and "giving meaning," without stopping to consider *what* and *how.*

Meaning always consists of responses and, therefore, it exists only in persons, not in things or symbols. Meaning is a subtle fusion of responses to present stimulation with the residues of responses to past stimulation, touched off through the mechanism of conditioning. Meaning is never something done *to us;* it always is something *we ourselves do.*

From these fundamental postulates certain practical conclusions may be drawn. When we look for meaning in words, we are in error. When we think that by the use of word stimuli we can call up meanings out of an experience vacuum, we will be disappointed. Meanings always have to be manufactured on the spot and at the moment by the one who "gets" them. If the listener does not have on hand the stuff (experiences) out of which the meaning can be made, there is no way in which the speaker can "give" it to him. How long would it take the average man on the street—or student in college—to accumulate the background of mathematical and physical experience he would need to understand Einstein's theory of relativity?

Naturally and naively, the speaker assumes that meanings which he understands will, *ipso facto*, be equally clear to his listeners. He fails to comprehend the basic fact that all his signs and symbols have to be filtered through experiences within the nervous system of his hearer.

How do we "get" the speaker's meaning? We do it by considering the ideas and feelings which he precipitates within us. We infer the speaker's meaning from the feelings and the ideas he stirs up within us.

One way of outlining the speech process is as follows:

1. Some happening, event, or combination of stimuli touches off a chain of responses in the nervous system of the speaker.
2. The speaker selects, out of the mass of his own responses, certain ones which he wants the listener to have.
3. The speaker encodes these inner reactions into what he hopes will be meaningful symbols which he produces with his audible and/or visible behavior.
4. The listener decodes the message by allowing it to stir up his past experience into what become for him meaningful patterns.

As we have seen in Chapter 2, the stimuli used by the speaker include verbal symbols (spoken words), tones, inflections, movements, postures, facial expressions, etc. Everything that the speaker does has to be decoded—interpreted by the listener—before it can become meaningful to him. Obviously, *de*coding is just as vital to the success of speech as is *en*coding and, in order to be sure of satisfactory decoding, speaker and listener must employ the same code. Even when they do, a good deal of meaning "leaks out" somehow in the channel between them.

Types of Meaning

There are two basic types of meaning: *extensional, denotative, logical, impersonal* meanings; and *intensional, connotative, emotional, personal* meanings. Extensional meanings are objective, definite, and explicit. They have to do with experiences which encoder and decoder can check against what we call outer reality—the world of things. When we talk about an apple, we can with relative ease procure an apple and together with the communicatee see it, touch it, smell it, taste it and thus exercise our senses in developing common experiences. When the speaker and the listener use sense experiences they have in common as the basis for developing meanings, we say they are talking "common sense." But when we talk about *honesty, patriotism, Americianism, communism,* etc., we are no longer dealing with anything that can be experienced through the senses. Such abstractions may take us further and further from sense experience until we find ourselves talking "non-sense." One of the reasons for the use of field trips, demonstrations, clinics, and laboratories in teaching is that they provide constant opportunity for the common checking of sense experience and thus make for clear extensional meanings.

Intensional meanings are hard to check against the inner, personal experiences for which they stand; they refer to subjective conditions, states of mind, which are accessible only to one individual. Of course, most meanings have both extensional and intensional aspects or elements. Barrett Wendell says,

> Every word we use must in greater or less degree possess two distinct traits—*denotation* [extension] and *connotation* [intension]. It denotes the idea which good use agrees that it should stand for; it connotes the very various and subtle *thoughts and emotions which cluster about the idea in the human mind.*

The word "cat" seems to be a clearly extensional term, but it can have a great variety of shades of connotation also. Different people have had a good many individual and peculiar experiences with the sort of animal referred to by the word. To one person who loves his pet cat, the word has completely different connotations from those stirred up in another person who is violently allergic to cat fur. Because intensional components are present in extensional words—in reactions to such words—a speaker must be very careful lest he stir up connotations which constitute obstructions in the route to his goal.

INFORMATIVE AND AFFECTIVE WORDS

Another classification of the meaning attached to words is the *informative* and the *affective*. Informative words are those which give us factual information, while affective words are designed to arouse our feelings and emotions. When the purpose of a speaker is to report factual information, he should avoid words which stir up emotions and impair the critical capacities of his listener; such words become "noise." On the other hand, affective language is very useful in motivation; it is the very bread and butter of the advertiser. (Of course, we do not endorse the indiscriminate and excessive use of affective language which sometimes is designed to obscure facts and anesthetize reason.) Purely informative language is rare in speech.

The news reporter should, so far as possible, confine himself to the use of informative language, whereas the news commentator may be expected to introduce into his message a considerable admixture of the affective. The minister and the candidate for political office inevitably find themselves faced with the necessity of using affective language if they are to influence the behavior of their hearers.

To illustrate: In reporting the results of Saturday's football game, one headline reads, "State University 24, State College 17." This language is approximately 100 per cent informative. Another newspaper heads its account of the same game, "State University Defeats State College, 24-17." Here the use of the word "defeat" injects a slight element of the affective into the report; it will stir the emotions of partisans of both schools. A third story carries the headline, "State University Clobbers State College, 24-17!" Here the language becomes definitely affective. Some of you may remember the police officer in the television serial whose trademark was his repeated warning to excited persons at the scene of a crime—"All I want is the facts, ma'am!" It may be noted, in passing, that very few reporters manage to state facts without some emotional coloring. It is a rare speaker who strips from his account of the facts all touches of emotion-laden and emotion-producing language.

The following paragraph is made up almost exclusively of extensional, informative meanings:

> This natural region, known as the North-West Frontier region, coincides very roughly with the North-West Frontier province, if we except the northermost part which lies amongst the Himalayan tangle, and, if we add to it the Punjab Districts of Jhelum, Rawalpindi, and

Attock. The region is thus divided into two parts by the River Indus. To the East of the river lie the Salt Range and the dry, sandy plateau of Attock which form part of the Punjab; to the west of the river are the hills and mountains of the North-West Frontier Province, interrupted by a number of valleys.

Perhaps it should be conceded that the foregoing has in it some words which may stir emotions, e.g., "Frontier," "Himalayan tangle," "river," "Salt Range," etc. If such words in such places do trip off emotional responses, the fact merely points to the inevitable conclusion that all words are likely to become loaded affectively through individual experiences. Nevertheless, if we were to make a trip to the region described in the passage, we could check these informative meanings against our firsthand sense experiences with the actual topography.

Now consider the sonnet by John Keats, "On First Looking into Chapman's Homer":

> Much have I travell'd in the realms of gold,
> And many goodly states and kingdoms seen;
> Round many western islands have I been
> Which bards in fealty to Apollo hold.
> Oft of one wide expanse had I been told
> That deep-brow'd Homer ruled as his demesne:
> Yet did I never breathe its pure serene
> Till I heard Chapman speak out loud and bold:
> Then felt I like some watcher of the skies
> When a new planet swims into his ken;
> Or like stout Cortez when with eagle eyes
> He star'd at the Pacific—and all his men
> Look'd at each other with a wild surmise—
> Silent upon a peak in Darien.

The meanings the poet is trying to stir up in us as he tells us about the moving experience that came to him when he first read the *Iliad* and the *Odyssey* in translation are almost wholly affective. The fact that Keats confuses Cortez with Balboa need not disturb us at all; the substitution of names does no damage to the fundamental emotional meaning. When some captious critic chided Keats for his error in names, Keats replied, "I was writing poetry not history." It need hardly be added that for a historian to place Cortez in Panama, where Balboa actually was, might seriously damage his reputation as a purveyor of information.

Nature of Symbols

A symbol may be defined as a response which is substitutable for another response. We find ourselves looking at a small, furry animal and we say "cat"; our pronouncing the word, either aloud or silently to ourselves, is substituted for the responses of fondling the cat, thrusting the cat away from us, picking up the cat—or any one of a hundred other responses we may previously have made to the visual stimulus, *cat*. As a matter of fact, saying the word may become a substitute for *all* of the other responses we ever have made to cats.

We often make the mistake of assuming that the *word* is substitutable for the *thing*—the objective reality—*per se*. It is not; it is substitutable for our past responses to the object which make up what we call experience. To put the matter in still another way, the spoken word "cat" represents (RE-presents) all our past responses to all the members of the feline family to which we ever have responded in any way. Although we may seem to be overstressing this point, it really is impossible to exaggerate its significance. The distinction between *the thing itself* and our *responses to the thing* lies at the very base of our understanding the whole communication process.

To make this point clear, let us look for a moment at the so-called "semantic triangle":

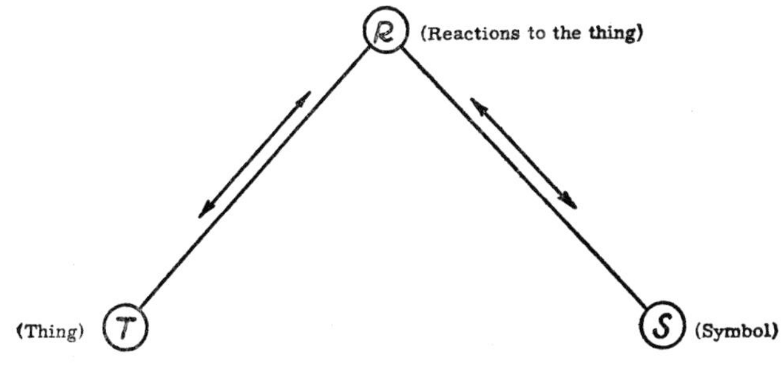

Note that there is no direct connection between "thing" and "symbol"; they are associated only through the responses of a perceiving organism. So let us insist again that symbols are substitutable for reactions to things and not for things themselves. The "semantic triangle" isn't really a triangle at all for it has only two sides; the base is absent. To put a base on it would distort reality by indicating a direct connection between the symbol and the thing. In the diagram, R indicates reactions; T, thing; and S, symbol. R is connected with both T and S. But confusion arises when we draw a line from S to T; this error tricks us into treating the symbol as if it were substitutable for the thing —or, worse still, identical with it.

A corollary of the truth just set forth is that although T may remain the same for different persons, their R's will always differ, and, consequently, S will have different meanings for them. The individual differences in R's are what make communication difficult. When once we have grasped the point we have been discussing, we come to wonder that two people ever can have sufficiently similar experiences to be able to communicate effectively at all.

Perception—Getting Meaning

Perceiving is the process by which meaning is manufactured. When a stimulus (or a complex of stimuli) affects our sense organs, nerve impulses travel to centers in our nervous system and we experience sensation. When we are stimulated by an object for the first time, our response is limited to a meaningless sensation. The life of the infant probably consists largely of such meaningless sensations. When we are stimulated by the same (or similar) object a second time, our response is different from our response the first time; our present sensation is fused with our former sensation and an element of memory or recognition comes into the pattern. Thus objects become meaningful to us. Only rarely do adults experience simple sensations; almost always some residues of past sensations are awakened when we are stimulated. We hear a strange sound. For a brief period we cannot identify it. But even while we are struggling to perceive it, it becomes more than a mere sensation; we begin to search among similar past experiences for possible meanings. At the minimum, it means "queer, unidentified sound." It is the nature of man to seek the meaning of all of his sense experience. He cannot rest until he has developed satisfying meanings.

Sinclair Lewis cites an excellent illustration of this tendency to find meaning in sensory experience. He pictures Babbit as just waking up on a cold winter morning. As he lies in bed, half conscious, he hears a heavy thud somewhere. His muscles tense as he lies and listens. There is no further sound. "What is it? It seemed to come from the front of the house. Yes, it sounded as if something had been thrown against the front door. What could that be? It is about the time at which the newsboy usually makes his rounds. Yes, that must be the answer; it was the newsboy tossing the morning paper against the front door." Babbit has developed a meaning which satisfies him and he turns over and drifts off to sleep again. This incident epitomizes all that we have been saying about the mechanism of getting meaning out of stimulation.

VERBAL STIMULI AND PERCEIVING

The most important meanings with which we have to deal arise from verbal stimulation. Typically, our response to *hearing* words is to *speak* words, either to others or silently to ourselves. Word responses to word stimuli are high-level mental responses. The deepest and most elaborate meanings with which we have to deal consist largely, if not wholly, of language tripped off within us by language stimuli, either other people's spoken or written words or our own.

Determinants of Meaning

There are six fundamental aspects or conditions of perceiving which we need to examine in some detail: (1) empathy, (2) verbal responses, (3) attitude, (4) habit, (5) homogeneity, and (6) primacy and recency.

EMPATHY IN PERCEIVING

Langfeld, an authority on aesthetics says: [1]

[1] H. S. Langfeld, *The Aesthetic Attitude* (New York: Harcourt, Brace and Company, 1920), p. 109.

> It is not necessary to lift a stone in order to know that it is heavy. The visual perception of the size and nature of the stone is sufficient to arouse within us, through association with previous experiences of lifting, the muscle sensations or motor set which would accompany the actual process of lifting. Without such previous experience there would be no perception of weight. The word itself would be without meaning. All our perceptions are dependent upon the motor attitudes that are assumed toward the object. The eye measures the extent of a line by moving over it, or there is an incipient revival within us of the muscular sensations of some other part of the body, such as the hand or leg; that is, we think of the movement of that member along the line, and thus have a clue as to the length of the line. . . . The meaning of facial expression is learned from the movement of one's own face.

Thus we come to understand that we derive meaning from situations, actions, and objects by "projecting" our ideas and feelings into them; they come to mean to us exactly what they stimulate us into doing. This tendency to project ourselves into what we see and hear we call *empathy*. This mechanism is a central factor in every speech situation. We must beware of the false notion that those who listen to and observe a speaker are like photographic plates recording passively everything to which they are exposed.

We all have experienced empathy in the football stadium as we have watched two teams struggling at the goal line; we may have projected our feelings into the action so completely that we have pushed our neighbor off his seat, trying to help our team score. We may have caught ourselves at a track meet trying to help the high-jumper or pole-vaulter over the bar by overt actions resembling, in part at least, what we have seen him doing. The contortions through which we go in following the actions of an acrobat performing a difficult stunt furnish another clear example of empathy.

Such empathic responses are vital determinants of the amount and kind of meaning we get out of the audible and visible behavior of other people by unconscious, subtle imitation of their actions. This empathic process is basic in all that goes on between speaker and listener. The listener inevitably empathizes in the behavior of the speaker and the speaker should, in turn, empathize in the behavior of the listener. Thus they may be bound together in a web of reciprocal perceiving which will lead to mutual understanding. Every attitude, every move, every sound of the speaker will be mirrored either for good or for ill in the empathic reactions of the communicatee.

VERBAL RESPONSES IN PERCEIVING

From what was said in an earlier section, it should be abundantly clear that talking is one of the most important ways of responding to talking. The psychologist, Woodworth, uses the interesting phrase, "words and other deeds." We must not overlook the fact that spoken words are actually deeds. And it is also true that speaking words to one's self is probably the most significant action in which the listener engages as he reacts to the speaker. Of course, it should be remembered that the responses of the listener may consist largely, or even wholly, as in a public speaking situation, of subvocal, silent, inner talking to one's self. In a public speaking situation the speaker utters a sentence; during the utterance and in the momentary pause before he begins the next, the listener speaks to himself and what he says to himself is for him the speaker's meaning.

Such "thought speed" is rapid. Recent investigation [2] has shown that information gain can be efficient even when rate has been increased beyond normal (by removing pauses and by speeding up the utterance of words). The gain actually is greater at moderately rapid rates than at slow speeds. However these studies have not examined what happens in persuasive speaking. When the forms of proof, including logic, are employed to effect attitude change, the thinking process undoubtedly becomes more complex.

It was formerly thought that a speaker must provide, through intelligent use of pause, time for his listeners to "talk ideas to themselves." Apparently in informative speaking this is not necessary. It is suggested by these investigators that the pause is valuable to the speaker because it permits him to do the inner talk-

[2] Grant Fairbanks has done much investigation in this area. See his "Auditory Comprehension of Repeated High-Speech Messages," *Journal of Speech and Hearing Disorders,* Vol. XXII, No. 1 (March, 1957), pp. 20–22, as an example of this research.

ing about his next idea and about what he sees and hears the audience doing. Certainly, when ideas are complex or abstract, use of pause also will assist the audience.

ATTITUDE OR SET IN PERCEIVING

The way in which attitude or set works in perceiving is illustrated by a classic experiment. A group is divided into two sub-groups. The individuals in one sub-group are asked to think intently about *buildings*, the others, to concentrate on *animals*. Both groups see letters flashed momentarily on a screen. The letters are H O N S E. Those in sub-group I report that they have seen the word, HOUSE, while those in the other group say that they have seen HORSE. All of which simply shows that expectation determines what meaning we derive from stimulation.

In the silhouette shown here, note the image that emerges when you concentrate your attention on the white part of the drawing. Now pay attention to the black part and observe the figure which comes out. Here we have a striking illustration of the effect of set or attitude on perceiving.

Often we see and hear what we are fearful of seeing and hearing; thus we suffer from illusions and delusions. The paranoid person is so certain that people are conspiring to do him harm that he interprets every action of those about him as hostile.

Every normal person experiences some measure of the tendency to interpret ambiguous behavior on the part of those around him as unfriendly. We walk into a room where others are talking. Just at that moment, all talk stops. How easy it is to suspect that the conversation has been about us—and uncomplimentary! We all make such mistakes in interpreting others' behavior.

HABIT IN PERCEIVING

When our responses become fixed into patterns which recur again and again, we call the patterns habits. When we know a person's habits, we may be able to predict his responses. We all tend to perceive meanings which fit easily and neatly into our habitual patterns of thinking, feeling, and acting. As one psychology textbook says: [3]

> Due to the dependence of perception on habit, the same combination of stimuli will be perceived differently by two persons. The tea taster's perception of tea, the florist's perception of roses, the fancier's perception of dogs, the entomologist's perception of bugs differ from the perceptions of untrained persons. Each of us has his private equipment of habit and perceives any situation accordingly.

The speaker must be mindful of the fact that whenever his listeners encounter an ambiguous combination of stimuli, they are prone to see it in the light of established habits. If we hear an alarm clock, it probably means "time to get up." If we are fishermen, minnows mean "baiting a hook." If we hear an icebox door slam, we may feel hungry. If we hear a speaker describing the flag passing in a parade, we may find ourselves applauding. If we hear a strong statement on a controversial issue, we may say to ourselves, "Now, hold on a minute! Do you have any proof for that?" However, if we have formed the habit of believing every thing we hear, we may unquestioningly accept extreme opinions offered by the speaker. Thus the meanings which come to us are determined by our habits of thought and feeling.

HOMOGENEITY IN PERCEIVING

Stimuli that have similar qualities seem to belong together. One type of homogeneity is that of position or proximity. A num-

[3] S. Smith and E. R. Guthrie, *General Psychology in Terms of Behavior* (New York: D. Appleton & Co., 1921), p. 167.

ber of different patterns, figures, or ideas may be perceived as belonging together simply because they are placed together. Consider the following groups of figures:

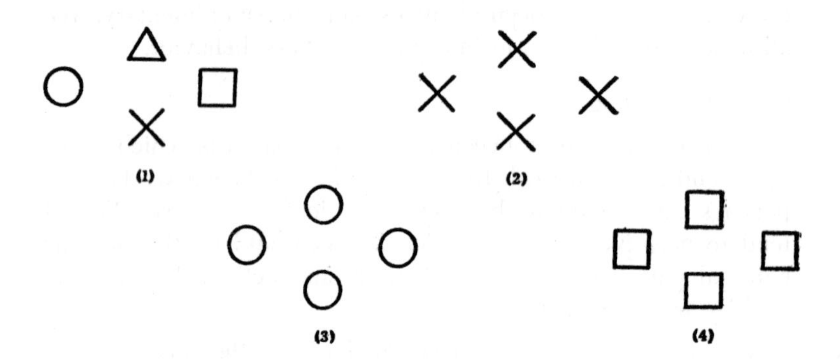

Each of the four groups is seen as a unit, yet, upon closer examination, we see that the items in Unit 1 are very different from each other, while those in the other units are like each other. The grouping of the figures in Unit 1 seems to modify their different qualities so that they take on a degree of homogeneity. This same sort of action takes place in the expression of attitudes and feelings in speech. If we discuss two ideas, one right after the other, they may seem to be alike and to belong together because of their proximity in time.

Senator Doe's opponent points out that the Senator voted for the construction of the Riverford Dam and then in the next sentence says, "The Communists also want us to spend our money building this dam." The unwary listener may transfer his attitudes about Communists to Senator Doe. This "guilt-by-association" technique is all too easy and common. Similarly, we may make an idea acceptable by placing it close to an idea which already is regarded as desirable and by making the two ideas seem similar.

PRIMACY AND RECENCY IN PERCEIVING

Finally, we should mention the role of primacy and recency in determining meaning. Although the experimental evidence is not uniformly consistent, the first and the last items in a series seem to produce more intense and lasting effects. The first may be a factor in establishing attitude or set and thus affect the meaning of all that is to follow. What one sees or hears first, to a marked degree, may color what he sees and hears subsequently. Solomon Asch, in his study of personality development, read two lists of traits to two groups of subjects. The two lists included the same traits but differed in the order in which they were presented. Group A heard, "intelligent, industrious, impulsive, critical, stubborn, envious." Group B heard, "envious, stubborn, critical, impulsive, industrious, intelligent." The subjects were asked to describe the personalities represented by the traits. The descriptions coming from the two groups were very different despite the fact that the traits were the same. The first traits mentioned gave a distinct slant to the thinking of the subjects so that the traits mentioned later were perceived *in terms of the earlier.*[4]

In other studies,[5] first impressions did not become lasting impressions. Arguments heard last were more effective. Although we cannot postulate an unequivocal "law of primacy" or "law of recency" in communication, we can state that both positions in a message are probably more effective than the middle positions, so far as perception is concerned.

Perceiving in Speech Situations

The speaker should remember that he is furnishing visual as well as auditory stimulation to his hearers and observers. Therefore, he should take care lest he make one speech to their ears and another to their eyes. Furthermore, the speaker, like every other source of stimulation, is perceived in context—that is, as a part of all the stimuli which go to make up the situation in which he is speaking. The listener always is bombarded by a multitude of diverse stimuli from sources other than the speaker. He is being stimulated by the external situation—noise, heat, bad air, movements of those around him, etc.; but he is also being affected

[4] S. E. Asch, "Forming Impressions of Personality," *Journal of Abnormal and Social Psychology,* Vol. 41 (1946), pp. 258–90.

[5] Carl I. Hovland *et al., The Order of Presentation in Persuasion* (New Haven: Yale University Press, 1957).

by what is going on inside himself—heart-beat, blood pressure, breathing, digestion, etc. One of the major problems of the speaker is to find ways of minimizing the distracting effects of marginal and irrelevant influences on his hearers and of counteracting them.

We should be alert to understand the attitudes and habits of those to whom we speak so that we may avoid, so far as possible, providing unnecessary opportunities to misinterpret what we are saying. We should remember that everyone likes to be stimulated into doing what he can do easily and comfortably and well. The speaker who wants to be liked will seldom ask his listener to do strange and unfamiliar things toward which the latter's attitudes are contrary or for which his habit patterns are inadequate.

The World Outside and the World Within

Without getting too deeply into metaphysics, let us say that we are not disposed to deny the common sense assumption that there *is* a real, objective world about us and that it is governed by dependable laws which living beings may ascertain and by which they may guide their conduct. All that we have insisted upon in this chapter is that each individual has to come to his knowledge of this outside world through his own sensory contacts with it, and through his language about it. Each individual must filter the world through his own nervous system and react to it according to his own physical equipment, his own past responses, his own points of view, and his own verbalization. It is not an empty phrase to say that each person constructs a world which is uniquely his own.

If this view is correct, the question inevitably arises—how can two human beings ever communicate at all? There are two answers: (1) Despite the fact that there are no two nervous systems exactly alike, any more than there are two faces exactly alike, nervous systems are more alike than different. (2) Many of the stimuli which the outside world furnishes are stable and uniform.

These two facts are reflected in the common core of experiences. We all have eyes, ears, skin receptors, touch receptors, temperature receptors, etc. We all experience sunshine and shadows, green grass, trees, flowers, spring, summer, fall, winter, other people, etc. Thus, when we attach symbols to our experiences, we find that the symbols often touch off in others responses similar to our own, and communication proves possible. Our everyday uses of communication convince us that it works. However, we cannot assume that two persons ever have identical meanings; they can have only overlapping and similar meanings. Communication never can be perfect.

What about the communication difficulties which result from sensory anomalies and defects? What happens when sensory avenues of approach to the world are blocked entirely? Consider the amazing case of Helen Keller who at the age of three lost both sight and hearing. She can describe a sunset or a symphony far more effectively than most of those who have all their senses. But we can never know just what her language symbols mean *to her.*

In no other area is this sort of speculation more fascinating than in the field of color vision. What is color anyway? How can it be defined? Color depends upon light. Color depends upon texture. But what *is* it? Under certain conditions wave lengths are yellow, while under other conditions the same wave lengths are green or blue. Why is it that a patch of pure "white" sunlight, when surrounded by purple becomes a *yellowish green* and, when placed in a green border, turns *pink?*

One expert in color perception says: [6]

> What we call color is a purely mental effect. It takes place only in our minds. . . . The light, our eyes, and our minds are the three phases of color. Each of them enters into every ordinary situation in which color is seen.

How do we account for the optical illusions to which every human eye is subject? Consider the two straight lines in Figure 1. Are they the same length? Look at the two lines in Figure 2. Are they parallel? Look at the line intersecting the columns in

[6] Ralph M. Evans, "Seeing Light and Color," *Scientific American,* August, 1949, pp. 52–54.

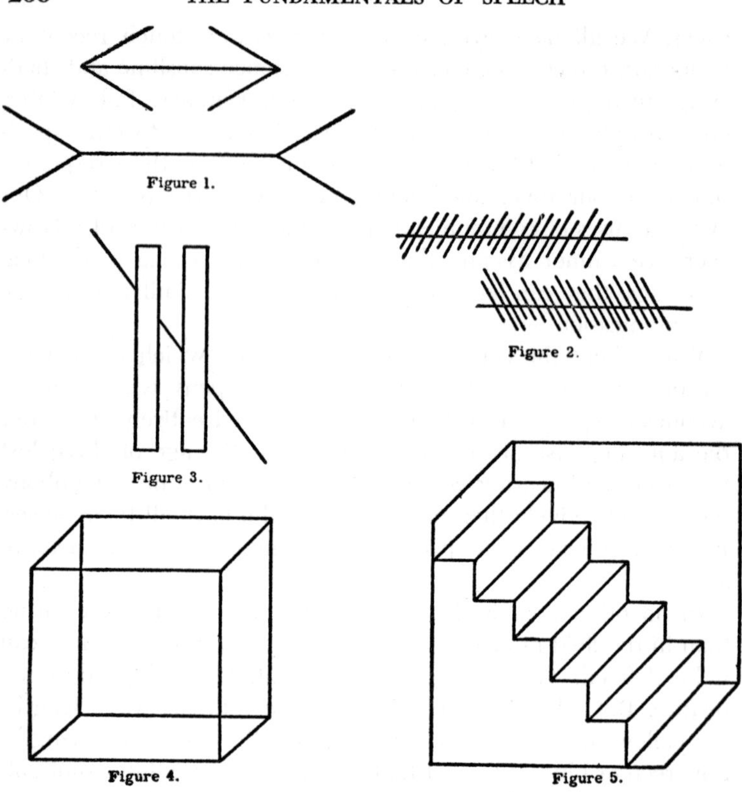
Figure 1.
Figure 2.
Figure 3.
Figure 4.
Figure 5.

Figure 3. Is it one continuous straight line? Fix your eyes intently on the cube in Figure 4. What happens? Study the staircase in Figure 5 until it seems to change. How do we explain these phenomena and how are they related to meaning?

> Seeing . . . is as much a matter of experience as of physics and physiology. It is always based in part on assumptions. We see what we believe we are looking at. Our mental pictures are our own. They are not necessarily shared either by others or by the objects themselves. . . . In order for anything to be 'seen,' in the ordinary sense of the word, it must tie in with experience in some way.[7]

As an old Arabian proverb puts the matter, "The eye is blind to what the mind does not see." In concluding this discussion,

[7] Adelbert Ames, quoted by Ralph M. Evans, *op. cit.*

we may add that what is true of vision is true of all the other senses. Meaning is always within a living organism reacting to its environment.

ADDITIONAL READINGS

Chase, Stuart, *The Power of Words* (New York: Harper and Brothers, 1954).

Gray, G. W. and Wise, C. M., *The Bases of Speech,* 3rd edition (New York: Harper and Brothers, 1959), Chapter 9.

Hayakawa, S. I., *Language, Meaning and Maturity* (New York: Harper and Brothers, 1959).

Johnson, Wendell, *People in Quandaries: The Semantics of Personal Adjustment* (New York: Harper and Brothers, 1946).

Langer, Suzanne, *Philosophy in a New Key* (Baltimore: Penguin Books, 1948), Chapter 10.

Lee, Irving J., *Customs and Crises in Communication* (New York: Harper and Brothers, 1954).

QUESTIONS AND PROJECTS

1. Prepare and deliver a 5-minute talk on interesting words. Find your material in the dictionary or some similar source. You may want to interview someone in the English Department for suggestions. Bring out the real romance in the way words have acquired and changed meanings.
2. Select ten words and read them, one by one, to five different people, requesting and recording their definitions. Tell the class what results you obtain. How do you explain the differences in meaning? Choose fairly common words.
3. Using the same words as used in Project No. 2, make a study of denotative and connotative meanings. What do you discover? Explain your findings as fully as you can.
4. Make a list of slogans that have been used in political campaigns with apparent effectiveness in influencing voters. Where do such stereotypes get their meanings? How does a word become "loaded"? Discuss your study with the class.
5. Select some printed matter which seems rich in intensional meaning and read it aloud to the class as effectively as you can. (4–5 minutes)
6. Study the accounts of the same event as they appear in two different newspapers or magazines. What major differences do you note? This project will be especially interesting if you can find two stories written by reporters who have strong opposite prejudices, economically, socially, or politically. Discuss your findings with the class.

7. Prepare and deliver a 5-minute talk on propaganda, showing how propaganda is related to the subject matter of this chapter.

8. Comment on the meaning of the following:

a. I usually play golf in the 70's. If it is either hotter or colder, I stay home.

b. The difference between a dedicated crusader and a meddlesome reformer lies in our agreement or disagreement with his objectives.

CHAPTER 10

Attention and Motivation

This chapter is based on two propositions or truths:

1. Speech has a chance for success only when, and as long as, the communicatee listens.

2. Speech will be successful only when the message satisfies the emotional and/or intellectual needs of the communicatee.

The prerequisites for the first of these are attention and interest; for the second, motivation and proof.

Gaining Attention and Maintaining Interest

As we noted in the last chapter, audiences listening to a speaker are being bombarded simultaneously by many stimuli, from within their own bodies as well as from outside. The speaker's supreme task is to see to it that his speech stimuli are the most potent in the situation and that no others distract the listeners' attention. There is probably no limit to what the speaker who can do this may achieve. A speaker who cannot do this can accomplish little.

All this seems obvious enough; yet, too often, the speaker assumes that all he has to do is to speak and let his audience make whatever effort may be necessary to get his meanings. For example, in a university faculty meeting, a professor had delivered a long and boring argument in support of a proposal for which he was asking approval. At the conclusion of his speech, another faculty member arose and complained, "I didn't get your argument at all." The speaker retorted testily, "Well, all *I* could do was state the argument."

Many speakers feel that their message is so important that they can't waste time making it interesting. They fall into the error of the ancient Greek orator who, when he saw his audience had become inattentive to his dry, dull argument, suddenly paused and said: "There once were two travelers on their way from Athens down to the Piraeus to take ship. One of them, having a great deal of baggage, had rented a donkey to transport it for him. At the noon hour, the two travelers stopped to rest. The one who had the donkey led it to one side of the road and lay down in its shade. The other traveler insisted that he be permitted to share the shade. The man who had the donkey contended that with it he had rented its shade. The other denied this and a heated argument began." At this point, the speaker abruptly walked off the platform. The audience shouted, "Come back, come back, and finish the story!" After a few moments, he reappeared and said, "Oh, men of Athens, when I speak about the salvation of our city, you fall asleep. But when I tell you the silly story of two men and an ass, you are all ears!" The point here is that a speaker who knew so well how to interest his audience should have been making use of his ability in presenting his cause. It does little good for a speaker to tell his audience that they *ought* to be interested in what he is saying or that he cannot understand why they are not interested. He bears the primary responsibility for interesting them.

Most definitions of attention are expressed in figures of speech; we speak of the *focus* and the *margin* of attention as if we were dealing with a purely visual function. It is true that we can learn a great deal from observing behavior characteristic of visual attention. We note how a person's eyes are fixed in the direction of the stimulus and how his muscles assist in orienting him to the source of stimulation. We observe the furrowed brow, the tense neck, the decreased rate of breathing of a person who is trying to see an object too distant or too small to be seen easily. Or consider the strained attitude of a person who is trying to hear a sound almost too faint to be audible. We see that attention is a unified, coordinated muscular set, or attitude, which brings sense organs to bear with maximum effectiveness upon a source of stimulation and thus contributes to alertness and readiness for further responses.

It has long been known that if we can get our listeners to attend to the ideas we want them to accept or to the courses of action we want them to take, we will be well on our way toward success. William James defined persuasion as the process of securing full and favorable attention to an actional idea. If we can *get and hold* 100-per-cent attention on an idea, we may be reasonably sure that whatever action belongs with the idea will be performed. A child who is tempted to draw a nail across the top of a polished mahogany table may suddenly find that, quite unconsciously, he has done it. This is because, as James would say, the idea of doing it "swelled" until it filled his consciousness.

One important characteristic of attention is its constant fluctuation. When we attend to an object or a situation, we focus on it intermittently, at brief intervals. The speaker should realize the impossibility of preventing momentary lapses of attention. He should concentrate on getting attention back every time he loses it. "Holding attention" really means getting it, losing it, getting it back, losing it again, gaining it again, and so on throughout the speech. Many speakers make the mistake of supposing that, once they have secured attention, they may count on keeping it as long as they commit no special error that would cause them to lose it. But this is not so; for the speaker, holding attention is a continuing problem.

BASIC FACTORS OF ATTENTION

All of us are engaged in a never-ceasing struggle to maintain feelings of physical fitness, adjustment, and well-being. As a consequence of this continual striving there is always a state of tension between us and our environment. We constantly seek adjustment, but we seldom attain it. We reach adjustment, only to slip quickly past it, into either too much tension or too much relaxation. When this delicate balance between *hypokinesis* (too little activity) and *hyperkinesis* (too much activity) is disturbed, we are predisposed to pay attention to those stimuli in the environment that may contribute to its re-establishment. We find such desirable stimuli in three general qualities of objects and situations—*intensity, movement,* and *change.*

Intensity. We instinctively pay attention to loud sounds; they produce emotional reactions and thus cause widespread tensions within our bodies. These make us uncomfortable until we unify and control them. In somewhat the same fashion, we are attracted by bright, vivid colors.

Movement. An object in motion will catch the eye, especially if it is the only moving object in the field of vision.

Change. When stimuli have called forth complete responses from us, they lose their power to hold our attention. For a while a particular musical rhythm will cause us to tap our feet. But if it continues, we eventually use our feet to propel us away from the source of the rhythm. However, when the rhythm changes from time to time, it is likely to retain our attention.

TYPES OF ATTENTION

Psychologists classify attention in three types—*involuntary, voluntary,* and *habitual.*

Involuntary Attention. When one or more of the basic factors—intensity, movement, and change—is present in a situation, our attention to it requires no effort of will; it is involuntary. The brightest and most vivid color in a field of colors; the loudest sound in a field of sounds; a moving object in a field of still objects (or vice versa); a vertical line in a field of horizontal lines; a definite rhythm in a field of irregular beats—these are examples of the type of stimuli that will gain the "right-of-way" to the central nervous system.

Mass communicators make use of these mechanical means of gaining attention. Note, for example, the bright colors of billboard and magazine advertising, the constant repetition of brand names in radio-television ads, and the repetition of campaign slogans in election years. The singing commercial makes use of rhythm and rhyme to direct our attention to a product or service.

The weakness of such devices, of course, is that they are composed of temporary stimuli. If the basic subject matter to which they call attention has no intrinsic interest for the listener or viewer, he will soon cease to pay attention. We frequently become negatively adapted to such mechanical devices. Therefore, in the use of repetition, for example, there is a point of diminishing returns.

In spite of the unreliability of involuntary attention, a speaker cannot afford to overlook its value. Judicious use of visible physical activity, an occasional well-told story or anecdote, variety in any or all the elements of voice will help to keep an audience listening. In using any of these, the speaker should remember that no device is to be employed for its own sake; it is to be used only as a method of getting the audience to think about and accept his ideas.

If you want people to watch you, give them evidence that you are alive. If they see nothing moving significantly when they look at you, they will not keep their eyes focused on you very long, and, once they have ceased to look at you, they are likely to turn their attention to other stimuli present in the situation which will divert them from what you are saying. Similarly, if it is difficult for them to hear you, or if your vocalization runs along in a monotonous pattern, there isn't much in your tone code to get and hold attention. Remember that when the attention of those to whom you speak has passed from you to incidental or irrelevant stimuli in the situation, your speech is over, no matter how much longer you may continue to gesticulate and vocalize.

Voluntary Attention. Voluntary attention involves an effort of the will; it operates when we force ourselves to attend. Our motive for attending usually is that we are aware of some possible reward for good attention or punishment for lack of it. If you expect an examination at the next meeting of your class and your instructor is conducting a review, you will likely force yourself to take note of what is said; you will shove into the background all competing stimuli. When a football team huddles to get the signals for the next play, they momentarily forget the cheering crowd, their aches and pains, even a low-flying jet; they make every effort to pay attention to what the quarterback is saying.

This voluntary type of attention is present in most speaking situations. A listener who is looking for information which he needs will attend voluntarily to what is said. Whenever a public speech is announced in advance and features a person of prestige or a subject of interest, the audience will bring to the speech a certain amount of conscious, purposeful, voluntary attention.

However, you, as a speaker, cannot be sure that voluntary attention will continue indefinitely. Unless the prospect of impending reward or punishment is extremely strong, your listeners will soon become fatigued from the effort of attending. Because of the very nature of the nervous activity involved in attention, the task of sustaining mental focus is difficult, if not impossible. Moreover, we are likely to react negatively to anybody or anything that wearies us excessively.

Habitual Attention. Habitual attention has characteristics of both the voluntary and the involuntary. It is willed attention because it is related to the listener's conscious needs and desires. At the same time it may have automatic and unconscious direction because the individual is "set," or ready psychologically and physically to pay attention.

A well-known *New Yorker* cartoon of some years ago depicted a "lady" artist seated in front of a painting, a small part of which she was copying. The larger work of art focused on central figures of a nude man and woman. Around these main figures was a border filled with flowers, birds, and leaves. The "artist," fitting the stereotype of a dowdy, buxom clubwoman, was directing all her attention to reproducing only one detail of the whole painting—a small hummingbird in a lower corner of the canvas. She was "set" to attend to the figure of the bird; perhaps she was a member of a bird-watchers' society. She was "set" to ignore the central nude figures. Probably she was consciously, involuntarily, and habitually attracted to the bird, and unconsciously unreceptive to the stimuli of the human figure. Habitual attention to your communiqué will be possible when you understand and appeal to your listeners' needs, feelings, attitudes, desires, and motives. Such attention is effortless, and yet conscious.

SELECTIVITY IN ATTENTION

Recent research in the mass media has pointed up a very significant characteristic of attention to communicative messages—its *selective* nature. Especially does this selectivity function in persuasive messages. From his examination of research, Klapper [1] generalizes that persuasion carried on through mass communications most often reinforces existing beliefs and attitudes, occasionally results in minor changes in the direction of the message,

[1] Joseph T. Klapper, *The Effects of Mass Communication* (Glencoe, Illinois: The Free Press, 1960), pp. 19ff.

and *only rarely* converts the communicatee. He ascribes this fact, in part, to people's tendency to listen to or to read only those persuasive messages which already agree with their points of view. Most studies of the effect of mass persuasion, in politics particularly, reveal this selectivity of attention.[2] Generally, in our two-party political society, only that minority of "independent voters"—whom Lippmann calls the "indispensable minority" —seem ready to listen to both sides.

We are also selective in what we attend to in face-to-face communication. We are more likely to go to rallies sponsored by our own political party; we listen to the ideas of those friends whose interests and backgrounds are most like ours; we often select our cultural entertainment on the basis of pre-judgments about its potential interest and reject other entertainments because we "know" we won't like them. All of this should suggest that attention is not easily gained, especially if there is any hint that the message is intended to persuade.

THE FACTORS OF INTERESTINGNESS

Many speech authorities differentiate the factors of attention and those of interest. Actually, when we use the factors of interestingness, we are drawing on the habitual attention of an audience. To interest really means to *keep attention.* Any speaker will find it valuable to determine what the listeners are interested in habitually and to what they spontaneously give their attention. Then, having identified some of these interests, he can begin with them and tactfully connect them with the ideas he wishes to present. As he proceeds, he can return again and again to these habitual interests, relating his ideas to them as he goes along.

What determines the interest "set" of an individual? What is it that makes him attend to specific portions of his surroundings and ignore others? Experimentation in this area suggests that two factors are especially important—*self-interest* (*the vital*) and *familiarity.*

[2] *The People's Choice,* by Paul Lazarsfeld, Bernard Berelson, and Hazel Gaudet (New York: Columbia University Press, 1948) is an account of a "classic" study of the effect of mass communication in political persuasion.

Self-interest or the Vital. Anything that affects us vitally is interesting to us. Matters associated with the satisfaction of our deep physiological needs or with our fundamental emotional urges command our continuing attention.

To illustrate, one evening a physician sat at the bridge table with three friends. Word was brought to him that a child had suddenly become seriously ill and needed immediate help. As he rose to go, one of his friends remonstrated, "Don't rush off; the child's mother is probably unduly alarmed over the situation. Stay and finish the game."

"That's what you think I ought to do?" queried the doctor.

"Yes," answered his friend, "fussy, nervous people have no right to call a physician after office hours, anyway."

"Very well," said the doctor, "I'll take your advice; it is your child who is ill."

You can imagine the rest of the story. The doctor's immediate departure suddenly became a *vital* necessity to the man who had been disposed to treat the illness so lightly.

Allport and Postman, in their study of the psychology of rumor, present striking evidence of the effect of self-interest. They showed a series of pictures to a subject and asked him to describe them to another subject who had not seen them. This second subject, in turn, described them to a third; the third, to a fourth; and so on. The descriptions given by subject No. 1 contained about twenty details for each picture, but in the retellings a number of changes took place. When the subjects were women, one picture which contained women's dresses became a story exclusively centered on the dresses. Another picture included a policeman as an insignificant factor. When the subjects were a group of police officers, the retelling of the description about the picture often centered entirely on the policeman. In other words, the subjects tended to note and emphasize those items which reflected their own personal concerns.[3] (Selective perception, as well as selective attention, operates in communication.)

The Familiar. We visit a strange city. One day we run into

[3] G. W. Allport and L. Postman, "The Basic Psychology of Rumor," *Transactions of the New York Academy of Sciences*, Series II, Vol. 8 (1945), pp. 61–81.

an acquaintance from our home town. At home, he never has been a special friend; in fact, we sometimes have avoided him socially. But, here, we greet him with a broad smile. We pat him on the back and spend hours with him, exchanging information and chit-chat about the home town and people we know in common. Have we changed our real feelings toward this person? Probably not. When we get home, we still will react toward him as before. But in this strange city, he is a symbol of familiarity to us, and we to him.

The Allport-Postman study of rumor also illustrates familiarity as an interest factor. The most frequently mentioned items in the later descriptions of the pictures were those most familiar to the subjects, even though in the original descriptions these items had been given only minor attention. The power of the familiar as a factor of attention probably results from the fact that it gives specific meaning to the situation which confronts us, especially if the situation is strange and unfamiliar. There is, of course, a point where this factor probably ceases to function as a means of gaining attention. If we become perfectly adjusted to situations, if they become "old hat" and offer no further challenge, we cease to be interested in them. The absolutely familiar has little or no interestingness.

A. E. Phillips [4] discusses five additional factors of interestingness. Most of these have been covered in our preceding discussion, but it may be helpful to consider them again briefly and more specifically. The list includes the *animate,* the *uncertain,* the *antagonistic,* the *novel,* and the *concrete.*

In psychological terms *animation* includes both movement and variation. We can never be completely adjusted to that which is changing, and, until we are adjusted, we continue to respond. Therefore, liveliness in a speaker is a great virtue. When we observe the crowds of pedestrians who stop and watch moving objects in store windows, we get some notion of the appeal of the animate. This factor can be introduced into a speech by using stories and anecdotes which involve action.

By the *uncertain* we mean the incomplete, or the partial, which

[4] A. E. Phillips, *Effective Speaking* (Chicago: Newton Co., 1938), pp. 63–78.

gives rise to suspense. We cannot adjust ourselves to a situation until we fully know what it is; our responses continue until it is complete. Suspense keeps us interested in a drama until the final curtain. This was one of the factors that held the audience's attention in the "Great Debates" of 1960.

Combat, conflict, and struggle between men or forces constitute another form of the uncertain. The element that again makes for interest here is incompleteness. We do not feel adjusted to the situation because it is constantly changing and evolving toward some unknown outcome. The fact that we are interested in a struggle does not mean necessarily that we are going to *enjoy* the outcome. Our interest in a game rests largely upon the *uncertain* and the *antagonistic,* although some of the other elements, such as the *animate,* and the *vital,* play their roles also. A dog fight is likely to take attention away from the world's greatest speaker. To present speech material in terms of struggle and contest will make it interesting.

We are attracted to that which is *novel;* but if the new departs too drastically from the old, our attraction to it may be short-lived. In presenting the new, the speaker must judiciously mix it with elements of the old. We like to hear old ideas and sentiments phrased in new ways. The fact that there is something new about the *familiar* gives us pleasant exercise in adjusting ourselves to it, while the fact that it is somewhat familiar guarantees our success in making a satisfactory adjustment after going through the pleasant exercise.

Why are people interested in *concrete* examples rather than in abstract ideas? Why is the *specific* more interesting than the general? An abstract concept is more or less an individual product. No two people ever have the same abstract thought; consequently, we find it difficult to respond to combinations of words that stand for abstractions. On the other hand, we can wrap our minds around concrete and specific ideas and respond to them in ways that give us pleasant feelings of adequacy. Certainly it is only the select few of us who ever move out beyond the concrete and the specific and acquire real capacity for handling the general and the abstract.

There are two special applications of this principle to be noted.

First, the average man is interested in personalities rather than in ideas. Compare the interest of the American people today in Abraham Lincoln with their interest in the political issues to which he devoted himself. Second, there is the inherent interestingness of an analogy; it brings the abstract and general down to where the average individual can grasp them. The parables of the New Testament are interesting because they reduce abstract, universal truths to specific examples.

To be sure, not all the problems of speaking are solved simply by getting and holding attention. A speaker may secure attention and yet fail to accomplish his purpose. Moreover, there is danger in using sensational and irrelevant means of obtaining attention. To take an extreme example, a speaker might capture and hold the attention of an audience by pointing a pistol at them, but he might find it difficult to make use of the attention thus gained. Similarly, a speaker may get and hold attention by eccentric personal appearance, unusual vocal patterns, or gymnastic antics and still fail to accomplish his purpose.

Motivating an Audience

A motive is a stimulus, a force, an influence which changes or establishes attitudes or beliefs, or moves men to action. Thus, as we use the term in speech, to motivate is to induce or to impel people to behave in ways which correspond with the wishes of the speaker.

In the preceding section we noted that, theoretically, if a speaker can focus the attention of his audience on an idea involving belief or action and hold it there, he may be reasonably sure that the belief or the action will be called out. However, since complete, continuous, unwavering attention is impossible, the public speaker who seeks to motivate his audience must use techniques which go beyond merely getting attention.

Aristotle used the word "proof" to denote the instruments of rhetoric which function to motivate—to persuade—an audience. He discussed three types of proof, as follows: [5]

[5] Aristotle, *Rhetoric*, translated by J. E. C. Welldon, London, 1886, 1923 edition, pp. 10–12.

> . . . The [first] instrument of proof is the moral character, when the delivery of the speech is such as to produce an impression of the speaker's credibility; for we yield a more complete and ready credence to persons of high character not only ordinarily and in a general way, but in such matters as do not admit of absolute certainty but necessarily leave room for difference of opinion, without any qualification whatever. . . . *Secondly,* proof may be conveyed through the audience, when it is worked up by the speech to an emotional state. For there is a wide difference in our manner of pronouncing decisions, according as we feel pleasure or pain, affection or hatred; and indeed the power of working upon the emotions is, as we assert, the one end or object to which our present professors of the rhetorical art endeavour to direct their studies. . . . *Lastly,* the instrument of proof is the speech itself, when we have proved a truth or an apparent truth from such means of persuasion as are appropriate to a particular subject.

We can paraphrase this by saying that "proof" inheres in three components of the speech situation: the character of the speaker; the feelings of the audience; and the content of the speech.

What the speaker is, the way he appears, how he acts in public and private life, the prestige and authority he possesses, all have definite effects on the outcome of his speaking; we call these elements *personal or ethical proof.*[6]

Residing in the minds of all members of an audience are such innate drives and learned motives as love, hunger, patriotism, desire for security, enjoyment of prestige, etc. In a sense, these motives are just waiting to be stirred up, to be brought to life in the minds of the audience. When properly aroused, they will help determine the reactions of the audience. These feelings are the basis of *emotional proof.*

Finally, the facts and opinions that the speaker employs, his methods of reasoning, the manner in which he organizes and arranges his ideas, these content factors are the elements of *logical proof.*

PERSONAL OR ETHICAL PROOF

When we like anyone, we find it easy to yield to his persuasion. If we dislike him personally, we may even take pleasure in re-

[6] The word *ethical* as used here is derived from the Greek word *ethos,* which means, loosely, *character.* It does not refer to morality.

fusing to do what he asks of us. We want to please our friends and we hesitate to displease them. When we say that we want to do what our friends want us to do, we simply are asserting that our affection for them somehow attaches to propositions which they lay before us.

In 1943, the Columbia Broadcasting System launched a War Bond Marathon which lasted eighteen hours. The radio star, Kate Smith, spoke for a minute or two at repeated intervals during the broadcast. On sixty-five separate occasions, she "begged, cajoled, demanded that her listeners buy war bonds." This appeal resulted in 39 million dollars of pledges in the course of one day. Shortly after the marathon, Robert K. Merton and a team of sociologists began to investigate why people did or did not respond to Miss Smith's appeals. One of the first and major findings that Merton noted was that the public held strong positive images of Kate Smith before the program began. She possessed prestige, not from any position as an authority on the War Bond Campaign, but as a person whom the large majority of those interviewed regarded with affection. Again and again, Merton found that this image of Miss Smith was a determining factor in the listeners' reactions. Some individuals were anxious to take this opportunity to express their feelings for Miss Smith; they said, for example, "Being an admirer of hers, I just called." Merton found a number of other factors operating in this persuasive speech situation, but one of the most powerful certainly was the ethical proof of the star.[7]

After noting a number of experimental and empirical studies in *ethos*, Hovland concludes, "*Who* says something is usually as important as *what* is said in the determination of the impact of a communication." [8] In one investigation it was discovered that attitudes toward an idea can be manipulated by assigning "favorable" sources to the idea, and also by assigning "good" and "bad" motives to the source.[9]

[7] Robert K. Merton, *Mass Persuasion* (New York: Harpers, 1946).

[8] Carl I. Hovland, "Effects of the Mass Media of Communication," in *Handbook of Social Psychology*, edited by Gardner Lindzey (Reading, Mass.: Addison-Wesley, 1954), Vol. II, pp. 1071–80.

[9] Nicholas Pastore and Milton W. Horowitz, "The Influence of Attributive Motive on the Acceptance of Statements," *Journal of Abnormal and Social Psychology*, Vol. 51, 1955, pp. 331–32.

Just how does a speaker's personality affect the reactions of his listeners? We may find answers to this question as we consider some of the principal factors that many people ascribe to personality. We have defined personality as an individual's potential meaning for those who come into contact with him. Persons are meaningful just as objects, situations, words, and other symbols are; the meaning of anything consists in the responses it evokes from those whom it stimulates. When a person stimulates us into doing what we can do easily and pleasantly, we tend to accredit him with an attractive personality. When he stimulates us into doing what we can do only with difficulty or with painful consequences to ourselves, we say that he has a disagreeable personality. The way an individual reacts to others conditions the way others react to him; his habits of reaction thus furnish the basis of other's judgments of him.

We have seen that a personality actually consists of a number of different, though integrated, roles. In a sense, an individual has a set of different "personalities," for by assuming different roles in different situations, he can be several different individuals. However, we readily may grant that certain persistent and consistent elements in the individual's behavior contribute to similarities in the judgments of those who *know* him, i.e., who have responded to him on a number of occasions.

Appearance. By appearance we mean the ways in which a person presents himself to the eyes of others. An attractive, impressive physical presence can be a real asset to a speaker. If he lacks natural physical attractiveness, he should cultivate compensating characteristics, such as alertness, pleasing muscle tensions, good posture, neatness of attire, etc.

Our impressions of another's personality depend to a certain extent upon muscle tensions that we can see. When an individual's tensions are such that our empathic responses involve either too much or too little tension on our part, we say he has an unpropossessing, unattractive, or negative personality. So also our impressions are affected by muscle tensions the results of which we can hear. From such simple reactions we tend to build up the complex structure of personality in those about us.

Intelligence. Usually we prefer a more intelligent person to a less intelligent one. Why? Because the behavior of an intelligent person is likely to be more predictable than that of one less intelligent. We can adjust ourselves more easily, and keep adjusted, to persons whose behavior is consistent than we can to those whose behavior is capricious. Then, too, we often get more satisfying reactions from an intelligent person.

One of the factors of intelligence is *sensitiveness.* Although we know that it is possible for a person to be too sensitive for his own comfort, it is difficult to overrate this quality in a speaker's personality. One who is sensitive to the responses of his listeners and shows respect for their reactions will be appreciated and liked.

Not only is the intelligent speaker more sensitive than the dull one, but he *reacts more quickly.* Of course, it is possible for a speaker to be too quick for an audience. Any good quality can be overdone, but a speaker who is slow and phlegmatic usually works against a considerable handicap.

Another element of intelligence is *discrimination.* The intelligent speaker understands the feedback he receives from his audience. He does the right thing at the right time, speaks the right word and thus creates a feeling of self-importance in others by his consideration and tact.

Temperament. Temperament is almost as difficult to define as personality itself. It has many elements in common with intelligence. We speak of a sensitive, quick temperament, and of an insensitive, sluggish temperament. Is the speaker nervous, high-strung, and excitable; or lethargic, relaxed, and calm? A speaker probably should seek the golden mean in temperament.

Suggestibility plays a role in temperament. The suggestible person lacks independence; he is pliable, easily influenced, likely to do whatever he sees other people doing, and to accept, uncritically, the opinions of those about him. We like a reasonable amount of suggestibility in our associates, but not too much. At the other extreme from the highly suggestible is the negatively suggestible person, who, when others in his group are inclined to respond in a certain way, will want to go in the opposite direction. A reasonable amount of negative suggestibility undoubtedly has its charm, but we can get too much of it rather quickly.

Society places a premium on intelligence and imposes penalties on too much *emotionality* and *sentimentality*. From our earliest years, we are trained to control our emotions. When we revert to overly sentimental types of reaction, we are likely to be considered childish or "dramatic." When we overdo sentimentality, we trip off embarrassed responses in others.

Of course, as we have said before, a speaker can overdo nonemotional behavior and thus give an impression of coldness or lack of feeling. We must not assume that emotional behavior is something of which we ought always to be ashamed. The good speaker must be emotional when emotionality will serve his purpose and intellectual when intellectuality is required.

The James-Lange theory of emotion, first announced more than seventy years ago, contains some features that may well be considered in a discussion of personality: [10]

> Common sense says, we lose our fortune, are sorry and weep; we meet a bear, are frightened and run; we are insulted by a rival, are angry and strike. . . . The more rational statement is that we feel sorry because we cry, angry because we strike, afraid because we tremble.
>
> Everybody knows how panic is increased by flight, and how the giving way to the symptoms of grief or anger increases the passions themselves. . . . In rage, it is notorious how we "work ourselves up" to a climax by repeated outbursts of expression. Refuse to express the passion and it dies. Count ten before venting your anger, and its occasion seems ridiculous. Whistling to keep up courage is no mere figure of speech. On the other hand, sit all day in a moping posture, sigh, and reply to everything with a dismal voice, and your melancholy lingers. There is no more valuable precept in moral education than this, as all who have experience know; if we wish to conquer undesirable emotional tendencies in ourselves, we must assiduously, and in the first instance cold-bloodedly, go through the outward movements of those contrary dispositions which we prefer to cultivate. The reward of persistency will infallibly come, in the fading out of the sullenness or depression, and the advent of real cheerfulness and kindliness in their stead. Smooth the brow, brighten the eye, contract the

[10] William James, *Psychology: Briefer Course* (New York: Henry Holt & Co., 1923), p. 382.

dorsal rather than the ventral aspect of the frame, and speak in a major key, pass the genial compliment, and your heart must be frigid indeed if it does not gradually thaw.

We have mentioned this theory in the discussion on stage fright; we re-introduce it at this point because an understanding of its implications may help the speaker who finds it difficult to arouse within himself the emotions that give warmth to his personality. He may accomplish much by working from the expression end of the emotional process. If he voluntarily assumes the external manifestations of the emotional pattern, he may stimulate himself into experiencing more feeling.

Finally, an attractive personality is *sympathetic.* Sympathy means understanding and appreciation of other people's feelings. Nothing is more important in the speaker's personality than this ability to enter into the emotional experiences of others.

Attitudes. Closely associated with temperament is attitude. One attitude of major importance for the speaker is self-confidence. Unless a speaker can feel a reasonable degree of confidence in himself, he scarcely can expect others to have confidence in him. One of the most serious weaknesses in personality is a feeling of inadequacy and inferiority which expresses itself in behavior that stirs up unfortunate responses in others. Of course, everybody feels inferior and inadequate in certain situations; the trouble with some people is that they have this feeling constantly. When it is extreme and chronic, it is an "inferiority complex."

Closely allied to our attitude toward ourselves is our attitude toward other people. There is a vast difference between a *social* attitude and a *reclusive* attitude. The social individual likes people, has learned how to adjust himself to them and finds pleasure in their reactions to him. His attitude is much more satisfactory as a basis for an effective speaking personality than a reclusive attitude. The social individual has confidence in his capacity for making the necessary adjustments to others. Other factors being equal, the successful speaker is the man who has wide interests outside himself. He finds that other people are interested in some of the same things and, thus, easily establishes common ground for getting along with them.

Of course, personality is not the sole factor in ethical proof. We have stressed it because it is the factor which most readily will be recognized in a speech class (where other elements of *ethos* are much less evident), and because it is the element for which training in speech can be most helpful.

Another important factor in this type of proof is the speaker's *prestige* and *reputation,* particularly as these relate to the subject about which he is talking. Prestige may result from an individual's position of authority—the President of the United States, a cabinet officer, a union leader, a football coach, a television network vice-president. Or, it may stem from the audience's recognition of the speaker's accomplishments and intense study of the subject matter—a professor who has just returned from a year's study of the Russian educational system, a playwright whose works have been seen on television and have won him an international award, a Pulitzer Prize journalist.

As we said in Chapter 4, this matter of authority is a relative thing. We need not be "expert" to have the right to speak on a subject—to have ethical proof. But, an audience does deserve to know why they should listen to us. A speaker can enhance his ethical proof by simply and sincerely explaining his qualifications, or he can ask the person who introduces him, if there is one, to do it for him.

Our American society has given rise to the "star system" in almost every profession. We even have star preachers, star doctors, and star teachers. Most of them deserve the ethical proof we assign to them in their individual professions. But Americans have a penchant for transferring the prestige of these personalities from their own to almost any other field. As we have noted in the chapter on "Listening," this transfer of prestige is a spurious use of ethical proof.

EMOTIONAL PROOF

In discussing emotional proof, it seems appropriate to consider what goes on when we "believe." Woodrow Wilson once said, "We speak of this as an age in which mind is monarch, but I take it for granted that, if that is true, mind is one of those modern monarchs who reign but do not govern. As a matter of fact, the world is governed in every generation by a great House of Commons made up of the passions [emotions]." [11]

No sharp line can be drawn between belief and action; for the speaker, the similarities are more significant than the differences. Our habits, our likes and dislikes, and our prejudices reside quite as largely in the symbolic world of language as they do in the direct and primary reactions to the objective world. The speaker frequently finds that his purpose cannot be attained unless and until he can modify the inner word-world of the reactor. At times, these internal language habits seem even more stubborn and resistant to change than does outward behavior. Moreover, the word-world is less subject to direct observation and much more elusive.

If a speaker expects to influence the feelings, beliefs, or actions of other people, he should study their behavior. Even more important, he must analyze and consider his own behavior and its motivating causes. He must ask himself *why* he thinks, feels, and acts as he does, and he should not accept in answer any rationalization that conceals his real motives. A good way to begin the study of motivation is to make a careful and searching inventory of one's own repertoire of emotions and their manifestations in varying situations.

Most of our beliefs have their roots deep in our emotional life. We always have multitudes of response tendencies on hand ready to attach themselves to propositions the implications of which are in harmony with our emotional state of the moment. An excellent example was the rise of spiritualism during and following both world wars. With many people mourning the loss of loved ones, there came a tremendous will-to-believe that the dead had not passed beyond reach. Distinguished and scholarly men like Sir Oliver Lodge and Conan Doyle credited the alleged phenomena of spiritualism upon evidence that, in other circumstances, would have seemed to them quite flimsy and untrustworthy.

On the other hand, there is also a will-to-disbelieve. It is impervious to all appeals; it doubts everything. There usually are

[11] Woodrow Wilson, "The American College," in J. M. O'Neill, *Models of Speech Composition* (New York: Century Co., 1909), p. 612.

conflicting elements in any proposition. We settle issues by following those tendencies that are emotionally reinforced. As Winans puts it: [12]

> One arrives at a decision by weighing the opposing arguments. Now, if he wishes to arrive at a certain conclusion, the arguments for it seem weighty, and those in opposition very light. He is likely to refuse credence to witnesses and authorities against the desired conclusion. He may even refuse to listen to opposing arguments; or he may listen in an attempt to be fair, but with a subconscious determination to discredit what he hears, saying all the while, That is not true; That is not important; or, That is insufficient. In other words, he refuses fair attention. No doubt you are a highly reasonable person; still, if you were to learn that your deceased uncle had cut you off from an expected legacy, you might find it easy to believe the old man *non compos mentis* when he executed his will. Learning later that he had added a codicil in your favor, you might find no difficulty in believing that at the approach of death his mind cleared.

Most people within a particular social group show rather uniform patterns of emotional response to symbols and situations. Every society has developed an extensive fabric of customs, manners, and folkways which bind together all of the individuals living in that society. In our Western culture, for example, we are almost unanimous in our emotional attitudes toward the family; we all tend to show sympathy for the underdog; we all believe in fair play; and we all respect our elders and love our children. Even if a person is so socially atypical that he does not "feel" these commonly approved emotions, he probably never will admit it. This unanimity of response toward a whole range of emotional situations is one factor which makes it possible for a speaker to influence a large group of heterogeneous individuals simultaneously.

Another strong and common basis for feelings, beliefs, and actions is our sense of solidarity with the social group. Men tend to follow what they believe to be accepted by those with whom they associate. Our conduct rarely rests solely and completely upon our individual experience. Men's acts are tinctured with tradition and dominated by social conformity.

One method a speaker can use in analyzing his audience's pos-

[12] J. A. Winans, *Public Speaking* (New York: Century Co., 1917), p. 251.

sible response patterns is to study the groups to which they belong. Knowing an individual's affiliations, however, is only a beginning. The speaker must also realize what attitudes, needs, and desires are associated with each of these affiliations. And when an audience is large, the task of identifying each listener's group memberships is impossible. In such cases, the speaker must determine as accurately as he can what group memberships his listeners have *in common.* George Gallup's extensive work in studying the formation of public opinion has led him to recognize that the most significant conditioners of attitude are occupational groups, sex, age, place of residence, political preference, income level, educational level, race, and religion.[13] These, then, can serve the speaker as categories for his analysis of the audience's feelings, sentiments, attitudes, and beliefs.

Emotional Motives. There are certain universal motives to which a communicator, regardless of the medium in which he works, may appeal in building his structure of emotional proof. Maslow [14] classifies human needs (motives) as follows: physiological needs; safety needs; belongingness and love needs; esteem needs; and self-actualization needs. He presents these in a hierarchal order (*a* to *e*), an order of ascendancy, which is loosely related to their relative degrees of universality. The physiological needs—hunger, thirst, etc.—are most universally felt. The need for self-actualization—an individual's need to attain the highest potential possible, not for power or prestige, but for self-satisfaction—is the least universal.

(*a*) *Physiological needs.* Although in our society there do not seem to be many people who suffer from hunger or thirst, freedom from want still remains a potential motive. Franklin Delano Roosevelt certainly used it as a powerful vote-getting appeal; it was a basic stimulus in his successful "New Deal" strategy.

(*b*) *Safety needs.* Self-preservation is the first law of life. We are deeply motivated to exist as long as we possibly can. The will-to-live forms the basis of all our plans. The millions of dollars

[13] George H. Gallup, *A Guide to Public Opinion Polls* (Princeton University Press, 1948), pp. 31–33.

[14] Abraham H. Maslow, *Motivation and Personality* (New York: Harper and Brothers, 1954).

spent annually in the purchase of patent medicines, the uncritical way in which we seize upon political and economic panaceas are but slight indications of the power of this impelling motive. Everyone wishes to keep out of trouble, is reluctant to go anywhere or do anything that will lead him into worry, discomfort or danger. Most people are concerned about their own security and well-being. They want to accept beliefs and follow courses of action that represent playing safe. In its broad application, the motive of self-preservation includes all sorts of activity intended to promote our security here and now, and "beyond this vale of tears." We dislike changes which may seem to threaten our security. The "in" group in a political campaign normally has the advantage, for many people fear what may occur if the administration is changed—even though they are not altogether satisfied with it.

(*c*) *Belongingness and love needs.* The third classification includes love, affection, and good will. We want to contribute to the welfare and happiness of those whom we love. Many a man is willing to risk reputation, money, health, or even life, in order to provide for those dear to him. It is possible for us to project ourselves into the lives of others to such an extent that we rate their welfare and their happiness above our own. If we can make people feel that the action we propose will contribute to the well-being of those they love, we shall enhance our chances of motivating them.

We are all members of many groups. We get a real satisfaction from belonging, and we attach our emotions to many of these groups. Especially when we derive religious or moral values from belonging, our association becomes a motive for action. Patriotism, the sentiment we derive from belonging to a national group, is a very powerful motive for which men are willing to sacrifice their more immediate affections, their reputation, their money, and their lives.

(*d*) *Esteem needs.* All of us want to be respected. We want reputation, social recognition, the attention of others. For some, this need may be met by securing property. The desire for property not only controls many individuals but it also controls social groups and nations to such an extent that the whole world plunges into devastating wars over economic interests. For others, this need is manifested in a search for power. Power doubtless means ease in relations with others. Whenever two people meet they must, consciously or unconsciously, agree to get along by submission one to the other, or by dominance and submission, in turn. It is pleasant for most of us to relate ourselves to others in the role of superiors.

Much advertising in the daily press and over the air makes its appeal to this motive of status-seeking. We are urged to enroll in a correspondence course, because if we do, we will be recognized as leaders in our community; and we will become executives, sit behind big mahogany desks, and press buttons to control the behavior of the others in the organization. The kind of clothes we wear, the books we read, everything about us may become models for imitation by others.

(*e*) *Self-actualization needs.* "What man *can* be, he *must* be." [15] In many men there is the deeply felt need to achieve a life not bound by material possessions, satisfaction of physiological urges, or personal esteem. "Their reach must exceed their grasp." Under this need we include all the motives involved in the satisfaction of artistic appetites, aesthetic cravings, love of literature, music, painting, sculpture, and drama. The pages of history are filled with the exploits of artists, scientists, and scholars, motivated, not by any of the "lower" needs, but by the desire to create and produce simply for the self-satisfaction derived from creation and production.

Many of the sentiments and virtues which are so impelling in our society derive from any or all of these needs—honesty, fairness, freedom, loyalty, and the like. The relative power of these needs varies with audiences, subjects, and occasions. There are significant differences among individuals in their susceptibility to various motives. We do know, however, that emotion is a powerful force in all normal human beings no matter how we may protest otherwise.

[15] *Ibid.,* p. 91.

LOGICAL PROOF

Usually when we use the word "proof," we refer to the type of support which is presented in the form of *argument*. We say that we have *proved* a proposition when we have established its soundness or correctness. Logical proof appeals to the intellect of the audience by developing *reasons* for believing the proposition.

Logical proof consists of two elements, *evidence* and *reasoning*. *Evidence* is of two main kinds—*factual*, and *authoritative*. Factual evidence consists of statistics, examples, analogies, verifiable data, etc. Authoritative evidence consists of "expert" opinion. From facts and opinions, the speaker "*reasons*" to conclusions. He may reach conclusions either deductively or inductively. Deduction is reasoning from the general to the particular. Induction is reasoning from the particular to the general.

Deduction. The general statement from which deduction starts is called the *major premise,* which is a statement already verified. There follows a second specific statement called the *minor premise* which also has been verified. From these two *premises,* the speaker draws a *conclusion.* This type of reasoning can be expressed in the format of a syllogism; for example:

> Major Premise: All men are mortal.
> Minor Premise: Socrates is a man.
> Conclusion: Therefore, Socrates is mortal.

An argument stated in this form is called a *categorical* syllogism.

Much of our reasoning, in conversation and on the public platform, is deductive. Seldom, however, do we reason deductively in complete syllogisms; we commonly omit one of the premises, taking it for granted. For example, we say: "Because all men are mortal, Socrates is mortal," or "Socrates is a man, therefore, he is mortal." A syllogism minus one of the premises is called an *enthymeme.* When we reason in enthymemes we must be very careful about the meaning and the scope of the omitted premise. When a speaker uses an enthymeme which includes too much in the omitted premise, he "begs the question."

A second type of syllogism is the *disjunctive.* Here the major premise states two alternatives and the minor premise affirms one of them. This process limits the conclusion to one of the alternatives. For example:

Major Premise: Either Jack failed to study for the exam or the test was beyond his ability.
Minor Premise: Jack studied hard.
Conclusion: Therefore, the test was beyond his ability.

Two tests may be used to determine the soundness of a disjunctive syllogism: (1) The alternatives must be the only possible alternatives, and (2) the alternatives must be mutually exclusive. The major premise in the foregoing syllogism seems to meet the second test. But suppose that Jack should explain his failure by saying, "I have a medical statement showing that I was ill on the day of the examination." The introduction of this third possible alternative would invalidate the reasoning. Or suppose that Jack could show that there were five pages missing from his textbook and that these pages had covered the very material which he had missed in the examination. Again, the conclusion would have been invalidated.

A third type of syllogism is the *hypothetical.* The major premise is a conditional statement, for example:

Major Premise: If we can get eight more votes for John, he will be elected.
Minor Premise: We have eight more votes for John.
Conclusion: John will be elected.

The first clause in the major premise is called the *antecedent;* the latter clause, the *consequent.* The minor premise *affirms* the antecedent. When our argument takes this form, we must make sure of two facts: (1) The antecedent and the consequent are so related that the implied causal connection is airtight, and (2) the minor premise is adequately supported. If we can prove that the antecedent condition has been met, the consequent will stand up. If we cannot prove the antecedent, we can draw no conclusion concerning the consequent.

Often we find that the antecedent is incomplete; we establish the condition only to find that it does not bring the consequences we have predicted. We get the eight additional votes for John, only to discover that he has lost four votes which we had thought were "in the bag." We then see that our statement of the antecedent should have been stated, "If we can get eight additional votes for John and *if the votes already committed to him do not shift,* he will be elected."

Induction. Inductive reasoning moves from the specific to the general. From the examination of a number of particular instances, we draw a general conclusion.

The scientist observes a wide range of phenomena (happenings) in his field of specialization, identifies common elements or characteristics, and builds up an hypothesis or principle which seems to generalize all the observed data. Thus scientific "laws" come into being.

By its very nature, inductive argument can never give us an absolutely certain conclusion; we can never observe every member of any class of objects or situations. There always remains the possibility of an exception to our generalizations. All that induction can give us is a higher or lower degree of probability. Icthyologists may assert with a very high degree of probability that all fish are cold-blooded, but no one can examine every single fish in the world. There remains the possibility, no matter how small, that some day, somewhere, someone may come upon a warm-blooded fish. When exceptions to generalizations come to light, conclusions are subject to modification. The advance of science can be described in terms of theories thought to be infallible having to be revised. Einstein even forced a reassessment of the "law" of gravitation.

Inductive argument is so slippery that we must be very careful in drawing conclusions from inadequate data. Before announcing a generalization, we should at least be sure that we have examined a sufficient number of particulars to have reached a high degree of probability. Hasty generalization can get the speaker into hot water with his audience very quickly. Before making general, all-inclusive statements about students, teen-agers, teachers, ministers, politicians, businessmen, football players, and other groups, we must be sure that we have observed a sufficient number of individuals in these categories to justify our inductive conclusions. Prejudiced or inaccurate observation (to say nothing of the misinterpretation of what we have observed) may lead to disaster in trying to prove or disprove a proposition to the satisfaction of a critical audience.

Cause-Effect Reasoning. Another frequently used method of reasoning is from cause to effect, and vice versa. (Actually, this method is employed in hypothetical syllogistic reasoning discussed earlier.) We attempt to prove that a given cause operates or has operated to create an observed effect and that no other cause is involved. Much forensic (court-room) pleading is based on causal relationships; circumstantial evidence is an example of cause-and-effect. In its basic form, this type of reasoning seems simple enough. But as our knowledge of the world about us has increased, we have come to realize that such reasoning often is difficult to substantiate.

To be accurate and effective, causal reasoning must be subjected to these two important tests:

1. Is the cause *adequate* to produce the observed effect?
2. Are we sure that *no other adequate causes exist* which might have produced the effect?

Most often we find that we are involved in relationships more complex than single-cause-to-single-effect. Especially as we work with social problems, we note multiplicity of causes. For example, thoughtful people who attempt to assess the impact of comic books or television on a child's behavior usually come to realize that these forces are only part of the situation—that the child's home life, his educational experiences, his "gangs," his religious training, his intellectual capacity, his social relations in dozens of seemingly unrelated circumstances, all act together to create the personality (personalities) which may or may not be susceptible to the particular comic book or television program.

Also, the basic or real cause of an event may be far removed from the immediate situation. A person becomes ill; the cause is diagnosed as a "virus." However, most people have not succumbed to this virus. This patient has been on a self-imposed crash diet and is actually suffering from malnutrition, which in reality could be considered the cause of his present illness. Often, understanding the immediate cause is not sufficient; we must follow the chain of causal relationships to the basic, original cause.

We also know that, after a time, causes and effects can become confused. Is the drunkenness of Mr. A the cause of his poverty, or the result of it? The answer probably depends on the moment at which the reasoning is applied.

Fallacies. A fallacy is an error in reasoning or argument. There are as many kinds of fallacies as there are kinds of arguments. Any violation of the principles of correct reasoning is a fallacy.

As we already have suggested, the most common of all fallacies is *hasty generalization* which results from imperfect induction. We observe narrowly and then jump to broad conclusions. A student who has had two or three unpleasant encounters with unsympathetic professors quickly concludes that all professors are hard task-masters. A Congressman receives half a dozen letters from his constituents protesting his stand on a particular bill and then announces that his "district" is against the measure.

Another very common error in reasoning is called the *post hoc ergo propter hoc* fallacy. ("After this, therefore because of this.") When we argue that, because one event precedes another, it is the cause of the other, without clearly demonstrating the alleged causal connection, we are guilty of the *post hoc* fallacy. The simple fact that A preceded B does not prove that A caused B. We are ill and take a certain medicine; we feel better and conclude that the drug has cured us. Fortunes have been built in the drug business on this fallacy! The football team has a long losing streak; a new coach is appointed; the following season is successful and, therefore, the new coach is credited with restoring the gridiron prestige of the college. Before we can properly argue that one set of facts is responsible for a consequent set of facts, we must demonstrate clearly that there is a valid cause-effect relationship between them.

A third type of fallacy is the careless use of *ambiguous terms.* In one part of an argument we use a word in one sense and then, in the conclusion, we use the same word in another sense. We must be careful not to shift meanings without realizing and indicating that we are doing so.

For example, two cities with approximately the same population show a startling difference in the number of arrests for "drunkenness." City A has 30 arrests for drunkenness in one month, whereas City B has 100 arrests for "drunkenness" in the same month. It is easy to claim that B has more "drunkenness" than A. But we may be overlooking the fact that the criteria used in defining "drunkenness" are quite different in the two cities.

A final common error in argument is *false analogy*. There are two kinds of analogy, literal and figurative. A literal analogy is an argument to the effect that since two things are alike in certain known respects, they are alike in unknown respects. The force of such a literal analogy depends upon the number of known agreements. If we have demonstrated that two chemical substances are alike in a number of characteristics, we argue that they probably are alike in ways that have not been demonstrated. A speaker attempts to show that, in several ways, conditions in America are closely similar to conditions in Rome just before its fall and proceeds to argue that what happened to Rome is going to happen to the United States. The fallacy lurking in such argument is that we may overlook differences in our eagerness to find likenesses. These differences may invalidate the comparison and prove the analogy false.

Many analogies are figurative rather than literal. When we compare the circulation of currency in a nation with the circulation of the blood in a human body, we are dealing in metaphor and we are likely to draw fallacious conclusions. Carlyle argued that democracy is bound to fail because a ship could not safely sail around Cape Horn if the captain were required to take a vote of the crew every time before changing course. The argument is meaningless because the differences between operating a government and sailing a ship far outweigh the superficial similarities.

During one of the famous joint debates of 1858 in Illinois, Judge Douglas asserted that Lincoln and the Buchanan Democrats had formed a coalition to defeat him. He drew an analogy between his position and that of the Russians besieged in Sebastopol by the allied armies during the Crimean War. He announced that he was going to defend himself against his enemies just as the Russians had defended themselves. He said, "When the Russians fired a volley, they did not care whether they hit an Englishman, a Frenchman, or a Turk." Lincoln turned the tables on him disastrously when he replied:

Well, now that's interesting! We have always thought of Judge Douglas as a lion but it turns out that he is the rugged Russian bear. If he is going to play the part of the Russians in Sebastopol while we occupy the position of the attacking armies outside, I hope that he will permit us to remind him that the allies took Sebastopol!

In speaking, you must:

1. Concern yourself with sound evidence, credible testimony, logical arrangement of materials;

2. Find words and phrases and ideas that touch off the tendencies of your audience to respond emotionally;

3. Develop the character, personality, and behavior that will dispose your audience to accept your ideas.

Do not depend upon any one of these alone!

ADDITIONAL READINGS

Brembeck, Winston L. and Howell, William S., *Persuasion* (New York: Prentice-Hall, 1952), Chapters 15 and 24.

Hovland, Carl I., Janis, Irving L., and Kelley, Harold H., *Communication and Persuasion* (New Haven: Yale University Press, 1953), Chapter 2.

Lippmann, Walter, *Public Opinion* (Baltimore: Pelican Books, 1946), Chapter 1.

Thonssen, Lester and Baird, A. Craig, *Speech Criticism* (New York: The Ronald Press, 1948), Chapter 13.

QUESTIONS AND PROJECTS

1. Analyze the advertising found in magazines, newspapers, billboards, radio, and television. (A) What "factors of interestingness" do you find? (B) How would you classify the advertisements in terms of the types of attention they are attempting to arouse? (C) Evaluate the effectiveness of the various advertisements.

2. Project No. 1 can be used as the basis for a panel discussion before the class. Each member of the panel can concentrate his analysis on one of the media.

3. Compare the advertisements found in several magazines, which are intended for different "publics" of varying degrees of sophistication (ranging, for example, from *True Story* to *The Saturday Review*).

What differences and similarities do you notice in techniques used? How do you explain these? (A similar analysis can be made of the advertising heard on different types of radio stations.)

4. Analyze your classroom "audience." What factors of interestingness seem to dominate their actual and potential behavior? Select a subject for a five-minute speech to convince. Write an introduction for such a speech that you believe will most likely capture their attention.

5. Select some unusually effective public speech, analyze it, and tell the class what you have learned regarding the use of emotional appeals.

6. Let the members of the class select topics from the following list. Each speaker will have from five to ten minutes to make the best speech he can on the topic he has chosen.

a. The Personal Equation in Persuasion
b. Argument That Generates Heat Rather Than Light
c. The Man Who Can Be Convinced but Would Like to See the Fellow Who Can Convince Him
d. The Emotional Behavior of Children and Adults
e. Is Seeing Believing?
f. The Power of a Conviction
g. Prejudices and Their Cure
h. The James-Lange Theory
i. Things That Worry Me and Why
j. My Life for a Single Day and Its Motivations
k. The Dominant Belief of My Hero
l. Sales Resistance

7. Make a three-minute speech that ends with a definite plea for some specific action on the part of the audience. See if you can get them to respond as you want them to. Try for a simple, yet overt, response, even if it is no more than a show of hands.

8. Turn in to the instructor an example of the use of each of the impelling motives in some advertisement, speech, letter, announcement, etc.

9. Attend a public speech. Before the speech begins, make an appraisal of the audience, noting particularly all the various group memberships (both formal and informal) that you think you find there. While the speech is in progress, note how the speaker does or does not seem to take these group roles and attitudes into account. Write a description of the audience and of the speaker's adaptation to the audience.

PART THREE

The Forms of Speech

CHAPTER 11

Public Address

The General Ends of Public Speaking

The three general ends, or purposes, of speaking in public are *to inform, to persuade,* and *to entertain.* In any given speech, these three general ends may support one another; that is, a speaker who wishes to move his audience to action (to persuade them), in the course of his speech may inform and entertain, though his final and dominant end is to persuade.

When the speaker's primary purpose is to get his audience to understand what he tells them, his general end is *to inform.* The teacher of physics, delivering a lecture on the construction and operation of a television set, is making a speech the general end of which is to inform, or instruct.

When a speaker's dominant purpose is to influence the attitudes, beliefs, or actions of his audience, his general end is *to persuade.* We can further classify persuasive speech situations according to purposes which are more specific. When a speaker primarily attempts to produce a strong emotional attitude toward his subject, he is making a speech *to impress.* When he desires to win belief for his point of view, he is making a speech *to convince.* When he wants immediate, specific action from his audience, he is making a speech *to actuate.* In all three of these, there is a common function—to influence the behavior of the audience toward the subject of the speech—to persuade.

When the speaker's principal purpose is to amuse, to create a mood of relaxation, good humor, and enjoyment, his general end is *to entertain.* After-dinner speeches, popular lectures, and travelogues frequently serve this purpose.

Section One—Informing an Audience

The speech *to inform* is often called an *expository* speech. The speaker describes, points out, explains the nature and characteristics of an event, an object, a circumstance, or an idea. He "exposes," or uncovers, the facts in the situation. Clearness is the main requirement in expository speaking. The task of the speaker is to tell his specific audience what he wants them to know about his subject.

Understanding, as we have explained in Chapter Nine, must occur in the mind of the listener; it is not sufficient that the *speaker* know what he is talking about. The purpose of informational speaking is to produce clear ideas *in the mind of the listener.* Such speaking begins, obviously, with clear ideas in the speaker's mind and becomes effective when it stimulates the listener into developing closely similar ideas. Assuming that a speaker understands what he is saying, he must:

1. Realize what knowledge his hearers already possess about his subject; and
2. Use what they already know in constructing the "new" meanings he wants them to grasp.

We stress this point because it is essential that a public speaker keep his purposes within the limits of possibility; these limits are prescribed by what the audience know as well as by what he knows. If the audience lack understanding of elementary facts, the speaker must fill in these gaps before he tries to give them information to which knowledge of these facts is prerequisite.

METHODS OF EXPOSITION

The following nine methods of exposition are most often used. You usually will employ combinations of these in your informational speaking.

Definition. Definition often makes up entire brief expositions and is almost always a part of any long or involved exposition. A good definition sets forth the distinguishing characteristics of what is defined. These characteristics are usually of two kinds—the general and the particular. The first indicates the group or class; and the second, the qualities by which the specific item is distinguished from other members of its class.

A good definition begins with the term to be defined and indicates the general class to which the term belongs and the specific differences between it and other terms within the same general class:

Term Defined	*General Classification*	*Particular Qualities*
A president	is an officer	who is the chief or head of an organization.
A bicycle	is a vehicle	having two wheels, one behind the other, propelled by the feet of the rider, acting on pedals.
Edible	is an adjective	meaning fit to be eaten.

We should avoid such expressions as "is where" or "is when" as predicates in definitions. Instead of saying, "Speech is where (or when) one person stirs up meanings in the mind of another person," it is better to say, "Speech is a process by which one person stirs up meanings in the mind of another person." A second look at this definition reveals that the predicate includes too much; it can cover any process by which one person stirs up meanings in the mind of another—e.g., writing, telegraphy, music, etc. So we use modifiers to limit the predicate: "Speech is a process by which one person stirs up meanings in the mind of another person through signs made by visible action and voice."

After having defined a term, it is sometimes desirable to give an example of what has been defined. But giving only examples when complete definitions are called for is usually not satisfactory. If asked, "What is a genius?" we should not reply, "Thomas Edison was a genius." This is an example, not a definition.

It is not always necessary or desirable to define a term formally. A dictionary definition often is dull and dogmatic, even though accurate. For many people, definitions have become associated with dreary classroom learning. Sometimes a concept can be explained by a connotative discussion which will enrich the meaning far beyond that provided by a denotative explanation. Consider, for example, the difference between what the dictionary says about "beauty" and what the poet says about it. In some cases, an amplified example may be the best way to give meaning. Although the statement, "Thomas Edison was a genius," tells very little about what "genius" means, a detailed description of the qualities which Edison possessed and which made him unique among men may define the word far more meaningfully than the dictionary does. In still other cases, it may be desirable to define a term by noting what the term *does not mean* as well as what it does mean. The essential duty of the speaker is to make his definition as meaningful as he can to his specific audience.

Remember that words and phrases may have many possible meanings. Whenever confusion is likely, be careful to explain which of the various meanings you intend. The cure for ambiguity and vagueness is precise definition. To define a term needing definition in terms which also need definition is to pile confusion on confusion.

Analysis. Exposition by analysis consists in breaking up a subject into its parts. We explain the government of the United States by stating the essential facts about each of its various branches; we explain, first, the legislative branch, then, the executive and, finally, the judicial. Each of these major divisions may be analyzed further. Under the legislative, we describe the Senate, the House, the committee system, etc. Under the executive, we discuss the President, the Cabinet, the agencies directly responsible to the executive, etc. Under the judicial, we explain the Supreme Court, the District Courts, the Circuit Courts of Appeals, etc. Many legal arguments and judges' charges to juries are excellent examples of exposition by analysis.

Examples. As one writer on public speaking has said, "Listeners like for-instances." We have noted how an example can amplify the meaning of definition. Examples add concreteness, color, and variety to a speech. By applying the meaning of a concept to the experience of an audience through example, a speaker can make use of the familiar, arouse curiosity, add humor, and appeal to the needs and desires of his listeners.

Examples may be long or short. Sometimes a word or two will suffice; at other times, it may be necessary to relate a complete story. Examples may be real or hypothetical. The latter usually are introduced by "suppose," "imagine," or "if"; they frequently are used to describe what will happen if a policy is (or is not) adopted. Hypothetical examples require careful creation and presentation. They must be within the realm of credibility. Ordinarily they should not be used if a *real* example is available. Examples from actuality have the advantage of authenticity.

Comparison and Contrast. As we have said, the best way to bring the unknown into the experience of our hearers is by relating it to what they already know. If they understand the judicial system of the United States, probably the most effective means of making clear to them the judicial system of Switzerland would be to compare it step by step with the familiar system. Drawing an outline of Belgium on a map of Wisconsin is an effective way of getting residents of Wisconsin to understand how small, or large, Belgium is. Contrasting English rugby with American football will be more efficient than explaining rugby of and by itself, for such a procedure will give us and our audience a familiar point of departure, a frame of common reference.

Illustrations. The late Joseph Jastrow, a great modern psychologist, frequently remarked that the human mind is more *analogical* than *logical;* that is, we have a natural tendency to see similarities in our experience. As a public speaker, you should make use of this tendency to see likenesses.

Illustrations, in effect, are comparisons of the subject under discussion with something that is familiar to the audience, but is not of the same kind as the subject. The *analogy,* the *simile,* and the *metaphor* are forms of illustration. Commencement speakers are fond—perhaps too fond—of drawing an analogy between the "game of life" and the "game of football," perhaps carrying the analogy throughout the speech. Hammerstein wrote about the corn "as high as an elephant's eye," using a simile to clarify and vivify the image he wanted to create. Theodore Roosevelt often talked of "speaking softly and carrying a big stick," a metaphor illustrating his concept of a strong foreign policy. In addition to aiding clarity, carefully constructed analogies add color and vividness. Many of the best remembered quotations from important public speeches of the past are such illustrations. (Other speech devices classified in this category are *fables, parables, stories,* and *anecdotes.*)

Statistics. Statistics can add meaning to a subject by describing it in specific numerical terms which make understanding more precise. Statistics also permit us to describe large subjects easily and economically. For instance, to depict the scope of juvenile delinquency, we would not have to detail every example. We can relate one or two specific cases and then, by using the total number of like instances, describe the whole situation.

Useful though they may be, statistics require careful handling. The following suggestions may be helpful:

1. *Use statistics sparingly.* Nothing will wear out an audience's attention more rapidly than a long list of numbers. The numerical retention span of the average person is short. If you must use many statistics, it is advisable to present them both orally and visually (by means of a chart or graph). Also, when possible, round out the numbers, especially when they are large. It is easier to remember "over half a million" than "526,321." Of course, you cannot do this when the exact number is needed.

2. *Make the statistics meaningful to your audience.* Most of us cannot comprehend "four hundred billion dollars." But if we are told that, to collect this sum of money, each man, woman, and child in the United States would have to put in $2,500, we begin to realize how large the total is. Proportions usually are easier to grasp than pure numbers; e.g., it is better to say "two out of every three Americans" than "119,700,000 Americans."

3. *Use the statistics accurately and honestly.* Statistics, if secured from a reliable source, probably are accurate. But they must be used to describe the area from which they were derived. Note how often rival politicians manipulate the same statistics to mean very different things; the chances are that they both distort the truth. Statistics become especially "sticky" when they are used to compare one unit with another. For example, comparing the number of people employed in 1960 with the number

in 1950 presents only a part of the picture. These statistics would be accurate only if presented along with statistics that compare the total populations in the two years—and that compare the number of people *un*employed. When you use statistics, be sure that your source is reliable. Be sure that the figures are up to date. Be sure that they actually measure what you say they measure. It often is advisable to cite the source of your statistics for the source may add weight to the numbers.

4. *When possible, try to dramatize your statistics by relating them to comprehensible and concrete situations.* For example:

> How much is a billion dollars? If a fund had started to accumulate at the beginning of the year 1 A.D., at the rate of one dollar a minute, it would have reached the billion mark in the year 1903. We talk very glibly about a national debt of 300 billion dollars. Suppose you were standing beside a great hole in the earth dropping in ten dollar bills, one every minute, twenty-four hours a day, and 365 days every year. How long would it take to drop in $1,000,000,000? Almost 200 years! And the national debt is 308 times a billion dollars!

Causal Relations. Sometimes the best way of making a subject clear is to discuss the cause-and-effect relations it presents. If we were asked to explain the present immigration laws of the United States, we might do so best by showing what conditions gave rise to each of the laws now in force; we might show how things "got the way they are." Or, we might reverse the process; if we were making an expository speech on reciprocal trade agreements, we might develop our outline in terms of the effects of the agreements upon the participating nations.

One of the fundamental facts about the world in which we live is that happenings, experiences, memories, thoughts, feelings, principles, etc., hang together in causal relationships. Cause-and-effect exposition is very common in teaching the sciences. We come to an understanding of causes by studying their effects, and vice versa. We know that oxygen is prerequisite to life. Scientific observation reveals that there is no oxygen on the moon, and we arrive at the understanding that the surface of the moon is lifeless. Someone tells us that a match has been dropped into a tank full of gas. We understand that a serious accident has happened. (Cause-and-effect is also an important method of logical reasoning, which we have discussed from that point of view on pages 229 and 230.

Restatement. The method of restatement in exposition consists in repeating the same idea a number of times in different language. When we can make two intelligent statements about anything, we say more about it than we do when we can make but one statement. When we can make ten accurate statements about a subject, we have a much richer meaning than we have when we have only one way of saying what we know about it. When we put an idea into different words, we are acting on the known fact that different phrasings have similar meanings for different people. Restating a thought is somewhat like picturing a structure from different angles and elevations. It is the same structure, but we gain a fuller understanding by looking at it from all sides.

Visual Aids. Graphs, charts, maps, models, samples, pictures, film clips, film strips, or diagrams often can make meanings clear with an economy of effort unapproached by any other device. There is a good deal of experimental evidence to show that we remember what we have seen better than what we have heard, and what we have both seen and heard still better. If we are explaining a gas engine, a model will be much more effective than language alone. A sample of the thing we are explaining which we can hold in our hands or pass among our audience, or a supply of samples large enough to present one to each member of the audience will give us obvious advantages. Pictures and models are more effective than graphs, charts, diagrams, and maps because they are more nearly equivalent to the things described.

We encourage you to use visual aids in your classroom speaking. You will find they can help you tremendously, making you feel more at home on the platform, giving you poise, and furnishing you something to do with your hands. Demonstrating such aids forms a fine approach to solving the problem of significant action in speech. However, when you are planning a speech in which visual aids may be a help, think out carefully just how you can employ them to gain maximum effect. Keep the following suggestions in mind:

1. Be sure that your visual aid is large enough to be seen

easily and placed properly to be seen by all members of your audience.

2. Do not "clutter up" your charts, graphs, maps, etc., with unnecessary details that have no direct bearing on your subject.

3. If you use a blackboard, practice your drawing or writing so that you can do it skillfully, unobtrusively, and quickly. Your performance at the blackboard must not detract from the data you put on it. Distraction will arise if you are inept or if you are unnecessarily ostentatious with a piece of chalk.

4. If you hand out, or pass around, samples or papers, plan carefully the time and method of distribution. See to it that the aids help and do not hinder you. Sometimes an unwise distribution of such material so completely takes up the interest of the audience that practically no attention is paid to what the speaker says. Be sure that your audience are listening to you. When their attention is wholly centered upon examining a visual aid, do not continue to talk as if they were still listening with undivided attention.

5. Keep your eyes in contact with the eyes of your audience. Resist the strong temptation to talk to the visual aid instead of to your audience. This suggestion is most often violated in the use of the blackboard, charts, and models. Use your hands to direct attention to the visual materials and your eyes to maintain a lively sense of communication with your listeners. If you are pointing out details in the visual aid, it is important, of course, to make sure that you are indicating the proper part of the aid; but sufficient familiarity with these details should enable you to do this with minimal breaks in audience contact.

6. When you have finished using the visual aid, remove it from view lest it divide the attention of your audience between itself and what you are saying.

When preparing a speech to inform, the speaker usually does not have to be concerned with motivating his audience; usually they are in a cooperative mood. His major concern should be his listeners' lack of information. It is a paradox, but true, that often those who know the most are least effective in explaining to others what they know. Knowing so much themselves, they find it hard to realize how little their listeners know and they become impatient and irritable when their listeners are slow in developing the meanings. Practically everyone can recall occasions on which our parents did a poor job of explaining what they wanted us to do and then held us accountable for our misunderstanding. Similarly, we all have had the experience of telling others what we wanted and later of being disappointed at finding that they did not understand. Life is filled with minor tragedies caused by an inability to inform.

Section Two—Persuading an Audience

As we have said, the distinction between expository speaking and persuasive speaking is not always clear-cut. Facts—the basic materials of the informative speech—can be most persuasive. A salesman, by simply demonstrating the features of a new automobile, can make you want to purchase it. After hearing an illustrated travelogue on the Scandinavian countries, you may pay a visit to a travel agent to arrange for a trip. The difference between the two speech goals, exposition and persuasion, sometimes can be determined only when we know the specific purpose of the speaker. In fact, persuasion may result accidentally even when to inform is the speaker's intent.

All the peoples of the world live in societies which are maintained primarily through persuasion of one kind or another. In a totalitarian or communist state, it is persuasion through coercion. In democracies, it is persuasion through discussion and verbal exchange of value judgments. Much of what we call "education" is really a form of persuasion. A child "learns" the basis of right and wrong because he is *persuaded* to accept the one and avoid the other. When we think of the teacher who most influenced us, we often remark, "He made me want to learn." Our economic system depends on persuasion through advertising and salesmanship. Our democratic political system was created by persuasion and can continue only through persuasion. Love may make the world go round, but persuasion most often determines the course of love.

TYPES OF PERSUASIVE SPEECHES

As we pointed out in our discussion of the general ends of public speaking, the term "persuasion" covers three purposes that are more specific—*to impress, to convince,* and *to actuate.*

Persuasion may be defined as the process of getting listeners to feel, think, or act the way the speaker wants them to. When we speak to impress, we are influencing feeling; when we speak to convince, we are influencing thinking; and when we speak to actuate, we are influencing objective action. It is well to remember, however, that the ultimate goal in all three types of situations is action of some sort, open or concealed, immediate or delayed, specific or general.

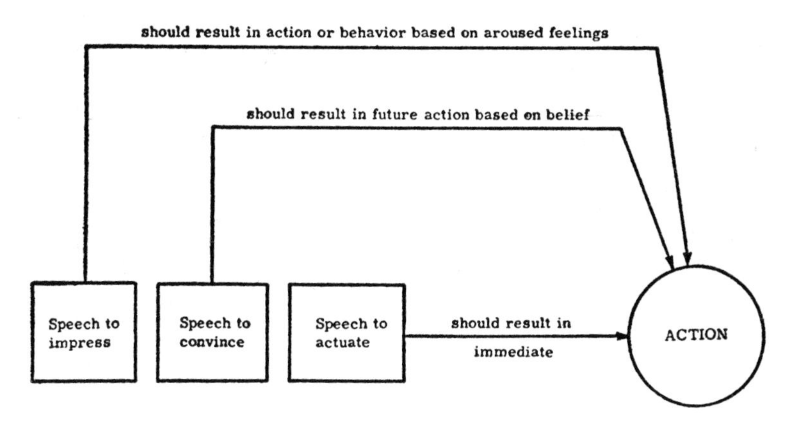

A single persuasive speech designed to get immediate action may include elements of all three types of persuasive processes. The speaker may first impress his audience with the problem confronting them; then he may convince them that his solution is the best that can be found; and finally, he may impel them to take immediate action to carry out his proposal.

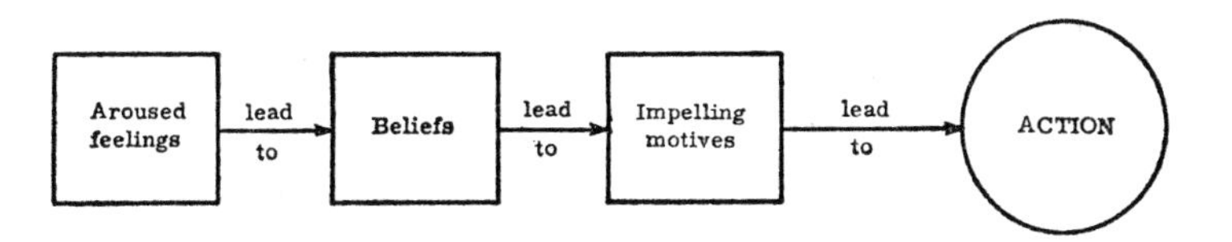

In many instances, however, it is necessary to pursue these ends one at a time in a series of speeches. Modern political campaigns for the election of a presidential candidate illustrate this differentiation of ends over a period of time. At the national conventions (which now, of course, are broadcast into the majority of American homes), specially selected party spokesmen try to impress the delegates and the home listeners with the achievements of their party and the shortcomings of their opponents; their appeals are basically emotional. Later, during the campaign, speakers at political rallies and over radio and TV use reasoning and evidence to get their listeners to believe in their platform and candidates. Then, on the eve of the election, or shortly before, the campaigners begin to call for specific action at the polls; they urge us to "get out tomorrow and vote for Senator X." But throughout the entire campaign the ultimate result these speakers are looking for is action.

Speeches to Impress. The speech to impress appears in many public speaking situations. One of the most common types is the sermon, in which the preacher attempts to reinforce the existing beliefs of his congregation in the hope that he may influence their general behavior and attitudes. "Good will" is another goal of many speeches to impress. A spokesman for industry talks to a service organization about the role of business in the community; his speech is clearly informative in nature, but he wants also to dispose his audience "favorably" toward the organization he represents. A considerable portion of mass-media advertising fits into this category; most businesses of any size employ public relations staffs whose primary purpose is to create in the mind of the public a favorable "image" of the organization.

Later we shall briefly describe what we call "occasional" speeches, speeches in which the occasion is the primary determinant of what the speaker says. Many of these can and should be speeches to impress. This is particularly true on such occasions as inaugurations, dedications, commemorations, and presentations. In some cases, speeches of introduction, welcome, and farewell are also designed primarily to evoke the feelings of the audience.

There are no special methods of preparing the speech to impress. Any of the methods of organization discussed in Chapter 4 can be applied to this speech purpose, depending on your subject and your audience. In many instances such a speech resembles a speech to inform. By careful selection and arrangement of details and by making these materials meaningful and vital to the specific audience, you can create an image of your subject that will arouse a favorable attitude. You do not distort facts; but by attaching your ideas to the emotional needs and desires of your audience and by making them vivid, you can stimulate your listeners' feelings.

Following is a paragraph from a speech delivered by Robert Green Ingersoll in 1876 at a reunion of veterans of the Civil War. It is a fine example of the use of evocative language, a type of language which is not much in vogue among speakers today, but which still can arouse the fundamental emotions of audiences, if skillfully used.

The past rises before me like a dream. Again we are in the great struggle for national life. We hear the sounds of preparation; the music of boisterous drums; the silver voices of heroic bugles. We see thousands of assemblages, and hear the appeals of orators. We see the pale cheeks of women and the flushed faces of men; and in those assemblages we see all the dead whose dust we have covered with flowers. We lose sight of them no more. We are with them when they enlist in the great army of freedom. We see them part with those they love. Some are walking for the last time in quiet woody places with the maidens they adore. We hear the whisperings and the sweet vows of eternal love as they lingeringly part forever. Others are bending over cradles, kissing babes that are asleep. Some are receiving the blessings of old men. Some are parting with mothers who hold them and press them to their hearts again and again and say nothing. Kisses and tears, tears and kisses—divine mingling of agony and love! And some are talking with wives, and endeavoring with brave words, spoken in the old tones, to drive from their hearts the awful fear. We seem them part. We see the wife standing in the door with the babe in her arms—standing in the sunlight sobbing. At the turn of the road a hand waves—she answers by holding high in her loving arms the child. He is gone and forever.

Read the following speech aloud.[1] What is the speaker's purpose? Is he trying to impress his audience? Can you figure out what the central idea is? Is it essentially a speech about Abraham

[1] Used by permission of the speaker, Bruce Barton.

Lincoln? Or is it a discussion of facts about Lincoln used as means rather than as ends in themselves?

We are met here to honor the memory of an American who was ill-fed, ill-clothed, ill-housed—and did not know it.

He was born in a log cabin without heat, running water, or any modern convenience. According to a philosophy now widely current, this was a hopeless environment; it should have convinced him from the start that he was doomed to failure.

His clothes were of crude homespun, ill fitting, and worn until the fabric would no longer hold a patch.

His diet of corn-pone and bacon lacked essential vitamins.

His schooling was limited to a few scattered weeks, under teachers whose own schooling had been meager.

In such circumstances he should have been told that there was no hope. But no one told him this. Instead, he was told that he was fortunate because he had been born in a country where any boy might properly aspire to even the highest success, even the Presidency of the United States.

He was told, also, that self-discipline and hard work were his only path to salvation, and that if he neglected them he would be poor and wretched all his life.

It was generally accepted in those days that the privilege of self-government involved the responsibility of self-support.

The rule of living was the rule of thrift. The first three commandments were:

"eat it up,"
"wear it out,"
"make it do."

He had every excuse for discouragement, self-pity, and revolt. He should have been good material for the Communist Party, an excellent professional delegate to Congress of American Youth. As such he might even have been invited to luncheon at the White House.

But no one let him know that the cards were stacked against him. No one suggested that it was useless to try. No one said: "It is too bad you did not come over here in the Mayflower because then you would have had a chance. Now it is too late. You were born poor and you will die poor. All the real chances are gone."

Instead, they said: "Root hog or die." And, though in later life he had his dark moods of spiritual depression, he never seems to have doubted that, given any sort of break, he could and would take care of himself.

The name is Abraham Lincoln. As our distance from him increases, his stature looms higher and his shadow lengthens. More and more he comes to be regarded as the greatest American.

Speeches to Convince. The goal of the speech to convince is belief. You may wish your audience to change their beliefs on a certain issue, or you may want them to accept a "new" belief. The subject of a speech to convince is a *proposition,* a declarative statement of the belief that you want accepted.

There are three main types of propositions. A *proposition of fact* declares that a certain condition exists *in fact;* it presents your analysis of a situation as being accurate and true. "Television instruction can alleviate the teacher shortage" is such a proposition of fact. When you speak to a *proposition of value,* you are dealing with right or wrong, with good or bad, with justice or injustice, as these "values" are applied to your subject; e.g., "Television instruction is the best answer to America's educational problems." The third type, the *proposition of policy,* avows that a certain action should be taken or a certain policy adopted; e.g., "Our college should employ television instruction in its large lecture courses."

In preparing to speak on any of these types of propositions, you must be able to answer certain pertinent questions:

1. For the proposition of fact: What facts will support my proposition? Do they really exist? Are they observable and can they be verified? What is the nature of the facts (e.g., circumstantial, statistical, empirical, hearsay, etc.)?

2. For the proposition of value: What standards of judgment shall I use (morality, material or spiritual benefit, justice)? Can I best judge this event by comparing it with some other similar event? Is my personal judgment sufficient? What evidence is required and available to support my judgment?

3. For the proposition of policy: Why is a new policy needed? What are the causes of the existing problem? Will my proposal solve the problem? Am I sure that it won't create new problems, or that there aren't better solutions?

In a speech to convince, you must prove your proposition. You do so by looking for the main "reasons" for accepting it, and then presenting them with all available means of support. The two best plans for organizing a speech to convince probably are the "logical" and the "problem-solution" methods described in Chapter 4.

The following brief speech is designed to convince an audience that the inflation of our currency is not a satisfactory economic policy. Can you determine what sort of a proposition the speaker is dealing with and how successful he is? Do you think that the analogy is sound? Does it prove the speaker's proposition?

A farmer out in Iowa had harvested his crop of corn. He found that he had 10,000 bushels. He was not satisfied for he needed more than that. He solved his problem by buying smaller "bushel" baskets. He measured his crop again and found that he had 20,000 baskets full. So he had plenty of corn!

This farmer was no more foolish than we are when we think that by printing more money we can increase our wealth. We have more dollars but they are fifty-cent dollars.

Note how, in an address delivered in 1946, Professor W. H. Kiekhofer, then a distinguished professor of economics at the University of Wisconsin, counters a widely-held belief about the size of our national debt: [2]

One of the most enticing snares and attractive delusions of these post-war years is the highly sponsored pronouncement that the size of the national debt is of no great importance since we owe it to ourselves. Even before our participation in the war, Marriner S. Eccles, then Chairman of the Board of Governors of the Federal Reserve System, said: "The burden of interest that we speak about is not of itself a burden if the debt is held within our own economy, because the interest which is paid also goes back to the economy as a whole, increases income, and therefore increases our ability to pay taxes." At about the same time and in similar vein President Roosevelt said: "And when this week you see all the crocodile tears about the burden of our grandchildren to pay the government debt, remember this: Our national debt, after all, is an internal debt, owed not only by the nation but to the nation. If our children have to pay the interest on it, they will pay that interest to themselves."

At a time when the national debt approximates 260 billion dollars, and the interest alone amounts to over 5 billion, the thesis that the size of the national debt is of no great importance because we owe it to ourselves would be highly comforting doctrine if only it were true. It

[2] William H. Kiekhofer, *To Thee, Wisconsin, State and University* (New York: Appleton-Century-Crofts, Inc., 1950), pp. 52–54. Reprinted by permission of the publishers.

is true that practically all of the debt is held by American citizens and institutions. It is true that in paying interest and principal over a long period of years the only thing necessary is to tax all of the people in order to pay some of the people what the government owes them. The payment of a domestically owned public debt effects a redistribution of income within a country. But it is not true that the size of a domestically owned national debt is of no great importance to the government and the people. If it were true, then the payment of taxes should be no burden either, since taxes too, are paid by the people to themselves, and soon get back again into the stream of national income. The anguished groans of suffering taxpayers are evidence that the burden is heavy, and only borne through the sacrifice of other outlays.

I cannot overlook the obvious facts that a public debt does create a burden for future taxpayers; that interest on the debt goes to individuals but not necessarily to the same individuals that pay the taxes, nor in the same proportions; that large public debts are apt to be inflationary because they require constant refunding and the line of least resistance is to borrow from the commercial banks, which means creating additional dollars; that servicing of the debt may handicap the government in making new expenditures that are necessary and desirable; and that the payment of a huge national debt, both interest and principal, presupposes a large annual gross national product, which it may be difficult to maintain steadily. But we have the large national debt. Monetary and fiscal stability requires that at the earliest possible date we begin to retire it. If we should manage the public debt in such a way as on the average, through the fat years and the lean, to reduce the principal by 1,000 millions of dollars per year, it would take us over 250 years to get back to the fiscal cleanliness and health we enjoyed in 1917 when our national debt was just under one billion dollars.

Speeches to Actuate. Each of the preceding types of speeches could be turned into a speech to actuate by including a special plea for immediate action. A speech in which you arouse good will toward the American Red Cross could close with your passing out pledge cards to be completed and turned in at the end of the meeting. A speech to build the belief that the voting age should be lowered might end with a request that the audience sign petitions which you later will mail to your Senator.

When you try to influence the actions of others, you must let them know precisely what you want them to do. Many times audiences come away from listening to a speaker, quite puzzled about what specific response he wanted. When we say to a friend, "Won't you come and see us sometime?" we are not nearly so likely to receive a call as we are when we say, "Won't you come over next Tuesday evening at eight o'clock?" A great deal of speaking to achieve action fails for this very simple reason—we leave the audience favorably disposed but confused as to how they can translate their attitude into specific action. A speaker announces: "The purpose of this meeting is to raise funds. We hope that we may have a large number of generous contributions." How much more effective it would be to say: "You will find a blank check attached to your program. Please write the name of your bank in the appropriate space, fill out the check for the largest amount you can contribute, and have it ready for the ushers who will collect it as soon as you have had time to prepare it." You must state clearly, definitely, and specifically the attitude you want your audience to assume, the proposition you want them to accept, the action you want them to take.

The speech to actuate requires no special format. Before you make your plea for action, you will want your audience to understand why they should act. You will want them in the proper frame of mind so that they will act. Whether you accomplish your purpose by informing them, impressing them, or convincing them will depend upon the specific setting of your speech.

On April 2, 1917, Woodrow Wilson delivered to the American Congress a stirring speech calling for a declaration of war against Germany. His words inspired the free peoples of the world to stand together against Imperial Germany. He concluded his address with the following plea:

> It is a distressing and oppressive duty, Gentlemen of the Congress, which I have performed in thus addressing you. There are, it may be, many months of fiery trial and sacrifice ahead of us. It is a fearful thing to lead this great peaceful people into war, into the most terrible and disastrous of all wars, civilization itself seeming to be in the balance. But the right is more precious than peace, and we shall fight for the things that we have always carried nearest our hearts—for democracy, for the right of those who submit to authority to have a voice in their own governments, for the rights and liberties of small nations, for a universal dominion of right by such a concert of free peoples as shall bring peace and safety to all nations and make the

world itself at last free. To such a task we can dedicate our lives and our fortunes, everything that we are and everything that we have, with the pride of those who know that the day has come when America is privileged to spend her blood and her might for the principles that gave her birth and happiness and the peace which she has treasured. God helping her, she can do no other.

Two and a half months later, Wilson closed his Flag Day address in which he exhorted the nation to an unflinching performance of its duty in the war, as follows:

For us there is but one choice. We have made it. Woe be to the man or group of men that seeks to stand in our way in this day of high resolution when every principle we hold dearest is to be vindicated and made secure for the salvation of the nation. We are ready to plead at the bar of history, and our flag shall wear a new lustre. Once more we shall make good with our lives and fortunes the great faith to which we were born, and a new glory shall shine in the face of our people.

The following two-minute speech is designed to impress, to reinforce an attitude, *and* to evoke a particular pattern of behavior: [3]

Last month a man in Chicago refused a million dollars for an invention he had evolved *in his spare time.*

You are interested in this because it confronts you with the possibilities of *your* spare time. Did you ever stop to think that most of the world's great men have achieved their true life work, not in the course of their needful occupations, but—*in their spare time?*

A tired-out rail-splitter crouched over his tattered books by candlelight or by fire-glow, at the day's end; preparing for his future, instead of snoring or skylarking like his co-laborers. Lincoln cut out his path to later immortality—*in his spare time.*

An underpaid and overworked telegraph clerk stole hours from sleep or from play, at night, trying to crystallize into realities certain fantastic dreams in which he had faith. Today the whole world is benefiting by what Edison did—*in his spare time.*

A down-at-heel instructor in an obscure college varied the drudgery he hated by spending his evenings and holidays in tinkering with a queer device of his, at which his fellow teachers laughed. But he invented the telephone—*in his spare time.*

Gentlemen, you, too, have spare time. The man who says: "I would do such and such a great thing, if only I had time!" would do nothing if he had all the time on the calendar. There is always time—*spare*

[3] Used by permission of the speaker, Bruce Barton.

time—at the disposal of every human who has the energy to use it. USE IT!

THE AUDIENCE IN PERSUASION

Throughout this book we stress the importance of understanding your audience, or adapting your ideas, organization, and presentation to each specific group of listeners. Every speech must be "audience-centered" if it is to succeed. You can understand how absolutely vital this is in persuasion. Consider, for example, the modern advertising agency whose reason for existence is to persuade the public to buy its clients' products. These agencies conduct continuing—and costly—research solely to learn the nature of the consumer, his attitudes, needs, and interests. Every speaker who wishes to persuade must conduct "research" in order to develop a satisfactory image of his audience. Here are some questions you should try to answer:

1. *How much do my audience know about my subject?* If they know little or nothing, you will have to help them understand the issues involved and your position with regard to them. In such an audience you need not worry about preconceived attitudes, for they probably will not exist. If the audience are well informed about the subject, you will want to determine the extent of their understanding and fit what you have to say into the framework of what they already know. It is most unpersuasive to ask the audience to accept something they do not understand; it is also unpersuasive to explain the obvious.

2. *How interested are my audience in my subject?* If they are indifferent, your first challenge will be to get them to want to listen to you, by using the techniques of attention and interest. If you know they have come to hear what *you* have to say about *your subject,* you can get into the meat of your argument more quickly.

3. *What is my audience's attitude toward my subject?* If they already agree with you, your task will be relatively simple. If such is the situation, you might use your speech to arouse open enthusiasm. A speaker at a pep rally does this, as does the keynoter at a political convention. The audience is "for" the same principles as the speaker; he wants to make them even more

conscious of these principles, hoping that the excitement he can generate will carry over to later action.

A hostile or critical audience presents much greater difficulty. Here you must use every psychological technique at your disposal to secure acceptance, first of yourself, and then of your point of view. Under hostile conditions, direct suggestion, the command, will undoubtedly fail. Your chances are much better if you can lead the audience, seemingly, to reach their own conclusions in favor of your proposal. Persuading a critical audience takes time; it is well to limit the extent of your purpose to that which you feel you can reasonably achieve at the time, leaving further persuasion for later speaking.

The neutral audience represent still different problems. Neutrality may result from not knowing much about the issues; in this case clear exposition will be an important part of your speech. Or, indifference may stem from a feeling that there is no urgency; here appeals to "the vital" may be primary.

4. *What is the audience's attitude toward me as a person?* Do they know me? Do they accept my authority on this subject? Consider an audience's reactions toward yourself in the same way that you have considered their feelings about your subject. In a situation where a master of ceremonies or a chairman will introduce you, he can take care of some of these problems. An audience will appreciate your showing them that you are worth listening to, provided you do so without either excessive egotism or undue humility.

5. *What are the attitudes of members of my audience toward one another?* Do the members of your audience belong to what sociologists call an "in-group" where they are all more or less of one mind and share the same feelings? Or do hostile factions exist among them? In the latter situation, diplomacy and tact are essential. An indispensable first step here is to find some common ground among the discordant elements in your audience and then to point up agreements between these common goals and your purpose.

The lines of influence between a speaker and his audience are established first between him and those persons who are most suggestible. Such individuals constitute centers of stimulation, which affect others around them. The speaker works through such susceptible and friendly individuals. It is an immense advantage to a speaker to have a number of these allies in his audience; without at least some of them he can scarcely hope to succeed. One enthusiastic auditor, by his open demonstration of approval, may start the logs moving when the jam of resistance otherwise might not be broken. Theater managers who employ professional claques understand this principle thoroughly. Half a dozen such mercenaries strategically placed in an audience, ready to laugh and applaud, may turn a "cold" audience into an enthusiastic one. Of course, we do not suggest that you hire such agents to subvert your audience; but we do urge you to keep your eyes and ears open for signs of such cooperation on the part of individual members of your audience. When you see heads nodding in agreement, facial expressions indicating willingness to accept what you are saying, and postural tensions manifesting interest and delight, try to utilize such feedback responses and strengthen them.

The individual in a group tends (1) to avoid extreme opinions and judgments, (2) to be less critical and discriminating in his evaluation of evidence, and (3) to find that while his associations flow more freely, his capacity for close logical reasoning is somewhat impaired.

The fact that a large number of people are being influenced by the speaker, while at the same time they are being influenced by each other, suggests that in order to deal effectively with the varieties of personality and experience before him, the speaker should search for common psychological factors. As we previously have said, human beings are more alike in their feelings than in their ideas. The individual in the group is more emotional and less intellectual than he is when alone. Therefore, it is in emotional behavior that the lowest common denominators of behavior usually are to be found. The speaker may have to rely upon emotional appeals to a much greater degree in addressing a group than he would in dealing with an individual.

Attitudes of submission and conformity characterize the behavior of the individual in a group and thus render him suggestible. The individual's tendency to react is powerfully reinforced by the sight of others doing the same things and by the feeling that social inhibitions in the way of carrying out common impulses have been removed. Allport says: [4]

Speakers who wish to stir their audience use special methods for eliciting responses of a *demonstrative sort,* so that an abundance of contributory social stimuli may be in evidence. The introductory humorous story arouses the individual's mirth, and facilitates through his laughter the laughter of others. Appeals are made to emotional rather than to thought responses; for emotional expression is the very material of which crowd facilitation is made. A crowd cannot be made up of reasoning individuals, because reasoning involves few outward responses through which individuals stimulate one another. Sentiments common to all are touched upon, since these involve expressive postures of stimulating value. Revered names are mentioned, and appeals are made in the name of justice, brotherly love, and patriotism. Routine activities such as reading or singing in concert, and rising and sitting together are familiar methods of making individuals more aware of one another, and so establishing a receptive attitude toward the expressive stimuli later to be evoked. Crowd building thus forms a vital portion of the forensic art.

If the individuals in a group are to influence the behavior of one another most effectively, they should be brought into close physical contact with one another. Therefore, experienced speakers often ask their audiences to fill the front seats or to move in from the sides to the center of the auditorium, in order to bring maximum interstimulation into play. Thus they attempt to "polarize" their audiences.

Speakers, realizing how prone the individual is to act in harmony with others, make use of devices that produce "an illusion of universality"; that is, a feeling that everybody else thinks what the speaker thinks, or approves of the course he suggests.

He harangues us in stereotypes as familiar as the air we breathe. He recalls the images of our cultural myths and legends. Stereotypes and images alike carry an enormous emotional significance; and as members of the crowd we give them our unreserved, if temporary, allegiance. Thus the speaker defines and crystallizes our group action.[5]

[4] F. H. Allport, *Social Psychology* (Boston: Houghton Mifflin Company, 1924), p. 300.

[5] Kimball Young, *Social Psychology: An Analysis of Social Behavior* (New York: F. S. Crofts & Co., 1930), p. 521. Copyright, Kimball Young. By permission of Appleton-Century-Crofts, Inc.

ETHICS IN PERSUASION

We cannot close our discussion of persuasion without a few words about the ethical obligations of the public speaker. Naturally, when one individual finds that he can exert influence over the feelings and beliefs and actions of other persons, he experiences an exhilarating sense of power. Whether we admit the fact or not, we all enjoy this feeling. But when we have it we should remind ourselves that power always brings with it responsibility for its legitimate exercise in the service of proper goals. Whenever a speaker awakens the emotions of an audience, he is dealing with what may become a Frankenstein monster which may get beyond his control.

When we use persuasion, we should ask ourselves: Do I have the right to ask my audience to accept my point of view? Do I really know something that they do not know? Is the response that I am asking of my audience justified by the facts? Will the course of action I am asking them to follow be good for them as well as for me? Am I seeking to develop in them feelings and ideas that they would be willing to assume if they really understood my purpose?

Moreover, we should bear in mind that attitudes, beliefs, and actions based largely upon emotional impulses may be shorter lived than those strongly supported by evidence and logic. Emotional behavior untempered by reasoning quickly becomes irrational and capricious. As speakers we can never escape a large share of the responsibility for what our audiences do when we have finished speaking.

Section Three—Entertaining an Audience

The third general end of speech is to entertain. Before the development of movies, radio, and television, the popular humorous lecturer who traveled the Chatauqua and Lyceum circuits was a principal source of entertainment for millions of Americans. Artemus War, Mark Twain, Irvin S. Cobb, Will Rogers, and others drew packed houses night after night as they "toured the provinces," creating good humor and enjoyment. Today the humorist has become the comedian, who usually works within a vaudeville, radio, television, or night-club framework rather than from the lecture platform. The few humorists who still appear in public lectures, e.g., Bennett Cerf and Ogden Nash, often purport to have something significant to tell us by way of information or inspiration, in addition to entertaining us.

Another type of speech often classified as entertaining is the illustrated lecture or travelogue. Such speeches, of course, are informative, but from the audience's point of view, entertainment may be the chief result. A speaker tells us how he traveled down the Amazon and shows us slides or motion pictures of his adventures. The information we gain, though it may be considerable, probably is not particularly vital. More important is the pleasure we feel because the speaker has let us share with him some beautiful, unusual, or exciting moments. This kind of speech frequently is filled with human-interest anecdotes; it often is accompanied by colorful pictures to attract the eye as well as the ear. We enjoy listening; we are entertained. The travelogue, too, is less frequently heard and seen on the public platform since the advent of radio, TV, and motion pictures, but it is still an important activity for many specialized groups.

Although entertainment as a principal end of public speaking appears relatively seldom, the factors of entertainment can be introduced with good effect into many speeches. Entertainment is not synonymous with humor; though, of course, humor is a common means of achieving entertainment. When we say that a speaker is entertaining, we mean that he makes listening a pleasurable experience. We attend to what he says with little effort. An anecdote, a bit of dramatized action, suspense, vivid language, a familiar quotation—any of these a speaker can use to make his audience want to listen. And when he does so, he is using a form of entertainment, not as his primary goal, but as a means of achieving that goal.

Employing humor, then, is one of the techniques of entertaining, and thus of gaining and holding attention. It also can help in creating good relations between speaker and audience. It may serve as the speaker's opening wedge in an uncomfortable or tense situation; it may even furnish him a way of making an unpopular notion palatable and acceptable.

TYPES OF HUMOR

Of what does humor consist? What makes us laugh? One theory considers laughter the result of feeling an emotional satisfaction from seeing another individual in an awkward, ludicrous, uncomfortable—even disastrous—situation, the witness realizing subconsciously that "there, but for the grace of God, go I." This theory accounts for the proximity of comedy to tragedy. It helps us understand the popularity, among comics, of such subjects as marriage, taxes, and death.

Obviously, a speaker usually cannot cavort about the platform to evoke laughter. But he can, by creating images through verbal, vocal, and physical symbols, give his audience a chance for the same type of emotional release. The principal means of humor at his disposal are caricature, satire, irony, exaggeration, ludicrous contrast, and understatement.

When we *caricature* a situation, person, or attitude, we distort it by playing up certain aspects way beyond reality. Note how the cartoonist exaggerates by overdrawing the nose, the teeth or the bald pate of his subject. Anna Russell, the Canadian comedienne, performs a hilarious routine in which she burlesques the "typical" ladies-club president introducing a guest artist. One of the foibles of this sort of person is the tendency to prattle on with all manner of extraneous small talk. Miss Russell begins with "Ladies and gentlemen—and others," tries vainly to extricate herself from the faux pas, announces all the club's up-coming events—with side comments on each, discusses the organization's financial straits—aggravated by the expense of paying the evening's artist, prattles on about her "beautiful corsage," finally gets around to introducing the guest, only to find that she can't remember her name. She pulls a sheet of paper from her enormous handbag, announces with gusto and confidence, "Miss Hamburger!" She realizes that the paper is her shopping list, is seized by a fit of sneezing brought on by the beautiful corsage, can't get out the name of the artist between sneezes, and finishes by throwing up her hands and shouting, "For gooness sake, clap!"

When the burlesque or exaggeration has behind it some moral purpose, we call it *satire*. If Miss Russell's purpose were to reform these omnipresent nuisances—the mistresses of ceremonies—we could call her monologue a satire. *Irony* goes a step further. When we make an exaggerated statement about a situation but mean something quite different, we are employing irony. Mark Twain's salty comments on humanity depended on irony for much of their effect. One of his best-known speeches was entitled "On Smoking," a humorous but compelling attack against the self-satisfied, "holier-than-thou" moralist. After telling of his having given up certain pleasures—for two days—to cure his lumbago, he said he had had occasion to recommend the remedy to an elderly lady friend whose ailments were not responding to medical care. "Give up smoking, drinking, eating, and swearing for a week," he advised her. But because she didn't smoke, drink, or swear, she couldn't give them up. "So there it was," he concluded. "She'd neglected her habits. She was a sinking ship with no freight to throw overboard. I guess one or two little bad habits would have saved her. But she was just a moral pauper." The thematic sentence of the speech is a delightful bit of irony—"Mind you, I have no objection to abstinence so long as it doesn't harm anybody."

We have discussed *exaggeration* as an element of caricature. Overstating a fact can be delightfully humorous. Note Mark Twain's description of Virginia City, Nevada, which he visited in the 1860's. Calling it a "good place for a man to lose his religion," he described it as having "wide-open gambling places, murders, street fights, riots, a whisky mill every sixteen steps, half a dozen jails—and some talk of building a church." In this quotation, note also the sudden *contrast* that Twain employs to point up his commentary. The juxtaposition of two incompatible ideas can create a *ludicrous* quality that is highly entertaining.

Understating a situation can also bring laughter. In *The Importance of Being Earnest,* Jack Worthing, who has reported the death of his fictitious brother with great pretended grief, is asked the cause of death. "A severe chill, it seems," he replies, and the understatement brings down the house. This technique is most effective when it follows close on exaggeration or is used as a commentary on a seemingly serious, significant situation.

One other form of humor that should be mentioned is the *pun,* or the play on words. For most of us, however, it is not a recommended technique, because it requires great ingenuity and care, for it may seem unadulterated "corn."

Probably few public speakers have amused and entertained as many people as did the immortal Will Rogers. On December 4, 1924, he delivered the following after-dinner speech at a dinner of the Alumni of Columbia University in New York City. The banquet was in memory of Alexander Hamilton and among the honored guests were Andrew Mellon and President Nicholas Murray Butler, both of whom also spoke.

Will Rogers chose as his topic, "Education and Wealth." He spoke as follows: [6]

President Butler paid me a compliment a while ago in mentioning my name in his introductory remarks, and he put me ahead of the Columbia graduates. I am glad he did that, because I got the worst of it last week. The Prince of Wales last week, in speaking of the sights of America, mentioned the Woolworth Building, the subway, the slaughterhouse, Will Rogers, and the Ford Factory. He could at least put me ahead of the hogs.

Everything must be in contrast at an affair like this. You know to show anything off properly you must have the contrast. Now I am here tonight representing poverty. We have enough wealth right here at this table, right here at the speaker's table alone—their conscience should hurt them, which I doubt if it does—so that we could liquidate our national debt. Every rich man reaches a time in his career when he comes to a turning point and starts to give it away. I have heard that of several of our guests here tonight, and that is one of the reasons that I am here. I would like to be here at the psychological moment.

We are here not only to keep cool with Coolidge but to do honor to Alexander Hamilton. Now he was the first Secretary of the Treasury. The reason he was appointed that was because he and Washington were the only men in America at that time who knew how to put their names on a check. Signing a check has remained the principal qualification of a U.S. Secretary of the Treasury. He was a Princeton man—or I believe it was Harvard—anyway it was one of those primary

[6] Reprinted by permission of Will Rogers, Jr.

schools. In fighting a duel, he forgot that in America our men over here could shoot. So unfortunately one of them was killed, which had never happened in the old country. So they did away with dueling. It was all right to protect your honor but not to go as far as you like.

If you are speaking of finances here tonight, I do not believe that you could look further than President Butler. Butler is the word—to dig up the dough. Columbia was nothing twenty years ago. Now he has gone around and got over a hundred buildings, and has annexed Grant's Tomb. He was the first man to go around to the graduates and explain to them that by giving money to Columbia it would help on the income tax and also perpetuate their names. We have an Alexander Hamilton Building. He landed these buildings and ran the place up to ninety millions or something like that. There are more students in the university than there are in any other in the world. It is the foremost university. There are thirty-two hundred courses. You spend your first two years in deciding what course to take, the next two years in finding the buildings that these courses are given in, and the rest of your life wishing that you had taken another course. And they have this society called the Alumni Association, a bunch of men who have gone to school and after they have come out formed a society to tell the school how to run it.

Do you sense any serious undercurrent in Will Rogers' humor? Is he trying to do anything more than amuse his audience? What are his real purpose and his actual theme?

USING HUMOR IN SPEAKING

Some special precautions and suggestions are necessary in the use of humor:

1. Avoid humor that is not in good taste and remember that taste varies from audience to audience.

2. Don't get carried away with your own humor. The speaker who laughs uncontrollably at his own humorous story often gets the reaction, "Well, it's not that funny!" Exaggeration and understatement are most effective when delivered in a dry, mock-serious manner.

3. Don't label your humor in advance. "Here's a funny one," may get the response, "O.K., show me."

4. Don't tell one humorous story after another just because you are getting a good response; such stories should be used to develop the serious idea you have in mind.

5. Practice your humor to improve timing and mood. If dialect

will enhance the story, be sure that you master the dialect before you use it.

6. Watch your audience's reactions. Let them have a good laugh if you can evoke it; don't cut if off until it has *almost* died down. If the audience is not responding the way you want them to, resist the temptation to try again with a broader sample of your fare.

7. Study the work of well-known humorists. Your library will provide you the writings of Mark Twain, Will Rogers, Artemus Ward, Robert Benchley, Stephen Leacock, Irvin S. Cobb, Cornelia Otis Skinner, and many others. Analyze radio and television comedians to learn their techniques of timing and mood. A number of recordings are also available for more leisurely and careful analysis. Among the best are *Mark Twain Tonight,* performed by Hal Holbrook, and several recordings by Anna Russell, Cornelia Otis Skinner, Shelley Berman, Bob Newhart, Bob Hope, and others.

Section Four—Speaking on Special Occasions

Certain occasions often prescribe special attention to purpose, composition, and delivery. The nature of the circumstances surrounding the speech on such occasions should be reflected in the content and presentation. What we will discuss here are "typical" speeches for the most common of these special occasions, realizing that any of these situations can be the proper moment for a speech very different from the typical ones.

AFTER-DINNER SPEECHES

The one occasion on which the speech to entertain most frequently is heard is the dinner or banquet program. The theory seems to be that after having gorged themselves on fruit cup, veal birds, and lemon meringue pie, the audience will want no intellectual stimulation, no interference with their fundamental attitudes, but only a pleasant interlude of relaxation and fun. This is not universally the case, however. More and more, organizations arrange banquets to serve serious purposes. Red

Cross workers meet at dinner to "kick off" the annual campaign or to celebrate achieving their goal. Democrats hold Jackson Day dinners to inspire their members to strive harder for the cause. Or, a dinner group may invite a certain speaker because they want to hear what he has to say about the subject on which he is an authority. Some college fraternities, for example, plan monthly dinners to which they invite faculty speakers; these men and women are asked, not to be funny, but to be informative or inspiring.

The "typical" after-dinner speech, however, is expected to serve the general end of entertainment. Its main purpose is to please the listeners. Three types of after-dinner speeches frequently heard are:

1. The *informal, topical* speech built around a central theme, serious or humorous. The organization of such a speech is loose; the speaker makes observations, tells stories to illustrate his observations, seems to let one idea remind him of another. The loose structure of the speech makes the speaker seem to be rambling—but in a pleasant, relaxed fashion that fits the mood and mental capacities of a "stuffed" audience. The subject usually is suggested by the occasion or the particular audience.

2. The *personal experience* speech. The speaker relates a series of anecdotes about himself or another person, e.g., the travelogue. If the subject is a person other than the speaker, the speech probably should not be a eulogy; the speaker probably will play up some human interest elements in that person's life. At a Lincoln's Birthday dinner, the speaker might discuss "Lincoln, the Teller of Tales," illustrating his speech with a variety of stories ascribed to Lincoln; or "Lincoln in the White House," describing Lincoln's relations with his personal staff, his guests, his family, the house itself.

3. The *prolonged caricature or burlesque* speech. The speaker delivers a mock-serious informative or persuasive speech on some outrageous subject. "What to Do with Discarded Banana Peels," "The Case for Ping-Pong Scholarships," "To Wear or not Wear—a Toupee," "How to Put an Audience to Sleep" are sample subjects. If skillfully done, such a speech actually may be effective persuasion, utilizing the element of irony. The ping-pong scholar-

ship speech, for example, could be a telling commentary on athletic scholarships, even though the real situation is not discussed directly at all.

A good after-dinner speech is usually from five to fifteen minutes in length. The time limits agreed upon or prescribed by the toastmaster should be carefully observed. An after-dinner speaker who steals the time properly belonging to other speakers is discourteous.

A good after-dinner speech is good-humored, friendly, happy, and informal. Contentious matters that arouse bitter feelings either should be excluded or treated with great tact. Skilled after-dinner speakers do not attempt to grind their own axes or to pay off personal grudges.

A good after-dinner speech is fresh and spontaneous. It is related to what has been said by others. It often is, at least in part, extemporaneous; it is manufactured as presented, but out of ideas that have been planned in advance. An after-dinner speech should be expressed in neat and understandable phraseology and closely adapted to the experiences and interests of the audience.

COMMEMORATIVE SPEECHES

Making a commemorative speech rarely is a utilitarian enterprise. In commemorative oratory the speaker is most like the poet and dramatist; he is the very voice and visible form of the occasion. He is expected to express, not so much his own thoughts, as the thoughts of the audience, to say what they would if they had his opportunity and his talent. The speaker must stress feelings appropriate to the occasion.

Eulogies. The eulogy is a common type of commemorative speech. The principal types of eulogy are the *chronological* and the *topical.*

1. *Chronological.* The chronological eulogy tells the story of the subject's life in time order; it is sometimes referred to as the biographical eulogy. When a eulogy is about a person whose life history is not known to the audience, this form may be useful and appropriate. Even so, however, great care should be ex-

ercised to make it an interesting, personal narrative and not a cold, impersonal setting forth of bare facts. The *meaning* of various incidents in the life of the subject should be emphasized.

2. *Topical.* The second type of eulogy is the topical; the speaker selects certain major aspects or incidents of the subject's life and dwells upon them, developing their significance, extracting lessons from them, and seeking to impress them deeply upon the audience. In such a speech it is very much easier to make a fresh, interesting, personal interpretation of the subject than in a chronological plan. In eulogies, the speaker should be careful to strike a note of feeling that fits the audience, the occasion—*and the time limit.*

Inaugurals. Inaugural speeches are essentially commemorative or dedicatory. In effect, an inaugural address dedicates a new administration. An inauguration is an appropriate occasion for a statement of principles and purposes. Ordinarily the speech should not be a campaign speech. Its purpose is to say the appropriate word, strike the right keynote, arouse enthusiasm for the tasks ahead, allay suspicion, and disarm opposition. Probably the most important inaugural speeches are those delivered by the President of the United States. Next in importance come the inaugurals delivered by governors of states, and presidents of colleges and universities.

Dedication and Anniversary Speeches. These commemorative speeches are delivered at such ceremonies as the opening of new institutions, the unveiling of monuments, the laying of cornerstones, etc. These are occasions on which sentiment and emotion are in the air. Here, as in eulogies, the end is impressiveness, rather than belief or action. Since there are many sorts of dedicatory exercises, there are many sorts of dedication speeches, ranging from Daniel Webster's "Bunker Hill Orations" to very brief and informal talks.

Anniversary speeches are much like dedication speeches; they are likely to look backward as well as forward. They are delivered on birthdays or other anniversaries of men or institutions. As in preparing other commemorative addresses, the speaker should avoid all business, professional, partisan, and personal ends, and serve the particular occasion in a way in keeping with its mood. Speakers on great occasions, particularly the anniversaries of institutions, are speaking not simply to the people of their own day; their message may be preserved and read and reread in later years. The speaker on such an occasion is speaking for the past and to both the present and the future.

SPEECHES OF INTRODUCTION

Anyone who takes an active part in the affairs of life is likely to be required at some time or other to make a speech of introduction. Therefore, it seems worth while to give a rather full set of suggestions to guide you in making speeches of introduction. The function of this kind of speech is to bring the main speaker and his audience together in a spirit of sympathy and understanding. If introducers would understand this function and keep it in mind, there would be more good speeches of introduction.

The material for speeches of introduction should be drawn from four sources—*speaker, subject, audience,* and *occasion.* The temptation is to say too much rather than too little in a speech of introduction. The following specific rules may help you:

1. *Make the speech short.* Rarely is there a situation in which the introducer is called on to make a long speech. Regardless of the number of interesting things you might say about the speaker, the subject, the audience, and the occasion, resist the temptation to say most of them. A good speech of introduction that accomplishes in nine words everything demanded by the occasion is, "Ladies and Gentlemen, the President of the United States."

2. *Make a speech of introduction only.* Never seize the occasion to make a speech of your own. In courtesy to the speaker you are introducing, leave him an attentive and unwearied audience.

3. *Never deliver an extravagant eulogy of the speaker.* Of course, it is perfectly proper to tell the audience important facts about the experience, training, or position of the speaker. Extreme praise, however, is in poor taste and is likely to be embarrassing to the speaker. A word or phrase referring to him as

being "accomplished" or "distinguished" is permissible, of course.

When you are in doubt about what you should include in your remarks, the proper and courteous thing to do is to ask the speaker what points he would like to have mentioned. Sometimes there are specific items of information that the speaker would like the audience to have and that he would prefer not to give himself. The speech of introduction should make the maximum contribution toward accomplishing *the speaker's* purpose.

4. *Do not discuss the speaker's subject.* While it is proper to refer to the speaker's subject as one on which he is well qualified to speak, or as one of importance or interest to the audience, you should not discuss the subject before the speaker has a chance to do so. The speaker should be permitted to present his material in his own way. Do not steal the speaker's thunder by telling the audience a few of the most interesting items; after all, he may prefer to reserve these for his own use!

Sydney J. Harris, a well-known columnist who does a considerable amount of special-occasion speaking, wrote recently: [7]

> I too have suffered from pompous, humorless and long-winded introductions, and I have often wondered what psychic mechanism prompts it.
>
> Audiences attend lectures, presumably to hear the speaker—not to hear announcements, greetings, or biographical sketches that sound more like obituaries.
>
> Only last week I went to hear a distinguished literary figure. He was flanked on the platform by three functionaries.
>
> Mr. A took the microphone and delivered a rambling speech of welcome, and introduced Mr. B. Mr. B added nothing of value to the proceedings, and after a few minutes handed the ball back to Mr. A who proceeded to introduce Mr. C, who proceeded to introduce the speaker of the evening with remarks that resembled a doctoral dissertation.
>
> By the time the featured speaker arose, we were hot, bored, sleepy, and overwrought. No human being could have lived up to his advance billing—and he didn't.
>
> I mention all this with kindly puzzlement, not in anger. I simply do not understand this obtuseness in otherwise sensitive people. Can they imagine that anyone is interested in their verbal contribution—or that both audience and speaker do not resent having ten minutes clipped from the main address?

[7] Reprinted by permission of the author. (Copyrighted by General Features Corporation, New York, N.Y.)

SPEECHES OF WELCOME

A speech of welcome should serve precisely the same function that a sincere greeting serves between individuals. Speeches of welcome are given on such occasions as a reception for a distinguished visitor, the greeting of a delegation representing an organization, a country, or a community, the return to the campus of an alumnus, or a meeting in honor of a new superintendent of schools or a new principal.

Speeches of welcome may contain:

1. An explanation of the nature of the occasion, as, for example, an explanation of the purpose of a convention.
2. An explanation of the purpose of the organization or institution by which the welcome is being given, as, for example, an interpretation of the spirit of a charitable, educational, or civic institution, as a part of the speech of welcome to a guest who is inspecting the institution or being entertained by it.
3. A tribute to the person or group being welcomed, as, for example, a tribute to University X as a part of the speech of welcome to its president when he visits University Y.

Speeches of welcome should be short, simply expressed, and free from insincere exaggeration. They should be in keeping with the atmosphere of the occasion. If it is one of serious dignity, the speech should be serious and dignified. On occasions of informal good fellowship, the speech may be light and humorous. If anyone makes a speech on a political or business topic when he is supposed to make a speech of welcome, he violates the proprieties.

In the spring of 1925 Glenn Frank became President of the University of Wisconsin. In September of that year he delivered an address welcoming a new freshman class into the university. Note the skillfully designed introduction in which he puts himself on common ground with his audience. Observe the clarity of thought and statement in which he presents his message. Consider particularly the effective use of repetition of sounds, alliteration, which makes the wording euphonious and musical and yet does not obtrude itself into the consciousness of the listener. This short speech, delivered in clear ringing periods by a master of communication techniques and supported by strong impressions of unusual personal charm, made a deep impression on the audience.

President Frank spoke as follows: [8]

As administrative head of the University, I welcome you to its halls and to its opportunities.

In a sense there is just a trace of impropriety in my presuming to welcome you to this University in view of the fact that I arrived on its campus only three short weeks in advance of your coming. But in a deeper sense I shall never again be as well fitted to welcome an incoming class as I am this morning, because, for the second time in my life, I know exactly how a freshman feels. I speak as a freshman to freshmen.

I know the ancient and anesthetic ritual of presidential welcomes. I think I know most of the stock advice that has been given to freshmen from the days of Abelard to the epoch-making entrance of the class of '29 to the University of Wisconsin. But I shall indulge in none of that advice this morning. I want only to share with you my feelings about this University, which is to you and to me alike a new world of allurement and challenge.

From slightly different angles, you and I are together setting out on a great adventure this morning. Together we are going to find out whether it is possible for young men and young women to make themselves really at home in the modern world, able to work in harmony with the creative forces of their time instead of at cross-purposes to them. This is the research magnificent which you are about to undertake. And unless I completely misread the genius of this institution, you could not find a better setting for your experiment.

You will find the University a very human place. The distinguished scholars of the several faculties with whom it will be your privilege to associate are not scowling taskmasters but sympathetic friends.

You cannot be long on this campus without discovering the kind of teacher who represents the authentic Wisconsin tradition. The University is not interested in teachers who are mere merchants of dead yesterdays; it covets and captures men who are guides into unborn tomorrows, men who have objects as well as subjects, men who refuse to put conformity to old customs above curiosity about new ideas, men who are not content to be peddlers of petty accuracies when they are called to be priests and prophets of abundant living. You will find among the scholars of these faculties men who know how to be great specialists without becoming specialized men, men who have reverence for their materials, men who have mastered the facts in their respective fields, but men who see that all facts are dead

[8] Reprinted by permission of Mrs. Glenn Frank.

until they are related to the rest of knowledge and to the rest of life. In short you are to have the high privilege of associating with distinguished scholars who know how to "relate the coal scuttle to the universe," men who are shepherds of the spirit as well as masters of the mind.

But you will not expect too much of these teachers. In the deepest sense of the word, they cannot teach you anything; they can only help you to learn for yourselves.

In the social associations of this University you will acquire a poise and polish that you might not otherwise acquire, but this is not the primary end and aim of this institution. The University of Wisconsin is not built around a ballroom. It would be a sorry sort of young man who had to spend four expensive years in order to pick up a valet's knowledge of dress and demeanor.

In the pomp and pageantry of great games you will come to know the thrill of athletic victories as you throw your bodies into play or merge yourselves with the cheering thousands in the stadium. But the primary end and aim of this institution is not athletics. At the University athletics will be no mere interloper in our academic life but a fine and fundamental part of our whole educational process; athletics will be a vivid symbol of the fact that here we recognize that the truly educated man must have not only a sound mind but a sound body. And you will find that under such policies a university will produce more winning teams than could possibly be produced by an institution that regarded athletics as a mere adjunct to the educational process, very much as it might play impresario to a bullfight in an arena.

In the classrooms of this University you will hear many doctrines discussed, but in the deepest sense of the word it is not the business of this University to fill your minds with doctrines. As I have said many times and in many places, it is not the business of a university to teach its students what to think but to teach them how to think, and then to trust them to decide what to think as year by year they face the changing facts of a changing world.

The University does not exist to furnish your minds as an interior decorator might furnish your house; the University exists to free your minds.

The University does not exist merely to train you to be clever competitors in the world as it is; it exists to help you to become creative cooperators in the making of the world as it ought to be.

The University wants you to know the past in order that you may live wisely in the present.

I hope that you may find in the University a temporary retreat from the world in which you may become emancipated from the dead dogmas, the obsolete opinions, the irrational inhibitions, the silly superstitions, the foolish fears, and the cowardly cautions that crush and kill the uneducated mind.

One would have to be very old and very cold not to respond to the prospect of life in a university the very air of which is electric with the thrill of intellectual and spiritual adventure.

It is the determined purpose of all of us who have anything to do with the purpose and procedure of this institution to see to it that the University be and remain such a place.

As the administrative head of the University, I welcome you to its halls and to its opportunities.

SPEECHES OF FAREWELL

The speech of farewell should express the speaker's sentiments on the occasion of his leaving a group, an institution, or a community. It may contain a response to some speech that has been addressed to him immediately before, or to some presentation that has been made to him. In other words, a speech of farewell may be at the same time a speech of response and/or acceptance. The graduating senior may deliver the valedictory address which is a typical farewell speech. Speeches of farewell usually should be short.

SPEECHES OF PRESENTATION

Good taste requires that a presentation speech should not overdo expressions of appreciation. It should not overpraise the person or group to whom the presentation is being made; exaggerated language should be avoided. Deserved compliments should not be withheld but restraint should be observed. A speech of presentation may well contain one or more of the following:

1. The reason for the presentation.
2. A description of the gift itself, its history, its associations, its meaning, or its use.
3. An appreciation of, or a brief tribute to, the person, institution, or group to whom the presentation is made.

SPEECHES OF ACCEPTANCE

What has been said about speeches of presentation applies also to speeches of acceptance. The warning about the need for restraint should be heeded, with the additional caution not to overpraise the gift that you accept or those from whom it comes. A speech of acceptance should always express the thanks of the recipient. It may also contain:

1. A brief discussion of the meaning, use, or significance of the gift, and a pledge to those making the presentation that it will be used as they would wish.

2. A brief tribute to the person, institutions, or group making the presentation.

SPEECHES OF RESPONSE

A speech of response should serve to express appreciation and other appropriate sentiments in answer to a speech of welcome, or the conferring of some particular honor—such as an honorary degree or some other token of esteem. The speech of acceptance is one type of speech of response. A speech of response may contain:

1. An appreciation of the significance of the occasion.

2. A tribute to the organization or institution or community conferring the honor.

3. An explanation of the organization or institution represented by the speaker.

On June 4, 1927, George F. Baker, Chairman of the Board of the First National Bank of New York, made the following brief speech in presenting to Harvard University a group of buildings comprising what is known as the George F. Baker Foundation of the Graduate School of Business Administration.[9]

Gentlemen: First I want to thank you for this kind and ever-to-be-remembered reception. These buildings have turned out so unexpectedly well that I must extend congratulations to you. I hope and believe that this School is to be the standard for all others, but it must be remembered always that the standards of excellence must be maintained, not simply on the outside of the buildings but in the work and training on the inside.

[9] This speech and the one following by President Lowell are reprinted by permission of Appleton-Century-Crofts, Inc., and are from *Contemporary Speeches,* compiled by James M. O'Neill and Floyd K. Riley. (Copyright 1930, The Century Co.)

Mr. President, it gives me great pleasure to present to you the keys to these buildings.

To this simple and brief speech of presentation, President Abbott Lawrence Lowell of Harvard replied as follows:

Mr. Baker: on behalf of Harvard University I accept these keys as a symbol of your great gift whereof the material proofs are about us. I hope that your happiness may be commensurate with the privileges you have provided for generation after generation of young men seeking to enter on the career which you yourself have adorned.

A well-nigh perfect speech made to fit a special purpose was delivered by Abraham Lincoln to his fellow townsmen in Springfield, Illinois, on a rainy February morning in 1861, as he was leaving to become President of the United States. Study it and try to discover the elements which make it an appropriate and beautiful speech of farewell.

My Friends: No one, not in my situation, can appreciate my feelings of sadness at this parting. To this place and the kindness of these people, I owe everything. Here I have lived a quarter of a century and have passed from a young to an old man. Here my children have been born, and one of them lies buried. I now leave, not knowing when or whether ever I shall return, with a task before me greater than that which rested upon Washington. Without the assistance of that divine Being who ever attended him, I cannot succeed. With that assistance I cannot fail. Trusting in Him who can go with me, and remain with you, and be everywhere for good, let us confidently hope that all may yet be well. To His care commending you, as I hope in your prayers you may commend me, I bid you an affectionate farewell.

Two years and eight months later, this same man stood on the battlefield at Gettysburg, in the midst of the turmoil and the uncertainty of the war's outcome, and, in 266 simple words, delivered a speech of dedication which probably never has been equalled in all human history. Even though it is familiar to us all, we set it down here as a model to be read and studied.

Fourscore and seven years ago our fathers brought forth upon this continent a new nation, conceived in liberty and dedicated to the proposition that all men are created equal.

Now we are engaged in a great civil war, testing whether that nation or any nation so conceived and so dedicated can long endure. We are met on a great battlefield of that war. We have come to dedicate a portion of that field as a final resting place for those who here gave their lives that that nation might live. It is altogether fitting and proper that we should do this.

But in a larger sense we cannot dedicate, we cannot consecrate, we cannot hallow this ground. The brave men, living and dead, who struggled here have consecrated it far above our poor power to add or detract. The world will little note nor long remember what we say here, but it can never forget what they did here. It is for us, the living, to be dedicated here to the unfinished work which they who fought here have thus far so nobly advanced. It is rather for us to be here dedicated to the great task remaining before us—that from these honored dead we take increased devotion to that cause for which they gave the last full measure of devotion; that we here highly resolve that these dead shall not have died in vain; that this nation, under God, shall have a new birth of freedom; and that government of the people, by the people, and for the people shall not perish from the earth.

When one hears these familiar words recited today by an effective speaker like Raymond Massey or Charles Laughton, one still feels their vibrant power. They were not for a day but for all time!

ADDITIONAL READINGS

Brembeck, Winston L. and Howell, William S., *Persuasion* (New York: Prentice-Hall, 1952).

Bryant, Donald C. and Wallace, Karl R., *The Fundamentals of Public Speaking,* 3rd edition (New York: Appleton-Century-Crofts, 1960), pp. 457–70.

Minnick, Wayne, *The Art of Persuasion* (Boston: Houghton Mifflin Co., 1957).

Winans, James A., *Speech-Making* (New York: Appleton-Century, 1938).

QUESTIONS AND PROJECTS

1. Explain one of the following, using the method of *analysis:*

Blue Cross	USSR	Organized baseball
SEATO	Africa	Federal court system
NATO	United Nations	Higher education

2. Give a five-minute expository speech on some mechanical device. Plan to use *visual aids.*

3. Give a five-minute informational speech on informational speak-

ing. Use a little material from the text and as much from other sources as possible.

4. Select a political speech as carried in a magazine or newspaper. Analyze it to determine: (a) specific purpose, (b) method of organization, (c) factual content, and (d) emotional appeals. Evaluate the speech. Prepare a four-minute speech in which you describe the political speech to the class and explain your reactions to it.

5. If a political campaign is being conducted during the term, listen to and read a substantial sampling of the presentations made in behalf of the candidates. Prepare an evaluation of the campaign from the point of view of ethics.

6. Prepare a listing of controversial issues that relate to your university or college. Select one of these and prepare a speech to *convince* your classmates that your point of view is correct.

7. Prepare a five- to seven-minute speech to actuate your class audience. Make it an actual speech to secure action from this class. Sell an article; ask for donations or pledges "on-the-spot"; present petitions to be signed; etc.

8. Your class might actually hold a dinner some evening. If this can be arranged, your instructor should cooperate with a committee to choose the toastmaster and the speakers. The instructor and the toastmaster should meet with the speakers and decide upon the topics. A large share of the success of the project will depend upon the care with which the plans are made and upon the skill with which the toastmaster executes his function. All too often, the toastmaster ruins a series of after-dinner speeches by being "reminded" of a lot of more or less inappropriate jokes that might better remain untold. The speeches should be short and snappy and the *introductions by the toastmaster should be even more so.*

9. Present a seven-minute speech in which you examine and explain some historically significant public address. To prepare this speech, you will perform research on the background of the speaker and the situation. Included in the speech will be excerpts of the speech to illustrate your analysis. Your speech will be prepared as a complete manuscript and will be rehearsed and presented to the class as an oral reading project.

CHAPTER 12

Discussion and Debate

Section One—Discussion

Ours is an era of discussion in business, in government, and in society at large. Much of the speaking that settles the issues of our daily lives occurs in conferences, committee meetings, and other discussion situations. Practically everyone participates in discussions. The dormitory "bull session" which centers around a controversial social problem and in which a solution of some sort is sought is one familiar type of informal discussion. Organized groups hold meetings to transact business and to make plans for future projects. When such organizations operate democratically, their decisions are reached after discussion. Standing and special committees discuss particular phases of any group's activities and prepare reports for consideration and action by the parent organization. And so, in every phase of public and social living, we find ourselves in the role of discussion participants.

Problem Solving

The initial purpose of most discussion is *inquiry*. A group, large or small, formal or informal, feel a need or realize that they face a problem which they must solve. "How can we get better grades?" "How can we increase the city's water supply?" "How can we settle this labor dispute?" "What should be our attitude toward Red China?" The ultimate goal of discussion is to find answers to such questions, answers which will seem satisfactory to all or at least to a majority of the participating group. To arrive at the answers, each participant will contribute his information, experience, and understanding. This pooling process, when carried on conscientiously and open-mindedly, results in a total sum of facts and opinions which no single individual would be able to assemble by himself.

If maximum results are to be obtained from the give-and-take of discussion, three essential elements must be present in the situation: (1) a method for attacking the problem, (2) sound leadership, and (3) full and thoughtful participation by members of the group.

A PLAN FOR DISCUSSION

Obviously, before any satisfactory solution can be reached, the problem must be explored and understood. All possible solutions must be examined to determine which is best. Here is an outline of suggested steps that may be helpful in a problem-solving discussion:

- I. What is the problem?
  - A. Why has the problem come to the attention of the group?
  - B. Who is involved in the problem?
  - C. When and how did the problem originate?
  - D. What causes the problem?
- II. What solutions have been proposed?
  - A. Who proposed them?
  - B. What are the arguments for each proposal?
  - C. Who will benefit most from the adoption of each proposal?
  - D. What evils or disadvantages seem to be involved in each proposal?
  - E. Which solution has the most support?
    1. What are its special advantages?
    2. Do its advantages outweigh its disadvantages?
    3. Will it remove the causes of the difficulty?
- III. How can we secure the adoption of the solution that seems best?
  - A. What plan of action shall we follow?
  - B. What opposing views will we have to meet?
  - C. How can we "sell" the solution to those involved?

The foregoing outline will not be suitable in all details for every discussion situation. But whenever we try to solve a social, economic, civic, or personal problem, many of these questions have to be answered if we want to be sure that the final solution is sound. Solving a problem of broad scope may take days, weeks, or even months if proper attention is to be given to the steps in the suggested outline. For example, consider the work of a legislative committee, one of the most important discussion groups in our democracy. Its function is to investigate problems, consider solutions, and report recommendations. And, finally, the committee usually plans strategy for gaining acceptance of the solution which it recommends. Its deliberation on a single problem often consumes months and even years.

Large organizations have to operate through committees because they are the only feasible means of handling problems. When committee recommendations are presented, discussion usually is superseded by debate in which members of the organization speak for or against the specific proposals in the committee report. At this stage, amendments may be offered, occasionally taking the form of a substitute solution, but ordinarily the debating leads to either the adoption or the rejection of the committee's proposal.

THE DISCUSSION LEADER

Leaderless discussion is likely to be confused and ineffectual. The first function of the leader is to work out a discussion plan. Usually he performs this function, not by himself, but with the active assistance of others in the discussion group. The plans should fit the specific purposes of the discussion, but they usually should cover the appropriate questions suggested in the problem-solving outline. Other general functions of the leader should be:

1. To introduce and explain the problem.
2. To introduce members of the discussion group to each other (and to the audience, when there is one).
3. To establish good feeling between himself and the participants and among the participants.
4. To get the discussion started, usually by raising some relevant and provocative questions about the problem.
5. To see to it that all members get a chance to participate.

6. To ask questions designed to clarify the contributions of participants, when necessary.

7. To keep the discussion moving, *on the track*.

8. To relieve emotional tensions which may be built up by violent arguments.

9. To make summaries and transitions to help participants see what has been accomplished and what remains to be done.

The leader should be a person with good humor, tact, poise, and an open mind. He should be able to guide and control without dictating. He should be well informed on the problem under discussion.

DISCUSSION PARTICIPANTS

The best-laid plans of the most competent leader will not guarantee success without full and intelligent participation by the members of the discussion group. All too often the participants in discussion come with little or no preparation. They seem to assume that because no one person is to monopolize the spotlight, nobody need be much concerned about his knowledge of the topic under discussion. "Somebody else is sure to have something to say in getting things started and I'll be able to think of an idea or two as we go along" expresses an unfortunate attitude which spoils many conferences and committee meetings. Preparation for participation in discussion should be just as thorough and careful as for any other form of speaking.

If a discussion is to produce a balanced and comprehensive view of a problem, the various participants must be prepared to understand and evaluate what they hear. Such appreciation requires as much preparation as does the communication of one's own ideas. Participants should examine critically and carefully every idea and piece of evidence contributed to the pool of information and opinion. They do this, not from a desire to pick at weaknesses and faults, but rather from an earnest desire to see the problem through to the best possible solution.

Therefore, each participant should anticipate being questioned about his statements and be prepared to present supporting evidence and reasoning when called upon to do so. He can also expect to be asked to re-evaluate his own ideas in the light of the materials presented by others. One who comes into a discussion with haphazard thinking, incomplete information, and nothing but opinions "off the top of his head" will be at a loss when his ideas are challenged. Hit-or-miss thoughts may have some value, but they are likely to be ignored because of the way in which they are presented. Discussions should proceed upon evidence, sound reasoning, and careful analysis. Adequate preparation is, therefore, prerequisite to effective participation.

A second important requirement for effective participation is an attitude of fairness and open-mindedness. One of the vital techniques of democracy is disagreeing without being disagreeable. Agreeing with opinions which are really repugnant to us merely to be polite should be avoided. When one understands a point, he should be willing to agree or disagree, but he should never terminate the discussion by a perfunctory agreement which misrepresents his true beliefs. If one honestly agrees with the position someone else takes, he should say so and then join in ferreting out the consequences of the point of view with which he has agreed. If one disagrees, he should say so goodnaturedly and seek the reasons which lie behind the disagreement.

When we feel obliged to disagree with others, we should take time to make a searching inventory of our techniques of disagreement. We should ask ourselves whether or not we can disagree with others and still maintain pleasant and cordial personal relations with them. When someone in our group makes a statement we cannot accept as true or correct, what do we do? Do we keep silent for fear of getting into trouble? Or do we manage to make our divergent point of view known without arousing antagonism? When we have expressed our convictions, do we close our minds to further evidence and argument? Or do we manage to keep our minds open and control our tempers while others express different or contrary opinions? On this point, consider the observation of George F. Kennan: [1]

> It is the real mark of self-assurance, the sign of inner strength, to be conciliatory and respectful and understanding of the neighbor's point of view. There is no uglier tendency in American nature than the

[1] Quoted in Irving Lee's, *How to Talk with People* (New York: Harper and Brothers, 1952), p. 43.

quickness to moral indignation and to wild suspicions of bad faith which many of us display when other people do not think as we do.

Professor Irving Lee analyzed two hundred actual discussions which occurred in trying to settle real problems. He discovered five "patterns of disagreement," or ways of dealing with differences of opinion. Examine your characteristic behavior in the light of these patterns.[2]

1. *Unwillingness to listen to others' points of view.* When someone states a position with which you disagree, do you say, quietly, "Well, now, that isn't quite the way I see the matter, but I shall be glad to have you tell me more about your views?" Or are you so eager to argue for your own point of view that you can scarcely wait for the other person to finish what he is saying? Or do you simply counter by announcing that you know you are right and that you do not want to discuss the matter further?

2. *Treating others' points of view as absurd.* When you hear someone make a statement that seems to you incorrect, do you raise your eyebrows and express surprise that any intelligent person can hold such a ridiculous view? If you do, you are simply trying to stop the discussion by throwing up a roadblock of cold contempt for the opinions of others.

3. *Poking fun at the opinions of others.* Many a good argument and worthwhile opinion have been laughed out of court. Making fun of arguments we cannot answer is an old trick which often is effective, but which leaves hurt feelings in others. The least we can say in condemning this tactic is that it is not helping to pool the resources of a group who are grappling seriously with a real problem.

4. *Charging an opponent with unfairness.* Instead of meeting an opponent's argument, we look annoyed and say that he is using underhanded, sly tactics to put us personally in an unfavorable light. We impute bad faith and unworthy motives to him. We charge that he is seeking to serve some selfish purpose. Of course, this sort of evasion constitutes the well-known fallacy, attacking the person instead of meeting the argument.

5. *Refusing to go any further.* All too often what might

[2] *Ibid.*, p. 44ff.

otherwise be a profitable discussion comes to an abrupt end because one side simply announces with finality that there is no use in continuing the discussion since no change of opinion is possible, so far as they are concerned. A discussion which ends that way might better never have been begun; it is likely to leave the discussants further apart than they were at the beginning.

It goes without saying that any of the foregoing patterns will nullify and ruin a discussion and the democratic process. But when we discuss problems in a spirit of willingness to listen to others' points of view tolerantly, we reach the goal which David Lilienthal set forth in his essay, "This I Do Believe": [3]

> One of the most beautiful phrases in our language are the words which an American uses when he says to those with whom he has been in disagreement: "I'll go along with you. That's not the way I see it, but I'll go along." Out of this precept of reasonableness and respect for the opinions of others often issues one of the finest fruits of thought; a composite judgment, the product of many minds.
>
> The considered judgment of men who reason together embodies more than "tolerance," which is, after all, a rather negative concept. It is rather based upon an affirmative belief in the value of blending diverse experiences, diverse backgrounds. Such a composite or group judgment can be sturdier than any one of the individual judgments that make it up. This harmonizing of conflicting views into a common conclusion is not merely the trader's "splitting the difference"; it is not compromise for its own sake. It is a doctrine in exact contradiction to the growing fanaticism and dogmatism in the world, in which differences from an official party line are dealt with as traitorous and in which the accommodation of conflicting ideas is regarded as a sign of weakness rather than what it is in fact: a mark of strength.

It should clearly be stated here that tolerance does not mean a wishy-washy lack of faith in one's own convictions; certainly it does not suggest that one should not stand up and maintain his ideas. Students sometimes mistakenly suppose that thorough preparation and a willingness to tolerate and conciliate others are incompatible, but it is not so. Knowledge and understanding bring real tolerance. The more we learn, the more we realize

[3] David Lilienthal, *This I Do Believe* (New York: Harper and Brothers, 1949), pp. 35–36.

how much remains to be learned. Therefore, we should prepare our potential contributions to a discussion so thoroughly that we can present our point of view clearly and concisely, support it so far as is necessary, re-evaluate it in the light of what others say, and evaluate what others say in the light of what we know and understand. We must be able to express our own ideas with brevity, clarity, and good humor and to listen patiently and appreciatively to the ideas of others. Above all, we should not waste precious time arguing about questions of fact. Such issues should be settled by consulting the facts. We may argue about the interpretation of facts, the meaning of facts, the implications of facts—but never about facts themselves.

Forms of Discussion

CLASSROOM DISCUSSION

One type of discussion with which we are all very familiar is classroom discussion. This usually takes place under conditions somewhat different from those which affect group discussion elsewhere. The teacher usually plays a dominant role in classroom discussion; he directs, supervises, and controls the process. Only rarely does a leader outside the classroom exercise anything approaching the degree of control that the teacher exercises. Moreover, the classroom situation is characterized by common information and thinking.

A good deal of classroom discussion is carried on for the purpose of clarifying the knowledge of the participants and demonstrating to the teacher and to fellow students an understanding of facts and principles. For example, suppose that in an economics class the subject under discussion is Gresham's law. Presumably, the teacher knows what the law is and so do most of the students. They discuss it for the purpose of making sure that all understand it. When it becomes evident that they do, the discussion is over. Classroom discussion abounds in expository rather than persuasive speaking.

CONFERENCE DISCUSSION

Conferences are valuable mainly because they permit us to assemble, through discussion, a number of items of information and fit them together into meaningful patterns. Too often those who manage conference procedures mistakenly assume that, although the several participants bring nothing but ignorance, it will be possible to distill wisdom from it through discussion. No one can manufacture wisdom by adding ignorance to ignorance! Furthermore, when conference discussion becomes a struggle between persons and factions seeking their own selfish interests, nothing very valuable can come out of it.

In planning for a conference discussion it is important that all the principal divergent points of view be represented. If we are setting up a conference on work contracts in an industry, we probably would have the following groups represented: labor, management, stockholders, and the public. The leader (chairman) well might be a prominent economist or a government official.

The participants should be tolerant and informed and motivated by a genuine desire to reach as much agreement and to avoid as much friction as possible. The discussion should be problem-centered and as free as possible from personalities. Collaboration toward a common goal should be the controlling objective. It is most helpful to have a leader who is respected by all factions—if there are factions. He should avoid arbitrary rulings; he should be tactful in suggesting a shift away from issues which, for the moment, seem to be made more divisive by discussing them. Often when a conference is about to break up because of seemingly irreconcilable differences, the leader may save the situation by suggesting a brief intermission during which heated tempers may cool and factions may hold subconferences independently and decide to make concessions which otherwise might not be made. Thus compromise solutions to vexing problems may be worked out. Often the effectiveness of a conference is promoted by having a comfortable and pleasant meeting place which puts participants into a good mood. A discussion rarely is improved by hurry; taking time is of the essence.

PUBLIC DISCUSSION

Thus far we have been concerned with discussions that are more or less private in nature—the classroom discussion and the conference. Here we have self-contained groups who discuss their problems while temporarily isolated from audiences. The participants are concentrating their attention on each other and on their problems. But frequently a discussion is conducted by a group before, and for the benefit of, an audience; this type we call *public discussion*. Usually, the participants are experts or, at least, persons intimately involved in the problem under discussion. The goal here is still inquiry and standard planning procedures can be followed. But the primary purpose, at the moment, is not necessarily to solve a problem but rather to inform the audience as to the issues and the various points of view concerning them. Such public discussion may follow a number of different patterns; indeed there are so many varieties of public discussions that it seems unnecessarily confusing to explain them all. Therefore, we shall describe only the three most popular types.

The Panel. A panel discussion is arranged as follows: A chairman, selected in advance, and four to six interested and informed persons make up the panel. They sit in full view of the audience, usually on a raised platform, and carry on an enlarged conversation among themselves for the purpose of presenting information and various points of view to the audience. To be really effective, the discussion must be carefully planned in advance. An outline indicating the order in which different phases of the problem will be discussed should be agreed upon and adhered to by all the participants in the panel, particularly by the chairman. A rehearsal sometimes is very helpful in preparing a good panel discussion.

The business of the chairman is to keep the discussion "on the beam" and to summarize what has been said when the other panel members have finished. Neither of these tasks is easy. The chairman has to be constantly alert to prevent profitless digressions. Whenever he detects a tendency to wander away from the main problem, he should interrupt the speakers tactfully and bring the discussion back to it.

A good panel discussion uses extempore speaking and is effective in proportion to the clarity and adequacy of the outline from which it proceeds and to the speaking skill of the participants. Members of the panel must participate at all times even when they are not speaking. Only one member should speak at a time; nothing can be more confusing to an audience than the jumble that occurs when two or three members talk simultaneously.

Usually, when a panel discussion has been concluded, the chairman asks for questions and comments from the audience. If this is going to be done, it is well to announce this *forum* period at the opening of the program. During the forum, the chairman should perform all the functions of a presiding officer, seeing to it especially that everyone who desires to participate is given an opportunity. If questions or comments are not directed to any particular speaker, the chairman can use his judgment as to which speaker should reply. There should be an advance understanding as to the length of questions and statements from the floor, and a maximum number of people should be guaranteed a chance to participate. The larger the meeting, the greater the need for formality and rigid rules.

The Symposium. The symposium differs from the panel in that (1) there usually are fewer speakers in the symposium, (2) the symposium speakers deliver carefully prepared talks, (3) each symposium speaker delivers one speech, under a definite time limit, and (4) the symposium speakers present their material more in the manner of a formal public address.

Suppose that the problem for discussion is, What Should America's Foreign Policy Be? A symposium might be made up of four speeches, as follows: (1) The Isolationist Point of View, (2) World Union Now, (3) The United Nations' Role in Our Foreign Policy, and (4) All-out Aid to the Free Nations. Each speaker might be allotted ten minutes. When the four speeches have been made, the chairman may ask each speaker to comment briefly on the discussion and then permit a brief period of questions and comments from the audience.

The Lecture-Forum. Any public lecture turns into a discussion situation when it is followed by a forum period which becomes an integral part of the program. This is the most common type of public discussion. If there is a chairman, either he or the lecturer may conduct the forum part of the discussion. Often it is difficult to secure audience participation at the end of a formal lecture, and those willing to take a hand in the proceedings usually are those who have the least to contribute but merely want to air their pet peeves and prejudices. A skillful chairman can minimize this menace.

Section Two—Debate

Debating and discussion have a great deal in common. As we have seen, discussion begins with an appreciation of the need for solving a problem through the cooperation of a number of interested people. We discuss problems in order to develop an understanding of issues and to bring to light various possible ways of thinking and acting concerning them. For example, as citizens, we face the problem of financing the ever-increasing cost of government. We may begin our discussion by considering the causes of the mounting costs, the value of various governmental activities, and the means by which additional revenue may be raised. Some participants in the discussion may suggest the elimination of certain government services; some may propose higher income taxes; others may argue for additional corporation taxes, etc. Out of such wide-ranging discussion, certain specific proposals for action may emerge and, when they do, the time for debating will have arrived.

In this section we refer primarily to the type of formal debating which most often takes place in college speech courses, in forensic meets, and before audiences. Such debating requires definite rules governing choice of proposition, procedure, selection of issues, clarification of the "burden of proof," etc. Such formal debate is most easily adapted to classroom practice. Of course, many of the same techniques and suggestions can be applied to the debating that takes place on the floors of legislatures or in an organization's business meetings.

Propositions for Debate

We *discuss* a *problem;* we *debate* a *proposition.* Discussion ends with a proposition; debate starts with one. All the speaking in a debate takes the form of argument for and against a specific proposal. We cannot debate "The Foreign Policy of the United States"; that is a problem for discussion. We can debate "The United States should enter the common market." We cannot debate the problem of federal taxation, but we can debate, "Federal taxes on corporations should be increased by fifty per cent." A good debater should also be an effective discussant but not everyone who can make a contribution to a discussion is necessarily a strong debater. Debating usually proceeds under more rigid rules than discussion does and is more formal.

There are seven characteristics of propositions suitable for debate:

1. A *good proposition is complete.* We cannot debate, "Congress vs. the Supreme Court." We can debate, "The Constitution of the United States should be so amended that any law declared unconstitutional by the Supreme Court shall become valid if re-enacted by Congress in the next succeeding session." No phrasing should be omitted that would make the proposition complete.

2. A *good proposition is declarative.* The proposition should be stated in a declarative sentence; it should not be phrased as a question. Instead of, "Should the states ratify the Child Labor Amendment?" the proposition should read, "The several states should ratify the Child Labor Amendment to the Federal Constitution."

3. A *good proposition is clear.* The proposition should be precise, specific, and unambiguous; it should state exactly what is to be proved or disproved and not something similar to it. For example, instead of debating, "Football is dangerous," we might better debate, "Intercollegiate football should be abolished."

4. A *good proposition is single.* We should debate one proposal at a time. "Military drill and final examinations should be abolished" is not a good proposition.

5. A *good proposition is brief.* It should be as brief as it can be and, at the same time, fulfill the other requirements. Instead of debating, "For the betterment of this university, a good course in debating, taught by a competent instructor, should be added to the curriculum, even if some other course has to be

dropped," we should phrase the proposition, "A course in debating should be offered in this university."

6. *A good proposition is stated affirmatively.* Those who are trying to change what *is* (the status quo) into what they think *should be* are the *affirmative.* The position they take should be expressed in the proposition. In the law courts, the plaintiff or the prosecution is the affirmative, the defendant is the negative. By definition, the defendant in a criminal case is considered innocent until proved guilty; those trying to prove him guilty are on the affirmative. We cannot debate, "The state should tax gasoline." Every state is doing that. We can debate, "All state taxes on gasoline should be repealed," or "The Wisconsin state gasoline tax should be increased two cents per gallon."

7. *A good proposition is debatable.* A debatable proposition is one with two sides for which arguments may be presented; it is one about which intelligent and well-informed people may hold opposing opinions even when the available facts are known. Better than debating, "The Nazi party leaders were guiltless," would be to debate, "The War-Crimes Commission should not have condemned the Nazi party leaders to execution."

Burden of Proof

The burden of proof in a debate is the responsibility for establishing the truth, the validity, or the desirability of the proposition. If the proposition is stated affirmatively (as it should be), the burden of proof rests upon the affirmative. Since the affirmative oppose the existing situation, are dissatisfied with things as they are, have a grievance and want a change, they bear the burden of proving that they are right. This responsibility never can be shifted to the negative. When the affirmative have presented enough proof to win unless the negative refute their "case," the responsibility for meeting the affirmative's argument then resting upon the negative is called the *burden of rebuttal.* This burden should not be confused with the burden of proof.

Issues

The issues are those vital questions which have to be answered "Yes" or "No" before one can be justified logically in being for or against the proposition. Most debates are on so-called "propositions of policy," i.e., they have to do with the advisability, the expediency, or the desirability of making specific changes in existing conditions. Two issues occur again and again in debating policy proposals and are known as "stock issues." These are:

1. Is there something seriously wrong in the present situation? Is some change needed?

2. If there is something demonstrably wrong with what now is, will the affirmative proposal remedy it?

However we phrase these questions, they are bound to appear in some form in almost every debate. The first demands that we consider the reasons for changing the existing situation or conditions. The second forces us to consider the adequacy, effectiveness, and practicability of the proposed remedy. The precise phrasing of the stock issues is determined by the proposition which is being debated.

The Affirmative Case

When the issues have emerged out of the controversy over the proposition, the affirmative have before them the complete picture of their responsibility in the debate; they have the "burden" of supporting adequately with evidence and argument their answers to the issues. The negative may choose to relieve the affirmative of some portion of their potential burden of proof by agreeing with them on one or more of the issues. If so, the conceded issue drops out of the affirmative's responsibility; their case then consists in sustaining their position on the remaining issues.

The Negative Case

To win the debate, the negative must prevent the affirmative from proving that the affirmative answer on at least one of the issues is correct. The negative case may take one of four forms:

1. *Pure refutation.* Here the negative point out all of the weaknesses they can in the affirmative's attempt to establish their position on the issues. They may do this by successfully blocking the affirmative either on all of the issues or on any one of them.

2. *Defense of the present.* This type of negative case goes beyond simple refutation. The negative argue that there is no foundation for the affirmative proposition because the present situation is reasonably satisfactory. They make the first stock issue the battleground by contending that there is no justification for any change at all.

3. *Adjustments or repairs.* The negative admit that the existing situation is not wholly satisfactory, but they argue that it can be patched up and made reasonably satisfactory by relatively minor changes. In using this type of case, the negative must be very careful not to concede too much ground on the first stock issue.

4. *Counter proposition.* The negative concede the first stock issue; they admit that the present situation is not satisfactory and that some change is desirable. However, they "counter" the affirmative proposal with one of their own. In effect they say, "We admit that something ought to be done but we have a better solution for the problem." A counter proposition must be really counter—i.e., it must be fundamentally inconsistent with the affirmative's proposition. If it is possible to adopt both the affirmative and the negative propositions, then the negative are not really offering a counter proposal.

Rebuttal Speeches

Rebuttal consists in attacking opposing arguments, answering opponents' questions, and reinforcing one's own case. It is very important to direct the rebuttal at vital issues; if the major points in the opponents' arguments can be met effectively, there should be little need for concern about trivial ones.

It is often effective to answer the main contentions of the opponents in the order of their original presentation. This procedure makes it easy for the audience to follow the ebb and flow of the debate and crystallizes the real issues. A common weakness in rebuttal speeches is that they lack any definite pattern; it is hard for the audience and the judge to know exactly what the refutation is intended to accomplish. The refutation of a point should involve three steps:

1. An accurate and fair statement of the precise point at issue.

2. A concise statement of the evidence and reasoning contrary to the opponents' point.

3. A clinching summary showing how the refutation of the particular point has damaged the opponent's whole case and strengthened one's own.

Forms of Support in Debating

Debating probably requires more attention to logical proof than any other form of speaking. But the emphasis on logic does not mean that effective debating should be coldly analytical, devoid of emotion and feeling. Debating is persuasive speaking. It is speaking to an audience. A debater's purpose should be to win support for his views about the proposition. And he can employ any or all of the forms of support required to explain and to persuade.

Often, significant portions of a debater's speech will be expository; any of the methods of exposition we have discussed in the preceding chapter can be useful to a debater. Motivation, of course, is his principal business. All the methods of proof and techniques of attention, described in Chapter 10, deserve consideration.

We also must mention here that delivery of a debate speech calls for the same qualities as any good public speech. The content and the delivery should be audience-centered. Such practices as addressing the judge ("Honorable Judge") or the opposition ("Honorable Opponents"), or speaking directly to the opponents, are no longer thought effective.

Chairman of the Debate

A formal debate before an audience requires a chairman to introduce the debate, to announce the speakers in turn, to explain the format of the debate to the audience if they are not familiar with it, to enforce time limits, to conduct a forum if it follows the debate, to announce the judges' decisions (or to administer the voting in an audience-decision debate), etc. The chairman should be thoroughly familiar with the procedures and rules of debating. In his remarks, he should never discuss the proposition for debate, except perhaps noting the significance of the subject and the occasion. His introductions should be brief and simple, usually indicating only the name and debate position of the speaker—e.g., "The debate will be opened for the affirmative by Mr. Charles Johnson of Midland University."

Types of Debate

Conventional debating pits two teams, usually of two speakers each, against each other, with each speaker given approximately ten minutes for a main or constructive speech and five minutes for a rebuttal speech. The debate proceeds as follows:

First affirmative constructive speech;
First negative constructive speech;
Second affirmative constructive speech;
Second negative constructive speech;
First negative rebuttal speech;
First affirmative rebuttal speech;
Second negative rebuttal speech; and
Second affirmative rebuttal speech.

(Sometimes the order in which the debaters have spoken in the constructive speeches is changed in rebuttal.) The reason for allowing the affirmative the advantage of the final rebuttal speech is that the affirmative bear the burden of proof. Timekeepers are used and debaters should stop promptly when notified that their allotted time has expired. The chairman, or the timekeeper, should enforce the time schedule rigorously.

Cross-Question debating originated in Oregon and is sometimes known as "The Oregon Plan." The procedure is as follows:

An opening speech by the first affirmative speaker;
A cross-examination of the first affirmative speaker by the second negative speaker;
An opening speech by the first negative speaker;
A cross-examination of the first negative speaker by the second affirmative speaker;
A summary of the negative case by the second negative speaker; and

A summary of the affirmative case by the second affirmative speaker.

In order to make this type of debate a success, the chairman must be competent and the participants must be experienced in the art of cross examination. The questions asked in cross examination must be clear, concise, and relevant to the issues. The debater who is being questioned must be given adequate opportunity to answer without being constantly interrupted with further questions. Confused haggling destroys any values which this format may possess.

The Direct-Clash Debate. There is an advance agreement between the two teams on the issues. The debate begins with a statement by the first affirmative speaker on any one of the issues. The first negative debater proceeds to discuss the issue which the affirmative has raised. This initiates the first direct clash. Following this initial rebuttal, there is a series of speeches and rebuttals in alternation until the judge announces that the first clash has been decided in favor of one of the teams. Then another clash starts and proceeds to the same conclusion. It is of paramount importance that there be clear-cut preliminary agreements on the details of the procedure to be followed in this type of debating.

Section Three—Parliamentary Procedure

Much of the discussion and debate in which we participate takes place in meetings governed by certain accepted principles and rules known as *parliamentary law.* In a democratic society, it is inevitable that most citizens will be called upon to participate in social, business, and civic organizations. Therefore, it is highly desirable that we should know how to contribute most to the work of the groups of which we are members.

Basic Principles

There is a great deal of misunderstanding of the purpose and function of parliamentary principles. It is often mistakenly supposed that they have been developed to hamper the transaction of business—because the rules of parliamentary procedure are so often misused by those who seek their own advantage at the expense of other people.

Efficiency is the first objective of parliamentary law. The essential difference between a group working under parliamentary procedure and one that recognizes no such code is that the first is a well-conducted, efficient organization while the second is a free-for-all, inefficient mob. The chief purpose of parliamentary rules is to make possible the transaction of the maximum amount of business in the minimum length of time. Anyone who uses it to waste time perverts its very nature.

Safeguarding equal rights and privileges is the second basic purpose. Parliamentary procedure is designed to protect the democratic rights of every individual and every group so far as that can be done consistently with promoting the welfare of the organization to which they belong. While the rule of the majority is assured, certain rights of the minority and of the individual are safeguarded.

Forming an Organization

There are two types of organization, the temporary and the permanent. Since the temporary organization has no constitution or bylaws, the parliamentary rules to be used have to be based on common consent. Usually when the people who are to form the organization have assembled, one of those who have arranged for the meeting calls it to order, makes a statement of the purpose and suggests ways and means of accomplishing the objectives. On such an occasion, it is proper for the presiding officer to say, "Unless there are objections, the rules of parliamentary procedure as laid down by Robert (or some other authority) will govern our deliberations." If an objection is raised, the assembly must decide by vote what code is to be used.

When a number of people decide to form a permanent organization, they should begin by notifying all those who may be interested of their intention to hold a meeting at a certain time and place. When the hour for starting the meeting arrives, someone who has played a leading role in calling the group together should take the chair and make a brief statement explaining the purpose of the gathering. Then he should either nominate someone to serve as temporary chairman and call for a voice vote on the nomination, or ask someone else to make a nomination and then call for a vote.

Upon taking the chair, the temporary chairman calls for the nomination of a temporary secretary who is chosen as the chairman has been. A committee to draft a constitution and bylaws should be appointed by the chairman or elected by the group. Obviously this committee can do its work best if it has the benefit of hearing a full expression of the desires, attitudes, and thoughts of those present regarding the nature of the permanent organization to be formed. Following this informal discussion, the chairman announces a date and place for the next meeting and declares the first meeting adjourned.

CONSTITUTION AND BYLAWS

The committee may well begin its work by examining the constitutions and bylaws of other similar organizations. A good constitution usually includes the following:

A preamble, stating the aims or purposes of the organization.
Article 1. Name of organization.
Article 2. Requirements for membership and method of electing members.
Article 3. Officers—length of terms, method of election, duties.
Article 4. Membership of Executive Committee and method of election.
Article 5. Time and place of regular meetings and method of calling special meetings.
Article 6. Methods of amending constitution.

Bylaws usually should cover the following items:

Section 1. Dues.
Section 2. Parliamentary authority.
Section 3. Definition of quorum.
Section 4. Method of changing bylaws.

Special attention should be given to specifying in Section 2 some final authority on procedure not covered by the constitution or bylaws. Some of the leading available authorities are Robert's *Rules of Order*, Sturgis' *Standard Code of Parliamentary Procedure*, and Auer's *Parliamentary Procedure.*

QUORUM

By definition a *quorum* is the number of members of an organization necessary for the legal transaction of business. The secretary is obliged to determine whether or not a quorum is present whenever a question is raised about it.

SECOND MEETING

The second meeting of the permanent organization will be devoted to the consideration and adoption of the report of the committee on constitution and bylaws. After calling the meeting to order the temporary chairman will ask for the report of the committee. The chairman of the committee should then read through the entire proposed constitution and bylaws. He should then go back and present the constitution article by article, or section by section (if articles contain more than one section). After each article, or section, has been read, the presiding officer asks whether there are any proposed changes or amendments. Changes agreeable to the committee may be incorporated without a vote. Those not acceptable to the committee must be adopted or rejected by a formal vote. After the assembly has acted on each article or section of the constitution, the chairman of the committee should move the adoption of the constitution as a whole, as it then stands with the amendments and changes that have been approved. The bylaws are then adopted in a similar fashion.

DUTIES OF OFFICERS

When the constitution and bylaws have been adopted, the next item of business is the election of officers and committees. Those elected usually take office at once.

Chairman. The presiding officer, variously called *chairman, president, speaker,* or *moderator*, bears the principal responsibility for maintaining order, seeing to it that all members have equal opportunity to participate in discussion, and conducting business according to the provisions of the constitution and bylaws and the parliamentary code. The chairman should be absolutely impartial in everything he says and does. He should not enter into the debate on any motion unless he has first called someone else to the chair and has taken his place on the floor with the other members. (This should be done very rarely and only under unusual circumstances, lest he impair his character as an impartial presiding officer.) He does not vote except when by so doing he can cause a tie or break a tie, or when the vote is by secret ballot.

The chairman should always have at hand copies of the constitution and bylaws and the recognized parliamentary manual. It is well for him to find out in advance what business is to come before the meeting, in order that he may be as helpful as possible to those who have matters to present. The good chairman does not parade his technical knowledge; he is tactful in dealing with members who lack information as to proper forms and procedures; he does not embarrass those who use incorrect techniques but restates their remarks or motions correctly without drawing undue attention to their mistakes. He always prefers the spirit of a rule to its letter. General Robert, the first great authority on parliamentary procedure, said, "Never be more technical or any more strict than is absolutely necessary for the good of the meeting." Of course, the larger and more formal the meeting, the more rigid and formal should be the conduct of business.

Secretary. The secretary is responsible for keeping accurate and complete records of the meetings. These records are called *minutes.* They should begin by stating the name of the organization, the place and date of the meeting, and the name of the presiding officer. They should include all motions and resolutions, with the names of their proposers and the seconds that have been presented, whether they have been passed or rejected. The minutes should show all committee reports in full, the actions taken on them, and any other facts that may be necessary to explain exactly what was done. The minutes should be completely impartial, impersonal, and factual; they should not contain the secretary's comments concerning anything that happened. For most organizations there is no objection to keeping the minutes in typewritten form and in a loose-leaf notebook. However, where matters of great importance are involved it may be wise to keep them in long-hand and in a bound notebook to prevent unauthorized changes or easy tampering. Usually, the secretary takes running notes and transcribes them into a complete record after the meeting has adjourned.

Treasurer. The treasurer keeps careful and detailed accounts of all financial transactions. It is important that he have on hand receipts for disbursements and specific written authorization from the president or secretary for the payment of bills. For his own protection, the treasurer should insist upon an official audit at the end of his term. A treasurer not familiar with accounting methods should seek the advice of someone who is.

Committees. A great deal of the business of every organization is carried on by and through committees. Committees save time, permit freer and fuller discussion, and bring out facts not available to all of the membership. The constitution usually prescribes what "standing committees" will function and how members of these are to be chosen. A standing committee is permanent in the sense that its membership is always complete and it is available at any time to consider matters which come under its jurisdiction. Social, finance, and membership committees are common standing committees. Often these committees are elected.

A special committee functions only with respect to the problem which makes its appointment necessary. It is sometimes called an *ad hoc* committee—a committee which pertains "to this" problem only. Most often such committees are appointed by the president.

In appointing committees, the president usually should select members who have a special knowledge of and interest in the matter "committed." Unless there is special reason to the contrary, parliamentary courtesy dictates that the member who makes the motion for the appointment of the committee should be named chairman of it.

Conducting Business

When a member wishes to present a proposal to the assembly, he should rise and address the presiding officer, "Mr. Chairman," "Mr. President," or "Madam Chairman." He should wait until the chairman recognizes him either by name or title, "Mr. Jones," "The Senator from the Third District," or the like. If two or more members address the chair simultaneously, the chair should recognize the one who has not previously spoken or one who will speak on the side opposite to that which has just been presented (if the chairman has any way of knowing).

MAKING A MOTION

When a member wants to have a matter discussed, he should bring it "before the house" by presenting it in the form of a motion or a resolution. If the motion or resolution is long or complicated, the member offering it should hand a written copy to the secretary. He should say, "I move that such and such action be taken," or "I move the adoption of the following resolution: 'Resolved – – –.'" The forms "I move you – – –," "I make a motion to – – –," and "I so move" are incorrect.

As soon as a motion has been made, the chairman should ask, "Is there a second?" A member desiring to second a motion may do so without rising or addressing the chair and being recognized. When the motion has been seconded, the chairman says, "It has been moved and seconded that – – –. Are there any remarks?" (Or "Is there any discussion?") The proposal is then "before the house" for debate. Unless this procedure is followed, a great deal of time may be wasted in vague talk about still vaguer proposals which have not been formally placed before the meeting.

VOTING

The common way of discovering the will of an organization is *viva-voce* voting, voting "by the living voice." When all those wanting to speak for or against a motion have been heard, the chairman asks, "Are you ready to vote?" Hearing nothing to the contrary, he then says, "The vote is on Mr. X's motion to – – –. All those in favor, please say *Aye*. Those opposed, please say *No*." After the vote, he says, "The motion is carried (or the motion is lost)."

If anyone feels that the chairman has misjudged the voice vote, he may "call for a division" as a point of personal privilege. When such a call is made, the chairman asks all those in favor of the motion to stand, or raise their hands. The secretary counts them. Then the chairman asks those opposed to stand, or raise their hands. The secretary counts again and then reports the tally to the chair. The chair then announces the vote and declares the motion carried or lost. Only on issues of great importance, where members should be allowed to vote in secret, is a written ballot used.

ORDER OF BUSINESS

The following order of business, sometimes called the *agenda,* is usually prescribed:

1. The chairman calls the meeting to order.
2. The chairman asks the secretary to read the minutes of the previous meeting which, following the reading, are corrected (if necessary) and then declared approved.
3. Unfinished business is considered. Any action that was in progress at the preceding meeting and left unfinished is then given further consideration.
4. Reports of standing committees are heard and acted upon.
5. Reports of special ("ad hoc") committees are heard and acted upon.
6. New business is considered.
7. The chairman adjourns the meeting, usually after a motion to that effect has been passed.

COMMITTEE REPORTS

After a committee chairman has presented a report, he should move that it be *filed* or *adopted.* A report that is strictly factual or informational should merely be filed. A report calling for specific action should be adopted (or rejected) or re-referred to the committee for further study. It is proper to adopt portions of a committee report while rejecting other portions. This action is accomplished by offering amendments to the motion to adopt the report.

Classes of Motions

So far as possible, motions are listed here in their order of precedence, starting with the lowest. (When a motion "takes precedence" over others, it must be considered and voted on before the others.)

MAIN MOTIONS

A main motion is one which brings a matter of business before the assembly for consideration and/or action. There are two kinds of main motions: *general* and *special.*

When the purpose of the motion is to initiate discussion on some proposal, it is a *general* main motion.

When the motion affects actions already taken or is designed to influence future action, it is a *special* main motion. There are four principal *special* main motions: *to create special orders, to rescind, to reconsider*, and *to resume consideration.*

1. *To Create Special Orders.* The purpose of this motion is to set a time for the consideration of a specific matter—to guarantee that it may be discussed fully at the specified future time. The passing of this motion gives the "special order" precedence over anything else that may be on the agenda, when the time set in the motion arrives. The form in which the motion should be made is:

> I move that the question of an assessment be made a special order of business at 8:45 P.M. in our next meeting.

2. *To Rescind.* The effect of a favorable vote on this motion is to undo or nullify the effects of a previous action. The proper form is:

> I move to rescind the action taken in February, levying a special assessment to be paid in April.

3. *To Reconsider.* The purpose of this motion is to bring back for further discussion some motion previously voted on. Its effect, if passed, is to reopen the entire matter for debate just as if no action had previously been taken. Traditionally, it has been parliamentary practice to require that a motion to reconsider be made only by a member who voted on the winning side when the original action was taken. For a number of rather persuasive reasons, this rule has now been relaxed and, in most organizations, *any* member is permitted to move a reconsideration. The proper form is:

> I move that our action on the proposal to levy a special assessment be reconsidered.

This motion is debatable only if the motion to which it is applied was debatable. Passage of the motion to reconsider does not void the previous action; it merely reopens the question for further discussion and another vote.

4. *To Resume Consideration.* When a motion has been laid on the table or postponed indefinitely or when adjournment has interrupted the discussion of a motion, it is proper to move for a resumption of consideration. The effect of an affirmative vote on this motion is to bring back to life some motion previously disposed of by an action less definite than rejection. The proper wording of the motion is:

I move that we resume consideration of the motion to increase the special assessment, which was laid on the table at our meeting of June 6th.

or

I move that we resume consideration of the motion to increase the special assessment, which was postponed indefinitely at our meeting of June 6th.

or

I move that we resume the discussion of the motion to increase the special assessment which was in progress at the time of adjournment on June 6th.

SUBSIDIARY MOTIONS

These motions are called *subsidiary* because they are dependent upon the main motions and provide various ways of disposing of main motions. They are presented here in the order of their precedence, lowest to highest.

1. *Postpone Indefinitely.* Passing this motion is almost equivalent to a negative vote on the main motion to which it is applied. It takes precedence only over main motions. The proper form is:

I move that the motion be postponed indefinitely.

The effect of passing this motion is to kill the motion to which it refers. It is frequently used to test the voting strength of the opposing sides in advance of a direct vote on the main motion; members may be willing to vote for indefinite postponement though they would not care to vote against the motion itself. A motion which has been postponed indefinitely can be resurrected only as a new main motion, or by a motion to resume consideration.

2. *Amend.* This motion takes precedence only over the *main motion* and *postpone indefinitely.* The proper forms are:

I move to amend the motion by striking out ---, by inserting ---, by adding ---, by dividing ---, or by substituting ---.

Such subsidiary motions as *postpone to a certain time, limit debate,* and *recess* are subject to amendment as to the time. An amendment to a main motion may be amended, but an amendment to an amendment to an amendment cannot be considered. Amendments must be germane but they may be hostile—i.e., they must have a clear bearing on the motion to which they are applied but their effect may completely defeat the purpose of the original motion.

3. *Commit.* This motion takes precedence over *main motions, amendments,* and *motions to postpone indefinitely.* The proper form is:

I move that the matter be referred to the committee on (designating the appropriate *standing* committee).

or

I move that the chairman appoint (or we elect) a special committee of (specify the number) to consider the matter.

Upon passage of this motion, the matter referred to the committee can be considered further only when the committee brings in its report.

4. *Postpone to a Certain Time.* This motion takes precedence over *main motions,* and motions *to commit, to amend,* and *to postpone indefinitely.* The proper form is:

I move that the question be postponed until (name the time).

It can be amended only as to the time. Matters postponed to a certain time become *orders of the day* when the time arrives. In contrast to the motions to *postpone indefinitely* and to *lay on the table,* which are unfriendly to the *main motion,* the motion to *postpone to a certain time* may be used in a way wholly friendly to the motion; its effect may be merely to delay consideration until a more favorable time.

5. *Limit or Extend Limits of Debate.* This motion takes pre-

cedence over *postpone to a certain time, commit, amend,* and *postpone indefinitely.* The proper forms are:

I move that the debate on this motion be limited (specify limitations—time of each speaker, total time of debate, number of speeches, etc.).

or

I move that the total time of the debate, the time allotted to each speaker, etc., be limited as follows: ---.

Since one of the cardinal freedoms in a democracy is free speech, any motion that limits or extends it requires a *two-thirds majority.*

6. *Previous Question.* This motion has precedence over *main motions* and all subsidiary motions except *lay on the table.* The proper form is:

I move the previous question.

The motion is *undebatable* and requires a *two-thirds vote* because it proposes a limitation on free discussion. When the motion is made and seconded, the chairman should say, "Shall the previous question be put? All those in favor, please rise (or hold up hands). All those opposed, please rise (or hold up hands)." A two-thirds affirmative vote has the effect of forcing an immediate vote on the pending motion, without any further debate. If the previous question is defeated, the discussion proceeds as if the motion had not been made.

7. *Lay on the Table.* This motion is sometimes called *postpone temporarily.* It takes precedence over all other subsidiary and main motions. The proper form is:

I move that the question be laid on the table.

This motion is not debatable and, if it is passed, it cannot be reconsidered. Laying a motion on the table takes with it any amendments which may be pending, and, likewise, laying amendments on the table carries with them the pending main motion. The vote on this motion is often used as a test of sentiment before voting on the main motion. (See discussion of *Postpone Indefinitely.*) A motion which has been laid on the table remains there until the assembly passes a main motion to resume consideration.

INCIDENTAL MOTIONS

These motions are so named because they arise incidentally as business is being conducted. In a sense, some of the following are not really motions at all since they do not even require a vote but are settled by rulings of the chairman. It is extremely difficult to assign any order of precedence to the incidental motions.

1. *Division of Assembly.* Proper form:

> I call for a division;
>
> or merely
>
> Division!

This call has the effect of a demand that a voice vote be checked as to its validity, as announced by the chairman, by a rising vote or a count of raised hands. Sometimes, when the chairman cannot be sure of the result of a voice vote, he himself may call for a division. No second is required and the call is not debatable.

2. *Division of a Question.* When a motion contains two or more distinct parts which can be considered separately, a member may ask that the question be divided and the parts each voted on separately. Proper form:

> I move that the motion be divided into two parts as follows ---, and that we vote on the parts one at a time.

This motion does not require a second and is not debatable. The chairman decides immediately whether or not the division shall be made.

3. *Objection to Consideration.* This motion can be made only before debate on a main motion begins. The proper form is:

> I object to the consideration of this question.

It requires no second, can be made while another person is speaking, is not debatable, and requires a two-thirds vote. When an objection is raised, the chairman shall immedately call for a standing or hand-raising vote, saying, "Shall the question be considered?" If there is a two-thirds negative vote, he says, "The objection is sustained; the question will not be considered." The motion takes precedence over all but privileged motions.

4. *Suspend Rules.* This motion takes precedence over all main and secondary motions. The proper form is:

I move to suspend the rules as follows: – – –.

The motion is not debatable and requires a two-thirds vote. The effect of passing the motion is to nullify specific rules for a specific purpose and for the immediate action to be taken. After the action has been disposed of, the rules go back into force.

5. *Withdraw a Motion.* This motion has precedence over *main motions, secondary motions,* and *suspend the rules.* The proper form is:

I ask leave to withdraw my motion.

The motion requires no second and is not debatable. When a request for leave to withdraw a motion is made, the chairman should say, "If there is no objection, the motion will be withdrawn." If there is objection, a majority vote is required to grant the request.

6. *Parliamentary Inquiry.* This really is a request for information and not a motion at all. It takes precedence over all motions except privileged questions. The form is:

I rise to a parliamentary inquiry.

The chairman asks the member to state his inquiry which usually is for information as to correct procedure, the stage which the discussion has reached, etc. The motion requires no second and is not debatable.

7. *Point of Order.* The object in raising a point of order is to draw attention to an alleged violation of the rules or an error in procedure. The form is:

I rise to a point of order.

No second is required and no debate is permitted. The chairman asks, "What is your point?" or says, "State your point." When the member has made his point clear, the chairman says either, "Your point is well taken," or, "Your point is not well taken." If the point is well taken, the chairman should try to rectify the mistake which has been made. A member should raise a point of order only when he considers the breach of rules or the departure from correct

Order of Precedence	Requires a Second	Debatable	Amendable	Required Vote	Applies To	Motions That Can Be Applied [1]	Can Be Renewed At Same Meeting	May Interrupt Speaker
I Privileged Motions								
Adjourn	Yes	No	No	Majority	No other motion	None	Yes [2]	No
Recess	Yes	No	Yes [3]	Majority	No other motion	Amend [3]	Yes [2]	No
Personal Privilege	No	No	No	None	No other motion	None	No	Yes
II Incidental Motions [4]								
Division of Assembly	No	No	No	None	Voting	None	No	Yes
Division of Question	No	No	No	None	Main motion; amendment	None	No	No
Objection to Consideration	No	No	No	⅔ (negative)	Main motion	None	No	Yes
Suspension of Rules	Yes	No	No	⅔	None	None	Yes [2]	Yes
Withdrawal of Motion	No	No	No	None	All motions	None	Yes [2]	No
Inquiry	No	No	No	None	None	None	No	Yes
Point of Order	No	No	No	None	Procedural errors	None	No	Yes
Appeal	Yes	Yes	No	Tie or majority	Chairman's rulings	Previous question, reconsider, limit debate, lay on	No	Yes
III Subsidiary Motions								
Lay on Table	Yes	No	No	Majority	Main; amendment	None	Yes [2]	No
Previous Question	Yes	No	No	⅔	Debatable motions	None	Yes [2]	No
Limit Debate	Yes	No	Yes [3]	⅔	Debatable motions	Amend	Yes [2]	No
Postpone to Certain Time	Yes	Yes [3]	Yes [3]	Majority	Main motions	Amend, previous question, limit debate	Yes [2]	No
Commit	Yes	Yes [3]	Yes [3]	Majority	Main, amend	Previous question, amend, limit debate	Yes [2]	No
Amend	Yes	Yes	Yes	Majority	Changeable motions	Reconsider, all subsidiary	No	No
Postpone Indefinitely	Yes	Yes	No	Majority	Main motions	Previous question, limit debate	No	No
IV Main Motions								
Resume Consideration	Yes	No	No	Majority	Main, amend, appeal	None	Yes [2]	No
Reconsider	Yes	Yes	No	Majority	Main, amend	None	No	Yes
Rescind	Yes	Yes	No	Majority	Main	All subsidiary except amend	No	No
Create Special Orders	Yes	Yes	Yes	Majority	Any specific matter	Amend	Yes [2]	No
General	Yes	Yes	Yes	Majority	None	Special main, object to consideration, all subsidiary	No	No

[1] In addition to Motion to Withdraw. [2] After change in situation. [3] Limited to specific issue covered by the motion itself. [4] No fixed order of precedence among II; each motion is disposed of as it arises. (The authors appreciate the consultation of Professor James W. Cleary, of the University

procedure serious enough to deny members their rights or to obstruct the will of the majority.

8. *Appeal.* The object of an appeal from the decision of the chairman is to obtain the judgment of the assembly on a disputed point. When a member disagrees with a ruling of the presiding officer, he rises and says:

I appeal from the decision of the chair.

This frequently happens when the chairman has turned down a point of order raised by a member. The chairman says, "Shall the decision of the chair stand? Those in favor of sustaining the decision please say *Aye;* those opposed, *No.*" After the vote he says, "The decision of the chair stands (or has been overruled)." A majority or a tie vote has the effect of validating the chairman's ruling.

PRIVILEGED MOTIONS

These motions have to do with the rights and privileges of members and with other matters of unusual and even vital concern to them. These motions have the highest order of precedence because time is of the essence in dealing with them.

1. *Point of Privilege.* A point of privilege is in order at almost any time, even when another member is speaking. The form is:

I rise to a point of personal privilege.

The chairman then says, "State your point." When the member has done so, the chairman rules on the request which has to do with such matters as the temperature of the room, draftiness, inability to see and hear what is being presented on the platform, etc. No second is required, the point is not debatable, and no vote is taken. A point of privilege takes precedence over all motions except *recess* and *adjournment.* If a question of privilege is presented as a motion, it loses its precedence and its privileged character.

2. *Recess.* The purpose of a motion for a recess is to provide a relatively brief intermission in a meeting without a final adjournment. The form is:

I move that we take a recess of ten minutes.

This motion takes precedence over all the other motions except *adjournment.* It is not debatable.

3. *Adjourn.* This motion has the highest precedence of all. The form is:

> I move that we adjourn.

It is not debatable. It may be made at any time except when another speaker has the floor. A motion to adjourn requires a second.

ADDITIONAL READINGS

Auer, J. Jeffery, *Essentials of Parliamentary Procedure,* 3rd edition (New York: Appleton-Century-Crofts, 1959).

Ewbank, Henry Lee and Auer, J. Jeffery, *Discussion and Debate: Tools of a Democracy,* 2nd edition (New York: Appleton-Century-Crofts, 1951).

Howell, William S. and Smith, Donald K., *Discussion* (New York: The Macmillan Co., 1956).

Haiman, F. S., *Group Leadership and Democratic Action* (Boston: Houghton Mifflin Co., 1951).

Robert, Henry M., *Robert's Rules of Order,* Revised: 75th Anniversary Edition (New York: Scott-Foresman and Co., 1951).

Sturgis, Alice F., *Sturgis' Standard Code of Parliamentary Procedure* (New York: McGraw-Hill Book Co., 1950).

Wines, Emma M. and Card, Marjory W., *"Come to Order!"* (New York: The Odyssey Press, 1941).

QUESTIONS AND PROJECTS

1. Listen attentively to a half-hour radio or television discussion on some problem of public interest. Note the organizational arrangement and procedures, the techniques of the presiding officer, and the contributions of the members. Write an evaluation of the program.

2. Divide the class into panels of 4–6 students each. The panel will choose a problem for discussion, and a leader. After studying the subject, the panel will meet again to plan a discussion which will be presented to the class. This discussion should terminate in a forum period.

3. Let the class, acting as a parliamentary body, formulate and pass resolutions on some of the following:

a. Campus social activities
b. House rules
c. Athletics

d. Student government
e. The college paper
f. Examinations, etc.

4. Spend several class hours demonstrating the correct forms in organizing a club, preparing and adopting a constitution and bylaws, electing officers, and transacting business. If this assignment is carried out with imagination and seriousness, it can be both entertaining and instructive.

5. Formulate good propositions for debate on the following topics:

a. Russia
b. The space age
c. Foreign aid
d. Taxation
e. Red China
f. Railroads
g. Capital punishment
h. The stock market
i. Sports
j. The American dollar
k. Senior citizens
l. Adolescents
m. College life
n. Racial equality

6. Consider the logic in the following:

a. All patrons of the arts are public benefactors. No poor people are patrons of the parts. Therefore, no poor people are public benefactors.

b. The courageous are confident. The experienced are confident. Therefore, the experienced are courageous.

c. All the members of the finance committee are members of the executive committee. No members of the library committee are members of the finance committee. Therefore, no members of the library committee are members of the executive committee.

d. I am sure that he knew the plan, for only members of the committee knew of it, and he was a member of the committee.

e. If he insists upon the present policy, he will fail; but he is willing to give up the policy. Therefore, he will succeed.

f. All who were pledged voted for him. This man was not pledged. Therefore, he did not vote for him.

g. Because poor people who own cows are the most industrious, the way to make poor people industrious is to give them cows.

h. There should be no restriction of speech in the Senate because freedom of speech is one of our fundamental rights.

i. We need not worry about the national debt for we owe the money to ourselves.

j. Since an article is sold for more or less than it is worth, either the seller or the buyer gets cheated.

k. No one can believe what he does not understand; therefore, there are no mysteries in true religion.

l. In a debate on government medicine, the affirmative argued that it had succeeded in England and therefore, in all probability, would succeed in the United States. The negative, however, argued that since it had failed in England, it probably would fail in the United States. Assuming that both the affirmative and the negative assumptions could be proved, which argument would be stronger?

m. Colonies should not rebel against the mother country because colonies are children and children should not rebel against parents.

CHAPTER 13

The Oral Interpretation of Literature

In our discussion of speech preparation and presentation we have stressed the desirability of learning to *speak extempore.* There is no more satisfactory manner of delivery for most public speaking situations and there is no better way of training the public speaker. However, there is nothing sacred about extemporaneous speaking. Throughout the long history of oratory, many of the greatest speeches have been read from manuscript or spoken from memory. Such speeches often reveal a precision of composition, word choice, organization, and style that an extempore speaker, no matter how skillful, cannot achieve. Some speakers prefer to speak from manuscript because they experience greater confidence in this form of delivery; others find that they can influence their audiences more effectively through the greater freedom and flexibility of the extempore technique. Nevertheless, the really effective speaker needs competence in all the different modes of presentation.

Men and women in important public positions frequently are asked to make speeches concerning policy. Sometimes these pronouncements have national, or even international, implications because of their controversial nature. To avoid governmental and personal repercussions, possible embarrassment, and long, tedious, ex post facto explanations, officials usually prepare their statements with meticulous care, often "clearing" them with government agencies concerned with the issues, and then read them verbatim to the public.

Scientists, doctors, lawyers, teachers, engineers, and others belong to local and national professional societies and may make significant contributions to their special fields of interest through research and study. Their contributions must be shared before they can become worth while; an important medium for sharing them is the paper read at meetings of professional societies. Frequently the paper is a report of scientific data which have been collected, organized, and interpreted. Almost always, such a paper can be only a short summary or digest of the speaker's total material on the subject. The need for accuracy in reporting scientific data and for stringent condensation requires the speaker to prepare a carefully worded and organized manuscript which he reads to the society.

In the next chapter we shall look at the requirements that radio and television impose on certain speech functions. Much of the speaking done by professional performers in these media—announcers, actors, news reporters, disk jockeys—is actually reading from scripts prepared either by the performer himself or by the station's continuity department. Even the "occasional" speaker who is given a one-time opportunity to use radio or TV is usually asked to prepare his talk in writing and to read it from the typed page.

Teachers at all educational levels read to their students. Perhaps the teacher of literature uses oral reading more extensively than others; one of his important goals is to create an aesthetic appreciation of the great fiction, poetry, and drama which make up our literary heritage. Many of these masterpieces come to life only when read aloud. The teacher of political science or history or economics or any other subject may want to acquaint his students with the theories of other specialists; to make certain that he presents these accurately and precisely, he chooses to read from these other authorities.

But not all oral reading is done in such specialized situations. Sometimes brief intervals of reading are introduced into extempore platform speeches. Perhaps the speaker wishes to use a statement from a recognized authority to support his position or just for a general prestige effect on the audience. Lines from Shakespeare, Robert Frost, Carl Sandburg, or T. S. Eliot may stimulate the emotion which the speaker is trying to arouse more succinctly and quickly than he himself can by using his own words. Therefore, he reads such quotations from manuscript.

In addition to these practical applications of reading skill, there is another reason for including training in oral interpretation in a beginning speech course. In Chapter 1, we presented the theory that personality development is to a large extent a matter of "role-taking." The individual who can adapt to many and diverse occasions is usually the person who has experienced, either actually or vicariously, the roles which he must assume in these different situations. Literature is one of the most important sources of vicarious experience. This fact has long been recognized by educators. The reason for including literature courses in all academic curricula is to furnish students with a body of ideas, the significance of which has endured, to let them experience the feelings, emotions, and thinking of men and women whose gifts of observation and description are extraordinarily acute, to let them learn something of the roles of these authors and of the characters they have created, so that these roles may become useful in future social situations.

All study of literature and literary appreciation most certainly works toward the achievement of these goals, but training in the oral interpretation of literature can be of special usefulness in achieving personality growth. Oral interpretation develops an intensive understanding of the works being studied which few literature courses, having to stress extensity as well as intensity, can offer. You will find, as you prepare your assignments in this phase of speech training, that you need more than an intellectual knowledge of the work to share the author's ideas effectively with your listeners; you also need an emotional and personal understanding. In the process of investigation and preparation, the literature truly may become a meaningful part of you, and certainly you will have to become "involved" in it if you are going to try to communicate its essence to someone else.

The following discussion will focus primarily on the oral interpretation of literature. The techniques used in any oral reading, whether it be of your own material or that of another, are essentially the same. This art of reading aloud cannot be mastered without an understanding of technique and a lot of practice. Indeed, many students find oral reading more difficult to master than the art of extempore speech. In a beginning course in speech, we can only touch on basic techniques. If, however, you are seriously concerned about developing your speech performance to the full, we strongly urge you to look over your institution's offerings in oral, or interpretative, reading. You will find that such courses not only can serve to improve your speech habits, but also can open up rich new experiences for you as you come to a greater appreciation of all forms of literature.

The Role of the Interpreter

Good oral reading of literature is an art. The artist—the interpreter—stands between the author and those to whom he reads as the translator of one language into another, written language into spoken language. It is his function to restate, in the symbols of speech, what the author has said, in the symbols of print, making every possible effort to retain every bit of the original meaning in the process. However, this function of restatement is not simple or passive. The reader does not stand inertly between the author and the listener. In a very real sense, the interpreter is a creative artist. In his reading he interprets, he adds something of himself, not only his technical ability in the use of his voice and visible action, but also his power to call up meanings in himself and his power to stir up similar meanings in others. The reader's imagination is his most important tool in oral interpretation. It is this imagination which permits us to say that the role of the interpreter is in reality the role of the artist. The following penetrating observations by Professor Frank M. Rarig deserve careful study and consideration: [1]

> Tolstoi says that the art impulse is the impulse to share experiences with others. . . . The function of interpretative speech in life, as in literature, is to bridge these gulfs that are constantly opening between the self and other persons. . . . It is this fact which may in part account for the persistence of the art of oral reading or the art of oral interpretation of imaginative literature. The thing that cannot be told by the individual immured within his walls of repression is told by the

[1] F. M. Rarig, "Some Elementary Contributions of Aesthetics to Interpretative Speech," *Quarterly Journal of Speech*, 26 (1940), 527–28.

poets, the makers of illusion. They put into words what the reader cannot put into words for himself. With words as their medium, they create forms of literary art within the conventions of which the reader may move and speak out the secrets of his life with articulate abandon.

Oral reading, then, may be defined as the sharing with others of the reader's experience as he has recognized it in stories, poems, plays, and informal essays. . . . Literature extends our capabilities for experience beyond the limits of any human life cycle. . . . The general purpose of all imaginative literature is transport or imaginative illusion. To incite transport or imaginative illusion in an audience, a reader must first have yielded himself to it. Two laws the creative artist must obey: he must first submit himself to his material; second, he must dominate that material, select from it the elements that affect him, according to his own predisposition and temperament, and impose on these selected elements an order that satisfies him. *Only in a limited sense is the oral reader a creative artist.* The writer has already done the work of observation, selection, and organization. It remains for the reader to submit himself, with all his powers of memory, imagination, and insight to the author's organization as recorded in words.

The role of the interpreter, then, is to translate the symbols of print into the symbols of speech so as to stimulate others into developing, *for themselves,* meanings which are as similar as possible to those which the reader has developed *for himself.* This statement implies that interpretation consists of two processes—first, the reader must get the meanings of the literature for himself; second, he must communicate those meanings to others. The effectiveness of interpretation depends upon the reader's complete accuracy in carrying out the first process and his technical ability in performing the second. A deficiency in either process will result in a poor interpretation.

Getting the Meaning

If we understand the complexities of communication, if we recognize, as we must, the individual differences in personalities, we will realize that getting complete and accurate meaning from a page of even the simplest prose is not easy. Consider again how often you fail to understand what your closest friend says. And yet your environments are similar, you have many friends in common, he is probably about the same age as you are, and many of his interests are yours also. Now think of your problem in trying to understand the writings of John Donne, a contemporary of William Shakespeare, who lived over 300 years ago in the England of Elizabeth I and James I.

As we have stated so many times before, comprehension of another's meaning cannot be achieved by passive listening or reading. We understand another person only insofar as we can fit that person into our own knowledge and experience. And so the reader has no way of realizing the author's meaning except by allowing the symbols to stir up his own past experiences. "We *receive* in reading; but we receive, not directly by what the author tells us, but indirectly by the new uses that he stimulates us into putting our experience to." [2]

Actually, complete accuracy in grasping the author's meaning is an impossibility. To be as true as possible to the purposes, the ideas, and the feelings of the author as they are translated into meaningful concepts for you is the end to which you should aspire.

DENOTATIVE MEANING

Your first task as an oral reader is to discover the denotative meaning that the author intends to communicate. As explained in Chapter 9, this denotative (or extensional) meaning refers to the objective significance of the language, to the logical ideas and the organizational framework of the material. To find denotative meaning, you might ask yourself questions such as these:

Do I know the ordinary dictionary meanings of all the words?

Can I state, in simple terms, the author's theme and purpose?

What is the logical pattern of the work? Can I put down on paper a clear outline of the ideas expressed, which will show their relationship to each other and to the major theme?

Is the author's grammatical technique clear to me in each and every sentence and phrase? Do I know how each phrase and clause is related to the rest of the sentences, and how each sentence is related to those before and after?

How does the author move from one idea to the next? What are his transitions? Are some ideas connected by means of contrast? By repetition of words or phrases? By the use of pronouns tied to antecedents used earlier?

[2] J. B. Kerfoot, quoted in R. L. Lyman, *The Mind at Work* (Chicago: Scott, Foresman & Co., 1924), p. 209.

A good way to check your answers to these questions is to write a précis, or brief summary, of what the author says, making sure that you include every important part of that meaning.

Some prose is almost entirely denotative in content. When the secretary of an organization writes the minutes of the preceding meeting, he limits himself to the facts; he does not indicate in his report the feelings of those who made the various motions, or the reasons back of the voting, or the moods of the committee chairmen who made the reports. Scientific papers presented at professional meetings are also primarily objective and denotative.

CONNOTATIVE MEANINGS

However, true literature abounds in the second type of meaning; indeed, it earns its place as great literature because of the author's ability to use and stir up the meanings which we call connotative (intensional). It is implied meaning which proceeds, not from the logical workings of the author's mind, but from his attitudes and emotions. This kind of meaning lies, not in the dictionary definitions of the words or the superficial ideas for which those words stand, but rather in the inner, subjective states of mind of the author. To decipher this meaning as completely and accurately as possible, you must try to appreciate the author's states of mind; you must seek out the underlying purposes and fundamental attitudes he held toward the ideas expressed. You might ask yourself these questions:

Why did the author write? Was he simply trying to entertain by telling a story or by creating a mood of beauty, relaxation, enjoyment? Or is there a significant thought he wants to get across?

What is the mood and atmosphere he is trying to create in the reader's mind?

What is the author's basic attitude? Sympathetic? Ironic? Amused? Satirical? Angry? Sorrowful? Straightforward? Humorous?

From what point of vantage does the author speak to the reader? Through himself in the first person? Through a character in the story or poem? Through a neutral observer? Through an interested observer? Through himself as an omniscient being? What effect does this choice of technique of orientation have on the emotional impact of the selection?

What is the locale or setting in which the action takes place? How does the author's choice of locale affect the mood and meaning of the work?

If the work is poetic, how do rhythm and rhyme contribute to the feeling of the reader? Does the author's choice of words enhance the meaning because of the sounds they call forth—i.e., does he employ such devices as alliteration, assonance, onomatopeia?

If the work is narrative, from what does the element of conflict result? How does the author present his characters, not only directly through description, but also indirectly through what they say, what others say of them, how they react within the plot structure?

Once again, a précis or paraphrase will help to make sure that the meaning is clear and complete. By paraphrasing we mean restating an author's meanings in language different from the original. Study the selection you are preparing to read until you can lay it aside and express completely and fully in your own words the meanings it contains. A nebulous general notion about the meaning is not enough. Until you can put the meaning into your own words, you may suspect that you do not really have it.

The following is a sample of an analysis of connotative meaning, illustrating the kind of digging and searching of which we've been speaking: [3]

. . . In Shakespeare's *Antony and Cleopatra,* for example, Cleopatra is telling Charmian, one of her attendants, how much she loves Antony. Charmian reminds her, none too subtly, that she once felt the same way about Julius Caesar. Cleopatra could have replied, "Oh, I was young, then, and didn't know any better." Instead she says,

> My salad days,
> When I was green in judgment, cold in blood,
> To say as I said then!

What are some of the allusions, what are some of the meanings of these words, these lines? "Salad" may have connotations of the relatively unimportant, since it is usually only an accompaniment to the substantial items in a meal; of weakness and lack of purpose, since it wilts quickly; of the first crisp, tender shoots that come from the ground, and hence of the spring of the year, or the youthful period of a life. The last connotation appears to be correct, since it is reinforced by "green" which, along with color, connotes immaturity, inexperience, freshness. The phrase "cold in blood," following "salad" and "green" and reinforcing both words, since salad greens are served

[3] Edward A. Bloom, Charles H. Philbrick and Elmer M. Blistein, *The Order of Poetry* (New York: The Odyssey Press, Inc., 1961), pp. 2–3.

cold, presents us with a rational statement on the difference between youthful and mature love. The phrase seems to imply that youthful passion is a temporary passion of the surface, since the blood below the surface remains cold. Mature love, on the other hand, is far more than skin deep; it heats the blood and is, therefore, more permanent, more sincere, more deeply felt than youthful love. The lines mean, then, much more than, "Oh, I was young, then, and didn't know any better." The poet has managed to strike all the chords of meaning that the words possess; he has explored words to their fullest appropriate limits.

IMAGINATION IN READING

The appreciation of meaning in literature is largely a function of the imagination. Over fifty years ago, Dr. S. S. Curry wrote, "The highest requisite of a good reader is the power to see what is not visible to the eyes, to realize in imagination every situation, to see the end from the beginning by the imagination, and to realize a unity of purpose in each successive idea."

What is imagination? It is the capacity for living in terms of symbols. When we have been so conditioned that words touch off within us patterns of experience in much the same way in which objects, situations, and relationships formerly have touched them off, we may be said to live and move and have our being in the realm of images. In another sense, imagination can be thought of in the terms of the role-taking concept. When we actively use our imaginations, we are really calling up in our minds roles which we have assumed in the past, which are part of our total personality. We use these roles (or images of roles) to help us understand the immediate context in which we are operating. This process occurs in every thought and action that we perform. However, in symbolic action, such as getting meaning from the printed page, this process frequently is at best haphazard and incomplete. Perhaps we have not experienced the roles necessary for full understanding. More likely we have not cultivated the power to call up these roles so vividly that we can use them imaginatively.

When we have acquired this power of imagination, we will have achieved a large measure of detachment from the workaday world about us. We will have equipped ourselves for the imaginative construction of those deeper realities which may never have actually existed before. Imagination is the key to mental freedom. We can put together past experiences which did not happen together originally and thus make something new and different.

As we have said, the basis of all experience is sensation. We stretch out our hands to the fire and get a sensation of warmth. The actual fire stimulates our sense organs. The next step in the growth of experience is achieved when we can look at a fire that is so far away that we cannot feel its warmth and yet perceive what it is and recall its warming properties. We carry the process one step further. We talk about a fire as that which has given or might give us the sensation or the perception of warmth. Now we are operating on the level of imagination.

Language is a device for manipulating this world of images. If we are to understand literature, we must have acquired the capacity to deal with images. As has been suggested, images are reproductions of sensations and percepts; but they are not exact copies. They are not candid camera shots; they are softened and diffused portraits. In the very process of becoming independent of outer reality they have undergone a transmutation. There has been some loss of detail. They are less photographic than sensations, but because of this, they are also more manageable.

There are as many kinds of images as there are distinct receptors, or sense organs. From sensations which come to us through the eye, we develop visual images. From those which come to us through the ear, we develop auditory images. From those which affect the sense organs of temperature, pressure, smell, and taste, we develop thermal, tactile, olfactory, and gustatory images. These different varieties of images furnish vital clues to the real meanings of literature.

Some images are primarily descriptive in purpose and nature. Take, for example, this stanza by Walt Whitman: [4]

Lo, 'tis autumn,
Lo, where the trees, deeper green, yellower and redder,
Cool and sweeten Ohio's villages with leaves fluttering in the moderate
wind,

[4] From "Come Up from the Fields, Father."

Where apples ripe in the orchards hang and grapes on the trellised vines,
(Smell you the smell of the grapes on the vines?
Smell you the buckwheat where the bees were lately buzzing?)
Above all, lo, the sky so calm, so transparent after the rain, and with wondrous clouds,
Below too, all calm, all vital and beautiful, and the farm prospers well.

Here the poet, through visual and olfactory images principally, produces an atmosphere of tranquillity, serenity, prosperity—a sense of well-being. Later in the poem he injects into this setting one of the typical tragedies of war—a family's being notified of the fatal wounding of their son. The juxtaposition of the sense of well-being achieved in the above passage with the sorrow and tragedy of the main theme serves to accentuate the meaning of the latter.

Images can do more than create a setting or mood. Often they are the principal devices for developing the real core of the author's meaning. Many such images are presented through figures of speech (metaphor, simile, contrast) to enhance their meaning values. In the following stanza by John Donne, the poet expresses the glories of being in love. In colloquial terms, a person "hasn't really lived" until this has happened to him.

I wonder by my troth, what thou and I
Did, till we loved? Were we not weaned till then,
But sucked on country pleasures, childishly?
Or snorted we in the seven sleepers' den?
'Twas so; but this, all pleasures fancies be.
If ever any beauty I did see,
Which I desired, and got, 'twas but a dream of thee.

Donne is not drawing literal images here, images of "not being weaned," or of "sucking on country pleasures" or of "sleeping." By means of these metaphors he is suggesting that all life, before he and his love met, was childish, meaningless, nothing but a dream. Except for this—being in love—all things that seemed pleasurable in the past were but fancies; every beautiful thing which happened to the lover previously had been nothing more than a dream of his loved one. The "sleeping" metaphor is complicated further by the "seven sleepers' den," a reference to the legend of the Seven Sleepers of Ephesus, seven people who drank a magic potion and slept in their cave for several centuries. This figure serves to emphasize further the poet's "dream" meaning.

Imagination performs a special service for you as interpreter in helping you to realize and to appreciate the connotative meanings in literature. It is only in proportion as your images (roles) are vivid that you can understand the attitudes and the feelings of the author. Imagination implies sensitiveness. To read well one must think the thoughts of the author clearly and feel his emotions deeply. Neither is possible without a live and facile imagination.

BACKGROUND PERSPECTIVE

To read a selection well, you may also need to understand its background. You may want to know the revealing facts concerning its authorship, the historical events connected with its composition, the sources of the material, the purposes of the author, and the reactions of those who previously have studied the work. In other words, to get complete meaning you may have to learn something about the role the author had assumed when he wrote the piece, and about the situation or scene in which he was playing that role.

Further, you should know all you can about the type of literature represented by the selection. If you are going to read an elegy, you should understand what an elegy is. If you are to interpret a lyric, you must study the nature of lyric poetry. If you read from a drama, you should comprehend the dramatic form in general, as well as the structure of the particular play. Each literary form must be understood before any example of it is interpreted.

Many facts about the author, his beliefs, convictions, prejudices, and devotions, may help you understand what he has written. Find out what you can about the circumstances in which the author spent his life, the influences which acted upon him, and the habits of thought and feeling which underlie his work. Of course, knowledge about the author will not have equal significance in all works of literature. For example, you never will know anything about the original author of an ancient ballad;

and it might not help you if you did. But you can realize how that particular literary form was first presented, how it was passed on from generation to generation, how it reflected the feelings and attitudes of the people to whom it was sung. And this information certainly will help you understand the poem.

In reference to this subject of authorship, a contemporary literary critic remarks upon [5]

> . . . the good fortune of Shakespeare, to walk the distance of life and to escape from the business of it without leaving a record of deed in any way comparable to the monuments of his poetic genius. He needs abide no question. Like a God he remains in the shadow behind his work. . . .
>
> It is perhaps our frailty that we insist on reading the poem by first knowing the poet. Surely there is some wisdom in the instinct. But let it once engender with a low inquisitiveness, and every creature born of it will bring a deadly dart to brandish against true judgment. When men cannot read *Don Juan* without first sinking deep into the Venetian sloughs or when they cannot open the *Essay on Christianity* without brooding over what may have been done passionately in St. Pancras churchyard, then it may be well for them to turn quickly to the book of Job, where all they shall ever know about the author is his book.
>
> . . . We must all treasure every truth which may be learned about a man. But we should always keep a clear distinction between the facts about a poet and . . . the intimate creativity of the man himself.

Doubtless, in some cases a familiarity with an author does not help us much in understanding his meanings. More often, however, it is prerequisite to any adequate reading.

Usually, also, it will help you to know all you can about the actual situation in which the material was written. How can any reader get the real significance of Lowell's "Ode on the Present Crisis" without considering the political issues with which the poem deals? Or of Lincoln's "Gettysburg Address" without realizing the emotional context of history in which it was spoken? Some compositions depend more upon the situation in which they were written than others do, but as a rule it pays to uncover the special conditions under which the author wrote.

[5] Bennett Weaver, *Toward the Understanding of Shelley* (Ann Arbor: The University of Michigan Press, 1932), pp. 1–2.

In all literature with any local setting, satires dealing with particular regions, speeches delivered in interesting places and at critical times, a knowledge of the exact circumstances is vital. A stage director who is about to produce T. S. Eliot's *Murder in the Cathedral* will do considerable research into the historical period in which the play's action takes place before he tries to direct the play. An oral reader of this play is, in a sense, both director and actor. He must know the full setting.

A CRITICAL PERSPECTIVE

Contemporary literary critics consider each piece of literature an emotional entity, a human experience, a "dramatic" event. They view each drama, novel, short story, narrative poem, lyric, or sonnet as the cumulative effect of some human action. Kenneth Burke suggests that each literary work has a scene (setting), actors, action, and dialogue. In the drama or narrative, these are likely to be explicit; in much poetry, for example, the love lyric or sonnet, the "dramatic" elements are only implied. They must be recreated by the imagination of the reader—for full appreciation of the event.

T. S. Eliot suggests that, in any form of art, emotion can be expressed only through an "objective correlative." A poet, for instance, selects a set of objects, a chain of events, or a situation as the "formula" of the emotion he wishes to express. The external facts are communicated in such a manner that sensory experiences are stirred up in the reader and the emotion is evoked. He points out that Lady Macbeth's state of mind as she "sleep walks" is communicated through an accumulation of many sensory impressions. The effect of the whole pattern of externals, the "objective correlatives" (the symbolic actions involved in the emotion), makes the human experience come to life.

Out damned spot! out, I say!—One; two: why, then 'tis time to do't:—Hell is murky!—Fie, my lord, fie! a soldier, and afeared? What need we fear who knows it, when none can call our power to account? —Yet who would have thought the old man to have had so much blood in him?

. . . .

The Thane of Fife had a wife; where is she now?—What, will these hands ne'er be clean?—No more o' that, my lord, no more o' that: you mar all with this starting.

. . . .

Here's the smell of the blood still: all the perfumes of Arabia will not sweeten this little hand. Oh, oh, oh!

. . . .

Wash your hands, put on your nightgown; look not so pale:—I tell you again, Banquo's buried; he cannot come out on's grave.

. . . .

To bed, to bed; there's knocking at the gate: come, come, come, come, give me your hand: what's done cannot be undone: to bed, to bed, to bed.

[*Exit*]

Such critical analyses as these suggest steps in the study of literature that seem particularly useful to the oral interpreter:

1. During the first readings, let the impact of the whole work be experienced—but not analytically.
2. Then, consider the elements of the human experience being communicated—the who, what, where, when, how of the event.
3. Next, study the process which the artist uses—the structure, the form, the relationship of parts to the whole.
4. Then, analyze the symbolic function of the situation, or the chain of events, or set of objects which the author employs to stir up sensory impressions.
5. Finally, again let the cumulative effect of the whole work be experienced.

At this point in your study, you will find the experience is now more meaningful, more alive and real. Now, you are ready to work on communicating your experience to someone else, through oral reading.

Communicating the Meaning

The real purpose of one who reads to others should be to make it easier and more certain for them to develop the complete meanings of the material than if they were reading it silently to themselves. The interpreter has at his disposal all the symbols of speech. They are more explicit and powerful in stirring up meanings than are the relatively lifeless symbols of the printed page.

PHRASING OR GROUPING

One of the most essential techniques for getting meaning across to another person is to group words into meaningful phrases, separated from each other by pauses of varying lengths, which break up the flow of language into units of meaning. Correct phrasing or grouping depends not only on combining the words into units but also on relating these units to each other in one harmonious whole. This second requisite is achieved by varying the length of the pauses between phrases and by using changes of pitch, or inflection, to combine or to separate the phrases and to indicate their relationship to each other. In the following sentence we have combined the words into phrases, or "thought units." In reading the sentence to convey the total idea, you will separate these units from each other by pauses. And you will also blend them together by the manner in which you regulate your voice changes. Notice, too, how the length of your pauses will vary depending upon the degree of blending between two phrases that is necessary for meaning.

> For no cause—in the very frenzy of wantonness and wickedness—by the red hand of murder—he was thrust from the full tide of this world's interests—from its hopes—its aspirations—its victories—into the visible presence of death—and he did not quail—not alone for the one short moment in which—stunned and dazed—he could give up life—hardly aware of its relinquishment—but through days of deadly languor—through weeks of agony—that was not less agony because silently borne.
>
> —*James G. Blaine,* "The Death of James A. Garfield"

It is essential that pauses be preceded and followed by the right voice modulations if the phrases are to hold together properly. A most unhappy tendency in reading is to break up a sentence into several parts, and then, through the use of downward inflections at the ends of phrases where the pitch should be sustained, to fail in putting these parts together again. (The exercises in Chapter 7, pp. 141–143, pertaining to *steps* and *slides,* may help you understand what we are talking about here.)

Pauses in reading do not necessarily parallel the punctuation. Punctuation on the page makes meanings clear to the reader.

Pauses in speaking make meanings clear to the hearer. If the pauses always followed punctuation, good phrasing would be impossible. For example, we write:

No, Sir! I was told that, if anyone called, it should be my business to answer all questions.

A speaker might phrase this as follows:

No Sir—I was told that if anyone called—it should be my business to answer all questions.

Another speaker might do it this way:

No Sir—I was told—that if anyone called—it should be my business to answer all questions.

But no speaker would follow the punctuation precisely in this particular sentence.

This does not mean that you should overlook commas, periods, semicolons, and dashes. They are guides to meaning, and often to phrasing. Consider, for example, the difference in meaning between the two following sentences, a difference which is achieved by the insertion of a comma in the second one. To show this difference in speaking the sentence, you will naturally insert a pause at the second comma as well as at the first.

A woman came in, while you were at the airport to meet your wife.

A woman came in, while you were at the airport, to meet your wife.

SUBORDINATION

If we are to put phrases together with proper regard for the larger meanings, we must observe that certain ideas are more important than others, and we must emphasize them and subordinate the less important. Subordination can be accomplished in a number of ways—slowing down the utterance on the more important and speeding it up on the less important, using more vocal force on the more important and less on the unimportant, making significant pitch changes between groups, in short, by applying all the vocal techniques of emphasis. Any adequate reading of the following sentences will bring out the important, main ideas and will put the less important, parenthetical phrases under them:

> If you believe that our civilization is founded in common sense, and it is the first condition of sanity to believe it, you will, when contemplating men, discern a Spirit overhead.
>
> —*George Meredith,* "The Comic Spirit"

> Hamilton, though of obscure birth and small stature, is represented by those who knew him to have been dignity and grace personified; and old Ben Franklin, even in woolen hose, and none too courtier-like, was the delight of the great nobles and fine ladies in whose company he made himself as much at home as though he had been born a marquis.
>
> —*Henry Watterson,* "Abraham Lincoln"

CAUSE-AND-EFFECT

Another relationship between phrases and ideas worthy of separate mention is "cause-and-effect." When an idea is expressed as resulting from another idea, you must show this understanding of the relationship by the way in which you join the phrases. An author may not explicitly express the cause or the effect in so many words; he may not use the words "because," "for," "therefore," or "and so." Perhaps he uses a simple "and" to connect the two ideas, as in, "Give a man an inch, and he'll take a mile." Sometimes only punctuation marks are used:

> He who disobeys any law of nature flings himself athwart her wheels, to be crushed to powder. And, if his disobedience is destruction, obedience is liberty. Obeying the law of steam, man has an engine. Obeying the law of fire, he has warmth. Obeying the law of speech, he has eloquence. . . . Nature loves paradoxes, and this is her chiefest paradox—he who stoops to wear the yoke of law becomes the child of liberty, while he who would be free from law wears a ball and chain through all his years.
>
> —*Newell Dwight Hillis,* "John Ruskin"

EMPHASIS

Emphasis is one way of revealing the relationship of words, phrases, and ideas to one another. Emphasis consists in contrast. Sometimes in speaking, emphasis is best secured by increasing the vocal intensity; at other times, by decreasing it; sometimes, by raising the voice to a higher pitch; sometimes, by shifting to a lower pitch; sometimes, by a pause; and sometimes, by a change of rate. If we have been using one kind of vocal pattern, anything spoken in a different pattern will be emphasized.

This technique may be used to point up certain words and phrases which deserve attention because of their purpose in the total context:

1. Those which are the most important and significant: "A stitch in *time* saves *nine.*"

2. Those which introduce new matter: "In addition to this technique we've been talking about, a reader requires *complete understanding of content.*"

3. Those which compare or contrast one idea or thing with another: "I am doing this, *not* for *myself*, but for *you.*"

4. Those which, if emphasized, will help suggest the author's attitude: If we say, "I don't want to go home," without any particular emphasis on specific words, we may imply an attitude of sorrow or resignation. However, "I don't want to go *home,*" may suggest the speaker's attitude toward his home. Or, "I don't *want* to go home," may imply an additional statement, "But I suppose I'll have to."

5. Those which intensify the emotion the author tries to create:

> *Who* made him *dead* to *rapture* and *despair,*
> A *thing* that *grieves not* and that *never hopes,*
> *Stolid* and *stunned,* a *brother* to the *ox?*
> —*Edwin Markham,* "The Man with the Hoe"

The following paragraph from one of the 1952 campaign speeches of Adlai Stevenson illustrates all of the above types. Try to bring out the full meaning of the words, both intellectual and emotional, and the correct relationship of the various words and phrases, by the way in which you employ emphasis:

> Yours is a democracy. Its government cannot be stronger or more tough-minded than its people. It cannot be more inflexibly committed to the task than they. It cannot be wiser than the people. As citizens of this democracy, you are the rulers and the ruled, the lawgivers and the law abiders, the beginning and the end. Democracy is a high privilege, but it is also a heavy responsibility whose shadow stalks, although you may ever walk in the sun.
>
> —*Stevenson,* "No Easy Way," Chicago, September 29, 1952

SPECIAL PROBLEMS IN READING POETRY

With the exception of oratory, poetry, of all the types of literature, profits most from the interpreter's art. Amy Lowell, who spent her life creating poetry, observes, "Poetry and oratorical prose have this in common, they are both intended primarily to be heard, not seen." And again, she says, "Poetry is as much an art to be heard as is music, if we could only get people to understand the fact."

The difference between prose and poetry is not a matter of *form* solely, or even primarily. The exclusive quality of poetry arises more fundamentally from the factors of *selectivity* and *concentration.*

Selectivity. No work of literature is a photographic presentation of the "slice of life" which it represents. The writer does not clutter up his picture with every detail that is present in "life." Rather, he selects, out of all possible items, those specific items which will best help him to get his meaning across to a reader. The poet employs *greater* selectivity than other literary artists; he may settle on one specific characteristic in describing a scene or an action where the short story writer might use three, or the novelist ten, or a hundred.

Consider Robert Browning's dramatic monologue, "My Last Duchess."

That's my last Duchess painted on the wall,
Looking as if she were alive. I call
That piece a wonder, now: Fra Pandolf's hands
Worked busily a day, and there she stands.
Will't please you sit and look at her? I said
"Fra Pandolf" by design, for never read
Strangers like you that pictured countenance,
The depth and passion of its earnest glance,
But to myself they turned (since none puts by
The curtain I have drawn for you, but I)
And seemed as they would ask me, if they durst,
How such a glance came there; so, not the first
Are you to turn and ask thus. Sir, 'twas not
Her husband's presence only, called that spot
Of joy into the Duchess' cheek: perhaps
Fra Pandolf chanced to say, "Her mantle laps

Over my Lady's wrist too much," or "Paint
Must never hope to reproduce the faint
Half-flush that dies along her throat"; such stuff
Was courtesy, she thought, and cause enough
For calling up that spot of joy. She had
A heart—how shall I say?—too soon made glad,
Too easily impressed; she liked whate'er
She looked on, and her looks went everywhere.
Sir, 'twas all one! My favor at her breast,
The dropping of the daylight in the West,
The bough of cherries some officious fool
Broke in the orchard for her, the white mule
She rode with round the terrace—all and each
Would draw from her alike the approving speech,
Or blush, at least. She thanked men,—good; but thanked
Somehow—I know not how—as if she ranked
My gift of a nine-hundred-years'-old name
With anybody's gift. Who'd stoop to blame
This sort of trifling? Even had you skill
In speech—(which I have not)—to make your will
Quite clear to such an one, and say, "Just this
Or that in you disgusts me; here you miss,
Or there exceed the mark"—and if she let
Herself be lessoned so, nor plainly set
Her wits to yours, forsooth, and made excuse,
—E'en then would be some stooping, and I choose
Never to stoop. Oh, sir, she smiled, no doubt
Whene'er I passed her; but who passed without
Much the same smile? This grew; I gave commands;
Then all smiles stopped together. There she stands
As if alive. Will't please you rise? We'll meet
The company below, then. I repeat,
The Count your master's known munificence
Is ample warrant that no just pretence
Of mine for dowry will be disallowed;
Though his fair daughter's self, as I avowed
At starting, is my object. Nay, we'll go
Together down, Sir! Notice Neptune, though,
Taming a sea-horse, thought a rarity,
Which Claus of Innsbruck cast in bronze for me!

The principal artistic purpose of the poem seems to be the revelation of a character. After studying the poem we learn a good deal about the Duke of Ferrara, much more than is explicitly stated in the lines. Notice, though, some of the selectivity which

Browning employs. First, he has selected a brief moment in the Duke's life, a seemingly insignificant moment, as the setting for the poem—though the moment becomes more meaningful when we realize the purpose of the Count's envoy in visiting the Duke. Out of the Duke's life history, Browning has selected only one significant set of circumstances—his relationship with his "last Duchess." Then, out of this entire relationship, he selects the Duke's growing jealousy as the primary theme. Finally, in revealing the emotion, the Duke refers to a selected number of his wife's actions; he expresses many of these either literally or metaphorically in terms of his wife's face, and even *more selectively*, in terms of the actions of his wife's eyes and mouth—her "smiles," "looks," "glance." Even when the Duke tells of having her murdered—or at least, disposed of—he does not say that she died, but rather that "all *smiles* stopped together."

The cumulative effect of these selected details gives us an impression of the Duke far beyond a simple sum of the details. In our mind's eye we can, if we only will, create quite a "complete" man. The interpreter must make sure that his listeners grasp the full significance of these selected details so that the totality is communicated, and not just the single items.

Concentration. The poet employs a powerful concentration of emotion and feeling in the presentation of these details. He concentrates, partly, by choosing words which carry a special impact and by using figures of speech which imply meanings beyond the words themselves. Note how much meaning has been concentrated into this line from "My Last Duchess":

"This grew; I gave commands; then all smiles stopped together."
There is no unnecessary verbiage here. The poet does not intend a literal interpretation; the metaphor implies an action much more consequential than the literal meaning. Note, too, how the *repeated* references to the Duchess' face throughout the poem also help concentrate our emotional attention.

Concentration is often achieved by employing onomatopoeia, alliteration, and assonance to suggest relations between sound and sense. In the phrase, "of all the bonny buds that blow," the word "bonny" sounds light and airy, in harmony with the meaning; and the repetition of the initial "b" phoneme further accentuates the feeling. Onomatopoetic words, such as "shiver," "throbbing," "moaning," "groaning," "whispering," "plashy," "murmuring," "rippling," "flapping," "zigzag," and others, carrying in themselves the music of poetry and frequently are important in determining the meaning of the material of which they are a part.

Rhythm (and rhyme) perform a concentrating function, too. In another of Browning's poems, "How They Brought the Good News from Ghent to Aix," the strong beat of speeding horses is suggested in the rhythm, and enhances the sense of urgency the poet wants to communicate:

> I sprang to the stirrup, and Joris, and he;
> I galloped, Dirck galloped, we galloped all three;
> "Good speed!" cried the watch, as the gatebolts undrew;
> "Speed!" echoed the wall to us galloping through;
> Behind shut the postern, the lights sank to rest,
> And into the midnight we galloped abreast.

These techniques of concentration deserve special attention in oral reading. The interpreter's utterance must be as "concentrated" as the writing. But this does not mean an arbitrary, superficial use of vocal emphasis, inflection, pause, or intensity shifts. These techniques must reflect the reader's full understanding of the meaning.

Form. Rhythm (which includes meter) is an essential part of the meaning of poetry; it may vary from the regular, rigid stress patterns that we find in many literary ballads to the highly irregular cadence of free verse. No interpretation that leaves out the element of rhythm can be considered either adequate or artistic. However, it is easy to overdo the musical element in reading poetry and let it run away with the sense. We all recognize that something very unfortunate is happening when we hear a poem read in a singsong fashion; the dominant impression we get is of a recurrent stress pattern. The correct handling of rhythm usually subordinates it to sense and mood. If over-dominance of rhythm is one of your problems in reading poetry, you might try the following suggestion in your practice sessions. Write out a poem in the form of prose. The usual typographical arrangement of verse, to some people, suggests regularity and rigidity of pattern. Ordinarily there will be plenty of meter and rhythm left in your reading even after you have transposed it into this prose form. But use this technique sparingly; you must never remove the basic rhythms completely.

Here is an example of rewriting poetry as if it were prose:

Proem

I shall not press the heavy gate to open it. I wait, I wait. I shall not wake the porter there who keeps the keys of paradise; I shall but hold the fair emprise of beauty close against my heart. When my God wills, I shall depart the windy street and enter in; the altars are but building where a priest shall serve the fanes of fate. I shall not press the heavy gate to open it. I wait, I wait.

—*Bennett Weaver,* "Sussex Poems"

After you have practiced reading the poem in prose form, try reading it from the verse form:

Proem

I shall not press the heavy gate
To open it. I wait, I wait.
I shall not wake the porter there
Who keeps the keys of paradise;
I shall but hold the fair emprise
Of beauty close against my heart.
When my God wills I shall depart
The windy street and enter in;
The altars are but building where
A priest shall serve the fanes of fate.
I shall not press the heavy gate
To open it. I wait, I wait.

In reading rhymed poetry, it is sometimes difficult to prevent too much emphasis from falling on the words that carry the rhyme scheme. The very fact that words rhyme with each other is sure to give them considerable prominence, without directing further attention to them by the manner in which they are uttered. Yet it is exceedingly difficult not to stress such words. Again, if this is a special problem, you might try to read the verse as if there were no rhymed words in it at all. Certainly such a technique would be necessary in interpreting "My Last Duchess." Browning has used the heroic couplet (iambic pentameter, with every two lines rhyming with each other), but within that pattern he has introduced a very conversational and irregular rhythm of grammatical construction. Over-emphasis on either poetic rhythm or the end rhymes distorts the meaning beyond comprehension.

"My Last Duchess" also illustrates the use of continued lines—lines of verse with no sense pause at the end. One of the most exasperating bad habits in oral reading of poetry is to pronounce each line as a unit in itself, with a mechanical pause at its end.

STYLE OF READING

No two readers will speak the same selection in exactly the same way. To do so would be simply impossible, and undesirable. However, we can categorize oral reading into two more or less distinct styles:

1. The *interpretative* or suggestive;
2. The *impersonative* or representational.

In interpretation, we try to stimulate the imagination of those to whom we read. In impersonation, we attempt to do more what the actor does, namely, bring the characters in the flesh before the audience. Miss Johnson's explanation of the difference between these two styles is excellent: [6]

> In complete impersonation we do *for* and *before* an audience for them to watch as they watch a play. . . . In interpretation we do *with* them, setting up our imaginative scene out in their realm, asking them, tacitly, to imagine scene, place, and all, as they may, not detracting from this by any locomotion of ours on the stage before them; not taking on, save in voice and facial expression, which must be *facile,* any *complete bodily* changes, from character to character, never changing our own imaginative concept of where our "scene" is located, by sometimes addressing characters as if they were somewhere in the audience, and then turning to address the next character as if he stood "on-stage" at our side.
>
> To me, then, there are two realms in which the interpreter may evolve his imaginary scene; the realm of the stage, a literal and objective realm whereon whatever we do will be looked *at* whether *into* or not, and the realm of the "audience," a suggestive realm, wherein we establish scene, character, and all pertaining to the impression as seen *in our mind's eye,* and in which we lead hearers to see with their mind's eye, always directing them suggestively, never literally, taking care indeed, that no literal actions, gestures, or movements shall interfere with the imaginative process of the audience. They do not look on, they look in.

[6] Gertrude E. Johnson, *Studies in the Art of Interpretation* (New York: D. Appleton–Century Co., 1940), p. 128.

Which of these two styles should the reader use? The answer to this question depends primarily on the reader's concept of his function and the nature of the material. The suggestions given here represent the philosophy of oral interpretation which emphasizes that the primary and sole purpose of reading should be to communicate, or stir up in the audience, meanings, feelings, attitudes, and emotions. The purpose of reading should never be to perform, to "show off," or to exhibit. If this is kept in mind, the following factors probably will influence your choice of style:

1. *Type of Material.* Obviously impersonation can be used only if there is a character, or characters, to "impersonate." Essays and lyrical poetry, therefore, should never be given the representational treatment. This does not mean that all fiction can be handled this way, however, for unless the author makes dialogue a primary device of evolving character and developing plot, the impersonative style will seem out of place. The reading of a play might be handled by impersonation, provided the other factors discussed below warrant such a style. Perhaps the dramatic monologue, where one and only one character is presented, is best suited for this impersonative type of presentation.

2. *The Performer.* First, is he reading from a book or manuscript? If so, we can say quite unequivocally that he should interpret and not impersonate. There is no possible way for a person who is actually reading while communicating to lose his own identity sufficiently to permit full-scale impersonation. The audience will always be aware of the book or script; it is a constant reminder to them that the speaker is *reading*. The vocal and physical contortions that the impersonator must go through if he is to "act out" the characters will only call attention to themselves, will seem out of place, and will destroy the directness necessary between reader and listener. When this happens, communication ceases and "performance" begins—and this must be avoided.

Second, if it is a memorized reading, or declamation, is the performer capable of "representing" the characters? This does not mean that complete impersonation is more difficult than suggestive interpretation, for the reverse actually is the case. But each individual, no matter how skilled, does have physical, emotional, and mental limitations which may destroy the illusion of character. A teen-age girl trying to make the audience believe that she "is" a condemned 60-year-old murderer (whether male or female), who is gradually going insane in a death-row cell, is simply too much. The physical traits of the character are beyond her without the help of extreme make-up and costuming; the mental and emotional experiences of the murderer are, we hope, completely outside the realm of her experience. What the audience sees is not the murderer, but a teen-age girl behaving hideously. The result is not communication but embarrassment.

3. *The Audience.* The principal characteristic of the listener which affects reading style is the age factor. A young audience (of kindergarten and primary school age) can take, and indeed, will want, a more exaggerated, more representational mode than will an older audience. The number of roles which the youngsters have integrated into their imaginations is still relatively small; they like to see things happen in front of them because their mental "stages" are not sufficiently equipped with characters and scenery. A person reading one of Kipling's "Just So" stories to such an audience would very likely want to broaden his characterization of the animal actors, and also the narrative and descriptive passages. Before an older, more mature audience, a more suggestive, more straightforward reading would be demanded.

4. *Setting.* Ideally, impersonation belongs on the stage, perhaps with considerable costuming, scenery, make-up, and lighting. However, most reading in public is not done in such a physical setting. It may be a classroom, a living room, or a banquet hall. The reader very likely will be dressed as the audience are dressed. There will be no special scenic or lighting effects in which he can work. To read impersonatively in such a situation is asking quite too much of an audience, and of a reader. The audience will see the realistic physical gestures and bearing of Queen Elizabeth and Essex; they will hear the vocal patterns of those characters. But at the same time they will see a person dressed in modern clothes, perhaps standing in front of a blackboard. They will be aware of the constant physical and vocal changes that the reader is going through as he shifts from being Elizabeth to being Essex. They will see only one person in front of them, although from the context of the material and from the contortions and glances of

the reader they will realize that they should be seeing more than one person. Because a part of the total context (the voice and action of the characters) is physically present within their line of sight, this aspect will get primary emphasis. The portion which they are called upon to imagine cannot help but be shunted into the background. It is difficult to focus on a total scene when some one element of that scene is extremely active before our eyes.

Even plays or dramatic scenes, therefore, may better be interpreted in most situations if they are being read. As we noted in our discussion of meaning in Chapter 9, an oral reading of a play actually may be more impressive than the stage performance of the same play, for the interpreter gives the audience freedom to use their imaginations. As we listen to the skilled interpreter, we people the stage with imagined characters more satisfying to us than those any producer could furnish. The experience of seeing a play after having heard it well read is similar to that which we have in seeing a motion picture made from a favorite novel. The cast of actors and the setting provided by Hollywood, with all its resources, often are less satisfying to us than were our imagined characters and scenes.

It should be clear that we prefer interpretation to impersonation for the oral reading of most literature. But it must be remembered that the interpretative style is not a cold, sterile, prosaic presentation. Interpretation must make the audience realize the emotional as well as the intellectual content of the material being read. This is accomplished by suggesting the emotion through vocal techniques and facial gestures, not by showing it in all its stark physical reality. The degree of suggestion used may vary from situation to situation, from material to material, from audience to audience; but as long as it remains only suggestion and does not become representation, the audience will be able to use their own imaginations to transform that suggestion into an understandable mental reality.

Whatever the style chosen for a particular reading, consistency is vital. To shift back and forth from one method to the other is ill-advised. For example, a reader begins by telling a story to the audience in a direct conversational way, maintaining his own personality. Then, as he comes to a particularly dramatic dialogue between two of the principal characters, he suddenly shifts from interpretation to impersonation. He faces first one way and then the other, in an effort to bring the two personalities to life realistically before the audience's eyes. Having finished with the impersonative episode, he returns to the interpretative technique. Each time he changes his technique, he jars the audience away from the story and intrudes himself into the limelight of their attention.

In concluding what we have to say about oral reading of literature, it may be well to state that interpretation, like all other forms of speaking, demands directness of communication. In our discussion of public speaking, we recommend direct audience contact for two reasons—to let the audience see that we are interested in having them understand us, and to let us see how they are reacting to what we are saying. Since effective communication is the goal of oral reading, audience contact will undoubtedly serve a vital purpose. To be sure, there may be some few highly emotional, introspective pieces of literature which might embarrass the reader or the listener if they were to be projected in eye-to-eye communication. Yet, even with such literature, it may not be the content that causes the embarrassment but the lack of skill and proper attitude on the part of the reader.

Our belief in the importance of directness is undoubtedly another reason for preferring the interpretative style in oral reading. Complete impersonation requires a high degree of "aesthetic distance" between the performer and the audience which usually causes the impersonator to avoid directness. This aesthetic distance is not attainable or desirable in most reading situations. (For a fuller discussion of aesthetic distance see p. 348.)

Reading a Manuscript Speech

Reading from your own speech manuscript, we repeat, demands the same sort of attention to understanding and techniques of communication as does the interpretation of literature. So often, however, this form of oral presentation breaks down badly, either because the speaker is not paying attention to his own meanings, or because he cannot translate the words he sees into meaningful audible and visible symbols—or because of both weaknesses.

In preparing a report to be read, you must keep in mind the

essential characteristics of oral style. We have considered these throughout our discussion of speech preparation and language, particularly in Chapters 4 and 8. At this point, we make two additional suggestions:

1. Rewrite and polish your manuscript until you are sure that you have said exactly what you mean. Do not be satisfied with your first draft. One real advantage in writing out a speech is that doing so makes possible the greatest possible precision of organization and language.

2. From time to time, while you are composing your manuscript, read it aloud to make sure that you are writing in a style that you can read effectively. If you have difficulty in phrasing any sentence with your tongue, you can be certain that your audience will find it even more difficult, perhaps impossible, to grasp it with their minds.

We are convinced that many speakers, when they read from manuscript, become almost oblivious to the meaning of the words they are uttering. They undoubtedly have used their best mental faculties in preparing the written speech, but when they get on the podium, in front of the audience, they seem to stop thinking. All of us have been subjected to this type of speaker. He buries his head in a sheaf of papers, pronounces the words one by one in a dreary monotone, apparently depending on some strange magic to give meaning to his language.

So the most helpful advice we can give you, in any reading situation, is *to think and feel while you read—think the thoughts* and *feel the emotions* you want your audience to understand and to feel.

The Art of Acting

Although the art of acting is not usually a part of a beginning speech course, it does deserve attention as an important speech form. During the last quarter century, interest in theater has grown remarkably. Hundreds of cities and towns maintain community theater projects, often under the sponsorship of boards of education or other municipal departments. Churches present dramatic productions. Civic and social organizations have drama-interest groups. Each year thousands of amateur actors "tread the boards." As a profession, acting still is a quixotic thing; we often hear that, at any given moment, 95 per cent of the professional actors are unemployed. But considered as amateur and non-professional functions, acting and stagecraft are significant avocational activities.

Acting and oral interpretation have a common basic attribute; both are *re-creative,* in the sense that the reader and the actor work with meanings originated by someone else. Both are concerned with stirring up, in the minds of the audience, the meanings, feelings, and attitudes of another person, the author. In both arts the primary task is twofold—(1) getting the meaning that the author intended and (2) communicating that meaning to an audience. Like the interpreter, the actor is also a *creative* artist. He brings to his characterization all of his powers of imagination. He calls upon his past experiences, both real and vicarious, in analyzing and understanding the role he is to play.

In effect, acting is an extension of oral interpretation; it is interpretation carried one step further. While it usually is desirable that the oral reader of dramatic literature interpret without acting, it is impossible for the actor to act without interpreting. Although an actor is primarily concerned with only one role and although he communicates the ideas and feelings of only one character, he has to know and understand the whole play. The dramatist has conceived ideas and situations which he presents through the interaction of a cast of characters. Every actor must know the relationship of his role to all the others so that this interaction can be demonstrated accurately. This is where the techniques of interpretation have especial value to the actor.

The two arts, however, are different as well as similar. And the difference is primarily a matter of how the reader and the actor apply two psychological principles of artistic performance —(1) empathy and (2) aesthetic distance.

1. *Empathy.* We earlier considered the operation of this principle in a number of speech situations, particularly with reference to the psychology of meaning. When we empathize, we "feel ourselves into"—project ourselves into—the situation confronting us, and we better understand the meaning of the situation because of our covert (implicit, or inner) physical partici-

pation. Now the oral interpreter is concerned with creating an empathic response in his listeners, not to himself but to the meaning expressed by the author. What the reader strives for is to build empathy between himself and his audience on the one hand and the ideas and feelings of the author on the other. The actor, however, wants the audience to participate in *his* activity, or, more accurately, in the activities *of the character he is portraying*. The difference may be shown as follows:

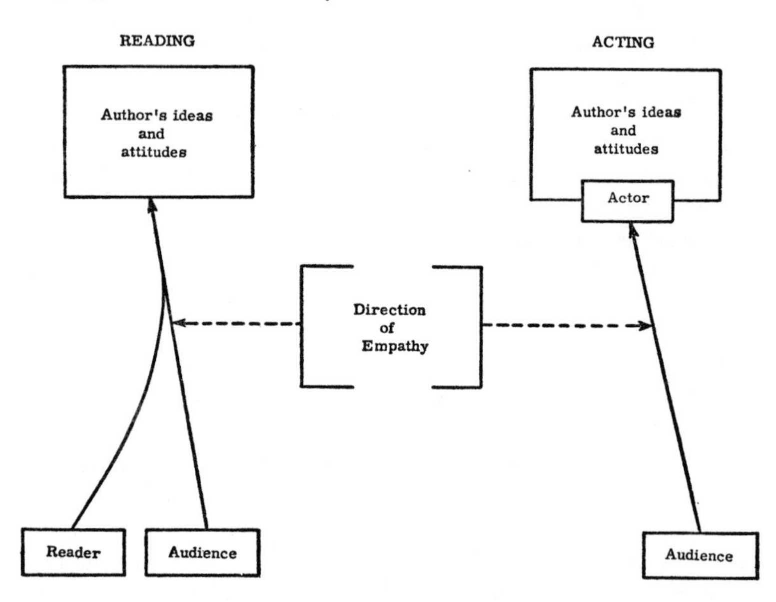

2. *Aesthetic Distance.* While it is desirable and necessary that an audience "participate" in reading and acting situations, it is important that this participation not be too complete. At the same time that the audience are empathizing, they must also remain somewhat detached. If they become too physically involved, if they become too much a part of the situation to which they are responding, they will lose their artistic appreciation of the situation. But if they participate only in their imagination and if their muscular activity is limited rather than complete, the audience will get a sense of aesthetic enjoyment from the reading or the acting. This attitude of detachment, which is necessary for

the appreciation of any art form, is called *aesthetic distance.* It is not a *physical* distance that we are talking about here, but a figurative, *mental* distance, a sense of being separated from the situation to which one is responding.

Aesthetic distance is necessary in both oral reading and acting, since both are art forms. The reading situation calls for the creation of aesthetic distance between the reader and the audience on the one hand and the work of the author on the other. On the stage, aesthetic distance must exist between the audience and the play; the actor, or rather, the character he is portraying, is part of the play.

There are probably as many "theories" of acting as there are actors. For some reason, most actors, who know what to do when they get on stage, do not know how to explain their procedures. Many of them claim they work from some sort of instinctive or intuitive approach which defies explanation.

The theories run the gamut from complete personal identification of the actor with his character to a cold, intellectual use of techniques. At the first extreme is the actor who enters into his character to the point where he loses his own personal identity and literally tries to "live" the character. At the other extreme is the actor who is all technique and no emotion. He has measured the length of every pause; he knows the precise timing of each gesture and step; he has calculated and habitualized every inflection.

For the beginning actor particularly, we suggest a compromise, which should perhaps lean a bit toward gaining control over technique, for without technique, acting can never become artistic. The actor certainly must work out the motivational pattern of the character's behavior, be able to explain every action and word of the character; but at all times he must maintain intellectual control over everything he does.

The general style of modern acting, especially in America, is tending toward realism, undoubtedly because much of the output of present-day playwrights is realistic or naturalistic. Professionally, this emphasis on realism seems to be creating a large number of good-to-excellent "type" actors, but very few great actors who are at home in a variety of styles and vehicles. It is perhaps too much to expect that a single actor can approach complete naturalism in more than a few, fairly similar roles. However, versatility can be increased by developing the necessary technical skills—and imagination.

Acting, like every art form, must be characterized by selectivity, restraint, and consistency. As we have said before, an artist is not a mere photographer. The actor does not simply "hold a mirror up to nature" or present us with "a slice of life." He selects, out of the complex of the character he is portraying, those elements that will best communicate the feeling and meaning he has in mind. He interprets these selected details for his audience so that they will more likely see the situation as he wants them to see it. If he does not, he cannot control the attention and motivation of his audience.

If the actor develops a character that is ultra-realistic in every minute detail, he may be presenting to his audience a hodgepodge of confusion that will cause them to react in dozens or hundreds of different ways. But if he chooses a small number of characteristics for special attention, he can control what his audience sees and hears. Dolman cites a famous and graphic example of selectivity: [7]

> Sarah Bernhardt, who could rant well enough on occasion, was never more effective than when she conveyed a whole tumult of feeling with a single significant gesture. In *La Tosca,* for example, when her lover was understood to be undergoing torture in the next room, she did not beat upon the door with both fists and shake her hair loose, as any good movie queen would do. She stood close to the door with her arm against it and her forehead against her arm, and the only movement was a convulsive twitching and clenching of the free hand.

Closely related to this concept of selectivity is the principle of *restraint.* An actor must always be in control of his own physical and mental processes; only restraint will insure this. And, even more important, restraint is necessary if the actor wants to control the empathic responses of his audience. Again we quote Dolman: [8]

[7] John Dolman, Jr., *The Art of Play Production* (New York: Harper and Brothers, 1946), p. 229.
[8] *Ibid.*, pp. 222, 226.

If the actor portrays unpleasant scenes too vividly there are too many unpleasant emotions aroused in us, and the experience becomes too harrowing; and if his portrayal reminds us too painfully of ourselves and our real troubles we lose our aesthetic distance.

In this connection, he cites the experience of the actress, Clara Morris, who in one play

portrayed incipient madness by clasping her arms about her knees and swaying, as she had seen a woman inmate of an asylum do; but at the first performance a young girl in the audience fainted and had to be carried out. She had recognized her mother's symptoms. . . . Clara Morris had the good sense to see that such effects were not those of legitimate art, and she took pains to avoid them in her later years.

Finally, acting must be *consistent.* When an actor has developed a realistic, selective, restrained character, he must keep *in character* every minute he is on stage. Actors often say that acting is 25 per cent action and 75 per cent reaction. If the actor drops character whenever he is silent or out of the center of attention, he immediately destroys any illusion of character that he has built up. When he is reacting, the actor must always keep in mind the principles of selectivity and restraint. Reaction that calls attention to itself or distracts the audience from the central action of a scene is worse than no reaction at all.

ADDITIONAL READINGS

Bacon, Wallace C. and Breen, Robert S., *Literature As Experience* (New York: McGraw-Hill Book Co., 1959).

Boleslavsky, Richard, *Acting: First Six Lessons* (New York: Theatre Arts Books, 1933).

Grimes, Wilma and Mattingly, Alethea S., *Interpretation: Writer-Reader-Audience* (Belmont, Calif.: Wadsworth Publishing Co., 1961).

Lowery, Sara and Johnson, Gertrude, *Interpretative Reading,* revised edition (New York: Appleton-Century-Crofts, 1953).

Smith, Joseph F. and Linn, James R., *Skill in Reading Aloud* (New York: Harper and Brothers, 1960).

Woolbert, Charles H. and Nelson, Severina E., *The Art of Interpretative Speech,* 4th edition (New York: Appleton-Century-Crofts, 1956).

QUESTIONS AND PROJECTS

(NOTE: We purposely have not included a selection of materials for practice in oral reading. When you do your own choosing from the large number of sources available in your library, you probably will find selections more suitable to your tastes and abilities than those we could suggest; and the process of searching undoubtedly will benefit you by exposing you to a greater volume and variety of literature than any we could include.)

1. Select a narrative passage from a contemporary novel, prepare a brief statement that will serve to orient your audience so that they may understand the material, deliver your introductory remarks, and then read the material as effectively as you can.

2. Select and read an article from a current magazine, dealing with a topic of vital current interest. Prepare the class to hear a reading of the article by telling them interesting facts about the author that will enable them better to appreciate his material.

3. Bring to class a narrative poem, make whatever preliminary announcement you think may be helpful, and then read the verse as well as you can. Be sure that you have selected *narrative* verse, not a lyric; the telling of a story must be its main objective.

4. Find a really good short story. Choose one with some literary merit. Abridge it so that you can read it in ten minutes, then present it as effectively as you can. Do it *interpretatively,* not impersonatively.

5. Prepare a 10-minute program of lyric poems, organized on some unifying principle. The poems may all deal with similar subjects or they may all be by one author. In any event, they should be read together because they belong together for some good reason. Remember that lyrics are songs. There must be music as well as language meanings in your reading.

6. Pick out a scene from a contemporary play and prepare to read it *impersonatively* .The scene should not involve more than two characters and at least one of these should be *very* different from yourself. The class will judge your effectiveness very largely in terms of your ability to make the characters live and speak before them.

7. Select some simple physical event or activity. Prepare a pantomime designed to communicate this to an audience, without the use of any vocalization. Practice the pantomime and present it to the class. If they easily can determine what you are doing, the chances are that your pantomime can be adjudged successful.

9. With one other student in the class, from a contemporary play pick out a scene which has two characters. The two of you will prepare to act it in front of the class. Memorize the lines, rehearse the scene thoroughly, and present it. Write a short essay on your concept of the character you are playing and the character's motivations.

10. Let the class be divided into groups of four or five each for play-readings. One member of each group will act as director or producer. It will be his responsibility to find a suitable play (or scene), to cut it down to not more than twenty-five minutes in length, cast it, rehearse it, and direct it before the class. The director will announce the play, introduce the characters and the actors, and see that all goes as it should. He may, or may not, play a part himself. The cast will sit in a semicircle on the platform before the class during the reading. Each reader should have a copy of the script. It is advisable to have not more than five or six characters in the play as presented. Each reader should be sufficiently familiar with his lines to be able to keep the reading moving properly by picking up his cues quickly.

CHAPTER 14

Radio and Television Speaking

Radio and television are not the sole domain of the professional performer, the station owner, or the advertiser. Those mystical air waves which carry electrical audio and video impulses and which transmit speech, sound, and music from the station to the receiver are *public property*. This may seem an anomaly in America where "air time" is bought and sold like a private commodity. But it is a reality, recognized as such by federal laws governing broadcasting within the United States. In effect, the station or network owner is a steward who has been given the right to use certain of these air waves for his own financial advantage, *in exchange* for his pledge to furnish *service to the public.*

At best, of course, this is a vague agreement. How to define "public service" has involved considerable controversy between the broadcasters and the Federal Communications Commission, the public's legal guardian in this contract. But, in general, the arrangement seems to be satisfactory and workable. Even the most jaundiced critics of radio and television are bound to admit that things could be worse. Certainly the FCC has had no small part in maintaining this agreement; it has formulated standards, flexible though they may be, which it can apply in its scrutiny of license and re-license applications. Realizing their responsibility to the public and their dependence on public favor, the broadcasters themselves have created additional auxiliary standards which they enforce upon themselves. And finally, the millions of listeners, by listening or not listening, by praising or condemning, and by buying or not buying the sponsor's product, have done more to determine what is carried over the air waves than any other source of control.

As in other communications situations, the member of a radio or TV audience is an integral active part of the communication pattern. Actually, though perhaps not ideally, he wields greater influence than the listener in most other situations. There seems to be a direct relationship between program content and audience interest, as it is observed by the station owner, the advertising agency, and the sponsor. There seems to be a direct relationship between the standards of listening and the standards of broadcasting. If that listening is uncritical, haphazard, relaxed to the point of laziness, it is likely that radio or TV programing will reflect those same qualities. If the audience is creative in its listening, if they demand high quality both in ideas and presentation, and if they are not easily satisfied, the programs will have to meet those requirements or go off the air.

Fortunately, many listeners have accepted their responsibility in this communication process. Fortunately also, most professional broadcasters and performers feel a strong sense of pride in their work which does not permit slipshod, careless programing and performance. In most instances, there seems to be a satisfactory balance between the standards of the listener and the standards of the broadcaster. But, as in all situations which depend on balance, both parties must constantly guard the equilibrium in order to maintain it. Every member of the radio and TV audience bears such a responsibility. This is especially true since he is one of the owners of this public property.

More frequently than before, the average American citizen has a chance to become a radio or TV performer himself. The terms of a station owner's contract with the FCC includes the words "in the public interest." One of the easiest and most satisfactory ways in which he can fulfill this part of his agreement is to offer his station's facilities for "airing" public issues, for disseminating information of interest and value to large segments of his audience, and for discussing public problems. Examples of this type of programing can be found in most station listings.

With few exceptions, the individuals appearing on such "public service" programs are not the regular talent of the station or network; they are lawyers, teachers, housewives, farmers, social workers, industrialists, labor leaders, artisans, clerks, and doctors, whose interests in the issues are firsthand and vital. Any individual who achieves public recognition for his work, no matter what his field, is likely to find himself in front of a microphone or camera. Local programs such as school broadcasts, interviews, "social calendar" shows, and discussion programs require the work of non-professionals, even though they may be professionally prepared and produced.

It is primarily with this type of participation that we are concerned in the following discussion of radio-television speaking. Such functions as directing, producing, sound effects, make-up, set design, and the like are professional aspects which must be learned in specialized courses and which, for the non-professional sometime participant, will be furnished by the station or network on which he appears. The focus in this chapter is on radio-TV *speaking*, on the principles of effective communication through these media.

Radio-TV Communication

Basically, the pattern of the communication process in radio and television is the same as that which we have stressed in earlier chapters. An idea originates in the mind of a communicator. He translates this as best he can into language and gesture symbols. In radio, he projects these verbal symbols into a microphone; on TV, he employs both the audible and visible codes. Electronic equipment converts the sound and light waves emanating from the speaker into electrical impulses which are carried from the station's transmitter to the receiver in a living room, bedroom, kitchen, or automobile, wherever the set may be located. The set re-converts these electrical impulses into sound and light waves which are picked up by the eyes and ears of the reactor. Finally, the reactor translates the symbols he has received into ideas and feelings.

The important difference between the two media, of course, is that the telecast impinges upon both the eye and the ear of the listener, while the radio broadcast works through the aural sense only. This difference seems sufficiently significant to warrant a separate consideration of certain aspects of the two media.

Radio Listening

Looking back over the communication process which we have described, we see that radio broadcasting can be pictured thus:

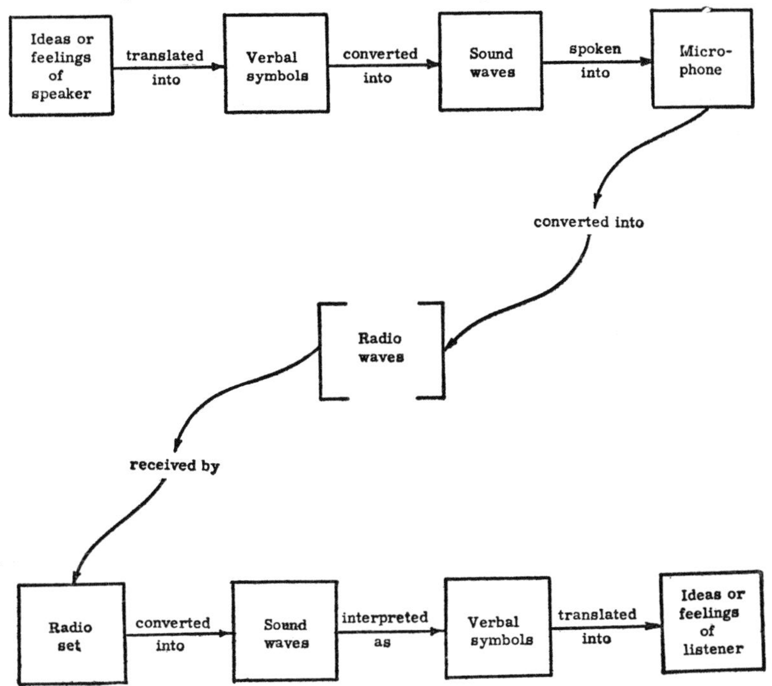

The pattern seems to differ from the face-to-face pattern primarily because of the intervention of electronic equipment and of radio carrier waves. Certainly, these are important variations. The condition of the equipment, the technical ability of the operators, the strength of the out-going signal, the atmospheric conditions through which the radio and video waves must pass—all of these can make or break the communication circuit. (In any of these, "noise" can be introduced.) But these are generally beyond the control of the individual radio performer. There are, however, secondary differences, the most important of which are found in the nature of behavior at the receiving end of the communication process:

1. *Radio listening is a private experience.* In large part, it occurs in a home, an automobile, or a small business establish-

ment. In this respect it is more like a conversational than a public speaking situation. In a very real sense, the radio broadcaster is a guest in the domain of the listener. But he will remain a guest only as long as the listener wants him around. Social protocol does not prevent the radio host from eliminating any influence which is disrupting his private, personal equanimity. In this respect radio listening is unlike that which takes place in conversation.

2. *Radio listening is distinctly an individual experience.* Except for situations where groups meet to tune in a particular program of interest to the group as an organization (e.g., classroom listening), the listener is alone or in the company of a small gathering of his family or friends. We have noted in an earlier chapter that people behave differently in groups from the way they behave as isolated individuals. They behave differently when they are members of larger groups from the way they behave when they are members of smaller groups. Auditors in individual or small, friendly group situations are more critical and more individualistic than they are when they are surrounded by many others. One of the principal effects of interstimulation among members of crowds is that the individual tends to avoid extreme judgments or opinions. The man in the group is anxious to identify himself as closely as possible with his fellows; he tries to conform to what he thinks the feelings and thoughts of those around him are; he wants to be as average as he can be and thus avoid drawing attention to himself. Members of the radio audience are likely to assume more extreme and non-conforming attitudes than they would if influences from other members of a larger audience were being brought to bear upon them. They may react more enthusiastically than they would in a public audience, or they may be more openly hostile to the speaker and his purposes. In short, they are free to be themselves without being bombarded by the social influences of a group.

3. *Radio listening is likely to be a part-time, secondary activity.* When this electronic miracle was in its infancy, listening often commanded the full and undivided attention of every member of the audience, in much the same way that TV does today, especially during the first two or three months after a new set is purchased. But over the years radio has lost its aura of novelty and glamor. It now frequently fills the role of a marginal interest

during other more immediate activities. This is perhaps even truer since the advent of TV, which in many homes has pushed the radio out of the living room into the kitchen, the workshop, the den, or the bedroom. Many people find it convenient to listen to radio while preparing or eating dinner, cleaning house, reading the evening paper—or even while studying. Certain programs, of course, do not lend themselves to this haphazard listening; talk programs frequently do not. Therefore, how to make a person stop what he is doing and concentrate fully on the radio speech must be a radio speaker's primary concern.

4. *The radio listener is autonomous and powerful.* Strictly speaking, a person listening to his radio cannot talk back. He cannot show the performer, by gestures, frowns, or smiles, how he feels about the speech he is hearing. There often is some delayed feedback through fan or protest letters; but the person who writes an unsolicited note of praise or condemnation is generally regarded as atypical. The principal retaliatory weapons in the hands of the radio listener are the dial and the on-off switch; these he uses whenever the spirit moves him.

This autonomy gives the radio listener tremendous power in a commercially-oriented system of broadcasting. Advertisers and broadcasters spend millions of dollars each year to determine how many people are listening to every type of program. If the Hooper, Nielsen, or Trendex ratings of any program are low, it is likely to be abandoned and a new one tried in its place. Producers of non-commercial public service programs are probably not so conscious of this audience-size analysis (except that on many commercial stations such programs are likely to be scheduled during "low-audience-rating" hours). However, any person using the medium for any purpose other than self-gratification must be aware of the listener's real importance in maintaining the communication.

5. *Radio listening is active, creative, and imaginative, when at its best.* The stimulus the listener receives is only an aural one, but the perceiving of the audible symbols involves all of his senses. In his mind's eye or imagination, he fills in the background for the words which he hears. And each listener does this in his own way. Except for engineering details, the only real limits of radio broadcasting are the limits of the audience's im-

agination. And so, while in one sense the unilateral nature of radio may detract from effective communication, in another sense this characteristic can broaden the scope of communication.

Television Viewing

The television viewer is not a different sort of individual from the radio listener; he probably is one and the same person. There is, however, a significant qualitative difference between the two media, caused, of course, by the addition of visual symbols in television. This combining of the visible with the audible gives us the communication pattern shown here:

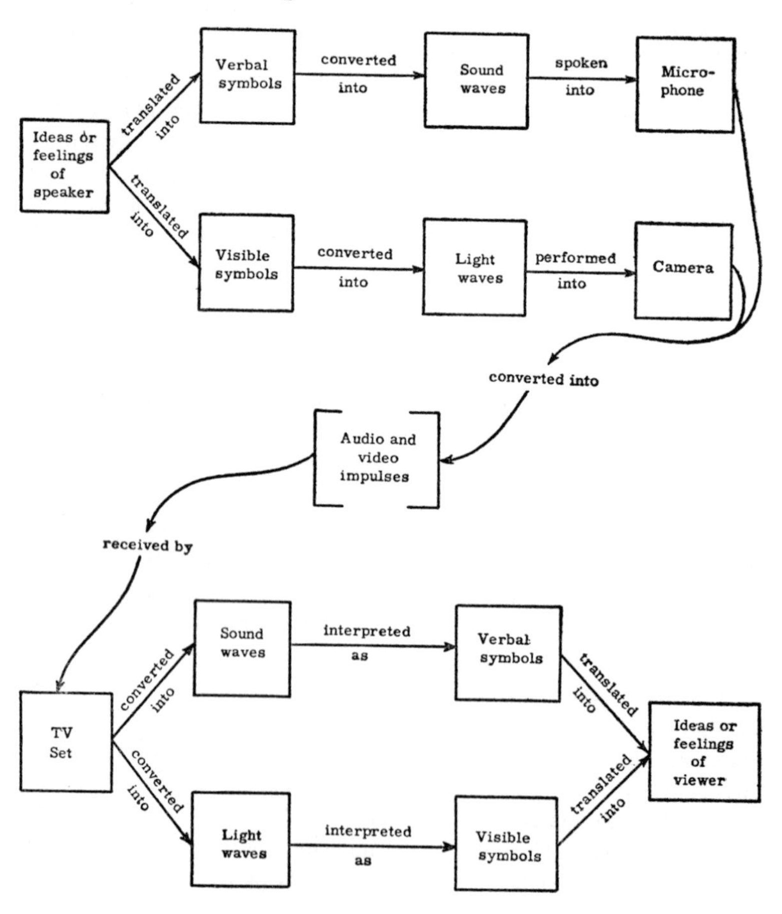

The introduction of the visible code imposes certain limitations on the communicative situation. These represent the main differences between radio and television, so far as the audience situation is concerned. Some of the more important of these are:

1. *At present, most TV viewing is concentrated in the living room of the American home.* The expense of receivers and certain other technical problems have prohibited multiple-set ownership by most families. So, the set is placed where it can serve the entire family most conveniently.

2. *TV viewing is likely to be a full-time activity.* Television does not lend itself to being a companion for other activities as readily as does radio. Because two senses are involved, a degree of concentration is required to get the full meaning of what is being telecast.

3. *TV viewing is more literal than radio listening.* From a psychological point of view, of course, the combination of video with audio strengthens the potential power of communication. But it also lessens the play of the audience's imagination and thus, in a real sense, limits the scope of ideas that can be communicated. In TV, the stage is set before the eyes of the viewer; in radio, it is set in the mind of the listener.

When nation-wide radio advertising first came into its own, there was an understandable desire on the part of the advertiser to reach a large segment of the listening audience and to please that segment. Undoubtedly a number of broadcasters hit upon the notion of finding the lowest common denominator within the audience and using it as the basis of program content. To some of them, this "l.c.d." seemed to be an intelligence equivalent to that of a 12- to 14-year-old. Today audience ratings are still very much in the mind of the commercial broadcaster, but he has begun to realize that high ratings are not attained by playing down to the listener. If ten million people listen to his program, he knows that they are ten million *individuals* of varying educational, cultural, and interest backgrounds. He knows there is no more a "broadcast-listener mentality" than there is a "crowd mind." Most modern broadcasters are interested in knowing not only how many people listen but who these listeners are. In planning and scheduling a program, he determines first what the purpose of his program will be. He then tries to determine to whom the program should be beamed and he schedules the show at a time when he knows he can reach the largest number of these people. He adopts a format and a type of presentation to fit his purpose, his program, and his potential audience. The end result of such audience analysis has been a varied and multiform program schedule on many stations.

Radio-TV Speaking

The speaking situation in radio and television differs from that in face-to-face speaking because of three factors: (1) The absence, in most instances, of a visible, reacting audience; (2) the presence of electronic equipment and personnel to control this equipment; and (3) the imposition of rigid time limitations.

1. *Radio-TV speaking is normally an isolated sort of activity.* In radio, for example, most speaking takes place in a soundproof studio, with no one present except a director—and he is often in another room behind a plate-glass window, perusing a script, studying a stop-watch, occasionally speaking to a control engineer and once in a while gesturing to the speaker to speed up, slow down, move closer to the microphone, or move away. In some cases, a studio audience may be present, but seldom is this the audience for whom the program is primarily intended. It is there because the producer feels that overt responses (feedback) from such an audience will add interest to the program for the home listener. Once in a while a microphone or camera will be placed in the middle of a public gathering to permit the radio audience to sit in on the proceedings, but even these situations are now being produced with a view toward satisfying the larger remote audiences.

The real audience for a radio-TV speech may be thousands of miles from the speaker. So far as the immediate situation is concerned, it is a reactionless audience. The speaker must, if he wants any success, imaginatively anticipate the responses of his listeners. He must build in his own mind an image of his audience, and, as it were, *speak to that image.*

2. *Radio-TV speaking often takes place in a highly distracting physical situation.* First, the speaker is confronted with a micro-

phone and/or a camera—or two or three of each. This experience can be quite disconcerting, even to the professional. "Mike fright" (or "camera fright") is essentially the same psychological phenomenon as stage fright. There are few among us who are not aware of the potential power of a microphone or a TV camera. For most of us, appearing before these pieces of equipment is a novel experience; it represents a role which we assume only infrequently. Like stage fright, "mike fright" is perfectly normal. Everything that has been said earlier about making stage fright serve a speaker's purposes can be said again. Have something worth-while to say; focus your thinking on your idea and not on your performance; want to communicate your ideas to others; and be thoroughly prepared.

Second, radio and television studios bustle with constant activity, which may seem extraneous and distracting to the speaker. Most radio programs will have a director, a control operator, perhaps a sound crew, and sometimes a number of performers. Many of these people may very well be within the speaker's line of vision, moving about, checking scripts, and preparing for later parts of the program. Usually the director will be within sight of the speaker, giving him signals which do not pertain to the ideas he is presenting but to the physical aspects of his speaking, such as microphone position, rate, timing, and the like.

In the TV situation, the addition of video greatly increases the size of the crew; cameramen, floor managers, scenery and make-up personnel must be present and must be permitted to do their jobs, frequently right in front of the performer. It takes considerable concentration to prevent these distractions from interfering with the performance of even the most seasoned veterans. Again, adequate preparation and constant focusing on the ideas being spoken are extremely important.

3. *Radio-TV speaking is rigidly controlled by the time factor.* Commercial broadcasters particularly are conscious of this need for strict adherence to program length. When thousands of dollars are paid for the use of a station's or network's facilities for a brief period, it would be economic suicide for the manager to permit another program to run overtime and encroach on it. Because Americans' listening habits have been geared to split-sec-

ond timing, non-commercial and educational stations also tend to operate on this same basis. Each and every element of a program must be carefully prepared with the time factor in mind. If a speech is scheduled to last five minutes, an error of thirty seconds either way may disrupt, not only the program at hand, but the following one as well.

For this reason, most radio and TV speeches are prepared in manuscript form and are read, not spoken extemporaneously. Even some interviews may be prepared in this manner, if there is any reason to believe that timing cannot be adequately controlled otherwise. Discussion programs usually are extemporaneous in style and presentation, but the participants' outlines probably will show, to the minute or half-minute, the length of time which is to be used for each major and minor idea.

A principal task of the radio-TV speaker is to maintain the "illusion of the first time" even though he actually is reading word-by-word a script he has prepared days or weeks earlier. It is here that the principles of oral interpretation apply to the radio-TV situation.

4. *Radio-TV speaking demands a disciplined and active imagination.* The speaker is addressing an unseen audience. He is doing so in the midst of a seemingly extraneous hubbub of activity. If he is to succeed, he obviously needs a clear, vivid impression of the audience to whom he actually is speaking his ideas—not a vague, amorphous concept of thousands of faceless people, but a distinct picture of one, two, or three individuals in an informal listening attitude. And he must discipline his attention so that the audience image remains strong at all times.

To summarize for emphasis: Effective radio-TV speaking is essentially the same as effective speaking in any other situation; every suggestion that has been given relative to the preparation of a public speech applies here as well. But we can point up, by way of review, a few of these suggestions which deserve especial attention because of the nature of the listening and speaking situations in these media. We will consider three speech forms in which the non-professional most frequently is involved—the talk, the interview, and the discussion.

THE RADIO TALK

1. *Have something worth-while to say.* This is, of course, the *sine qua non* of all effective speaking. But, when we recognize that the radio talk usually encroaches upon the time and hospitality of many more individuals than any other type of public speech, this rule seems to deserve even greater emphasis. Remember that radio listeners are likely to be more critical of what is said than are members of a public gathering. And they have at their disposal the most effective "speech-stopper" available—the on-off switch!

2. *Limit the scope of your central theme.* The radio talk ordinarily is shorter than the average public speech; therefore, the ideas which can adequately be presented are, of necessity, usually fewer in number. Also, because of the dependence on aural stimuli alone, a single idea may need more development, more explanation, more repetition, in order to insure complete understanding.

3. *Work for maximum clarity during all phases of your preparation.* Instant intelligibility must be your goal. Your organization must be precise and easy to follow; transitions between major and minor ideas, which in the public speech may be helped out by physical movement, must be distinctly woven into the verbal text. Because you cannot create visual pictures through models, gestures, and facial expression, you must build up mental images in the minds of your listeners by word pictures, examples, concrete descriptions, and vivid language. Break up long sentences into shorter ones wherever you can. Remember that your listener cannot tell you when he wants an idea repeated or expanded. You must anticipate how much development each thought is going to need.

4. *If you are preparing a message to be read from manuscript, make sure that it reads well.* As you write the speech, test out its readability. If it is not easily spoken because of complex construction or obscure wording, make the necessary changes immediately. Even better, try out the talk on your family or friends, or read it into a recorder and listen to it yourself.

5. *Work for a relaxed but animated conversational style of de-*

livery. The present-day concept of effective public speaking delivery is one of enlarged conversation. But the radio listening situation is not an enlarged situation; it is small, intimate, and personal. Animated conversation implies vocal variety. Variety is necessary not only to maintain interest, but also to help you create clear, vivid images. However, this variety must be disciplined and controlled. A microphone has limitations in transmitting the tonal code of the voice, especially loudness or volume. Sudden bursts of intensity will blast the equipment and disturb the listener. Changes in volume ordinarily should be compensated for by shifts in position before the microphone. The microphone will accurately pick up and transmit shifts in quality, pitch, and tempo, all of which can be used with excellent effect.

6. *Time your message with precision.* The broadcast situation simply will not permit vocal meandering. If the speaker is allotted ten minutes, he will have ten minutes and not one second more. And, if he ignores the warning of the director, the studio engineer simply will push a button on the control panel and the speech will be over. Speeches that are too short also are not desirable; if you have something worth-while to say, you certainly should utilize your full opportunity for saying it.

When you have prepared the speech, time it carefully, not just once, but again and again until you are sure that you can say what you have to say in the time given you. This must be done with the realization that, when you get in front of the microphone, your timing may become distorted. Metabolism changes resulting from the newness of the situation may have an unconscious effect on your rate of speech. The more adequate your rehearsal, the less disturbing will such changes be. You also will have the help of the director who is trained to estimate what is happening during the final presentation and to forestall any major catastrophe.

THE TELEVISION TALK

Each of the six specific suggestions for radio speaking applies to television as well. TV speaking is a matter of adapting your role to certain new circumstances, most of them external in nature.

1. *Remember that you are being seen as well as heard.* Empathy will directly affect the listeners' reactions to what you are saying and doing. If anything, the visual aspect is more significant here than in public speaking, chiefly because the camera can select and magnify the elements of visible behavior, facial expression, etc.

2. *Utilize visual aids.* In making your speech interesting and clear, you can have at your disposal any number of visual aids—pictures, charts, film strips, models, scenery, actors, even a short motion picture. Any of these, of course, must be integrated into the organization of the speech. They must be carefully prepared and rehearsed. Talk over their use with the producer or director. If they require the assistance of another person, that individual should rehearse his part of the performance. Scripts showing the placement and timing of these devices should be prepared for the director and his assistants so that the technical problems of camera placement and focus can be worked out. For the nonprofessional, most of these matters are the task of the station crews and supervisors, but it is the speaker's responsibility to work them out with these persons and, once the pattern has been perfected, to stick to it in later preparation, rehearsal, and performance.

3. *Keep in mind that TV speaking is not public speaking.* Like radio, television is beamed into private, often informal, listening situations. The auditory presentation should be similar to that recommended for radio speaking, and the visual, of course, must fit the auditory.

4. *Accept the advice of the director or producer.* TV cameras are peculiarly sensitive to certain colors, textures, and physical characteristics. How to dress, what make-up to use, whether to use "chest" or "boom" microphones, how to interpret the signals of floor managers and assistant directors, all of these are essential considerations for the TV speaker. If the station makes rehearsal time available, use all of it intelligently.

Early in the preparation for any TV performance, it would be well to learn the station's policy regarding the use of a manuscript. Some will allow or prefer an extemporaneous delivery of a short speech; others may insist that the talk be read, either from papers on a desk or rostrum, or from a teleprompter or prearranged "goof" cards (large cards held outside camera range but within the visual line of the speaker). If the presentation is extemporaneous, you must have rehearsed the speech thoroughly with careful attention to the timing aspect. If the speech is read, you should read with all the directness and audience contact you can muster. You must have the message so well in mind that you need not be glued to the typed page but can appear to be talking with your listeners. If you use a teleprompter or goof cards, practice using such devices. Only a few sentences can be printed on a single goof card or be seen at one moment on the prompter; to avoid seeming as though you are reading individual phrases or sentences, and to give movement and unity to the speech, you must have your ideas and all of your plan well in mind. And, of course, the principles of effective oral interpretation must be used.

THE RADIO-TV INTERVIEW

The primary purpose of the broadcast interview is to entertain or to inform. Occasionally, it may be used for persuasive ends. A personality interview often is used as part of a public relations campaign in behalf of a new book, a movie, or a commercial product. An authority, being interviewed about a controversial issue, may turn his answers into appeals for his way of thinking, even though the program is intended for information purposes only. A purportedly objective interviewer asks a candidate about his platform, his promises, his qualifications; the questions are made to seem spontaneous and to be the ones the public would ask if they had a chance—but they have been prepared carefully for persuasive purposes.

In broadcasting, a principal difference between the speaking done in an interview and that in a talk is the relationship of the speaker to the listener. The audience, in effect, listens *in* on an interview, while it listens *to* a talk. The interview is intended for the entertainment or edification of the broadcast audience, not the interviewer, but the goal is accomplished indirectly. The participants focus primary attention on each other, but they realize that what they are saying reaches far beyond the immediate interview situation.

An extended interview needs as much preparation as a talk, though the kind of preparation will be quite different. The success of this speech form depends to a large extent on the rapport between the interviewer and the interviewee. Such rapport ordinarily cannot be created on the spur of the moment, but results from a feeling of mutual respect stemming from previous periods of communicative interaction. Pre-program conferences—really interviews in themselves—are necessary and important. Here the interviewer will learn most about his "subject"; here the skilled questioner will determine the direction he will give the final interview. Techniques of seeking out information about a person or his ideas vary greatly. But primarily, the interviewer must remember that he is sitting in for the listening public, that he is asking questions for them.

An interview needs organization that is rigid enough so that the final program seems to have unity, but flexible enough so that relevant, on-the-spot ideas can be introduced. The interviewer should be in control of the situation, but not to the extent that he deprives the interviewee of primary attention or destroys the feeling of spontaneity. Much of the desired quality will result from the way in which he handles his questioning. For example, if, from time to time, he can ask a question which seems to result from a statement made by the guest, the interview will appear to move forward with purpose. At all events, helter-skelter, random questioning should be avoided.

The success of an interview is not the sole responsibility of the questioner. The interviewee should be willing to furnish ideas and information during the planning stage, and be willing to respond freely and fully during the final interview. The biggest headache of any interviewer is a subject who "clams up" in the broadcast, whose answers are limited to a "yes" or "no" or an occasional "I think so." (This, of course, can be prevented partly by avoiding questions which make that sort of answer possible.) Almost equally distressing is the interviewee who rambles, digresses, and reminisces for minutes on end. The interviewee must recognize and accept his responsibility for creating an interesting and worthwhile program.

No interview, other than the man-on-the-street type, should

be tried without some advance preparation. On the other hand, no interview should be so precisely planned and rehearsed that it seems to be read or memorized. Certainly some attempt should be made to determine quite specifically the scope of the ideas to be presented. Unless the interviewer purposely is trying to put his subject on the spot, it seems desirable to plan in advance all or most of the questions so that the interviewee can consider his answers prior to the actual broadcast. One important reason for such preparation is to put the subject at ease; there is no real substitute for some rehearsal to accomplish this.

RADIO-TV DISCUSSION

Several factors have limited the use of discussion in broadcasting, in spite of its obvious potential in public service. First, sponsors have been reticent about picking up the tabs for such programs because the listening audience usually will be small. Second, because these programs may deal with controversial issues, their presentation often calls for careful scrutiny by station manager and participants, who are aware of libel laws and the danger of offending important segments of the listening public. Third, taking part in discussion programs is no easy task. If the discussion has spontaneity and if it involves different sides in a controversy, the speakers know that they must be ready for any turn of events; if a forum or audience participation is part of the format, an even greater amount of knowledge and tolerance may be necessary.

In spite of these limitations, program managers have not by any means neglected the use of discussions. In its recurring examination of stations' scheduling policies, the FCC has looked with favor on this type of program; if for no other reason, many broadcasters will include this program type among their public service features. Service organizations like the League of Women Voters, the Parent-Teachers Association, and the American Legion often have been able to arrange one-time presentations or even a short series of programs, whenever a local issue seemed to warrant it. Educational stations—and these are increasing in number and importance—can usually offer many such programs; ordinarily they have available the talents of a good-sized faculty who are knowledgeable about a number of current problems and events.

Any of the types of public discussion described in Chapter 12 can be adapted for use on radio and television. The two most frequently employed are the panel and the symposium.

The primary requisites for successful participation in broadcast discussion are (1) as complete a fund of knowledge about the subject as possible, (2) a thorough understanding of discussion techniques and of the responsibility of the participant and the moderator, and (3) a realization of the limitations imposed by the media. The first two of these have been explained in detail in Chapter 12. The last requires only a few specific suggestions in addition to what has already been said about radio-TV speaking:

1. *Discussion, over radio especially, requires constant attention to clarity, not only of ideas, but also of the identity of the participants.* Particularly is this a problem in the panel discussion where focus shifts from individual to individual frequently and rapidly.

Four things can be done to prevent confusion. First, in his introduction, the moderator can clearly name each of the discussants and identify him as to position and prestige qualifications. Second, as early as possible each participant can state clearly his particular point of view if the subject is a controversial one, or his special type of information and orientation toward the problem if it is an exploratory discussion. Third, all members frequently should use proper names when answering or directing questions or commenting on one another's contributions. Fourth, in his transitions and summaries, the moderator can identify points of view with the individuals who have expressed them.

2. *Radio-TV discussion should exhibit a strong sense of interaction among the members.* This interaction may run the gamut from cooperation to conflict. Listeners get a kick out of a good fight; they also enjoy seeing people settling their differences in friendly fashion. From the audience's point of view, a good discussion should show both conflict and cooperation, provided the conflict does not become a brawl and the cooperation does not turn into passive, uncritical acquiescence. Above all, the discussants must seem to be working together toward a sound under-

standing of issues. In public discussions from the platform of an auditorium, where an audience is present, this interaction also usually involves that audience; not only the moderator, but individual members as well frequently may "take in" the audience when they make some of their comments. In broadcasting, however, there seems to be a preference for limiting such listener contact to the function of the moderator. Producers want the person at home to listen in on or look in on a discussion in progress. Members concentrate their attention on each other at all times; usually only the moderator makes any attempt to address the listener or viewer directly. This does not mean that the participant can neglect the listener. Everything that is said must meet the criteria of effective audience-centered communication. In the symposium, of course, the speeches are intended to be directed to the listener, not to the other speakers. But in this type, too, the members must recognize that they are part of a larger discussion; their contributions should show an awareness of the ideas of the other speakers and of the purpose of the whole group.

3. *Like all good public speaking, broadcast discussion should be an extemporaneous and spontaneous activity.* Certainly, an agenda or organization outline should be set up well in advance of the final presentation. The panel may get together for preliminary and even practice discussions. At least one of these rehearsals should be "on mike" or "on camera" so that the members can accustom themselves to these pieces of equipment. However, the director or moderator should watch for signs of staleness or too much exact repetition from one rehearsal to the next; these may indicate over-rehearsal and a lack of active thinking. The illusion of the first time is important here as it is in all speaking. This is achieved, not by lack of preparation, but by creative use of rehearsals and conferences and by a lively *desire* to present one's ideas as lucidly and interestingly as possible. In broadcast speaking, as in all speaking, no amount of technique can take the place of this *desire to communicate.*

ADDITIONAL READINGS

Chester, Giraud and Garrison, G. R., *Television and Radio: An Introduction* (New York: Appleton-Century-Crofts, 1956).

Head, Sidney W., *Broadcasting in America* (Boston: Houghton Mifflin Co., 1956).
Lawton, Sherman P., *The Modern Broadcaster* (New York: Harper and Brothers, 1961).
Schramm, Wilbur (ed.), *The Process and Effects of Mass Communication* (Urbana: University of Illinois Press, 1954).
Smead, Elmer, *Freedom of Speech by Radio and Television* (Washington, D.C.: Public Affairs Press, 1959).

QUESTIONS AND PROJECTS

1. Make radio-TV speaking the subject of study from the receiving end of the process. Begin by selecting a number of programs of various types, listen to them critically, and analyze them to discover their strong and weak features.

2. Any public-address system provides the essential apparatus for practicing radio speaking. Many interesting facts can be learned even without a P.A. system by having speakers and readers stand behind a screen as they speak and read to the class. In this way you become aware of the vital part played by the visible code in normal speech situations and of the burden that radio places upon the unaided audible code.

3. Prepare a 5-minute speech in manuscript form. Time it precisely. Record the speech with the idea in mind that the tape will later be played over the campus or local radio station.

4. Work in pairs to prepare and present a series of radio interviews, again using some recording device. Perhaps most of you will choose to do personality interviews—though some members of the class may have a position of authority in a campus activity which could serve as the basis for an authority interview.

5. Contact the program director of a large radio or TV station and ask him to send you copies of any good scripts he may have available, especially those of programs with which members of the class are thoroughly familiar. Examine and discuss these scripts in class.

6. Arrange for the class to visit one of the local radio or TV stations to observe operations involved in actual broadcasting.

Index

J

K

L

M

N

O